A HISTORY OF AFRICAN CHRISTIANITY 1950–1975

AFRICAN STUDIES SERIES

The African Studies Series is a collection of monographs and general
studies which reflect the interdisciplinary interests of the African
Studies Centre at Cambridge. Volumes to date have combined
historical, anthropological, economic, political and other perspectives.
Each contribution has assumed that such broad approaches can
contribute much to our understanding of Africa, and that this may in
turn be of advantage to specific disciplines.

BOOKS IN THIS SERIES

A HISTORY OF AFRICAN CHRISTIANITY 1950–1975

ADRIAN HASTINGS

CAMBRIDGE UNIVERSITY PRESS

CAMBRIDGE
LONDON · NEW YORK · MELBOURNE

Published by the Syndics of the Cambridge University Press
The Pitt Building, Trumpington Street, Cambridge CB2 1RP
Bentley House, 200 Euston Road, London NW1 2DB
32 East 57th Street, New York, NY 10022, USA
296 Beaconsfield Parade, Middle Park, Melbourne 3206, Australia

First published 1979

Phototypeset in V.I.P. Times by
Western Printing Services Ltd, Bristol

Printed in Great Britain by
The Pitman Press, Bath

Library of Congress Cataloguing in Publication Data
Hastings, Adrian.
A history of African Christianity, 1950–1975.
(African studies series; 26)
Bibliography: p. 303
Includes index.
1. Christianity – Africa – Addresses, essays, lectures.
I. Title. II. Series.
BRI360.H33   276   78–16599
ISBN 0 521 22212 5 hard covers
ISBN 0 521 29397 9 paperback

Contents

Preface

While working as a Research Officer at the School of Oriental and African Studies I resolved to write a history of modern African Christianity. It became part of the project I was engaged upon in association with Professor Richard Gray, the core of which was the running of a series of seminars to consider the evolution of the Christian Churches in independent Africa. Our seminars formed part of a wider international project of research which culminated in a Conference at Jos in Nigeria in September 1975. A large selection of the papers presented at Jos or written for the SOAS seminars has now been published by Rex Collings in a volume entitled *Christianity in Independent Africa*, edited by Edward Fasholé-Luke, Richard Gray, Godwin Tasie and myself. These papers have been of immense use for the writing of this history; indeed it would have been a nearly impossible task without them. At the same time the weight of concern in the SOAS and Jos discussions was much more thematic than chronological and my brief *African Christianity* (Geoffrey Chapman, 1976), written immediately after returning from the Jos Conference, was intended to draw together the findings of the whole project from this standpoint. Personally I was, however, convinced that the time had come for a fairly straight history of contemporary African Christianity and I set about planning it in 1974. The present volume is the result.

I must express my great gratitude to many people: first to SOAS which made me a Research Officer for three years with a wonderfully free rein, and to the Leverhulme Foundation which provided the grant to make this possible. I would also like to thank all those who took part in a seminar at the Institute of Commonwealth Studies in January 1975, in which the plan of the work was discussed, and another smaller seminar a little later in John Lonsdale's rooms in Trinity College, Cambridge. Professor Richard Gray has read much of the book most carefully and my indebtedness to his comments and to his help in so many ways is profound. Dr John Lonsdale has expended many hours reading and commenting upon the typescript, some parts more than once. Dr Jocelyn Murray has meticulously revised the notes and constructed the bibliography and index. Mrs Mary-Ann Sheehy has retyped the text with the greatest care. My mother has read through the

Preface

whole book spotting grammatical infelicities with her usual keen eye. I have benefited enormously from the collections of recent material on missionary history and new religious movements assembled in the Department of Religious Studies at Aberdeen by Mr Andrew Walls and Dr Harold Turner. To all these and other friends who have helped very considerably in one way or another, many, many thanks. Whatever qualities the book possesses derive from many minds, its defects are all my own.

ADRIAN HASTINGS

King's College, Aberdeen
9 January 1978

Abbreviations

AACC	All Africa Conference of Churches
ABAKO	Association des Bakongo pour l'unification, l'expansion et la défense de la langue Kikongo
AICA	African Independent Churches Association
CMS	Church Missionary Society
CPP	Convention People's Party
DP	Democratic Party
EJCSK	Église de Jésus Christ sur la terre par le prophète Simon Kimbangu
FNLA	Frente National de Libertação de Angola
Frelimo	Mozambique Liberation Front
MPLA	Movimento Popular de Libertação de Angola
MRP	Mouvement Républicain Populaire
PARMEHUTU	Hutu Emancipation Movement
TANU	Tanganyika African National Union
UMCA	Universities' Mission to Central Africa
UNIP	United National Independence Party
UNITA	Uniao Nacional Para la Independência Total de Angola
WCC	World Council of Churches
ZANU	Zimbabwe African National Union
ZAPU	Zimbabwe African People's Union

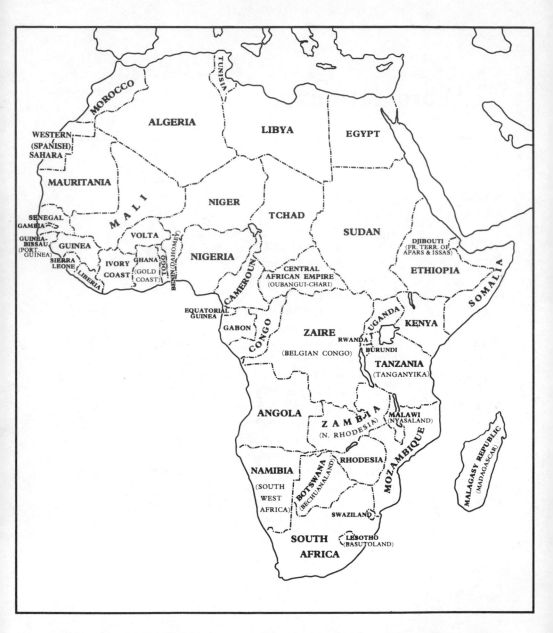

1. A political map of Africa (with the addition of names of countries as they were in 1950, when different from today).

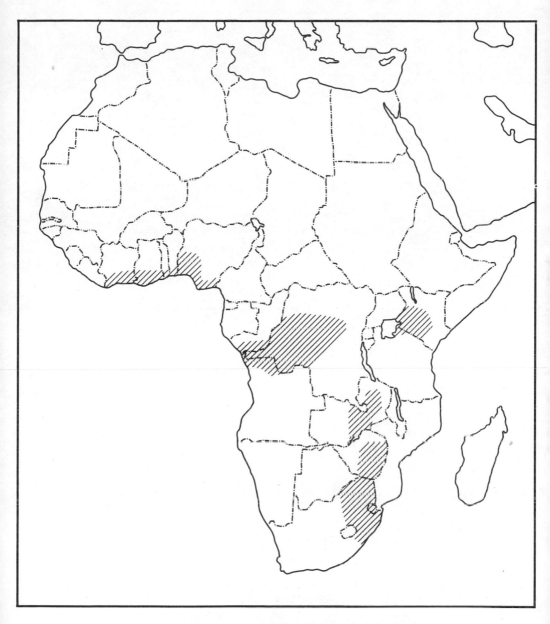

2. Principal areas of religious independency 1950–75.

Introduction

The importance of the religious dimension within modern history should be clear enough to anyone concerned theoretically or practically with the life of contemporary Africa. This is by no means something unique to Africa but the vitality of contemporary religion and its intricate relationships with many other sides of life is there particularly manifest. African religion includes three main strands – the traditional, the Christian, and the Islamic – and a full religious history must do justice to all three and to their inter-involvement at many levels. Most Christian Africans share significantly at least in the traditional strand, and some in that of Islam too. These are by no means watertight compartments. Nevertheless the Christian churches have for the most part a quite clearly recognisable character, distinguishable if not wholly separable from that of other religious traditions; their role has been crucial to the political and social history of most countries of black Africa and it is certainly justifiable to look at them on their own. They have indeed been studied to a far greater extent than the other traditions, perhaps because they are a great deal more accessible to the western minded people who carry out 'studies' of this sort. Yet these studies are themselves patchy and seldom attempt to paint any overall picture, at least in other than very simple terms.

It has been my conviction that the immense importance of modern African Christianity both for the wider life of the continent and for that of the world Christian community, of which it has become a very significant segment, more than justifies the attempt to assess historically what has been going on as a whole in the last quarter of a century: that is to say, how the Christian churches have come through the era of decolonisation from an ecclesiasticism of dependence centred, at least publicly, upon the missionary to an age of independence.

It would be impossible to do any justice to this story as a whole, its balance, its gains and losses, its sheer complexity, without drawing into a single web the history of the Catholic and Protestant mission churches as well as that of those churches founded in Africa and today normally identified as 'independent'. Moreover there is a geographical unity about the history of twentieth-century Africa which makes it unrealistic to draw a hard

1

dividing line anywhere between the Sahara and the Cape. Consequently the intention of this book, while resisting the temptation to tell the story of every country and every church for the sake of material completeness, is to see black Africa as a whole and Christianity as a whole over twenty-five years, from the last decade of colonialism to the independence of Angola and the World Council Assembly in Nairobi at the end of 1975.

Doubtless such a study could still proceed thematically, denominationally or regionally, and to some extent this book follows all three paths. But I have believed it best to control the treatment of the whole with a strongly chronological matrix: to write in fact a fairly straight history. This is, I am convinced, fully justified in the better attainment of an overall unity of assessment than seems attainable any other way, and it naturally follows from the belief that without an adequate understanding of the quickly changing political history of these years, very much ecclesiastical history drifts dangerously out of focus. It has to be admitted that the partial subordination of thematic, denominational and regional considerations to a fairly firm dividing up of a mere quarter century can contribute to the complexity of the narrative; but the complexity is not finally in the narrative but in the events, and if the book has a moral it can be this as well as any: we simplify at our peril. I can only pray the gentle reader, including fellow scholars, to bear with me if I have shunned more than I should the allurement of a streamlined story, of the over-arching generalisation. There are, I suspect, temptations of simplification to which students of religious phenomena still seem particularly drawn.

The chapters of this book have, then, a firmly chronological shape. The first attempts to establish a comprehensible base in an assessment of the shape of things in 1950 – an assessment which has, of course, to look back a good deal on the past. After that, three chapters carry the story forward across three periods of eight years each; this division grew naturally and seemed to propose itself in terms of both political and ecclesiastical developments, even if quite inevitably the dividing lines pinch the foot a little here and there and have, of course, to be over-stepped when required. Within this chronological framework the chapters themselves are divided with a certain uniformity by theme and denomination. That is to say, each begins with a political history and proceeds from that to the field of church–state relations. There are subsequent sections on Protestant, Catholic and Independent churches. It is possible, then, for the reader to use the book more thematically than it is presented. Each chapter is divided into three parts: A, B, and C. A comprises the political history and that of church–state relations; B the more purely ecclesiastical account of Protestant and Catholic mission churches; C independency. These sections are not, of course, fully autonomous: there is much about independency within the church–state sections, for instance, each chapter being intended as a coherent whole. Nevertheless it is possible to read the book following the order A, B, C, instead of 1, 2, 3, 4, if one should choose to do so. The regional division is less systematic. Increasingly throughout the period southern Africa presents a different pattern from the rest and in chapters 3 and 4 it was found necessary to divide the matter firmly from this point of view in the discussion of church and state. Elsewhere this has not been done consistently and it would, I believe, be a pity to do so.

The final chapter offers some more general considerations, the indication of some underlying trends and recurring themes, but it does not attempt to point morals, to indicate an overall conclusion or to prophesy the future prospects of African Christianity. Such aims would be beyond my purpose or ability. I have no doubt, all the same, that the story has its morals, many of them, for human history has an inescapable in-built morality and this can only be excluded by a scholarship of dehumanisation. That indeed I have endeavoured to avoid. Certainly, this is a story which includes its measure of folly, of mediocrity, of insignificant ventures, but it is also a record of faith and hope and fellowship and subtle imagination and striking courage and hard endeavour, and of all these things as being inalienable and significant elements within the total history of a society and its culture. It is written by one who now stands more apart from his subject than he had once intended, but who in one way and another shared in much that this book recounts, who resolved in 1949 as a very young man to serve the church in Africa and who, through the whole quarter century, had his mind on little else. He is then an outsider who has participated quite deeply in various ways in the 1950s, the 1960s, the 1970s, and much that is written here draws directly upon one facet or another of his personal experience. It is offered to those to whom the history of African Christianity belongs more absolutely than it can to the author as a tribute of affection, written in the belief that a humane discernment of the tangled web of historic truth is the kindest service a friend can provide.

1

1950

A. Church and State

In 1950 Africa was predominantly a colonial, and even a quiet, continent. In Ethiopia the Emperor Haile Selassie I, King of Kings, Conquering Lion of Juda, Elect of God, ruled on the throne from which he had temporarily been driven by Mussolini. With the exception of five years of exile (1936–41) he had ruled Ethiopia since his appointment as regent in 1916. In 1930 he was crowned emperor. Already in 1950 a ruler with a long history and a considerable international reputation he had shouldered the task of combining the divine right of kings with the modernisation of his poor and inaccessible kingdom, particularly in the field of education. On his return to Addis Ababa in May 1941 he had declared his intention of 'establishing in Ethiopia Christian ethics in government, liberty of conscience and democratic institutions'. For the next thirty years he would be engaged as he grew older with, perhaps, diminishing success in combining such ideals with the practice of a divine monarch, a narrow feudal aristocracy and a privileged state church which included scarcely half the inhabitants of the country. While the reality of his rule hardly measured up to that programme of 1941, the power of its symbolism throughout a colonial continent was immense.

Besides Ethiopia only Liberia, Egypt and South Africa were independent African states in 1950, and even there the independence was incomplete. In King Farouk's Egypt the Wafd swept into power with an overwhelming electoral victory in January of that year; its programme was to establish the political unity of the Nile Valley, of the Sudan with Egypt, under the Egyptian crown, and at the same time to bring about the withdrawal of the British army from the canal zone. In neither aim was it to be successful. In Liberia, President Tubman had been ruling for the last seven years, the leader of the 'True Whig Party'. The son of a Methodist minister and himself a lay preacher in the Methodist Church, he had undoubtedly done much to modernise Liberia, improve its international image, and weld together the Americo-Liberians of the coast and the tribes of the interior. Amendments to the constitution in 1947 had for the first time given representation in parliament both to the hinterland provinces and to women. At the same time, better than anyone else in Africa, Dr Tubman represented in 1950 and for two decades to come that essentially Victorian tradition of Christianity and social prestige which was constituted by a certain fluency in the English language, Protestantism, legal monogamy and symbolised by the tie and the frock coat.

South Africa was now ruled by Dr Malan, a former Predikant of the Dutch Reformed Church, leader of the Nationalist Party which had come to power, on a minority of votes, in the general election of 1948. Despite the stated policy of the Nationalists, South Africa in 1950 was still a Dominion within the British Commonwealth under the British monarchy, and the right of appeal to the Privy Council was only now being terminated. To the north of it Rhodesia was a self-governing but not an independent territory, led by its prime minister, Sir Godfrey Huggins.

The Emperor Haile Selassie, President Tubman, King Farouk, Dr Malan and Sir Godfrey Huggins – these were Africa's only representatives of independent or quasi-independent rule. There were, of course, many other men of power – from the King of Morocco and the Bey of Tunis to the Asantehene, the Sultan of Zanzibar and the King of Swaziland – but they were firmly, if generally courteously, subjected to governors appointed by, and responsible to, a European government. Africa from Algeria to Basutoland, from Senegal to Zanzibar, was ruled in 1950 in the name of the Kings of England and Belgium, the Presidents of France, Portugal and Spain. Mr Attlee, M. Bidault, Senhor Salazar and M. van Zeeland were the effective masters of nine-tenths of Africa and the only man on the continent to whom they had really to pay much attention was Dr Malan.

It was a colonial world and on the surface a relatively quiet one. Disturbances and riots there were indeed from time to time, on the west coast (as at Enugu in November 1949), in Kenya, in Buganda, on the Rand, but they were rather limited both in local scale and in their wider impact. The African news items which produced the widest coverage in 1950 were the after events of Seretse Khama's marriage to a white girl and the collapse of the Labour government's ill-planned groundnuts scheme in Tanganyika. In 1950 the world was too concerned with Asia to have much time for Africa. 1950 was Asia's year. The preceding twelve months had seen the communists sweep across China replacing Chiang Kai Shek by Mao Tse Tung as ruler of the world's largest nation, and in December Indonesia had become independent under Sukarno. In January India became a republic. A few months later the United States began its military assistance in Viet Nam where the French were being forced back in the far north. In June the Korean War broke upon the world and for the rest of the year it dominated the news: the rapid intervention of the UN, principally the Americans, to save the south from being overrun; the advance of the northern troops in spite of that almost across the whole country; the successful Allied counter-attack in mid-September; the subsequent Allied conquest of most of the north; the Chinese intervention in November bringing yet another reversal of fortune; the Allied retreat back again to the 38th parallel.

All this took place at the height of the cold war. The communist world and the western world were never more hostilely entrenched right across the globe than in 1950. It was the year of Europe's rearmament; likewise of a bitter attack upon the churches and the clergy in Hungary, Czechoslovakia and other countries of eastern Europe. African affairs, in so far as they had any recognised wider significance, were seen within the context of this world struggle of ideology, political system and military might. The continent was occasionally adverted to as a future ally for the free west, a potential target for communist propaganda: subversive pamphlets, it was said, were being mysteriously distributed here, some dynamite had been stolen there, while the communist menace could be freely used – and not only in South Africa, where the Communist Party was suppressed by law that year – to justify 'continued European leadership for an indefinite period'. As Major-General Foukes, acting president of the Kenya Electors Union, declared in a speech in Dar es Salaam on 4 April: 'If Europeans went down, all the Asians and Africans could hope for was a slave's life in a Communist police state'.[1]

Nevertheless things were moving in Africa in 1950 all across the continent from south to north. The profound consequences of the Second World War were still working their way through society. They had been chiefly economic and psychological. The West's need for raw materials – at a time when much of Asia was lost – had brought about an immense expansion in production in many parts of Africa: the Allied need for the copper of Katanga and Northern Rhodesia was the most striking example but not the only one. The uranium for the first atomic bombs came from Africa. The difficulty of importing manufactured goods brought about at the same time a considerable expansion of secondary industry, notably in South Africa and Rhodesia. There was in consequence a sharp increase in the number of Africans in regular employment, including skilled or semi-skilled work. Psychologically, the defeat of France and Belgium, the manifest vulnerability of the colonial powers at world level, the wide experience of tens of thousands of black soldiers fighting for democracy in north Africa, Asia and Europe, the world-wide ideological quickening produced by the founding of the United Nations Organisation – all this had brought about a profound alteration in African attitudes towards the status quo, and even in European attitudes. Colonial rule had now to be carefully justified and regularly assessed. A series of international conferences, beginning in 1948, was examining a whole range of aspects of African life from labour and rinderpest to treatment of offenders and the protection of fauna and flora.[2]

7

Africa was indeed already, as a sharp-eyed Dutch journalist described it, 'the continent of tomorrow's trouble',[3] above all because of the strongly and obviously contrasting directions which developments were now taking. The Union of South Africa was 'the great power of Africa' as *The Times* called it,[4] and since the elections of May 1948 it had been set upon a course in which equality between the races was systematically rejected in favour of partial segregation (apartheid) and total domination (baaskap) by the white fifth of the population. Until May 1948 South Africa had not been in principle fully committed to such a policy though its practice had been essentially of this nature for decades, and white majority opinion had shown itself time after time wholly unwilling to move even slowly in the opposite direction of racial equality.

The prime minister until May 1948 was Jan Smuts, a man with a vast liberal international reputation but a constitutional inability to see that his universal ideas must apply also to black men; he was, anyway, in his late seventies and much out of the country. While ineffectually anxious in his last years to find some sort of racial new deal, he knew well enough how short a distance even his great prestige would carry the white electorate in that direction. But he had in Jan Hofmeyr a brilliantly able deputy prime minister who had publicly committed himself to supporting the eventual entry of all races into parliament. Hofmeyr was the proto-type of the Christian Liberal in power: committed by his political position to upholding a system which on point after point he rejected in his heart yet finally distrusted by that system's out and out supporters because of the occasional almost academic expression of his deepest personal beliefs. The very ambiguity of the position of Smuts' government meant that, while effectively increasing the discriminatory character of South African law, it had yet lost the confidence of those most wanting discrimination. Dr Malan appeared a more reliable, if less sophisticated, upholder of white supremacy than General Smuts who had always to mind his international reputation. Luthuli called him 'A world statesman beyond the Union's borders, a subtle and relentless white supremacist at home'.[5] It was, after all, he and no one else who had the responsibility for removing Africans in the Cape from the common voters roll – perhaps the single most significant step of all away from the ideal of a non-racial state.

It could be that Hofmeyr cost Smuts the 1948 election; he died six months later, December 1948, and Smuts followed him in 1950. With the death of Hofmeyr there remained no major creative political opponent to the apartheid policies of the nationalists, and white opinion moved steadily further in their favour. The Mixed Marriages Act, the Immorality Act, the Group Areas Act, the fiercely contested abolition of any representation of the Coloureds in parliament – all this quickly followed. The Suppression of Communism Act of July 1950, and the massive powers with which it endowed the Minister of Justice, profoundly changed the character of South African government.

In October 1950 Dr Hendrik Verwoerd became Minister of Native Affairs. The great theorist of apartheid, he had not as yet played a very active part in politics. He was now entrusted with its implementation – an unswerving application of religious-political theory to the re-ordering of millions of defenceless lives. He was the son of a missionary, a man with a coldly ideological approach to politics, a long record of anti-semitic and Nazi sympathies, but an almost messianic conviction of both the justice of his policies and his own divine mission to bring them to realisation.

The same year it was announced that no further reports on the mandated territory of South West Africa (Namibia) would be sent to the UN. In May the International Court of Justice in the Hague took up the question of its status for the first of many times. In August six representatives – all national-ists – were elected for the first time by the Europeans of the territory to sit in parliament at Cape Town, and by doing so greatly strengthened the govern-ment's majority. In 1950, furthermore, the government of Dr Malan pre-pared to re-open the issue of the transfer of sovereignty over the 'High Commission territories' – Basutoland, Swaziland and Bechuanaland – from Britain to the Union, while African leadership in the three countries and liberals in Britain prepared to resist his claim.

This new South Africa's glorious day had been the 16 December 1949, 'Dingaan's Day', when 250,000 people – one tenth of all the whites in the country – had assembled outside Pretoria and to a salute of twenty-one guns inaugurated the Voortrekker Monument. Though the tone of the celebra-tion was intended not to be offensive, and Mr Havenga even declared that it was a good day for the blacks too, for they had been relieved through white victory of Zulu tyranny and had learnt to look to the white man as their sure guardian, Dr Malan stressed that the battle was in no way over: 'The struggle for racial purity' must go on together with the war against 'godless commun-ism' which 'continued to act like a destructive and deadly canker'.[6] The message of the festival was proclaimed loud and clear in *Die Kerkbode*, official newspaper of the Dutch Reformed Church: 'Awake Afrikanerdom, which has celebrated the Voortrekker festival, awake for white South Africa and a sound Christendom for our children and their children'.[7]

If what was happening in South Africa was in one way a stronger assertion than ever of white power over black, it was in another way an anti-colonialist development: the Afrikaner tribe, which had fled from colonial rule in the 1830s, which had nevertheless been conquered by the British in the 1890s, had now at last fully recovered the initiative and was asserting its power alike against the surviving fragments of colonial rule and against less fortunate tribes, at present in a relatively subservient state but a potential future threat to Afrikaner domination. A similar pattern was to reappear more than once

9

in one or another part of Africa in the coming years, with black tribes as well as white. Nowhere else, however, could a considerable group of white inhabitants so securely and confidently disassociate itself from the restraint but also the support of an overseas colonial power. Elsewhere (until Rhodesia's Unilateral Declaration of Independence) the movement towards independence must also be a movement towards the political elimination of white superiority.

It was in Italy's old empire that the most immediate developments were taking place, and the UN were called upon in the course of 1950 to settle the fate of Eritrea and of Libya. The future of the former was much debated between those who supported Ethiopia's claim for its total amalgamation, those who proposed a federal relationship with Ethiopia, those who wanted it to remain virtually autonomous for another ten years or so (perhaps, like Somalia, as an Italian trust territory) and those who wished to split it between Ethiopia and the Sudan. In the end it was given to Ethiopia within a federal constitution which did not endure, and if Eritrea was a political problem in 1950 it would be a still greater one in 1975.

The question of Libya proved more simple and the UN agreed that it should be independent by the beginning of 1952 – the next state to join Ethiopia, Egypt, Liberia and South Africa. A *Times* editorial commented upon its poverty but concluded that 'if it is given sufficient financial and technical aid, it can grow the flocks and crops necessary for subsistence and a small export trade'.[8] How far away any vision of Libya's oil millions!

Elsewhere in North Africa there was a noticeable political advance in 1950 in Tunisia, where in August a new cabinet was appointed half of whose members were Tunisian and in which Habib Bourguiba's Neo-Destour Party was represented. Bourguiba, who had recently returned from Egypt to lead the nationalist movement, had declared that 'it would be criminal not to grasp the hand stretched out towards us'. Tunisia's advance towards self-government was soon to be its neighbour Algeria's problem, for there a million French settlers were prepared to bar the way.

The constitutional advances which by 1950 were taking place widely across Africa, but particularly in British Africa, were a response to rising economic prosperity, the growth of an educated elite and its inevitable demand for increased participation in government, within a wider context of history. The current cold war, the political emancipation of the great nations of Asia, India above all, the establishment and anti-colonialist ideology of the UN, the weakening of the European colonial powers as a consequence of the Second World War, the Labour government in Britain, the return to their homelands of thousands of black Africans who had been recruited, indoctrinated with the struggle for a free world, and sent across the globe in the wartime armies of the colonial powers: all this stimulated a movement towards political independence which was well, if quietly, underway by 1950.

Gatherings such as the Pan-African Congress in Manchester in October 1945, in which Kwame Nkrumah and Jomo Kenyatta had taken a leading part, set the coming course more decisively than did any meeting of the British cabinet. The next year Kenyatta returned to Kenya after fifteen years of absence, and in 1947 Nkrumah went back to the Gold Coast after twelve years away. This double return, coupled with the nationalist victory in the Union in May 1948, really set the scene for the African politics of the next two decades – a triangular pattern well symbolised by Nkrumah, Malan and Kenyatta.

Ten years before, 1938, Kenyatta had published in London his remarkable *Facing Mount Kenya*, an assertion of the worth of African culture, undermined and scorned by westerners, which had massive political overtones. But Paris, far more than London, had been for years a centre of black cultural renewal in which the lead was taken chiefly by West Indians of whom the best known is Aimé Césaire. In 1950 this already dated back more than twenty years. Césaire and Léopold Sédar Senghor, a brilliant young teacher from Senegal, had between them developed the theory of *négritude*: a powerful and emotional assertion of black culture over against European culture and, in particular, the French policy of assimilation. Across poetry, traditional oral literature, music and dance, a philosophy of the black way of life was being sought to withstand the crushing effect of an entirely French pattern of education. But it was not anti-French. By 1950 Senghor himself was a distinguished political as well as literary figure, a member of the National Assembly, the author of several volumes of poetry, a close friend of Georges Pompidou – as much a Frenchman as an African. A convinced Catholic in the liberal Jacques Maritain mould, his dictum was 'culture first' not 'politics first', and his development of *négritude* was not a rejection of French culture but rather an appeal to the enrichment of complementarity. The writer René Maran wrote of him at that time: 'Senghor . . . is the prototype of what should and will be one day the French-African community. He carries within him two differing cultures which complement each other. And in his heart he carries both France and Africa'.[9] In 1947 Senghor and Alioune Diop had established the magazine *Présence Africaine* in Paris. It was to have a very considerable influence in the coming years – a forum open to a wide range of viewpoints, but with a very considerable liberal Catholic influence. There was a tension here as elsewhere between Marxist and Christian connections.

The underlying significance of the consciousness all these men represented was at once cultural and political: a reassertion of the worth of the black race and of black achievement across a necessarily somewhat mythical delineation of the blissful state of pre-colonial Africa, and in a few years time

11

it would burst forth not only in political independence but also in a spate of creative literature in both English and French. For the time being its widest expression was a new thirst for secondary and higher education of an admittedly western type. Until this time there had been next to no university education provided inside black Africa – only a trickle of graduates emerged from Fourah Bay College in Sierra Leone linked with Durham University since the nineteenth century. To gain an education one had either to go south towards the Union or overseas to Europe or America. A few went south. A young man from Buganda, who had recently left the army, Benedicto Kiwanuka, travelled down to Roma in Basutoland in 1950 to study there for two years, before going to London, while a few months before, late in 1949, another young man, this one from Mozambique, who had previously done well at the Hofmeyr School and then entered the University of the Rand, was deported from the Union. He had been backed by the Christian Council of Mozambique and his name was given as 'Eduardo Monjane'.[10]

But most went to Europe – to Paris, London, or still further afield. In 1950 Julius Nyerere, a qualified teacher from St Mary's Tabora, was studying history at Edinburgh. This pattern was now, in part, to change. As the numbers of those desiring a university education much increased, together with the need within the evolving institutional system for such men, it became clear that the time had arrived for new universities within Africa. Ibadan was founded as a university college in 1948, to be followed almost at once by Legon in Ghana, Khartoum, and Makerere in Uganda. All these were affiliated to the University of London. Fourah Bay College was given a new lease of life. Lovanium in the Congo was founded in 1949 and moved from Kisantu to Leopoldville in 1950 – although the lack of secondary education in the Congo meant that its first strictly academic year began only in 1954. Further to the west an Institut des Hautes Études was established at Dakar in 1950.

All these were to be decisively important institutions for Africa in the coming years, providing for the emergence of a new middle professional class, a new bureaucracy, a relatively numerous educated elite which would make the transfer of power from white hands to black an unrevolutionary process, not as such requiring any very drastic institutional change. But in 1950 not one of these institutions, except Fourah Bay, had as yet produced a single graduate.

The political objectives of the colonial powers were not the same. In 1950 Belgium could be said to have no political objective other than the maintenance of a benign, but firm, paternalism. Unlike Britain, France and Portugal it had opted neither for ultimate political independence nor for political assimilation. It simply avoided a consideration of the political future, rather as Smuts avoided it. Nor in 1950 was there much political unrest in the

Belgian Congo. Unlike most of Africa, but like the Portuguese territories, it had been rather little affected by the Second World War. All the same it was the year of the foundation of what was to become a powerful political organisation – ABAKO, the Association des Bakongo pour l'unification, l'expansion et la défense de la langue kikongo. Founded by M. E. Nzeza-Landu as a cultural society, it was within a few years to become the political party of Kasavubu, the Congo's first president.[11]

Britain had opted for the road of political independence, France and Portugal political assimilation. In the Portuguese territories in 1950 political assimilation, nevertheless, meant little indeed. The colonies had been declared in 1935 to be part of the territory of Portugal, but in 1950 they were still – even officially – entitled 'colonies', though the next year they were redesignated 'overseas provinces'. But no part of Africa was more political-ly, economically or educationally quiescent. In French Africa the position was very different. By the Constitution of 1946 all French territories were represented in the French Parliament, and black Africa elected 32 out of 627 deputies in the National Assembly and 34 senators out of 320 members of the Council of the Republic. At the same time the overseas territories elected their own territorial assemblies. France had excluded the option of differentiation and individual independence, choosing instead that of assimi-lation and political integration and for the time being it almost seemed to work. Political parties had sprung up all across French Africa. Nowhere else in colonial Africa could individual Africans rise to so high a political posi-tion. Léopold Senghor of Senegal was not only a deputy in Paris but a member of the European Assembly in Strasbourg. Until 1948 a member of the French Socialist Party, he had then joined a group of overseas deputies, the Indépendants d'Outre Mer, influenced by the Christian Democratic Mouvement Républicain Populaire (MRP).

His rival, and at the time apparently a more radical figure, was Felix Houphouet-Boigny of the Ivory Coast. He too had been elected as a deputy to the National Assembly in 1946 – on which occasion he had added the 'Boigny' to his name (signifying 'irresistible force'). The same year, rather than join a French political party, he had organised the inter-territorial Rassemblement Démocratique Africain, closely linked to the French Com-munist Party although its overall character was far from communist. By 1950 his power in the Ivory Coast was great indeed and, as the French government looked with increasing suspicion at the powerful movement which had taken shape there under his leadership, tension grew and there were major riots, notably on 24 January 1950. A warrant was issued for Houphouet's arrest though in fact he was protected by parliamentary immunity. In the course of 1950 he altered direction; in October he announced that the Rassemblement was breaking all its connections with the communists, on the grounds that it was 'a purely African party and it will

13

remain as such'. In the following years Houphouet was to take an increasingly 'moderate', pro-French and pro-western line.

If in principle British and French colonial policies were poles apart, Houphouet's position in the Ivory Coast at the beginning of 1950 was not unlike that of Kwame Nkrumah in the neighbouring Gold Coast, where January had equally been a month of disturbances culminating in Nkrumah's arrest on the 21st. It was the Gold Coast which was to be Africa's pace-setter during the next decade and Nkrumah its most messianic figure: the Pan-African liberator. In 1946 a new constitution had established an African unofficial majority in the legislature; in November of the following year Nkrumah returned to the country from Britain as general secretary of the United Gold Coast Convention; a sudden heightening of political tension produced the major riots in Accra of February 1948, and they in turn led to the appointment of an all-African constitutional committee under Mr Justice Coussey whose report was published and accepted in the course of 1950. The Legislative Council was now to be wholly elected and the executive council would operate ministerially and include a large African majority. This arrangement really constituted the crucial constitutional breakthrough for black Africa – the irreversible step across the line towards political independence not only for the Gold Coast but, by inference, for everywhere.

In the middle of 1949 Nkrumah had founded his own radical party, the CPP, the Convention People's Party, and after a few months of hectic political activity was arrested following the disturbances of January 1950. But his support in the country as a whole was now overwhelming and when, in February 1951, a general election was held to elect a legislature on the new formula, he won it hands down. He was released from prison a few days later amidst wildly enthusiastic scenes, the singing of *Lead Kindly Light* and the slaughter of a lamb at his feet. The political destinies of Africa were now divided firmly between the line of Dr Malan upon the one hand and that of Kwame Nkrumah upon the other. If each was the standard bearer of a nationalism absolutised by an at least quasi-religious appeal, their claims upon the future were clearly incompatible: the black continental universalism of Nkrumah could not conceivably be reconciled with the white particularism of Malan and Verwoerd, but both had an unselfcritical determination finally denied to the imperialisms of Europe. J. H. Huizinga remarked that very year: 'As we all know, while the Gold Coast Africans are about to achieve almost complete home rule, the native peoples of South Africa are now about to achieve almost complete suppression'.[12] Or again, in the words of Margery Perham: 'two utterly opposed principles are now at work in the African continent and, as things are moving at present, it seems they must ultimately come into collision'.[13] The political history of Africa in the next twenty-five years would in a very real sense be the working out of that

14

prophecy of 1950, though it would also demonstrate that race was by no means the only major issue of social and political structure. Indeed the 'two utterly opposed principles' would at times appear able to coexist almost amicably so long as a still deeper principle of the basic class differentiation between elite and mass was still retained by both.

If the constitutional progress of the Gold Coast was unparalleled in its rapidity, comparable developments were going on elsewhere. In both Nigeria and Sierra Leone, despite the particular internal problems they had to face, deriving from a lack of confidence in the former between north and south, in the latter between colony and protectorate, new constitutions providing for assemblies with an elected African majority were to be adopted in 1951. The leading political figure of Nigeria in 1950 was undoubtedly the Igbo Dr Azikiwe, then a man of forty-six. His party, the National Council of Nigeria and the Cameroons, was striving to be national rather than regional. The owner of a chain of newspapers, the master of his own ginger group, 'the Zikist Movement', an intensely exciting and excitable leader of the masses with a great capacity both for foresight and for producing divisive personal conflict, Zik was one of Africa's half dozen best known personalities.

There could be no doubt of the general direction of British West Africa's political future in 1950, or of South Africa's. The greatest question lay in between particularly in the British territories of the east and the centre. Were they to go Malan's way or Nkrumah's?

In regard to Rhodesia this seemed hardly an open question in 1950 for its small white settler group had been granted internal self-government nearly thirty years before; its prime minister since 1933 had been Godfrey Huggins, a doctor from Malvern. By 1950 the Rhodesian whites were some 120,000 strong and being reinforced annually by about 10,000 further immigrants. The age of the pioneers was over and full dominion status seemed nearly in sight. When in September the diamond jubilee of the arrival of the first column at Fort Salisbury was celebrated in Salisbury and London, many hoped that they were on the point of seeing a large new dominion of Central Africa, different from South Africa in that it would be controlled by English speakers not Afrikaners, but no less surely a 'white man's country'. While the Union Jack was solemnly hoisted in Cecil Square, Salisbury, by one of the few survivors of the pioneer column, in London the occasion was marked by a celebration at St Martins-in-the-Fields with an Address from Mr Amery in the presence of the High Commissioner and representatives of the King and Mr Attlee.

The crucial question now was that of a wider federation of the two Rhodesias and Nyasaland, urged by most white people in the three territories (who had earlier wanted a simple amalgamation, at least of Southern and Northern Rhodesia), but increasingly opposed by African opinion. The

15

Labour Government in Britain was reluctant to sanction a federation except on terms which were unacceptable to most whites, that is to say on terms which somehow guaranteed African political rights at least in the two territories still under effective British rule. In the words of Huggins during an important policy speech at Gatooma in December 1949: 'I gather that the United Kingdom Government would require representation of Africans by Africans from the start. I am quite sure that the time has not arrived for that, and further that there are as yet not enough civilised natives to justify one constituency; so, while the ultimate participation of Africans in the Central Government was accepted, the fact that they are not ready seems to provide a complete deadlock'.[14] That deadlock was not to be broken – and then only in a delusory manner – until a Conservative government was returned to power in Britain in 1952.

In the meantime all across East and Central Africa there was constant jockeying for some increase in power both by white and black. There were constitutional advances here too, if far more cautious than on the west coast. The Legislative Council of Uganda, another country in which there had been serious rioting in 1949, a consequence of the Bataka movement, was expanded in 1950 to include sixteen unofficial members, Africans increasing from four to eight. In Kenya, where the first African had been allowed onto the Legislative Council in 1944, and a second in 1947, there were now four; in 1951 they were to increase to six, but the Indians were to be six as well, Arabs two, and the representatives of the European settler community fourteen. A proposal to make some slight constitutional advance in Tanganyika had recently caused a storm not only from the quite small white settler community there but also from the Kenya Electors' Union which envisaged in the future an 'East and Central African federation' under European leadership, and would 'not tolerate restriction on European settlement'.[15] Major Keyser, leader of the European unofficial members in the Kenya legislature, visited Southern Rhodesia for consultation; Huggins discussed East African affairs with the Colonial Office in London, and Dr Malan even ventured to announce that he was prepared to receive a deputation from Kenya and Tanganyika settlers.[16]

Doubtless there was an element of unreality in much of this, but the possibility of a self-governing white-ruled state from Kenya to Rhodesia did not seem fantastic in 1950 to many people, both white and black.

Black political organisation in these parts of Africa was mostly rudimentary or non-existent. In Northern Rhodesia an African Congress had been founded in 1948; it had as yet little strength though it may be noted that in March 1950 a small group of men led by Kenneth Kaunda, a part-time teacher, set up a local branch in the remote rural centre of Chinsali. He already spoke clearly of racial oppression as a 'great burden of evil' and was seeking a way to combat it.[17] Only in Kenya was there any widely organised

16

African political opposition and its leader was Mr Kenyatta. For decades there had been a series of Kikuyu political organisations, long led by the veteran Harry Thuku. The Kenya African Union was founded shortly after the Second World War and in June 1947 Kenyatta was elected president and set about building up its organisation much as Nkrumah was doing at the same time in the Gold Coast – only that Kenyatta's approach was a more restrained one, and his appeal to the whole country more limited. Still by 1950 he was holding meetings of many thousands of people, the only African politician of the first rank east of Nigeria. He challenged the aspirations of the white settlers just as they were riding at their highest; perhaps only with the power of hindsight could one see that he was essentially a Houphouet-Boigny rather than a Nkrumah. But the explosion of Kikuyu tension which had built up, apparently almost unnoticed, over the years in the face of the growth of white settlement and land ownership and out of a deep sense of alienation within their own country, was now something which Kenyatta could help to release but certainly not control – any more than a government largely insensitive to its deeper rationale could control it. Already in 1950 the name of Mau Mau and the reports of secret oathings were occasionally heard, and soon central Kenya would be the scene of the greatest emergency British colonial rule had had to face in Africa for many decades.

White rule or black in this generation – Nkrumah or Huggins, let alone Malan – or was there some third way between, an enigmatic 'partnership' now starting to be talked of? If so, what in practice did it mean? These were the political questions of 1950 – the questions of a still colonial world, undoubtedly, but of a colonial world where the cracks were beginning to appear upon many sides.

The Christian churches were so much part of this world, and even of its political structures and motivation, that it could certainly not be properly described without them. The one thing almost everyone claimed in Africa in 1950 was the sanction of religion in some form, from the Emperor of Ethiopia to the small groups in the Kikuyu countryside beginning a revolutionary movement with the secret taking of oaths. Religion – be it Christianity, Islam or that of African tradition – was the sanction for all that was most traditional in Africa; it was closely linked with all that was most colonial, and it would seldom be far away from all that was most revolutionary. In the most ancient of Africa's empires Haile Selassie was the 'Elect of God' and his system of governance most intimately linked with the clergy and ethos of the Orthodox Church; in white South Africa parliament in Cape Town opened every morning with the saying of Christian prayers; in Morocco, in Zanzibar, in Sokoto the sultans and their governments were equally strengthened by the saying of Islamic prayers, while the rites and intercessions of traditional religion remained a central concern of the Oba of Benin or the Ngwenyama of Swaziland. In the last case, however, a gentle fusion of religious inspiration was permitted within the ritual of government for while the Christian missions had shunned the great national ceremonies, the Zionists had entered in and by 1950 a colourful group of their bishops enhanced by their presence the spiritual validation of the great annual Incwala festival.

While Christianity was the religion of a relatively small minority of Africans in 1950 it was still – south of the Sahara – in one or other of its many forms the continent's dominant religion at the level of government and of political life. The religion of the colonial ruler was becoming the religion of the colonised. Yet Christian conversion, worthwhile and useful as it might be in all sorts of ways, undoubtedly created a deep question of institutional authenticity for any king in Africa, just because it could cut so deeply into the mythical and even institutional under-girding of his office and authority. It bit into the cultural context of political institution just as it did into marital institution. It may take generations for a replacement of comparable credibility to be found for what was lost with conversion. Yet efforts were made to establish that replacement. The solemn coronation of the Kabaka Daudi Chwa of Buganda in 1914 on Budo Hill and of his son Mutesa II nearly thirty years later, with its intimate interlacing of Ganda tradition and Christian ritual, was the expression of a consistent attempt to re-root the ancient Ganda monarchy in a new religious context and in terms which would accord both with the tradition of the nation and the example of Westminster.

It was taken for granted in most colonial circles that church and state should go hand in hand, even if there were some agnostic exceptions and certainly many degrees of cooperation. Not all churches would be included – some governments took a very firm line in excluding the ones they judged less respectable or potentially subversive; nor was the church–state relationship seen in the same light by all governments. Indeed the disjunction between the two in French Africa was considerable, while in Portuguese Africa their conjunction – particularly since the Concordat of 1940 – was remarkable. In France a long governmental tradition of anti-clericalism in the Third Republic resulted in a wariness upon either side about cooperating in the colonies; only with the Second World War did this appreciably change. In the Portuguese colonies a comparable anti-clericalism in the early part of the century had been sharply reversed by Salazar. Here the Catholic Church or – as it was officially named – 'The Portuguese missionary organisation' was now effectively tied to government in numerous ways, above all financial, spelt out not only in the Missionary Agreement between Portugal and the Vatican attached to the Concordat of 1940, but still more in the Portuguese Government's Missionary Statute of the following year. The Church's general missionary work received an annual subsidy by diocese and missionary society, all the travel expenses of mission staff were paid, together with the regular salaries of the bishops.

In those colonies having a governor-general the Bishops will receive a stipend, equal to the salary of a governor of a province which is not that where the capital of the colony is situated, from the budget of the colony where they exercise their spiritual jurisdiction. In other colonies, the Bishops will receive a stipend equal to the salary of the best paid head of a service. The Archbishops of the archdioceses of Luanda and Lourenco Marques will receive stipends equal to the salary of the governors of the provinces of Luanda and Lourenco Marques respectively.[18]

In return for these and other privileges, including what was not far off a monopoly of education, the Catholic Church accepted a state veto over the appointment of bishops, the submission of annual reports to the government covering all aspects of church work, and an effective commitment to further Portuguese colonial policy. On the other hand Anglican and Protestant missions were clearly discriminated against, particularly as the reverse effect of the Concordat – their position had been very much better prior to 1940.[19] This was specially true in the field of education. While tolerated, they were regarded as potentially dangerous, almost necessarily incapable of furthering that policy of 'Portugalisation' of Africa to which the government was committed, for next to none of their missionaries were Portuguese.

In Belgian Africa the position had not been so different; the Concordat which the Vatican made with Leopold II in 1906 had established the Catholic church in a position of great privilege while guaranteeing that the great majority of its missionaries would be of Belgian nationality. It was 'the National Mission'. The strength of the Catholic Party in the Belgian government ensured that this position did not change. Catholic schools had for long alone received financial support from government and the effective power of the missionaries to get their way over many matters by appeal to the civil authority was vast. It was not without reason that the veteran Bishop de Hemptinne could be known as 'the son of King Leopold'. Protestant missions, however, were stronger than in Portuguese Africa and had powerful international backing, though they were unsubsidised. The position here greatly changed after the Second World War and from 1946 Protestant and Catholic schools were supported on the same terms. When a Socialist–Liberal coalition came to power in Brussels in 1954, it would be anxious to diminish the clerical appearance of its colonial system, but in practice in the eyes of Africans the union of church and state was probably little impaired.[20]

Despite the formal establishment at home of the Church of England, there was never so close a link in British Africa between the colonial power and a single church. The rival claims of Anglicans, the Presbyterian Church of Scotland, the free churches everywhere, and the Catholic Church were all too powerful for this to be possible. The Anglican missionary effort was itself relatively small in the overall picture, yet the Union Jack still tended to carry

19

with it something of an Anglican quasi-establishment. The Archbishop of Cape Town and his colleagues elsewhere had enjoyed a political role decidedly superior to that of the representatives of any other church – and they could always appeal quietly back to Canterbury: a letter from the archbishop at Lambeth Palace to 10 Downing Street on some matter of colonial concern was not unusual. Indeed in this very year, 1950, the Prime Minister replied to a letter of the Archbishop of Canterbury to assure him that the decision to ban Seretse Khama and his white wife for five years from the Bamangwato Reserve did not mark any change in British policy in race relations.[21] Max Warren, General Secretary of the CMS (Church Missionary Society) all through these years, was the man who probably saw the working of this relationship most closely from the inside. He has pointed out one among many visual instances of it, so striking and yet so entirely taken for granted:

Readers of Sir Michael Blundell's autobiography – *So Rough a Wind* – will find opposite page 192 a photograph taken at the new Legislative Council in Nairobi, Kenya, in 1951. In the foreground is Michael Blundell standing at the Despatch Box. In the Background sits the Speaker under the Royal Arms. On the Speaker's right is the Governor-General in full uniform. On the Speaker's left is the Bishop of Mombasa in Convocation robes. In those days the boundaries of Mombasa coincided with the political territory of Kenya. That photograph is good documentary evidence of the reality of the Anglican quasi-establishment.[22]

And so is the very location of the Bishop of Mombasa's residence in Nairobi – immediately outside the gates of Government House.

By and large, however, in British Africa, at least outside the most strongly Muslim areas, all the mainline churches tended to stand in a position of considerable colonial privilege, sharing in the subsidising of their educational and medical work. But the degree of social identification between mission and administration, or mission and white settler society greatly varied. Many missionaries held themselves firmly aloof, never joined the local white club and might hardly have been considered sufficiently respectable to be offered a place on the verandah for a sundowner. The national and class background of the missionary, as well as his church, were here important. Irish Holy Ghost Fathers tended to have a very different social relationship with the settler community from Italian Consolata Fathers in Central Kenya where both groups worked as Roman Catholic missionaries, and Africans could note clearly enough the way the two were treated: a Consolata Father might be left standing outside the door as they themselves were. In some areas missionaries were undoubtedly regarded as belonging to the class of 'Europeans', but in other areas this was not the case – they were honorary 'non-Europeans'. But where a settler community existed, it always required either some sharp difference of background or a very clear-sighted missionary decision to steer clear of an at least apparent identification: the identification of the golf course.

There were many places where some considerable acceptance of a colour-bar by the church quite clearly indicated a large measure of political harmony between the church and the colonial–settler establishment. Prestigious missionary-run schools for white children only, with educational standards and equipment far higher than those offered in any African school and involving a large number of the best qualified mission staff, showed only too clearly the basic political stance and priorities of a particular church or missionary society: such was the Jesuit-run St George's in Salisbury, or St Mary's of the Holy Ghost Society in Nairobi. Elsewhere there might even be a colour-bar in church or at communion, while African priests were in more than one place treated in a discriminatory manner even by the white clergy – for instance, they had to approach a white presbytery by the back door and were never shown into the room where Europeans were entertained. This could be the case in the Congo, in the Rhodesias, in South Africa.

Beyond the church's political position as demonstrated through law and concordat, by the almost ritual denunciation of communism, by financial support, by participation in state ceremonial, by the structures of ministry and worship, and by the life style of the clergy, there was its position as emerging from the explicit pronouncements or actions of church leaders or other prominent Christians.

A large number of missionaries and African Christians doubtless believed that there was little or no connecting link between their religious concerns and the present political state or future constitutional prospects of the lands where they lived and worked, though many who were quite unconcerned with wider political issues would certainly have agreed that particular acts of injustice on the part of the authorities could call for a protest from the church. They would too have had no doubt that 'communism' was a politically unacceptable alternative for the Christian and should be denounced in no uncertain terms, primarily doubtless because of communism's atheistic character, but 'communism' in 1950 was easily made to cover a vast range of ideas and attitudes. In an uncompromising anti-communism, church and state were at one almost everywhere in the Africa of 1950.

There had long been a small but influential minority of missionaries – drawn particularly from British Presbyterians, Anglicans and Methodists – who went much further in a political direction, who saw it as their task 'to watch native interests' quite consistently, to stand up for the immediate land rights and long-term political prospects of Africans wherever they seemed in danger either from government or from settlers. Men like Archdeacon Owen in Kenya, John White and Arthur Shearly Cripps in Rhodesia and Andrew Doig in Nyasaland had been of such a kind, and they could generally rely on the support of a strong church lobby in Britain, marshalled as likely as not by J. H. Oldham from Edinburgh House.

In 1950 in Africa there were at least five different types of voice hailing from Christian churches in response to the contemporary political scene, over and above routine acceptance of the status quo. It was in South Africa, with its more complex society, its universities and varied ecclesiastical traditions going back a century and more, its growing racial and cultural polarisation, that they were most clearly heard.

The first was the voice of the liberal English-speaking church establishment. Understandably, it did not favour any very radical approach to the stirring or satisfaction of African political aspirations and it did not question the overall propriety of established government, but it was increasingly sensitive to racial discrimination in all its forms. The sort of thinking on church and society associated with Archbishop Temple, Bishop George Bell and J. H. Oldham, with the Oxford Conference of 1937 on 'Church, Community and State', at which the formation of the World Council of Churches was in fact agreed, with the Malvern Conference of 1941, was inevitably permeating through to some of the church's leaders in Africa. It is not surprising then that South African legislation, particularly where it most directly affected traditional areas of church ministry, such as the Mixed Marriages Act, produced protests and resistance of a sort. The British Council of Churches in 1950 recorded its determination 'to oppose any tendencies towards racial discrimination in any territories for which the British Government is responsible',[23] while in October the South African Methodist Church at its annual conference condemned the actions of the government as leading gradually to a totalitarian state and the restriction or removal of the African and coloured franchise. The Catholic Bishop of Cape Town, Mgr Hennemann, had already in September 1948 described apartheid in a letter read in all Catholic churches as 'noxious, unchristian and destructive' and had gone on to condemn 'attacks on the personal liberties and dignity of the non-white citizen' together with the removal of such limited franchise as he then possessed.

The most consistent and powerful witness to the rights of man, regardless of colour, to be found within the institutional leadership of the church came at this time from Geoffrey Clayton. He had been Anglican bishop of Johannesburg since 1934 until becoming Archbishop of Cape Town in 1948. It could be argued that in 1948 the Anglican archbishopric of Cape Town was, at least potentially, the most influential ecclesiastical position on the whole continent, and in Clayton the church had appointed a man of immense ability and experience, clarity of intelligence and sureness of touch. He was an ecclesiastical statesman, shrewd, masterly, somewhat insensitive, a straight Anglo-Catholic, without doubts and without any striking originality of mind, entirely confident in the pattern of a ministry which put the church and religious things very decidedly first. He had the deepest suspicion of any priest who saw things differently, particularly anyone whose apparent primary concern was with the needs of the world rather than with those of the church: Raymond Raynes and Trevor Huddleston, Michael Scott and Bishop Ambrose Reeves, they all irritated him. It was partly a matter of sheer temperament. Dry, unemotional, distrustful of populism of any sort – pentecostal or political – an English upper-middle-class type who was con-stitutionally as incapable of identifying with blacks as with women, or with the poor anywhere in his own life style, he was yet able to assess the general situation with courage and a very clear judgement, and did not for one moment question that the church's task – secondary but still immensely important – was to speak up for the poor and the weak.

The report on 'the Church and the Nation' produced in the Johannesburg diocese under Clayton's leadership towards the end of the war by a large and able commission was, without doubt, the church in Africa's most pondered attempt in that period to tackle not just particular injustices but the underly-ing system. Its recommendations for a wide extension of the franchise to African, coloured and Indian men and women were, for their time, revolu-tionary. In this, as in many other things that Clayton advocated – such as government recognition of the African Mineworkers Union – he had gone far beyond the occasional protest against the latest scandal, far beyond what could really be expected from most of his fellow bishops. If his report had little influence upon the overall direction of society, it undoubtedly greatly affected some individuals. Alan Paton, later chairman of the Liberal Party and one of South Africa's most valiant and unextinguishable warriors for radical change, has written: 'I must record that being a member of the Bishop's Commission was one of the seminal events of my life, after which I was never the same again . . . having lived for 38 years in the dark, the Commission opened for me a door, and I went through into the light'.[24]

Despite all this and the great gratitude which many non-white people undoubtedly felt towards Clayton, it is necessary to take note also of the apparent weaknesses in his type of approach. First, it was essentially one of the whites speaking to whites about 'natives'. There seems no evidence that Clayton ever saw the need to meet seriously with African leaders, work with them, or even find out how they saw the situation. Existentially he appears little if at all affected by the agony of the situation and almost brutally unsympathetic with a priest like Michael Scott who was literally carried away by that agony. Next, the policy he advocated was essentially of a gradualist and rather paternalist type at a time when such an approach was more and more unacceptable even to moderate Africans. There should be 'a gradual removal of the colour-bar'. But if the colour-bar is evil, why should the church call only for its gradual removal? Clayton would have replied that only a fool could imagine that it could be immediately removed. Does a church lose its moral authority if it tempers its public teaching to what it judges to be pragmatically possible within an evil situation? Finally, as Afrikaner critics so often pointed out, the English-speaking churches – including very much the Anglican Church – in fact practised racial discrimination in all sorts of ways within their own life, and there is little evidence that Clayton bothered much about this or set his face firmly against it.

Yet, when all this is said, Clayton remains a figure of quite exceptional importance in the world of 1950: the one sustained, unsuppressible and very authoritative voice of protest over things political to come from the very heart of the ecclesiastical establishment.

Our second voice expressed a quite different view of Christianity and politics. For it, Christianity went with white men and white rule, providing an ideology and a justification for white supremacy in one form or another. In June 1950 the European Electors Union in Kenya urged the British Government 'to issue a restatement of colonial policy which will make it clear beyond all question or doubt that the British people will remain in East Africa as builders of Christian Civilization, and that it will be the privilege of the British people for a very long time ahead to be the controlling directing force in East Africa'.[25] Such an identification of 'Christian Civilisation' with European rule was very widespread, but from the church viewpoint by far its most serious expression was to be found in two very different areas: upon the one side in the 'Portuguese missionary organisation' which we have already considered; upon the other in the Dutch Reformed Churches of South Africa.

After the nationalist victory in the 1948 South African general election *Die Kerkbode* declared 'We as Church give thanks with humility that the members of our Government are all bearers of Protestant belief and members of the Christian Church'. A little later it wrote:

The day is coming when the non-white races and power will stand mobilised against the white for their supposed rights. So also will the time come that the mobilised powers of unbelief under the leadership of the Prince of Darkness will rise up in bloody strife against the real Christendom. These events summon us as Church today. MOBILISE – MOBILISE – MOBILISE TO THE UTMOST.[26]

The Nationalist Party had for its part explicitly based its policy of apartheid on 'the christian principle of right and justice', as in its major pre-election policy document, the so-called 'Sauer Report'. Dr Malan himself had been a minister of the church and his approach to political issues was heavily religious. 'Christian nationalism' was in fact the favourite name for the party's policy, and there was particular stress upon this in the educational field where the principles of 'Christian–National Education' were constantly reiterated.

In April 1950 a major conference of the Dutch Reformed Church at Bloemfontein chaired by Dr G. B. A. Gerdener called for the complete

24

segregation of the races without racial hatred so that justice could be done to all. Only with separate development could Europeans and Africans both live happily in southern Africa. 'It was essential that all native labour should be systematically and gradually superseded by European labour in all European industry, including farming . . . Apartheid is the declared policy of the Government, and . . . the Congress is convinced that there are basic principles of God's word supporting apartheid'.[27] But any such systematic and total segregation was immediately rejected by Dr Malan himself as 'impracticable', and there is no evidence that the Dutch Reformed Church has ever attempted to work for it. Thus, if it could rightly criticise the other churches for hypocrisy in denouncing discrimination and segregation when they practised these things themselves in their own church life, the Dutch Reformed Church – even at its most reasonable – could be criticised for justifying government policy in terms of an aim which the government itself consistently (and rightly) rejected as entirely impracticable.

Nowhere perhaps in Africa has there been a more consistent fusion of politics and religion than in the theory and practice of the Nationalist Party and the Dutch Reformed Church. The power kernel within both has been the secret organisation known as the *Broederbond*, founded in 1918. Malan, Strydom and Verwoerd are all thought to have been members. As to its fundamental philosophy, its general secretary declared in 1944 that 'The Broederbond is born from a deep conviction that the Afrikaner nation has been placed in this country by God's hand.' P. J. Meyer, a former chairman, said of it in 1966:

The main purpose of this cultural movement was to purify Afrikaans nationalism of all elements by which it could destroy itself and to build it on a Christian–Protestant basis, with (as yardstick) the legal principles of the Holy Writ, the guidelines of our Christian national tradition and the demands of the time in which we live, in all spheres of life to full independence and maturity.[28]

The Broederbond with its carefully formed cells of influential Afrikaners, many of them Predikants, was behind that mobilisation of the Afrikaner people and the Dutch Reformed Churches which produced the 1948 election victory and the subsequent ruthless implementation of the policy of apartheid. While the Church's voice as represented by Archbishop Clayton had effectively failed to mobilise white or black, English-speaking Christians or anyone else, the Church's voice as represented by *Die Kerkbode* had powerfully contributed to the mobilisation of a sufficient part of the population to project South Africa in a 'Christian national' direction wholly different from that of the liberal non-racial Christianity advocated by Clayton or Jan Hofmeyr.

One had popular appeal, the other had none. But when Bishop Clayton found himself reinforced by clerical populists who really wanted to apply the kernel of his teaching in the market place, he himself turned distinctly sour.

South Africa in these years had to undergo the extraordinary experience of Michael Scott in his prime. Both he and Trevor Huddleston had arrived in the country in 1943, but while the latter settled down to a vigorous but geographically very limited ministry in the slums of Johannesburg's Sophiatown, Michael Scott felt called to an entirely personal type of peripatetic ministry and very soon became a national figure. A curate in Johannesburg with an unsettled background, no university degree, no clear vision of what he either sought or believed in, no great capacity as a public speaker, an Anglican priest who had previously drifted about Asia and Britain on the fringe of the Communist Party, he was within a few months of arrival helping to organise, and then chairman of, a national non-party organisation called the Campaign for Right and Justice. After two years of struggle, he found the Campaign was changing its character – it was being taken over by its Communist members, partly doubtless because they were the most cohesive and committed group in it. Men like Michael Scott had no group support behind them.

I felt overcome [he wrote later] by a sense of betrayal and frustration in face of what seemed the overwhelming forces of oppression both on the Government side and in the Opposition. Against these our efforts seemed so puny and were made even more ineffectual by the intriguing methods and cynicism of the Communists towards everything that was not controlled by them or harnessed to their own cause. Their support, though, was in a sense a kiss of death. I felt instinctively from that time that there was no recourse left open to me but the path of passive resistance. I felt betrayed by my own Church. Though, admittedly, my tactics had been at fault they had not been so much at fault as to give the hierarchy any justifiable pretext for their lack of support, if not open opposition to what we were trying to do.[29]

While his bishop, Geoffrey Clayton, was filled with the calmest of certainties about God, the world, the church and his own ministry, Michael Scott was a prey to every sort of uncertainty. He lived his life with an agonising doubt about fundamentals, a deep diffidence about himself, and a troublesome unreliability over little matters such as keeping appointments or mentioning to his superiors where he was going or why. He had no ambitious desire to be in the centre of any stage and no great practical ability for organisation, speech or even political analysis. He was simply filled with a passionate concern for justice, for the defence of the poor. And in this his life was spent.

The Campaign for Right and Justice was followed in 1946 by a visit to Durban where the Indians had organised a Passive Resistance Movement in opposition to the new Asiatic Land Tenure Bill. Their silent protesters were being brutally assaulted night after night by companies of white thugs. Scott felt he must stand beside them. Arrested under the law of trespass, he spent three months in gaol. On returning to Johannesburg he lost his post as a curate, because Clayton would not permit him to keep it without giving an assurance that he would not undertake further action of this sort without permission. In the next three years he took up residence for a time with a poor African minister, the Reverend Theophilus, in 'Tobruk', one of the most appalling and crime-ridden of shanty towns, until he was again arrested, for living in a native area. After investigating labour conditions in the notoriously slave-driving farms of the eastern Transvaal and publishing an article on the subject in the *Rand Daily Mail* to the fury of the farmers, he was drawn into the defence of the rights of the Herero people in South West Africa. Appointed by Chief Hosea as their representative at the United Nations, he went to the UN year after year to plead their cause.

In 1950 Scott became a prohibited immigrant in the Union of South Africa, but by now – in the judgement of the not very friendly editor of *African Affairs* – it was 'perhaps no exaggeration to say that his name is known to a greater number of people than anyone else of any race connected with Africa'.[30] An apparently insignificant Anglican padre, practically disowned by his own church, with 'no showmanship, only conscience', he was now writing frequent and important letters to *The Times*, a voice of international significance. He spoke at major meetings at Central Hall Westminster in April 1950 and in the Town Hall at Oxford in June; he preached in St Paul's Cathedral in May. In May, too, the International Court of Justice at the Hague for the first time took up the question of the status of South West Africa and it had to be admitted that it was Michael Scott who had 'succeeded practically single-handed, in forcing the Herero issue in South West Africa before the International Court'.[31]

The fourth political voice of the church in 1950 was a voice of middle-class Africans. Our first three voices have all been white voices, and indeed the upper ecclesiastical leadership in all except the independent churches was almost totally white in 1950. Yet the immense majority of church members was black. If the independent churches, in South Africa particularly, for the most part eschewed politics, there were many African political leaders who were committed members of other churches, indeed whose politics had grown almost naturally out of their sense of Christianity, rather little as they might influence their own ecclesiastical authorities.

Professor Z. K. Matthews was the pre-eminent figure here. In 1950 he was Professor of African Studies at the University College of Fort Hare and had been so since 1936. Since 1941 he had been a member of the Native Representative Council, now about to be abolished by government, and since that same year he had been a member of the African National Congress. If he had been willing to stand he would most probably have been elected President-General of Congress in December 1949. He was soon to leave for a year in America as Henry Luce Visiting Professor of World Christianity at Union Theological Seminary. His distinguished colleague, Professor D. D. T. Jabavu, a rather older man, had been at the missionary conferences of Le Zoute and Jerusalem in the 1920s, as Albert Luthuli went to that of Madras in 1938. Matthews and Luthuli had earlier been together for years on the staff of Adams College, Natal – after Fort Hare and Lovedale the most distinguished African educational centre in southern Africa. By 1950 Luthuli was a vice-president of the Christian Council; he had only recently joined Congress, being the very epitome of the Christian moderate who long preferred to work through mission school and a chief-tainship; yet in 1952 he was to be elected its national President. Behind such men were others like the Anglican priest James Calata, Secretary-General of Congress from 1936 to 1949 but president too of the African Ministers' Association.

These men and those closely linked with them were the natural leaders of the nation, men of very high ability but also representative of a remarkably mature Christianity with its social and political implications firmly but rather gently thought through. They had tried hard over many years to reconcile white South Africa and their own people on terms more than fair to their oppressors but had been rebuffed time and again; by the end of the 1940s they had come one by one to the conclusion that they had next to nothing to hope for from the white leadership, be it that of Smuts or Malan, and that their own hitherto remarkably conciliatory line could not be continued. As Hofmeyr wrote a little pathetically in 1946 to Smuts, away at Lake Success preaching his gospel of international non-racial liberalism, apparently only inapplicable at home:

It seems that the (hitherto) moderate intellectuals of the Professor Matthews type are now committed to an extreme line against colour discrimination, and have carried the chiefs with them. We can't afford to allow them to be swept into the extremist camp, but I don't see what we can do to satisfy them which would be tolerated by European public opinion'.[32]

At the same time Matthews commented sadly upon a most unsatisfactory speech of Hofmeyr's to the Native Representative Council – 'It seemed merely an apologia for the status quo.' The gentleness of his comment was always remarkable; he was indeed somewhat too gentle to be the effective political leader of an oppressed people. Not without reason when he died Professor Monica Wilson described him as above all 'a man for reconcilia-tion – reconciliation without capitulation'.[33]

In a splendid statement of August 1950 James Calata called Christ 'the champion of Freedom'[34] thus enunciating a theological theme more associ-ated with 1970 than 1950. Two years later when Luthuli accepted the presidency of the Congress and had been dismissed from his position as Chief, he issued a statement upon his position. For thirty years, he said, he had been pursuing 'the path of moderation', 'knocking in vain patiently, moderately and modestly at a closed and barred door', now he saw no other alternative than that of Congress and the Passive Resistance Campaign. He ended with the famous words 'It is inevitable that in working for Freedom some individuals and some families must take the lead and suffer: The Road to Freedom is via the Cross'.[35]

There can be no question but that with these men Christian belief was stimulating and guiding political action, and one could reasonably claim that their voice and the political position it expressed was both more internally consistent and more consonant with the universal Christian tradition than either that of Clayton and Hofmeyr upon the one hand, or that of Dr Malan and the Dutch Reformed Churches upon the other.

It was in a very real way Christianity as taught and practised in the best liberal missionary institutions such as Fort Hare and Adams College which stimulated and even unified African nationalism up to this time; the next generation of leadership would be much less concerned with Christianity, and a dual role for men in both Congress and Christian Council would become increasingly improbable. Yet even the new generation of the Congress Youth League, founded in 1944, was at first much influenced by Christianity. The Young Turks of the Youth League, men like Nelson Mandela, Walter Sisulu and Oliver Tambo had as their first president Anton Lembede, a very active Catholic, who died in 1947; but the increasing feeling of their betrayal by the churches, coupled with new types of international influence, would mean that while some of the leaders might remain Christians, their religion would be increasingly peripheral to their public voice.

In most countries outside South Africa there was in 1950 very much less of a recognisably African church voice in the field of politics, though in Sierra Leone, Nigeria and the Gold Coast it had for many years been by no means absent. The leaders of West African coastal Christianity had taken it for granted that their religion, racial equality and political rights were linked at least by congruity. By 1950 Léopold Senghor was the leading political figure in Senegal, a predominantly Muslim country, though he spent much more of his time in Paris than he did in Dakar. A former seminarian, who had since come deeply under the influence of liberal and neo-Thomist French Catholics – Peguy, Maritain and Mounier – he represented the finest form of contemporary Catholic political thinking. In this, however, he was a somewhat isolated figure far more easily placeable in Europe than in Africa, though since 1948 he had joined the overseas political group, the Independants d'Outre-Mer, led by the Catholic Actionist, Dr Aujoulat. Less of a liberal was the Abbé Barthelemy Boganda, a brilliant young priest, who had also been in the National Assembly in Paris since 1946, representing his native Oubangui-Chari on the Catholic MRP ticket. In 1950 he had just married, been consequently defrocked, but neither lost his popular support nor greatly changed his point of view. He moved from the MRP to ally himself with the right-wing 'Peasant' group.

29

In both French- and Portuguese-speaking Africa the seminaries were a natural breeding ground for politicians. Indeed in Belgian and Portuguese Africa there might be almost no other road to a full secondary education. In the Congo there was already a considerable body of black Catholic priests as well as a still larger penumbra of ex-seminarists, and it is not surprising that an able young man like Abbé Joseph Malula in Leopoldville was at this time gathering a group of like-minded people around him under the name of Conscience Africaine to articulate a common concern for the problems of their society. Its occasional journal would be edited by Joseph Ileo, a future prime minister.[36] Further south again, in Angola there was in 1950 a lively group of students in Christ the King seminary at Nova Lisboa who set about spending their vacations organising a programme of general education in the villages with a significant political overtone. Not surprisingly this was not allowed to last long and most soon quit the seminary, but it provided one of the roots for the growing Angolan nationalism of the next decade.[37]

In English-speaking Africa politicisation sprouted from much more Protestant ground. In the Gold Coast, to take the most politically mature of the countries of Black Africa, Doctors Danquah, Busia and Baeta were something of the equivalent to Matthews and Jabavu in South Africa, if a little younger. Methodist or Presbyterian, they were men prominent alike in ecclesiastical, academic and political life. The Reverend C. G. Baeta was appointed in 1950 lecturer in religious studies at the new university college where he would later be professor; at the same time he was a member of Legislative Council. Neither he nor Busia nor Danquah were carried away by any great enthusiasm for the new leader; Busia was later to head the opposition until he went into exile, while Danquah would die in Nkrumah's prison. The latter's charismatic return and the emergence of the Convention People's Party could be compared with the contemporaneous rise in South Africa of the Congress Youth Group with its powerful new ideas, but in South Africa – perhaps on account of the far tougher challenge which had to be faced – the older element was not simply swept aside politically by the young men as practically happened in the Gold Coast. Furthermore the rapid emergence of Albert Luthuli, who had been almost apolitical until 1950 but represented a remarkable combination of the older Christian commitment and chiefly links with the new forcefulness proper to a nationalistic mass movement, helped at this time to avoid a collision of the sort which left the Gold Coast's senior Christian leadership somehow imprisoned within what was for the time yesterday's discredited party – the United Gold Coast Convention. The political problems which the Church would shortly have to face within the new system of a nationalist one-party state were, anyway, of so different a character from those of the colonial period that the legacy of Christian political attitudes derived from the immediate past was likely to be of limited lasting usefulness.

Elsewhere a specifically Christian political voice is often hard to detect. On one side African political structures were either very carefully circumscribed by the colonial authorities or of an inchoate or intermittent character; on the other the churches tended so strongly to disapprove of the independent expression of political views by their members that the aspiring politician was more likely to be an ex-churchman than a church goer. The able Rhodesian protopolitician Charles Mzingeli was such a one: a Catholic who finally broke with his church when he saw that even its more liberal representatives had no time for his political stance. His own independence was guaranteed by a modest grocery store and he had sound reason for complaining that no one in mission employ, such as catechists and teachers, was allowed to participate in political activities.[38]

North of the Zambezi too, while Welfare Associations and Congress Parties were almost inevitably inaugurated by the cream of the mission trained elite – the Presbyterian centre of Livingstonia, in particular, providing the seedbed for a rich series of political and religious initiatives – in almost every case the links between them and their churches of origin turned into a sense of antipathy. For a while at least the African Methodist Episcopal Church with its black American origins proved a more congenial environment for worship. When in 1946 John Membe, its indefatigable Zambian propagator, wrote in simple explanation of this all-black church to a sympathetic District Commissioner 'We as Africans are trying to exercise the self-help and worship God under our own Vine Tree',[39] he was asserting an at least potentially political position and only a few years later he would be enthusiastically preaching at meetings of the Northern Rhodesian Congress Party.

The fifth and final voice of the church in 1950 seldom reached print; it was less articulate than Membe's, and was probably not often heard in a European language: it was the rumbling, frequently incoherent, frequently suppressed voice of the common man, sharing to a greater or lesser extent in Christian faith as he shared too, almost invariably, in the faith of his ancestors and in the humiliated condition of a colonised race. It is by far the most difficult voice to detect, long silent, and when it did express itself it was often across supposedly non-political matters that, almost unconsciously, it evoked a political judgement. Thus the recurrent use of the term 'Ethiopian' to name apparently apolitical little independent sects a thousand miles away from Ethiopia surely represented a yearning as profoundly political as it was religious. Many a millennialist movement or church of the saints, with its mind set upon the eradication of witchcraft and sorcery and its confident hopes that a new age would soon arrive, lacked any recognisable political programme, yet its vision of the future almost invariably included some sort of reversal of roles in which the humiliated black would at last come into his own. Dangerous stuff in a colonial society it was easily judged, and all such movements were viewed by the authorities with the very greatest suspicion.

Waves of such religious dissidence, with its nearly inevitable political overtones, had swept the Congo in particular for decades – in the western Congo they usually invoked the name of Simon Kimbangu, while in the eastern Congo they drew rather on the legacy of 'Watchtower', *Kitawala*.[40] The predominant form such unrest was taking in the west in the 1940s was that of the 'Khaki movement' inspired by Simon Mpadi who emphatically proclaimed 'The Lord Simon Kimbangu' to be 'the sacred sceptre of empire whom the Lord God has given to the black race':[41] Kimbangu was in fact still in prison at Elizabethville where he had been ever since 1921 and where Mpadi was soon to join him. Dissidence could take many forms in which religious expectation and political protest were almost inextricably mixed; yet however purely religious their devotees might think some of them, the Belgian authorities proscribed them all. Thus the governor of Kasai, reacting to a new wave of Kimbanguist activity in the late 1940s, banned, on 18 November 1949, Kimbanguism, Ngunzism, prophetism, the Mission of the Blacks, the Bantu ba Simon, the Bana ba Simon.[42] Whatever it was, it was to be banned.

So when, again in 1949, the Angolan Simao Toco, a former Baptist teacher who had been living in the lower Congo, founded his own Pentecostal church, he too was at once arrested with a large crowd of his followers and on 10 January 1950 handed over at the frontier to the Portuguese authorities. Similarly just four months later Simon Mpadi arrested in the French Congo was handed over, on 17 May, to the Belgian authorities. The Tokoists appear in fact to have been one of the most politically harmless of groups and the Portuguese administration did not treat them too hard but they were at once committed to various camps and restricted areas. Toco himself was moved from place to place but, as he continued far too active and persuasive a preacher for the liking of the authorities, he was at length appointed keeper of an isolated lighthouse! – a minor political victim, like so many others, almost despite himself.[43]

On the other side of the continent on 24 April 1950 at Kolloa in western Kenya there was a bloody battle between another little group, though a more militant one, the Dini ya Msambwa (the Religion of the Ancestors), fighting beneath their green flag, and the police. Twenty members of the Dini were killed including their current leader, Lukas Pkech, as were four policemen. The Dini, traditionalist and polygamous, had been founded by Elijah Masinde, formerly an adherent of the Friends African Mission. By 1950 Elijah had already been deported to Lamu. Hardly countable as a Christian church, though much influenced by biblical and Christian themes, it advocated the eviction of Europeans and proclaimed the dawning of a new age. An obstinate handful of confused men and women, it struggled on through many years despite repeated official efforts at suppression, with a mixture of bible and African tradition, strange but not uncommon hopes for a religious–political utopia round the corner. Its sad uncertain history points not only towards the larger appeal of Mau Mau but still more poignantly to the vast mental unsettlement on the wide borderlands of old and new, of religious belief and political action.[44]

One man who might fairly be said to represent the fifth voice of the church, with a far clearer Christian conviction than Lukas Pkech, spent the whole of 1950 in prison in Uganda. It was the Archpriest Reuben Spartas Ssebanja Mukasa. He was at that time fifty years old.[45] Twenty years earlier he had founded in Uganda the African Greek Orthodox Church with its headquarters at Namungona, four miles from Kampala, being ordained a priest by Archbishop Alexander, an African from South Africa, who had obtained his orders from a mysterious succession going back to a Jacobite bishop in Malabar. While the Orthodox Church never grew very large in Uganda it had some 10,000 adherents in 1950. Although Spartas' original intention was undoubtedly one of asserting African ecclesiastical autonomy – a thing never entirely unconnected in his eyes with political autonomy – absolute independence was certainly not crucial for him and within a few years he had gravitated into the Orthodox Communion of Alexandria after a visit from a Greek priest working in Tanganyika, the Archimandrite Sarikas. In 1946 Spartas even visited Alexandria, was blessed by the Patriarch and appointed his Vicar General.

Spartas' interests, however, had always been political as well as religious. Back in 1925 he had tried, unsuccessfully, to found an African Progressive Society. Now, after his visit to Alexandria, he rather quickly became absorbed in the Bataka movement which culminated in the Buganda riots of April and May 1949. Linked with the African Farmers Union it was a people's movement against the political oligarchy which now effectively ruled Buganda, as well as a general restlessness with the new order whether represented by British governors, Catholic or Anglican missionaries or the chiefs and African clergy who cooperated with them. It was an upsurge of anxiety whose aims were largely unformulated, a harking back to what were seen as the traditional values, both religious and social, a reaction from the immense enthusiasm with which thirty to fifty years earlier the Baganda had turned en masse to a new Christian and political order. That enthusiasm had turned somewhat sour, partly because while many of the chiefs of the first Christian generation had been men of spiritual power, their successors inherited their wealth and privilege but little of their personal commitment. Probably the most clear-minded leader of the Bataka at this time was that mysterious man Semakula Mulumba, formerly a Catholic religious brother (a Munnacaroli) who left for England, settled in Hampstead, and directed the movement from there, not returning for over twenty years but continually subsidised by his supporters. It was in his village of Kirumba, in the heart of the Catholic county of Buddu and the vicariate of the first African bishop, Mgr Kiwanuka, that the symbolic pattern of the movement first developed. Children were withdrawn from the Catholic schools and an independent one set up instead. The Word 'BU' was clearly displayed on all houses. The men grew hair and beard long, the women left their nails uncut and wore bark cloth on all occasions.[46] Their protest, if somewhat incoherent, was a comprehensive one, religious and political.

It has never been clear exactly what the Archpriest or the other leaders of the Bataka really intended to achieve. They were against both western ways and the chiefly oligarchy, calling for an alliance of king and people. Their immediate demand was for an elected Lukiko (Buganda's own national council). Maybe only Mulumba among them became clearly committed to political revolution. Sentenced after the riots to six years imprisonment, Spartas was in fact released in late 1953. While the Bataka had become a threat to the Kabaka's own government in 1949, they became his firmest supporters when he was himself sent into exile four years later and Spartas was even nominated by the Kabaka personally as a member of the Lukiko in 1956.

Spartas in prison in 1950, as indeed Semakula Mulumba in Hampstead, might seem an odd but not a very significant figure. And yet in the very ambiguity of his position Spartas could be seen to represent much in the church of his time: extremely enterprising, constantly seeking both for the old and the new, and yet dissatisfied too with both. A traditionalist who was a continual innovator, a Christian who resented missionary churches and yet submitted most attentively to the Patriarch of Alexandria; a man above all whose mind went restlessly back and forth between religion and politics, 'President of the Baganda Landlords' at one moment, Vicar General of the Patriarch of Alexandria at another; finally, one might admit, ineffectual enough, but not finally pointless: a voice both of the church and of the people.

B. The historic churches

In his conversion to the Orthodox tradition Reuben Spartas was very much of an exception, although in central Kenya too there was in 1950 a small black Orthodox Church. But the principal representative of eastern Christianity in black Africa has been, of course, ever since the fourth century, the Church of Ethiopia, dependent as it remained upon the see of Alexandria.

The Church of Alexandria is indubitably the primal see of Africa, one of the three original patriarchates of the ancient church. Egypt in the third, fourth and fifth centuries was probably the most forceful and creative province of Christendom – the home of Origen, Athanasius and Cyril, the cradle of Christian monasticism. Then came the great Christological schism of the fifth century when Egypt and Syria were unable to accept the Council of Chalcedon, a theological divide which reflected all too obviously an underlying cultural divide between the Greek–Latin imperial world upon the one hand and that of African and Asian nationalisms upon the other. From then on the Coptic tradition of Egypt, like the Syriac tradition, was out of communion with the West and became the core of so-called monophysite or 'non-chalcedonian' christianity.

It was from Egypt and Syria that the Ethiopian Orthodox Church was founded and fed, and it remained subject through the ages to the see of Alexandria from where it always received its Abuna or archbishop and to which it owed its creed, liturgy and monastic spirituality. Nevertheless its practical isolation for so many centuries and its social and cultural requirements, so different from those of the lower Nile Valley, permitted the development of a unique ecclesiological, liturgical and artistic tradition.

The most unusual element in this tradition was its Hebraic substructure. It seems undeniable that in some way the ancient Aksumite kingdom, from which that of Ethiopia has grown, had been profoundly influenced by Judaism before the coming of Christianity in the reign of Ezana. This pre-existing Judaism both rendered Christian conversion easier and in an extraordinary way controlled its institutional evolution so that the resulting pattern of Orthodox worship and religious life was as much one of the Old Testament as of the New.[47] The way the interior of church buildings was divided into three upon the model of the Temple, the observance of the Pentateuchal dietary laws dividing clean from unclean, the holding of the Sabbath equal to Sunday, circumcision on the eighth day – these are but some of the more striking instances of the Judaic character of the Ethiopian Church. In no other major branch of Christianity has there been such continuity maintained with Judaism.

This continuity was not only a matter of practice but also of ecclesiology: the Ethiopian kingdom and church have been seen as the exact inheritor of the Judaic kingdom. The key to this can best be found in the fourteenth-century document, the *Kebra Nagast* (the 'Glory of the Kings') which tells how the Queen of Sheba visited Solomon, returned home pregnant with his child who became Menelik I of Ethiopia, founder of the Solomonic dynasty; further how Menelik later visited his father and carried off the Ark of the Covenant which he bore back to Aksum, the original capital of Ethiopia.[48] The *Kebra Nagast* concludes with the following words: 'Thus hath God made for the King of Ethiopia more glory and grace and majesty than for all the other kings of the earth because of the greatness of Zion, the Tabernacle of the Law of God, the heavenly Zion.' While a fourteenth-century text incorporating still older traditions about the mythical history of two thousand years earlier may seem a very long way away from twentieth-century Africa, it yet remains extraordinarily apt to throw light upon much that is contemporary. Its confident conviction that the holy city of Aksum is no other than Jerusalem for it actually possesses the Ark of the Covenant, and that the Ethiopian people are no other than the chosen people of God, has been the central theme of Ethiopian Christian thought ever since. 'Siyon' was the symbolic name of the kingdom itself: Ethiopia is Zion,[49] Zion realised and renewed upon African soil.

Preoccupation with Jerusalem has proved a potent and recurring theme within the Ethiopian tradition. The holy city of Lalibela with its wondrous rock churches seems to have been devised as a new Aksum in the safer and more accessible highlands, a new Jerusalem and a centre of pilgrimage. Its foundation is linked with the pilgrimage of its founder, King Lalibela, to Jerusalem. It was to have its own Jordan, its own mount of Transfiguration, above all its own Golgotha. This passionate re-enactment of Jerusalem in Ethiopia had as its anchor a continuing bond with the historic Jerusalem. Nothing is more impressive than the tenacity manifested through the centuries by the Ethiopian monastery in Palestine.

There was here a profound identification in principle of religion and national identity: being Ethiopian at bottom meant being Christian, even though as a matter of fact many Ethiopians were never Christians – not only in the newly conquered lands but in the historic heart land of the northern highlands. But the Old Testament sense of mission, of being a chosen nation, now a Christian nation, 'God's holy people' was immensely strong though it generally coexisted with a considerable tolerance of non-Christians in their midst as also with the survival within Christian life of local religious and magical practices deriving from many sources. There was a rich and uncontrolled syncretic character in Ethiopian religion assisted by the absence of most of the hierarchical and administrative institutions one is accustomed to in a western church; yet despite the vast isolation this never affected its unquestionable adherence across the centuries to the essentials of Christian belief and sacramental practice. For this the monasteries and the link with Alexandria were above all responsible.

The Ethiopian model of Christianity coupled its Old Testament observances with a liturgy, carried out by a multitude of white robed and turbaned clergy, centred upon the sacraments and the great festivals which is entirely recognisable as part of the world Christian tradition, if at the same time highly distinctive. One thinks of the splendid ceremonies at Aksum for Hosanna, the Palm Festival, or for the Feast of Our Lady of Zion, or at Tamkat, Epiphany, the Baptismal feast, when the faithful are annually 'rebaptised' after the sacred crosses have been solemnly dipped in the waters of the river. A form of Christianity emerged here in very special circumstances which yet seems almost archetypal in a number of important ways for the rest of the continent. And from the late nineteenth century its independent existence appeared as a symbol for dissatisfied searching Christians to the south and the west – as a justificatory charter for being themselves, a constant source of inspiration and of nomenclature. It would be foolish to describe modern African Christianity in terms of acceptance or rejection of the sources of western Europe and north America, Protestant and Roman Catholic, while ignoring this great additional source, already so deeply adapted culturally, in the horn of Africa.

The Ethiopian Church has grown very greatly in size during the last hundred years, particularly towards the south, as partner of the expanding Ethiopian monarchy since the days of Yohannes IV (1872–89) and of Menelik II (1889–1913). The church had no formal missionary institutions and the expansion southwards was in the first instance an expansion of northern Christians – governors, soldiers, traders, clergy – taking up residence, occupying land, building churches.[50] Such Galla and Sidamo as were converted had no long catechumenate nor, any more than their Cushitic predecessors in the northern highlands, were they expected to withdraw categorically from all the beliefs and practices they had hitherto cherished. In southern Ethiopia Christianity spread much as it had done on the borders of an early medieval Christian state in northern Europe or as Islam still spread among the subjects of a Sudanic Sultan. In places a chief sought baptism with many of his followers; in places some holy priest exercised a powerful influence upon those among whom he had settled; at times a forceful northern governor set up a school and put pressure on his more accessible subjects to accept the imperial religion.[51] If Christianity spread in such ways, it was also resisted by many of the new subject peoples precisely because it was experienced as a function of Ethiopianisation. Certainly a governor like the stern warrior Balča, who ruled over the largely non-Christian southern province of Sidamo for many decades following the Battle of Adwa, saw it as part of his task to build churches and to patronise

37

the priests and deacons who taught church songs and traditional poetry in his court school. He would have the Lives of the Saints read to him each day.[52]

The Ethiopian Church had no alternative to dependence upon the monarchy and such lay magnates as Balča. Its strength lay in the monasteries and the villages, above these there had been next to no superstructure at all. Until 1929 there was but one bishop and that an Egyptian who was often not even fluent in Amharic. In that year, as part of the reforms of the early period of Haile Selassie, five assistant Ethiopian bishops had been consecrated in Alexandria. During the Italian occupation the Ethiopian Church had been forcibly separated from the Coptic and, much as the Ethiopians disliked the Italians and all their deeds, on this they did not wish to go back. There was a strong nationalist sentiment at work in the church only partially restrained by the Emperor. While the aged Egyptian primate, Abuna Kyrillos, was accepted back in principle, negotiations were at once begun to ensure that future primates would be Ethiopian.[53] The Copts were at first quite unwilling to allow this and the lengthy negotiations almost ended more than once in deadlock and an Ethiopian declaration of ecclesiastical independence; this, however, was avoided and in July 1948 it was agreed that the next primate should be an Ethiopian backed by an enlarged Ethiopian hierarchy. So when Kyrillos died in October 1950 the Abuna Basilios, prior of Debra Libanos and already acting archbishop, was elected in his place and solemnly installed in Cairo in January as Primate of Ethiopia.

It was a symbol of the growing strength and confidence of Ethiopia which went with the restored rule of Haile Selassie, and if black men all over the continent had been shocked by Mussolini's conquest in the 1930s,[54] they could now rejoice and take heart in the triumphant vindication of black independence and majesty in both state and church. But the appointment of Basilios was not merely an expression of Ethiopian independence, it was also a practical step in the process of providing the Orthodox church with an institutional structure and leadership more or less comparable with that of churches elsewhere.

The Ethiopian Church had no organised presence whatsoever beyond its political borders (except in its ancient monastery in Jerusalem). Perhaps so much the better: if its impact on its immediate neighbours was often a matter of imperial institution rather than of charisma and such as to produce considerable antipathy, its vast remoter impact was quite the opposite: a mysterious counter-symbol to white western Christianity. Certainly by 1950 when the Prior of Debra Libanos was preparing for his consecration in Cairo, European missionaries who had brought extensive churches into being all across Africa had no intention of encouraging consideration of the Ethiopian model: for them it was rather a corrupt and almost irrelevant religious backwater.

For a hundred years they and their predecessors had been unfailingly at work up and down the continent, engaged in a seemingly strange variety of occupations: exploring rivers, tending gardens, buying and freeing slaves, building schools and hospitals, preaching their doctrines, translating their bibles and prayerbooks into scores of languages, holding services, even running little enclaves of society as if they were semi-independent fiefs. However pietistic or 'other-worldly' missions might be in inspiration, it is remarkable how in practice they generally got down within a few years to grappling with such strongly this-worldly concerns and to taking for granted that the liberation of man from famine or the slave trader was a proper, even a central, aspect of their work and the only plausible vehicle for a more ultimate message. Doubtless the point of it all remained in their own minds a fairly simple one: to produce conversions to Christian faith and so establish churches (of their particular denominational brand) where hitherto there had been but paganism or Islam.[55]

The nineteenth century was the golden age of the Protestant missionary and Africa his most challenging field of work. The Catholic missionary effort seemed limited in comparison and a bit out of the main stream. In earlier ages it had been the other way round – there was a striking absence of missionary concern in Reformation Protestantism – but the considerable Catholic mission effort born of the sixteenth-century spiritual and institutional revival known as the Counter-Reformation had almost collapsed by the close of the eighteenth. The main missionary society had been that of the Jesuits, which was dissolved by the Pope under political pressure in 1773 and only resurrected fifty years later. Following upon this and the general lassitude of institutional religion in the later eighteenth century came the French Revolution to break up the structures of the Catholic Church not only in France but throughout much of southern Europe. The consequence was a hiatus in the Catholic overseas effort just at the time when the great Protestant missionary thrust was getting under way under the inspiration of Pietism and the Evangelical Movement.

The British Baptist Missionary Society was founded in 1792 and the non-denominational (but largely Congregationalist) London Missionary Society in 1795. The Evangelical Anglican Church Missionary Society followed four years later, the Basel Mission in 1815 and that of Berlin in 1824. And so it went on all across the Protestant world. Their missionaries led the way in the opening up of the interior of Africa to European knowledge, trade, settlement and conquest. While there was always a handful of Catholic missionaries at work along the coast, notably some Holy Ghost Fathers, the Catholic missionary revival really came a good deal later – after the middle of the century with de Marion Bresillac's foundation of the Society of African Missions at Lyons in 1856 and Daniel Comboni's call to arms, his *Piano per la rigenerazione dell'Africa* published in 1864. In the next five years the Verona Fathers were founded by Comboni in Italy, the

White Fathers by Lavigerie in Algiers and the Mill Hill Fathers by Vaughan in England. Other societies, both of nuns and priests, followed in many countries but the effective impact on the mission field took time to develop, and in many parts of Africa the impression was given that the Catholics were rather irritatingly dogging the footsteps of the Protestant pioneers. At its most memorable the epoch had been a Protestant one, its abiding names Moffat and Livingstone, Coillard and Rebmann, Mary Slessor and James Stewart, Robert Laws and Bishop Mackenzie.

Other factors helped to strengthen the Protestant ascendancy over the nineteenth century. The effect of the British blockade on slave ships had been to land many slaves at Freetown in Sierra Leone, a Protestant stronghold since its foundation by returned black Nova Scotians. Fourah Bay College was set up by the CMS for their education and soon some among them were returning to evangelise their own peoples along the coast. The impact of this upon the character of West African coastal Christianity was, all in all, immense and it was almost entirely a Protestant one: a few returned Catholics from Brazil should not be forgotten for their influence in Dahomey or Lagos, but they did not turn into evangelists as did many of their Protestant cousins from Freetown. Of these Bishop Samuel Ajayi Crowther, a Yoruba who became bishop on the Niger, was the most distinguished. He and his colleagues, while frequently treated none too well by their own British-based missionary societies, ensured that West African Christianity would have at first a strongly Protestant ethos.

The presence of the old Dutch settlement at the Cape brought about much the same result for southern Africa, coupled as it was with an ever growing spate of British missionaries, many of whom nevertheless were as far from seeing eye to eye with the Dutch Calvinists as were their contemporaries from appreciating very whole heartedly the native Christian tradition on the west coast. It was the shadow of Britain which established everywhere, west, south and east, something of a Protestant ethos for colonial Africa. Britain was Africa's primary imperial power and Britain in the nineteenth century was undoubtedly a Protestant state, if one which could not afford to be too unfair to Catholic interests – Ireland was, after all, an increasingly vociferous part of the United Kingdom. While France also obtained considerable, if far less populated, areas of black Africa, and was in some sense a Catholic country, it was at the close of the nineteenth century ruled by rather anti-clerical governments. There was none of the steady sympathetic convergences of outlook and action between church and state in France which could exist in Britain, though that by no means diminished the nationalism of many a French missionary. Germany, Africa's third colonial power, while it had a large Catholic minority at home, was also dominantly Protestant in leadership and sympathy. In Catholic Portugal the church was inert and the government anti-clerical so that it was only in Belgian Africa that, effectively, there had been a positively different image and with a good deal of governmental favouritism Christianisation appeared as primarily a matter of Catholicisation.

This missionary weighting of the nineteenth century was still to the public eye the dominant one in 1950 – at least for British Africa. It could be said with some over-simplification that Africa, in so far as it was Christian, was seen as primarily Protestant and Protestant of a certain kind. Its missionaries had been predominantly from Europe and from Europe's main historic churches: German and Scandinavian Lutherans; French, Swiss and Dutch Calvinists; Scottish Presbyterians; British Anglicans, Methodists and Baptists. The defeat of Germany in two world wars and the loss of its colonies in the first, together with the numerical weakness of French Protestantism, ensured that Britain emphatically took the lead ecclesiastically as politically: the nerve centre for the mission enterprise was Edinburgh House in the heart of London. While American Protestantism with its far stronger 'sectarian' emphasis had since 1920 sent out an ever increasing number of missionaries, they had hitherto mostly been destined for Asia or South America, though they were numerous enough in the Congo. In 1950 Africa as a whole had still experienced rather limited American interest in church or state. It remained Europe's continent and by reputation Protestant Europe's continent: its historic hero was Livingstone; its living hero was the theologian, musician and missionary doctor, Albert Schweitzer, labouring in his hospital at Lambarene in the Gabon as he had been for most of the time since his first arrival there in 1913; its chosen author was the scholarly Edwin Smith who had been born on a South African mission station in 1876, had become a master of Bantu languages as well as a Methodist missionary in central Africa, the writer of a prodigious number of books about African and missionary subjects and, in 1950, had only just given up the editorship of the International African Institute's quarterly *Africa*; its senior statesman was the quietly omniscient Scot, J. H. Oldham.

For world Protestantism this was a moment of a wider enlightened assurance: the ending of the Second World War and the establishment of the United Nations Organisation appeared to spell a possible new era for the world in which the prevailing inspiration would be that of the Christian Protestant West. The seventh and final volume of Kenneth Latourette's *History of the Expansion of Christianity*, published in 1947, is instinct with a sense of confidence and superiority; the following year the World Council of Churches was constituted at Amsterdam. The calibre of intelligence and leadership taken for granted in these ecclesiastical circles was certainly very high: they were the circles of Visser't Hooft and Bishop Bell of Chichester, of Canon Charles Raven and Pastor Niemoller, with theologians to turn to such as Barth, Tillich and Kraemer. If there were sides to this establishment too liberal and too ecumenical to be other than a source of suspicion to more fundamentalist missionaries, it was nevertheless an establishment into which the top echelon of the missionary leadership was naturally slotted. One may think of Geoffrey Clayton, J. H. Oldham, Max Warren. Archbishop Clayton of Cape Town – at that time the only Anglican Archbishop in Africa – was a former fellow of Peterhouse, Cambridge, who towered above African Church circles with a hard, rather clerical, far-sighted clarity of mind and firmness of purpose.[56] J. H. Oldham had never lived in Africa but few people had influenced its progress more, the most liberal and far-sighted of paternalists. The secretary of the World Missionary Conference at Edinburgh in 1910 and for many years of the International Missionary Council, first editor of the *International Review of Missions* and author (in 1924) of *Christianity and the Race Problem*, he was a layman whose ecclesiastical status was worth that of twenty bishops, a man who had negotiated time and again with the British government over African interests, a principal architect of the World Council and still, in 1950, aged seventy-six a powerfully influential figure behind the scenes. Max Warren was of a younger generation, thirty years younger than Oldham.[57] In 1950 he had been General Secretary of the CMS for eight years – arguably at that time the most influential position in the whole of the Protestant missionary world. He was to continue for another thirteen. Like Clayton a Cambridge man, he was one endowed with all the comfortable, urbane confidence of the upper-middle-class Anglican Evangelical: so sure in his faith and so firmly on beam socially that he could quietly innovate as the years passed and he perceived the political and ecclesiastical environment changing about him. Like Oldham, Clayton, or Archbishop Fisher with whom he had so much to do, Warren moved very easily back and forth between his own church establishment and that of British government, yet he could evaluate both pretty shrewdly, forseeing more than most that in a profound way the line would end with him: the 1950s were really to be the last decade for the ecclesiastical statesman of this type.

In 1950, however, the shape of the future and the speed with which it would descend upon the churches to transform their missionary structures were far from evident. On the contrary, the old confidence was simply reinforced by a sense of wider horizons and more effective ecumenical co-operation than had ever before been practicable. There were plenty of remarkable men at work on every side: Bishop Stephen Neill was that year travelling all across Africa surveying the state of theological education; Carey Francis, another former Peterhouse fellow, was headmaster of Alliance High School in Kenya, building it up as a superbly efficient Evangelical tool of African education; then there was Geoffrey Parrinder, lecturer in Religious Studies at Ibadan, whose book on *West African Religion* had just appeared. There was John V. Taylor in Uganda, Trevor Huddleston on the Rand and many others – people of great ability and dedication, rather more conscious than their predecessors of the wider religious, social and political implications of Christian mission.

Perhaps the missionary figure with the greatest African sensitivity was the young Swedish Lutheran, Bengt Sundkler, who had been serving as Research Secretary of the International Missionary Council. He had already done important work in South Africa and Tanganyika and published a seminal study of Bantu prophets; now Professor in Uppsala he gave a lecture in 1950 to the Nordic Missionary Conference in Oslo on the 'Indigenous Church' which pointed, as this gentle seer was so often to do, at the *punctum stantis aut cadentis* of the missionary movement. As a Swede he represented a group of relative 'outsiders' in the colonial world and this is important, a missionary element not to be overlooked. Swedes, Swiss, Danes, while not so numerous, were able to bear a greater role of disinterestedness which generated both vision and confidence.

Certainly if one looked around Africa in 1950 the achievement of the missionary enterprise could not but appear very considerable. With a helping hand from most colonial governments and in many lands little less than a monopoly of primary and secondary education, the perseverance, wide-ranging ability and money of the missionary societies had combined with the eager response of many Africans to produce churches whose size and character was now remarkable. If in the nineteenth century and even the first years of the twentieth the labours of pioneer missionaries had frequently been crowned by a mere trickle of converts, except in a few favoured and untypical places, from about 1919 onwards with the clear establishment almost everywhere of the colonial economy and the arrival of the bicycle this very clearly changed. Baptisms mounted by leaps and bounds as missionary stations multiplied even in the most out of the way areas, and village churches multiplied still more; the catechist became the great new figure of rural Africa, while white missionaries spent more and more of their time supervising and continually extending a complex network of schools ranging from the crudest village huts to elite boarding establishments.

By 1950 there were at least twenty-three million Christians in the Continent between the Cape and the Sahara.[58] Of these, very roughly, eleven million were Roman Catholics, ten million Protestants and two million members of independent churches. Of the Catholics three-and-a-half million were in Belgian territory – the Congo seemed clearly destined to provide the real heart of Catholic Africa; there were also very strong churches in eastern Africa – one million in Uganda and 700,000 in Tanganyika. The west was comparatively weak with one-and-a-half million all the way from Senegal through Gold Coast, Ivory Coast and Nigeria to the British Cameroons: Dahomey and Igboland were here the strongest points. The Union of South Africa was still weaker with but half a million, black and white together.

The Protestant (including Anglican) pattern was different with its strongest bases just where the Catholics were weakest – in South Africa and the west coast, especially Nigeria.[59] Of its ten million about half (two million white and three million black) were inside the Union of South Africa, but there was also a remarkably strong church developing in the Belgian Congo – claiming some one-and-a-half million adherents. It is interesting that one of the most vigorous sections of Protestant Christianity should have emerged in the Congo where the colonial government had been least favourable. They may indeed have secretly benefited from this situation which made the independent character of the missionary a great deal clearer in African eyes and also better reflected the inner sense of the Protestant vocation than the rather more establishment status Anglicans, Methodists and Presbyterians easily enjoyed elsewhere beneath the Union Jack. It corresponded too with both the Baptist and the American background of so many of the missionaries.

There were fewer Protestants than Catholics in French Africa, in Tanganyika and (probably) Uganda, and far fewer in Portuguese Africa. In the latter they were facing an increasingly unfavourable position since the Concordat of 1940 which had provided so very privileged a status for Roman Catholic work. But in Liberia, Sierra Leone, Gold Coast, Nigeria, Kenya, Nyasaland, the Rhodesias, Bechuanaland and South Africa they were considerably more numerous. If there were some eight million black Protestant Christians, they were certainly heavily weighted to the south. In South Africa itself there were over a million non-white Methodists, 750,000 Anglicans, 550,000 Dutch Reformed and 450,000 Lutherans.[60] Congregationalists numbered over 200,000 to which should be joined the large Congregational church in neighbouring Bechuanaland, the fruit of the work of the London Missionary Society.[61] Elsewhere the main Lutheran presence was in South West Africa, Tanganyika and the Cameroons – old German territories where Scandinavian as well as German missionaries had worked devotedly for decades – for instance Finns in South West Africa. From Scandinavia again the Free Swedish Mission had built up a sizeable church in the French Congo around Brazzaville. From Protestant Europe too were the strong missions of the Paris Evangelical Missionary Society in Basutoland and Barotseland. The Basel Mission, the Church of Scotland and the Free Church of Scotland (reunited to the former in 1929) had served vigorous Presbyterian missions in the Gold Coast and Togo, Nigeria and the Cameroons, Kenya, Nyasaland and Northern Rhodesia as well as South Africa.[62] The Dutch Reformed Church of South Africa was responsible for work of a particularly high quality in the Tiv country of Nigeria, Nyasaland, Northern and Southern Rhodesia. Baptists were strongest in the Congo and northern Angola but were present too in Nigeria, the Cameroons and elsewhere. Not far removed from them were the 'non-denominational' societies, fundamentalist and mostly American based. The largest of these were the Sudan Interior Mission and the Africa Inland Mission. The former was at work principally in northern Nigeria and Ethiopia, the latter in Kenya and the Congo. These had not been large societies in the past but by 1950 they and the Baptists were expanding in a way many others were not.

There was an Anglican presence in every part of British Africa and almost none beyond (except for Rwanda and Burundi), but its strength varied greatly: massive in Nigeria and Uganda, moderate in Kenya and Nyasaland, weak in Gold Coast and Northern Rhodesia. The largest missionary society involved, the CMS, was responsible for all the work north of Tanganyika except for the tiny mission in the Gold Coast.[63] This had produced a predominantly evangelical tone to the Anglicanism of West and East Africa but in southern Tanganyika, Nyasaland and Northern Rhodesia the high church UMCA (Universities' Mission to central Africa) introduced a very different tradition of churchmanship with its celibate missionaries and its emphatic commitment to Anglo-Catholic teaching and spirituality. Probably no other part of the world Anglican communion had so unequivocally 'Catholic' a character as the dioceses of Zanzibar, Masasi and Nyasaland. Further south in South Africa and Rhodesia, Anglicanism, backed by the old established Society for the Propagation of the Gospel had also developed on 'high' rather than 'evangelical' lines. Hence (with the minor exception of the Gold Coast) Anglicans were being taught to be Evangelicals in one half of Africa (Sierra Leone, Nigeria, Uganda, Kenya, Rwanda, Burundi, northern Tanganyika) and high church in the other (southern Tanganyika and all to the south of it): the first group took it for granted that they were 'Protestant' Christians; the second would have been distressed to be so described.

Methodists were at least as widely spread across the continent and were much less confined to the British Empire, but they could vary significantly depending on whether their origins were British, American or continental. Thus in Rhodesia two separate Methodist churches were developing because there were two Methodist missionary societies working in the country, one British, one American. The Methodist was in 1950 the largest church among Africans in South Africa and also in the Gold Coast. It was strong in southern Nigeria and central Kenya, but also in several non-British parts of the continent. There was a thriving church in the Ivory Coast largely springing from converts of the Prophet Harris (see page 81) and there were also significant American Methodist missions in Katanga and central Angola.

All in all the Protestant map was anything but a simple one. While in a few countries, such as Uganda, Tanganyika and much of French Africa, there was very little overlapping between Protestant missions, in many others – particularly the more salubrious parts of British Africa – there was a great deal. In Uganda there was a single significant Protestant church, the Anglican, served by the CMS and its various subsidiaries. Even when the Africa Inland Mission, by no means an Anglican body, decided to start work in Uganda, it agreed to do so in conjunction with the CMS so that in the West Nile District, where it laboured, its converts became members of the one Anglican Church. South Africa presented the most extreme contrast to this – Livingstone long ago had already protested about how Protestant missionaries huddled together in its more settled parts.[64] Yet they seldom worked together: even Lutherans from one country could find it hard, or impossible, to cooperate with Lutherans from another.[65] Something similar happened in parts of Nigeria, the Gold Coast, Kenya and the Rhodesias, so that a wide range of western denominations took root in each country.

In the Belgian Congo by 1950 there were forty-four different Protestant missionary societies at work and 1,699 missionaries.[66] Though they were so many, they mostly shared something of a common viewpoint, many being definitely Baptist (British, American or Scandinavian) and all needing to stand up to the clear favour the Belgian authorities had shown the Catholics. As a consequence the Protestant societies had for years worked fairly harmoniously together through the Congo Protestant Council in a way which was not so often achieved elsewhere.

The Protestant and Anglican missionary commitment to Africa can never have seemed more impressive than in 1950, and yet beneath the surface much was not well. Bishop Neill's survey provided one key pointer here: while the churches had worked hard since the 1920s on the development of schools and hospitals, a development that actually seemed to necessitate the continued presence and control of foreign missionaries, they had done strangely little in most places to train a local clergy which could possibly replace the missionaries outside the villages. Apart from the Catholic Church, what ministers were trained had nearly all an extremely low standard of education. While such a standard was very likely the right way to begin in the early stages of a mission, and while such men could be admirable village pastors, they were not such as to cater well for the modern side of society or to take over the leadership and administration of large churches organised in a western way. It could easily look as if many missionaries did not want such clerical leaders to arise, or at least not to rise too soon or too far; indeed when able men did emerge they often received the impression that there was little question of their attaining to positions of major responsibility: however experienced and competent, an African would still be left technically subject to some newly arrived European. In the Congo there was as yet not one African member of the Congo Protestant Council.[67] Until 1947 there had been no single African Anglican bishop in east, central or southern Africa and since then there had been only one, Aberi Balya, an assistant bishop in Uganda.

Yet at the same time the need for a great increase in able African leadership was, even on the most obviously practical grounds, extremely grave. The churches were rapidly expanding, there were new opportunities of work on every side, young missionaries were just not appearing in the numbers needed. Nor was there money to support them. The main churches of Britain and Europe, upon whom the major responsibilities for the mission lay, had in fact entered into a long and apparently unalterable process of missionary decline. It had begun with the world slump of 1929, if not before;[68] it had been accentuated by the Second World War, and now – despite an immediate post-war enthusiasm and the fact that many posts could qualify under new arrangements for governmental financial support – the main Protestant churches were more and more conscious that their personnel simply could not keep pace with that of the Roman Catholics upon the one side and new American fundamentalist agencies upon the other.[69]

Furthermore, some of the most important older Protestant missions were also grievously weakened by schisms, and even when these did not finally result in the establishment of new independent churches of any great size in comparison with the parent body, they did carry away too many of their abler ministers and senior members not seriously to jeopardise the maturing of their work. An example among many is that of the Livingstonia mission in northern Nyasaland, the pride of the Free Church of Scotland, established by that remarkably equable and persevering man Dr Robert Laws in 1875 and supervised by him for over fifty years.[70] For many Livingstonia has seemed almost the ideal mission and its Overtoun Institution was undoubtedly the major educational influence in Central Africa; yet from the time of its golden jubilee its history was one of many disappointments. Between 1928 and 1934 there were four major secessions. The first, out of which came the African National Church, was founded by five middle-grade Livingstonia graduates: three were teachers, one a printer and one had been a mission storekeeper. The other three secessions were all led by experienced clergy, one of whom, Y. Z. Mwasi, had been the first African Moderator of Presbytery. They linked together to establish the Black Man's Church in Africa. Livingstonia had a far better record of early ordination and devolution of authority than most missions. Indeed the greatest danger seemed to be just here: some promotion was allowed but this made it all the clearer that essentially control remained in white hands. The very authority which an African minister had acquired compounded the frustration, particularly if he also had other personal problems to contend with. At Livingstonia things may have been made worse by something of a trough following the ending of the long reign of Laws. And then, of course, there was the sheer ethos of the Free Church. If the men of the Free Church had proudly withdrawn from the Church of Scotland in the 'Disruption' of 1843, a fact which was by no means hidden from their converts, why should not Mwasi and Chinula now do the same? As Chinula himself declared, it was the 'Livingstonia Mission which trained me' to seek God 'according to the liberty of my own conscience'.[71] Neither of these churches became very large but the loss of leading men and the undermining of confidence inside Livingstonia could not but be serious.

In West and South Africa particularly the Protestant churches had what was probably their clearest success in the engendering of a small church-linked elite of the highest quality. On the west coast a lively, out-spoken, self-confident urban society had grown up in Lagos, Accra, Freetown and Monrovia. Dependent on Protestant mission schools, its leadership constituted the elite of the Anglican, Methodist, Presbyterian and Baptist Churches. This group certainly did include some clerics such as the Gold Coast Presbyterian theologian Baeta and Anglican bishops like the Sierra Leonean T. S. Johnson and the Nigerian Akinyele.[72] These last two were both over seventy in 1950 and had been consecrated as assistant bishops in the 1930s. In 1950 there was as yet no diocesan bishop appointed since the death of Crowther in 1891, though Akinyele would become one the following year with the erection of the new diocese of Ibadan. Johnson and Akinyele were both Fourah Bay graduates and had both been secondary school headmasters for many years. Johnson had retired in 1947 to spend his final years in his home village of Benguema where he wrote local history and introduced a machine for cracking palm nuts. All the same the church seemed to find it a lot easier to encourage a lay elite than a clerical one. There was in 1950, as there had been for years, a distinguished Protestant lay professional leadership in the main towns along the west African coast which included such people as President Tubman of Liberia, Dr Francis Ibiam, a Presbyterian Igbo, who would be knighted the next year in the New Year Honours List, and J. B. Danquah, again a Presbyterian, the idiosyncratic Gold Coast journalist, lawyer, politician and author of *The Akan Doctrine of God*.

If Fourah Bay, an old CMS foundation later linked to the university of Durham, was the most respected educational institution in West Africa, Lovedale and Fort Hare standing side by side in the Ciskei were the most distinguished in South Africa. Here again the roots of the tradition lay in the Free Church of Scotland; Lovedale had blossomed as the most exciting sign for the inhabitants of southern Africa of high education, Christian integrity and the practicability of fellowship between white and black. Its paper, the *South African Outlook*, founded in 1870, had consistently across the decades proclaimed its conviction that a policy of 'widening the chasm' between black and white was both unchristian and disastrous.[73] Its finest white workers had been fully matched by their predominantly Xhosa pupils and colleagues. On the one side one may think of Neil MacVicar who had

48

just died in 1950: an intensely humane and highly capable Scottish mission-ary doctor, a pioneer in the training of African nurses. He had met and been recruited by James Stewart for Lovedale in 1900, Stewart having been Principal of Lovedale since 1870 and before that a companion of Living-stone on his Zambezi expedition. On the other side one may think of Professors Matthews and Jabavu,[74] men of very considerable learning and still greater humanity. They were certainly lights to their people; they were also at the centre of a relatively small circle of teachers, doctors, journalists, amateur politicians – all in all at that time a fairly confident Christian professional core, as yet not too uncomfortably squeezed between white rulers and black masses.

In people such as these, from Bishop Johnson in Sierra Leone to Professor Jabavu in his comfortable old house at Middledrift by Fort Hare, we see the fruits of a century of Protestant missionary effort at their richest and most clearly recognisable. But such people were, inevitably, few and the norma-tive picture of 1950 Protestantism cannot be one of Fourah Bay and Fort Hare or even of the Livingstonia Institute or Alliance High School. Nor can it be one of an urban working or lower middle class. Africa was the most rural of continents and if, in some countries, the town population was already considerable, it was certainly not here that the core of mission Christianity was to be found. With the somewhat ambivalent exceptions of the west coast, the main missions, Protestant and Catholic, had almost everywhere established a strongly rural base, shunning emerging towns in a way that they would soon come to regret. Hence the normative picture, in so far as such a thing is possible at all, has to be one set squarely in the countryside, its many catechists and its few priests, above all its lay congrega-tions existing for the most part almost apart from any regular clerical ministration at all.

By 1950 there were in fact numberless little village congregations in those parts of Africa where evangelisation had struck root fairly early and where as a consequence a church of some sort was now a taken-for-granted element within local society. John Taylor gave a classic account of one such area of village Christianity in the 1950s in *The Growth of the Church in Buganda*. The CMS began work in Buganda in 1877 and the quick response of the Baganda to Christianity is well known. Before the end of the century there were already tens of thousands of Christians and Bishop Tucker ordained the first Baganda priests in 1896. Yet more than fifty years later there was still no bishop and even relatively few priests. By 1950 there were scores of little village churches up and down Buganda, some in good stead, others almost fallen down; some had only recently been built, some were already old; some were looked after by probably aged catechists, others by young farmers who had simply taken a lead in the matter of church worship. To most of these churches a priest hardly ever came. On average an Anglican priest had some fifteen such churches in his care, but he had only a bicycle at best to help him get around, and normally ministered only in his main pastorate church; some priests, however, had far more churches than that – thirty or even ninety.[75] In these circumstances the regular worship and church life of the great majority of African Christians were by and large priestless. As a matter of fact most adults in such congregations were excluded from communion even if a priest should come and celebrate a communion service, this for marital reasons: one had two wives, another had married a Catholic, a third and a fourth and a fifth were monogamous, but they had married by customary law and never in church. Strict church laws over marriage excluded a very high proportion of believing and even practising Christians from full church membership, not just for a time but generally for life. Yet this was coming to matter rather little because 'full church membership' was really a clerical concept and the clergy were singularly scarce on the ground. It did not signify very much to be excluded from communion if a communion service was almost never celebrated in your village church anyway. A high proportion of such Christians no longer came to the village church for regular services, partly because the services were so poorly conducted, partly because years of marital irregularity or participation in 'pagan' practices had sapped their enthusiasm. They were Christians, they had little doubt about that, but with unbending ecclesiastical legislation and little or no pastoral encouragement they had drifted into a state far indeed from what the missionaries who had called the church into being a generation or two before had intended. But, practically speaking, there were no longer any missionaries about. They had 'withdrawn upwards' into higher levels of ecclesiastical administration and specialised tasks; outside the capital there was hardly a missionary left engaged full time in pastoral work.

The picture which John Taylor presented of Christian life in his Kyagwe villages was a somewhat extreme one: in few places was a Protestant church so rurally rooted, and most missionary societies had not withdrawn so completely from rural pastoral care as had the CMS in Buganda. Nevertheless it could be paralleled well enough from other older churches. To some it was a highly dispiriting picture, showing little else but apathy and syncretism. To others it was rather one of a quiet symbiosis in which, despite failure and a mistaken rigidity in the clerical pattern which was theoretically being followed, in fact a deeply rooted African Christianity was emerging, already effectively independent of European missionaries and European funds, though it was by no means an 'independent' church.

It is with this background that one must consider the range of African initiative and ministry, beginning with a well-built new village church described by John Taylor; it had been put up and finely furnished by a local carpenter, a polygamist who was, therefore, ineligible to take the services but that was done by another local farmer.[76] There never had been a time in which African Christians were not givers as well as receivers in the process of Christian growth: the early Freetown evangelists of the west coast, the Baganda martyrs of the 1880s, and countless catechists and evangelists up and down the continent are proof of that. In 1950 there were many senior men like Bishops Johnson and Akinyele, if less widely honoured than they, who had carried the burden of the day and the heat for many a decade. One such was Andreya Kajerero, a hardy Muhaya Lutheran who had led his church in the north-west of Tanzania through two world wars in which German missionaries had been taken away; he had stood up fearlessly to Wesleyan 'poachers' at one point, an Anglican bishop at another, and troublesome revivalists at a third. For him there was no other way than the Lutheran order though it could be rightly backed up by African dreams. And there was many an old and faithful minister whose approach was not dissimilar.

The scale of African ministry was, however, in process of expanding very considerably after the Second World War with many new ventures both planned and unplanned. For one thing European bishops and superintendents were starting to recognise the crying need for a far larger number of black ordained men than they had hitherto planned for. Thus in 1948 the Danish Lutheran mission in Adamawa, Nigeria, had ordained its first five ministers, to be followed by six more in 1955.[77] At Michaelmas 1950 the Anglican Bishop of Masasi ordained nine men to the priesthood – the largest number since the UMCA first began.[78] Each of these men was likely to have a very considerable local influence in the area where he was settled, but vital initiatives were often taken more informally. For instance, after many years of little progress, the United Methodist Church began to grow quite encouragingly in the Mende interior of Sierra Leone at this time; a main factor here was that of two blind itinerant preachers, Pa Mbovai and Matthew Moamie, who made their way from village to village. They had memorised whole sections of the bible and themselves composed Christian songs in the Mende manner.[79]

An interesting church growth entirely dependent upon black initiative was that of the African Methodist Episcopal Church. An American Negro body in origin, AME had come to South Africa at the end of the nineteenth century in response to an invitation from the first wave of 'Ethiopians' and had become widely established there. By 1950 it had 38 Presiding Elder Districts and 215 ordained ministers. While its bishops remained Americans, there were never more than two or three missionaries from America in Africa – to rule as bishop or to teach at the Wilberforce Institute in Transvaal. It was essentially a self-propagating church responding to many of the needs catered for by independency. From the 1920s it had spread rapidly across Central Africa under the careful leadership of Zephaniah Mtshwelo, a Tembu from Cape Province, who was from 1927 AME's Presiding Elder in Southern Rhodesia. Hanock Phiri, a remarkable Mchewa from Nyasaland and Dr Banda's uncle and mentor, had established the church there, while in Northern Rhodesia it had grown most of all, multiplying first in the townships along the line of rail and then in many more remote country parts. Unlike the mission churches which spread from the country to the town, AME spread from town to country.[80]

In 1950 AME's Presiding Elder in Lusaka was the very enterprising John Membe who had already worked extremely hard for seventeen years to develop AME in central Africa and would continue for many more. Beginning as minister at Abercorn in the far north of Northern Rhodesia he had not only established a fair number of congregations in the neighbourhood but also endeavoured to press on into Tanganyika. From Abercorn he had been moved to Nyasaland to replace Hanock Phiri on retirement and in 1950 he had only recently taken up his post in Lusaka. In Abercorn he had been succeeded by Johannes Mabombo, a much-loved Xhosa from South Africa who worked for the last twenty-five years of his life in Northern Rhodesia, dying at Mbereshi. These men and their colleagues represented an earnest and responsible African commitment to missionary evangelism; they were not much interested in politics and certainly not in millenialist doctrines; they were not even seeking any very extensive 'Africanisation' of Christianity. They accepted Methodist doctrines and practices in their AME form unhesitatingly. They showed an easy ability to cross frontiers, to learn new languages and to build up little congregations without any foreign financial support; they were not anti-white but they did appreciate a scope for ministry and responsibility which AME offered but which they could not have found at that time in any of the mission churches.

The most considerable and best-known area of independent initiative within the mission churches was that of the 'Revival' in eastern Africa, the *Balokole*.[81] The movement had begun in Rwanda in the 1930s and spread in waves, first across Uganda and then through other Protestant churches of East Africa, carrying everywhere its triumphant Luganda hymn *Tukutendereza Yezu*: We praise you, Jesus. In 1950 it was at the height of its influence and making a particular impression both in central Kenya, and in north-western Tanganyika. While it had many of the characteristics and group mechanisms of classical Protestant revival the world over, drawn doubtless from the Keswick Conventions and the 'Oxford Group' of Buchman, it quickly developed an African form and impetus of its own – a form frequently bordering on that of an independent church of a withdrawing type. Instead of being a short, sharp renewal of religious commitment engineered – as so often in Europe and America – by the famous preacher with something of a religious personality cult, East African revival developed as an essentially lay community of prayer and fellowship; while it did indeed draw on mass conventions and passing preachers and included

52

clergy in its ranks, it remained a very unclericalised movement, tending indeed to withdraw its members from the wider responsibilities of the church as of secular society. It did not make its members refuse to pay taxes, but it did encourage them to become pacifists – to the annoyance, during the war, of the colonial government – just as it encouraged them not to accept the customary bridewealth for their daughters.

The Revival expressed an uncompromising rejection of the sort of assimilation of church and world, of Christianity and African custom, which had been going quietly on within the church among the mass of not too enthusiastic Christians. It is curious that a movement which from one point of view is the solidest proof of 'Africanisation', something which missionaries could assuredly not control and of which many were not unreasonably suspicious, was at the same time a movement to reject the Africanising symbiosis which was inevitably growing in momentum in a third-generation church. If the Revival brought a much needed new outburst of commitment to the confession of faith and high moral standards, an intense personal loyalty to Christ which would prove decisive for many in moments of crisis, it also brought conflict, narrowness, spiritual arrogance and near schism. It had almost all the characteristics which brought other movements to full independency and if it did so here only with a few, this was due both to a wise restraint on the part of its ablest leader, William Nagenda, as on that of Bishop Stuart of Uganda, and to something rather deep in the mentality of the Baganda and related peoples than whom no one has a greater sense of authority and institution.

Nevertheless Revival was divisive and could be as bitterly criticised as it was enthusiastically welcomed. The comment upon it of old Kajerero in Buhaya was sufficiently caustic:

When sinners had confessed their sins the revived sang: *Tukutendereza Yezu*. They hopped and danced and despised those who had not been revived. They refused to eat coffee-beans or groundnuts or to use ornaments or spears. They soon started to have their own services and despised their former friends saying: 'You have not yet been saved.' In that way they refused to obey their missionaries and pastors and they said to them: 'We have no fellowship with you.' The leaders of the church reproved them and showed them the way of salvation according to the Bible but they refused to listen and made their own laws and elected their own leadership.[82]

In this instance Revival did actually for a while bring schism. For the most part it did not, but provided instead something of a lay religious order subsisting uneasily if vibrantly within the church and combining, as such bodies so often do, a certain self-righteous exclusiveness with high faith, intense prayer and the mutual support of close fellowship.

Hanock Phiri and John Membe had been in part educated at Livingstonia; Johannes Mabombo had been a Wesleyan deacon in South Africa. It is difficult to see that the kind of Christianity they subsequently taught was so greatly different from that of their 'mission church' days, or that Mwasi and Chinula so greatly changed as ministers in moving from the Presbyterian Church to the Black Man's Church in Africa. If circumstances had been slightly different all these might well have worked and died as Presbyterian or Methodist ministers within a white-founded church – as many of their colleagues did. The Revival carried off a Ugandan Masaka shopkeeper, Crisafati Matovu, to preach the gospel in Buha, western Tanganyika, where he eventually became a priest and Anglican rural dean. If a German Lutheran missionary had not arrived back in the nick of time when the Lutheran Christians of Buhaya were quarrelling with their unwelcome Wesleyan missionaries, or if Bishop Stuart had been more autocratic than he was, Andrea Kajerero might not have gone down in history as a pillar of the Lutheran mission church and William Nagenda as an Anglican revivalist, but both as heroes of independency.

African Christians seldom had anyone to appeal to when in disagreement with their missionaries; the options were too often abject submission or complete separation. Yet in many cases they were never in fact so driven to the wall and a sufficient sphere of independence had *de facto* if not *de jure* already been achieved within the mission church by 1950. Certainly the patterns of rural Christianity which were emerging, both lay and clerical, cut across the frontier of 'mission' and 'independent', and indeed across that of Protestant and Catholic too. Upon each side there were tendencies both to tolerance and intolerance: to putting up with polygamy and beer and dancing and bridewealth and the veneration of ancestors, and to banishing all such things as godless and pagan; to live with witchcraft, somehow countering it in a quiet way with blessed water or pagan amulet, or to banish it in some great public outburst of hysteria; to enter the hierarchy of civil society, the power politics of tribe or the new political parties, or to scorn all such things as worthless and meaningless when once one has entered 'the new tribe' of Christ.

At the level of high leadership the Protestant churches looked overwhelmingly white and missionary in 1950, as dependent as ever upon earnest committees in London or New York. That level was not unimportant and it did frequently impinge in one way or another upon many aspects of popular church life, sometimes helpfully, sometimes destructively; yet at the level of much of the membership, at least in the larger and older churches, the missionary and his concerns were already receding into the distance. The village with its own narrow tangled hopes and fears, its grass-roofed chapel, its poorly trained catechist, its occasional visits from a native minister on his bicycle, was the place where the church had now to stand or fall.

The Holy Year of 1950 was a high watermark for the Roman Catholic Church and it was the first of such jubilees in which its young African wing was able to take a notable part. The years immediately subsequent to the Second World War were for Catholicism ones of a certain *éclat*. If on one side they witnessed the painful harassment of the great Catholic churches of eastern Europe in Lithuania, Poland, Hungary and Czechoslovakia by communist governments, on the other they saw the last and most successful era in the long resurgence of Roman authority, the doctrinal, spiritual and institutional assertions of ultramontanism. In 1950 Pius XII had been reigning for twelve years and would continue for eight more. His, undoubtedly, was one of the great pontificates of the modern church – longer than any since that of Pius IX, painstakingly systematic, utterly Roman of the most uncompromising hue.

There was great institutional achievement in these years, most evidently in Latin America and in Africa, and there were also many significant reforms, even liturgical and theological, as witness the encyclicals *Mystici Corporis*, *Divino Afflante Spiritu* and *Mediator Dei* on the church, scripture and the liturgy all dating from the 1940s. Yet here as in every side of the work of Pius XII the pattern of an unquestioned Roman authority over the whole church and over everything to do with the church, of a Latin clerically controlled society centralised in Rome, of neo-scholastic philosophy and theology as the only acceptable Catholic medium of thought, was not only maintained but pressed at least as consistently (if not as cruelly) as had ever been the case. As regards Vatican policy towards the social and political order, there had likewise been no change in direction, though there was one to some extent in methods. The Catholic social principles as established in the encyclicals of Leo XIII and his successors were to be guaranteed in so far as possible through concordats and backed by Catholic Action and by Christian Democratic political parties. Communism was the great enemy; Fascism, never much liked but not greatly feared either, had proved an increasingly dangerous yet not always unwelcome alternative. Over Franco and Salazar the Vatican had few worries and the Concordat with Portugal in 1940 which had given the Catholic Church so many privileges in Africa while tying it closely to Salazar's regime was certainly not a source of unease to the Pope. Elsewhere in the post-war world the defeat of the Nazis had brought to power in western Europe parties with whom Rome had more sympathy than any it had to live with for a hundred years. The Catholic political leadership of western Europe – De Gasperi in Italy, Adenauer in Germany, Bidault and Schuman in France – was a new and welcome phenomenon. The pattern of the Christian Democratic party, predominantly Catholic in inspiration but including some Protestant participation, upholding western democracy and capitalism and backed by a strong Catholic Action organisation firmly controlled by the hierarchy, was proving a most effective and reassuring one. It was the model that missionaries were already endeavouring to export to other continents.

55

At the same time Catholic participation in many other central aspects of western life, academic and professional, was far more considerable and more public than in previous decades. There was a sense in which the Catholic Church was coming to terms with modern society, but as yet without sanctioning modification in its post-Tridentine theology and spirituality or its organisational centralisation. On the contrary. A certain relaxation on some fronts seemed acceptable if counter-balanced by a tightening up on others. Large new seminaries were being opened in Rome to ensure that the leaders of the church from every country of the world were trained in the Roman schools. Such religious orders as had their headquarters in other countries were being pressed to move them to the holy city. No pope ever had a greater personal ascendancy over the whole church than Pius XII with his almost daily public audiences and incessant allocutions upon this topic or that. The year 1950 with its hundreds of thousands of pilgrims coming to Rome from every part of the world was the apogee of it all. There were two major papal pronouncements that year. The first, the encyclical *Humani Generis*, firmly condemned new theological trends which were gaining strength in France, Belgium and Germany, but which with their greater scriptural, patristic and ecumenical emphasis or again with their increased preoccupation with modern scientific and philosophical attitudes, appeared to threaten the amalgam of neo-scholasticism and theologised canon law dominant in Rome. The second was the infallible declaration of 1 November of the Assumption of the Virgin Mary into heaven. Together they represented a Roman Catholicism which was both self-confident and almost wholly divorced from the preoccupations of the non-Catholic Christian world.

While there were theologians in northern Europe preparing the ground in learned but prudently phrased tomes for a very different approach, there can be no doubt that the Catholicism of Pius XII was most warmly embraced by the missionary societies and, through them, the young churches of Africa. The great African Holy Year pilgrimage had been carefully prepared by two Apostolic Delegates – Archbishop Lefebvre in Dakar and Archbishop Mathew in Mombasa. The pilgrims of the west coast were gathered by boat and sailed round the coast to Rome led by Lefebvre in person. It was perhaps his greatest moment. In Rome they were met by Mathew and the pilgrims of the east. For the first time hundreds of Catholic Africans, priests and laity, were gathered in the holy city and exposed to the electrifying effect of its fervent and triumphalistic ceremonies. Certainly the Holy Year represented for the leading figures of the time a sort of symbolic model of all they were working for.

Lefebvre and Mathew were both exceptionally able and influential figures. Vicar Apostolic of Senegal as well as Apostolic Delegate for all French Africa, Marcel Lefebvre was already what he was to remain for the next twenty-five years – a highly masterful person with a very clear idea of how the church should be run. As a Holy Ghost Father he could operate from inside the missionary system as David Mathew could not. The latter was, perhaps, the most unexpected person to be found within the Catholic missionary world of that time. For the most part that world was decidedly non-academic, its recruitment was from the rural working class, it was a world of religious orders and societies, it did not write at least for publication, it was predominantly continental and hardly at all English. In all of which it found both strength and weakness. Yet David Mathew, Apostolic Delegate to British Africa for seven years, was its exact opposite: the secular priest, the upper class Englishman, a Balliol historian before he became a priest and a prolific writer not only of history but also of rather poor, slightly indiscreet, fiction. The Catholic missionary world neither understood nor liked Mathew, but he was respected both for his learning and for his ability to obtain the governor's ear. A very loyal servant of Roman policies, if at times in a rather un-Roman way, his main preoccupation was the promotion of the African clergy at a time when they were almost wholly subject to missionary rule. His commitment to their cause was manifest and they have never forgotten it.

Apostolic Delegates represented Rome. Behind them stood the Secretariat of State and the Prefect of Propaganda Fide, in 1950 Cardinal Fumasoni Biondi. Their power was certainly not to be despised but in practice it was often a great deal less than that of the generals of the major missionary societies. Rome had parcelled out Africa between the different orders and in 1950 the vicariates and prefectures into which it had been divided remained firmly within the control of these great ecclesiastical baronics. If the papal policies were to be implemented, it really depended more upon such a man as Louis Durrieu than it did upon David Mathew. Durrieu was General of the White Fathers, a Frenchman stern in temperament and ultramontane in loyalty. He had been a missionary bishop in Upper Volta previous to his election and was the first White Father general to live in Rome whither he had moved their headquarters from Algiers. His policy was to enforce in almost everything the contemporary Roman line, even to the extent of ensuring that young White Fathers should no longer study theology in the university of Louvain but only in Rome. His 'Romanitas' did not, however, go so far as agreeing to send African seminarians to study at the College of Propaganda away from the White Father run seminaries of Africa. That he considered, with some reason, ill advised, and it was a bold White Father bishop who would heed the call of Propaganda and disregard the wishes of his general.

The White Fathers were the society with the largest number of men at work on the continent but they were not the oldest. A striking characteristic of the modern missionary history of Africa has been the relative insignificance of the older orders – Benedictines, Cistercians, Dominicans, Franciscans, Redemptorists, Passionists, even Jesuits. The dominant orders of Europe, they maintained their position in the Americas and largely in Asia too, but their contribution in Africa has been more limited. Here the lead was taken and held by the specialised missionary societies of the nineteenth century.[83] The first to arrive in force had been the Holy Ghost Fathers who began work in the middle of the last century on the coasts both west and east. In 1950 they remained the principal society in Senegal, Sierra Leone, Nigeria east of the Niger, the Cameroons, Gabon, the French Congo, eastern Kenya and Tanganyika. On the west coast they had early been reinforced by de Marion Bresillac's SMA (Society of African Missions). Theirs was Nigeria west of the Niger, Dahomey, Togo, most of southern Gold Coast and Ivory Coast.

The White Fathers had followed a different strategy, that of avoiding the coast and striking at the far interior. In West Africa, most of which was sparsely populated and much of which had a considerable muslim population, its most fruitful field lay in Upper Volta and just over the border in northern Gold Coast. In the east its area was known as the 'Great Lakes' – the eastern Congo, western Uganda, western Tanganyika, Rwanda, Burundi, northern Zambia and northern Nyasaland: all in all, this was by far the most successful Catholic mission area in the whole continent.

The Verona Fathers had concentrated from the beginning upon the Nile valley – southern Sudan and northern Uganda; the Oblates of Mary Immaculate became the largest society to work in southern Africa; the Belgian national society, the Scheut Fathers, were numerous in western and central Congo; Mill Hill worked principally in eastern Uganda, western Kenya and the British Cameroons. The German and Swiss missionary Benedictines of St Ottilien developed two great abbeys (Peramiho and Ndanda) in southern Tanganyika, while another German monastic group, originally Cistercian, established the abbey of Mariannhill in Natal. The young Irish missionary society of Kiltegan had taken over Calabar from the Holy Ghost Fathers. Jesuits were at work in Southern and Northern Rhodesia as well as western Congo.

Certainly the specifically missionary societies, growing fast as they were, had not the resources to spread across the whole of Africa in the comprehensive manner Rome desired; hence it was one of the key tasks of Propaganda Fide to find other religious orders willing to take over a vicariate here or there. In the Belgian Congo this began earliest and for rather different reasons: under pressure from Leopold II the Congo had been accepted as a national responsibiltity by the Belgian Catholic Church so that almost every order at work in Belgium adopted one or another section of its cherished colony. Hence besides the White Fathers, Scheut Fathers and Jesuits who came first, there was a motley assortment of Premonstratensians, Re-

58

demptorists, Benedictines, Capuchins, Salesians, Dominicans and others. As the years went by Rome persuaded more and more societies to enter the work somewhere and a number of other countries became almost as variegated from a Catholic missionary viewpoint as was the Belgian Congo. Thus in Tanganyika the original three societies of the Holy Ghost, the White Fathers and the Benedictines had been joined by 1950 by Swiss Capuchins in Dar es Salaam, Italian Passionists in Dodoma, Italian Consolata in Iringa, and Irish Pallottines in Mbulu; to all these were now being added Rosminians in Tanga and Maryknollers in Musoma. The last was a notable addition in marking the late but vigorous arrival of the American Catholic Church upon the African scene.[84]

It would be a great mistake to imagine that the missionary societies had all a uniform style of work. They varied immensely in spirituality, in the type of work they were fitted for, in capacity and level of education, in national background. Undoubtedly there was much in common, particularly at the level more apparent to the visiting European, but it would be unwise to overlook deep differences of emphasis and a certain almost anarchic character in the Catholic system. There was not only a surprising absence of collaboration between societies, there could even exist a quite hostile rivalry. Certainly Mill Hill Fathers in Kenya could cooperate closely with Mill Hill Fathers in Uganda but hardly at all with Consolata or Holy Ghost Fathers at work in neighbouring Kenyan vicariates. Much the same was almost everywhere true. It was a struggle for Apostolic Delegates to insist upon a minimum of common policy and this was often only achieved as an essential requisite for acquiring government grants in the fields of education and medicine.

There were great differences in the sheer quality of missionary work. The professional missionary societies for the most part had a tradition of work and a sense of what they were meant to be doing often sadly missed in the activities of some of the late arrivals – men sent out by Orders in no way prepared for this sort of activity. These latter too often fell back on poaching the members of other churches. Certainly if one thinks of the mastery of African languages, the translation of biblical and liturgical texts, the training of catechists and of priests, there was a very wide range of practice. One finds the highest standards in the White Fathers, the Swiss Bethlehem Fathers at Gwelo in Rhodesia, the German Benedictines in southern Tanganyika. While the continental missionaries – French, Germans, Swiss and Dutch – were best at these things, the Irish and the Canadians excelled in the provision of education and as the development of a relatively sophisticated schools system became a crucial part of the missionary effort, so did the Irish come more and more into their own as Catholic propagators of the English language and the British boarding school.

While the discussion hitherto has been wholly in terms of missionary priests and this is necessary in as much as they, and they alone, controlled the government of the church, its sacramental system and pastoral organisation, it must be remembered that the number of nuns was equally great and if their work was done still more quietly than that of the priests, it was hardly, if at all, less influential. In no other way had the Catholic Church such an enormous advantage over other missions. The dedication, continuity and sheer numbers of missionary sisters involved in educational, medical and wider pastoral and community work was an immeasurable strength for the Catholic mission. There were women missionaries married and unmarried, in all churches but their impact was seldom quite comparable with that of the nuns. Furthermore their foundation of African sisterhoods would prove, particularly in eastern Africa, one of the most crucial factors in establishing the physiognomy of the new churches.

A large section of Africa hitherto, perhaps surprisingly, not mentioned, is that of the Portuguese territories. In 1950 there was only one cardinal in Africa, Clemente Teodosio de Gouveia, Archbishop of Lourenco Marques. One might presume from this that Mozambique was one of the most developed parts of Catholic Africa; in fact this was not so. In few countries was the church weaker. His creation had been a political gesture of goodwill towards Portugal in the wake of the Concordat. The Catholic Church in Angola and Mozambique had a long history but in the latter at least it had never taken firm root among Africans. While elsewhere the church in Africa was dependent jurisdictionally upon the Roman Congregation of Propaganda Fide, there it was not, being instead a juridical extension of the church in Portugal. There were dioceses instead of vicariates and each diocese had as bishop a Portuguese diocesan priest. The international missionary societies had hardly entered these countries, with the important exception of the Holy Ghost Fathers in Angola, who were unusual in having a sizeable Portuguese province. The church in Portugal was itself, however, very short of priests and had few to spare for its overseas territories. Most of those who did go went chiefly to serve the white Portuguese population, not to establish an African church. A change here had been effected by the Concordat: a more open door was to be allowed to non-Portuguese Catholic missionaries and the international societies were now entering Mozambique, though of course remaining closely subject to the Portuguese hierarchy.

While the impression a study of the missionary map can easily give is one of formidable overall Catholic strength, in fact this needs to be modified very considerably. It is true that Catholic missionary numbers were steadily mounting and could hardly do other than produce alarm in many a rival Protestant heart. As a consequence almost nowhere was there any question of a missionary 'withdrawal' – in fact the number of ordained black priests was so small that this was neither practicable nor contemplated. But the very scale of the Catholic missionary presence could be itself a source of great and inevitable weakness, extremely little room being left for black initiative. The need for that was recognised in theory but in practice too often left to a hypothetical future. In many parts of Africa the Catholic Church in 1950 was little more than a network of schools and catechists supervised by a missionary clergy which, while growing ever more numerous, was often less close to the people than had been the pioneers of earlier generations. In a number of areas, however, strong Catholic communities were now in existence and the real map of Catholic Africa needs to pay most attention to what existed on the African side rather than the complexities of the white mission network, however much the latter was in control.

There was only one black bishop in 1950 – Joseph Kiwanuka, Vicar Apostolic of Masaka in western Buganda since 1939. He had certainly proved himself a shrewd and effective bishop during many years when his appointment was regarded with less than enthusiasm by many missionaries and every failure in Masaka was seized upon as evidence of the unwisdom of promoting black men. Throughout the 1940s he had held what was certainly a position of unique responsibility and influence for an African in eastern Africa and the policies he consistently followed show him as considerably in advance of most of his episcopal colleagues. On one side lay the development of strong lay participation in church planning through the establishment of elected parish councils and parents associations, on the other the sending of his ablest younger priests and seminarians for higher studies abroad. On both points he was quite resolved, quite out of step with most bishops of the 1950s but fully vindicated in retrospect.

Masaka vicariate, however, was still more important than its bishop.[85] Consisting chiefly of the county of Buddu, it was one of the most Catholic areas of the whole of Africa, grounded in a mass conversion movement of the 1890s. At least half the total population was Catholic, there had been a regular succession of priestly ordinations since 1913 and there were large numbers of African nuns and some teaching brothers too. No white missionary had done pastoral work in the vicariate since 1934. Here indeed there had been a clear withdrawal deliberately planned by the old missionary bishop, Henri Streicher, who had arrived in Uganda in 1891, retired as bishop in 1933 but was still living in 1950 at his original mission of Villa Maria, a very old and saintly man vastly revered by the Baganda Christians around him. In the judgement of many he was the greatest missionary of the twentieth century.

Masaka was a clear example of a peasant Catholicism which had by 1950 really taken root in this fairly out-of-the-way but not unprogressive corner of rural Africa. One could find much the same already in existence in a number of places, particularly around the great lakes. In Tanganyika there was Buhaya, which bordered Masaka, and Ufipa, a particularly poor and remote area east of Lake Tanganyika. There were too the Ngoni people at the

61

northern end of Lake Malawi served by the Benedictines, and the Chagga on Mount Kilimanjaro who were clearly divided, as was Buhaya, into two religious groups – Lutheran and Catholic. West of Masaka and Buhaya were Rwanda and Burundi. In each a movement of mass conversion dating from the 1930s was still in full flood in 1950 with 167,000 catechumens in Rwanda and 210,000 in Burundi. The former might have appeared to the observer the nearest approach to a Catholic country in black Africa. Its king, Mwami Rudahigwa, had been solemnly baptised in 1943 and had dedicated his country to Christ the King. Most of the chiefs were Catholics and there were already eight-five local priests, most of them members of the dominant Tutsi minority. In Burundi where the conversion process had got under way rather later there were thirty. Elsewhere in Africa the protectorate of Lesotho, the coastland of Dahomey and Togo, and the Igbo parts of eastern Nigeria were other areas where Catholicism had already quite clearly taken deep root.

There were some 800 black Catholic priests at this time. Two-thirds of these had been ordained within the last ten years and the great majority of them were in western Uganda, western Tanganyika, Rwanda, Burundi and the Congo.

Buganda, Igboland, Chaggaland, Rwanda, Burundi were all areas in which a movement of mass conversion had established what was already recognisable as a Christian social atmosphere, something in the nature of a collective public commitment. In some of these places there was a sharp division between Catholic and Protestant and the excitement of such a movement had further exacerbated rival denominational loyalties. In others, such as Ufipa, the Catholics had almost had it to themselves. The dynamics of such movements and the methods of the missionaries varied considerably – the schools race in Igboland between Irish Holy Ghost Fathers and British CMS presents a very different picture from the White Father evangelisation of Ufipa with its lengthy catechumenate and the relative absence of schooling, which could have much less appeal in its poor and isolated highlands.[86] Yet in many ways the pattern of religion which tended to emerge after some years with its sacramentals and angels, its relative absence of priests and of regular sacraments, its profound dependance on catechists, was a common one.

It is clear statistically that the giant of Catholic Africa was already the Belgian Congo. With well over 3,000 missionaries – priests, sisters and brothers – in twenty-five different vicariates, with twenty-four different orders of priests and fifty-eight of sisters at work (almost all Belgian) it is not surprising if the number of converts had mounted rapidly to reach the figure of three-and-a-half million. What is surprising is that there were little more than one hundred African priests and two hundred nuns. Rwanda alone had almost as many with one-tenth the number baptized. Certainly the Catholic

Church in the Congo had gone in for numbers on the grand scale, as it had gone in for a fine rural health service and for primary schools. But again there were within the country major differences of policy. The two Jesuit vicariates in the west, Kisantu and Kwango, had fifty-one African priests between them, trained in the great seminary of Mayidi. The Benedictine vicariate of Katanga, on the other hand, did not have a single one.

Bishop Jean de Hemptinne, Vicar Apostolic of Katanga, was one of the most powerful figures of his time and it is worth pausing to consider his career and attitudes because they illustrate, perhaps better than those of anyone else, the colonial temper which so greatly affected the missionary church at the time. He had been appointed Prefect Apostolic of Katanga as a young monk of Maredsous in 1910. As a member of a wealthy, devoutly Catholic, newly ennobled banking family, de Hemptinne was a natural member of the Belgian colonial establishment and a personal friend of King Albert with whom he had a special private audience before leaving for the Congo. When Albert visited Katanga eighteen years later and laid the foundation stone of the new church of St Theresa at Likasi, de Hemptinne used the occasion to make a speech on the relationship of church and state in the development of 'Christian civilisation' which lauded the Belgian colonial system without reserve; the atmosphere, we are told, was one of 'ardent loyalism'.[87] In 1932 de Hemptinne became Vicar Apostolic and such he was to remain until 1958. As a man with the ear of Brussels and a member of the Provincial Council of Katanga, his political influence was immense. It was used to acquire as near a religious and educational monopoly as was possible, to keep Kimbangu in prison, and to suppress any independent voice in church or state. When Fr Tempels' *Bantu Philosophy* was published in 1945 de Hemptinne put pressure on the Vatican to ensure that he did not return to the Congo.[88] The same year he had opposed the development of Congolese trade unions at the bishops' conference; here, as on other matters, he found himself in disagreement with the far more flexible approach of Mgr Dellepiane, the Apostolic Delegate.

At least as enduring was de Hemptinne's unflinching opposition to Protestant missionary work, believing as he did that there was an 'identity between the political programme of the American missions and the political programme of Moscow'.[89] Even when after 1946 government policy was to subsidise the schools of all missions without discrimination, the Catholic position in Katanga remained highly privileged because of the close alliance established between the Benedictines and the Union Minière du Haut Katanga. The Union Minière had placed its schools under Benedictine control and de Hemptinne guaranteed that he would produce what the mining companies needed and that no one else could. He defended the arrangement at a quite fundamental level:

Protestantism gnaws at the principle of authority wherever it can. With Belgian money principles are spread which will end by undermining the authority of the Belgians in the Congo. That is certainly one of the greatest mistakes which can be committed at this time. The big companies, on the other hand, understand that Catholicism represents a stable factor, and it is to us they have given the responsibility for education.[90]

That was October 1950. de Hemptinne is important because of his immense personal influence on the development of Christianity in Africa over many years, but also because he represented a point of view that very many Catholic missionaries shared and not only in the Congo. But it was not a universal viewpoint, nor one in all ways in line with Roman policy, though it was closely akin to the official Portuguese position. His was certainly a different tone from that of the learned Jesuit, Fr Van Wing, who was struggling behind the scenes in the late 1940s for the development of higher education in the Congo, or from that of the Franciscan Fr Tempels whose discovery that the Bantu had a philosophy of their own had so disturbed the bishop, or again from that of Fr Aupiais in Dahomey whose identification with African interests was so manifest that he had been elected to represent them in Paris.[91] There was very much more than one voice in the Catholic missionary world of 1950; nevertheless few were more potent than that of Bishop de Hemptinne.

There was, without doubt, very much less of an articulate African voice in the Catholic than in the Protestant church. The universal Catholic system of the time, together with a steady increase in white missionaries, saw to that. Yet we have seen Bishop Kiwanuka and the able group of priests around him in Masaka, and they stood for men all over the continent – the scores of young priests now being ordained each year, the rising lay elite of teachers, clerks and small businessmen, the many thousands of poorly trained and still more poorly paid catechists – many of whom were increasingly irked by the absence of media to express their views. African Catholic history does remain somewhat anonymous, yet it is not difficult to find figures in the local scene who made an impact and in some cases clearly did their own thing too. Four of wider significance we may recall here, all four clearly unrepresentative and yet for that very reason important to remember because the picture of a society can only begin to be true when stretched to include at least some of its unusual members who fully belonged to it and yet represented no one but themselves.

Living near the old mission headquarters at Karema in Ufipa on the shore of Lake Tanganyika was an old gentleman still in the 1950s dressed in white stockings, black cotton breeches, embroidered jacket and red fez.[92] It was Dr Adrian Atiman who had been born nearly a century before on the other side of the continent near Timbuktu and had as a child been sold into slavery. Ransomed by the White Fathers, he had been trained as a medical missionary in Algiers, Malta and Rome. Early in 1889 he had arrived in Karema, later married a Bemba girl and got down to sixty years of quiet work. There he still was, a doctor who supplemented the learning he had acquired in Europe with local Fipa remedies and who had proved himself a successful surgeon. The recipient of numerous medals from international organisations, he remained an extraordinarily dignified and quiet figure and a living witness to various ways in which the missionary gospel had been indeed a liberating one.

In 1950 one of the senior Igbo priests left Nigeria never to return. Fr Michael Tanzi had, in the memory of all who knew him, an extraordinary personal sanctity of a very traditional kind.[93] If he had a model it must have been that of St John Vianney, the nineteenth-century curé of Ars. It does not seem to have been that of any missionary he had ever met. From childhood on he committed himself to hours of private prayer and to the most intense asceticism, especially of diet. For him this world meant simply nothing, the next everything. What he had, he gave away. As parish priest he had a profound spiritual influence on many who had come into contact with him. And then in 1950 he left his ministry to become a Trappist monk at the monastery of Mount St Bernard's in England. There he died fourteen years later, a man who fits into none of the conventional fashionable models of protest and liberation. He was nevertheless both liberated and liberating through the intensity and sincerity of his commitment to an old-fashioned gospel which he found fully valid without the slightest need for cultural adaptation.

For another priest, better known to his contemporaries, the need for such adaptation was only too obvious. Alexis Kagame in Rwanda was a young poet and scholar of brilliance searching for the harmonisation of his Tutsi court culture and Catholicism; a man bitterly critical of Belgian colonial domination over the historic monarchy of Rwanda but utterly committed to the maintenance of the traditional Tutsi domination over the Hutu majority. He was a close friend of the Mwami and a person whose influence was already very considerable. In 1950 his epic poem *La Redemptoriade* was published in the White Father review *Grands Lacs* but still more important was the vindication of the whole Tutsi regime which he was working upon and shortly to publish, *Le Code des Institutions politiques du Ruanda*. The Belgian authorities feared his presence in Rwanda and, despite their general policy of opposing the study of Africans overseas, arranged for him to be sent on a very long course in Rome.

Finally, Senghor, a poet who had benefited from the freedom of the layman and the French policy of the total assimilation of an elite, in such strong contrast to that of Belgium. He represented, as did Protestants like Danquah and Ibiam, the tiny apex of a new West African Christian bourgeoisie, but he sensed too the dangers that lay therein and upon it he had made in the mid-1940s the following observations:[94]

Catholicism must remain close to its Gospel sources. It cannot flourish on the soil of Africa if it appears, as it does too often even in France, as a set of polite manners for decent middle-class people or as a weapon for subjugation in the hands of a paternalistic capitalism. In the provincial capitals of French West Africa I am afraid it has already begun to take this appearance. It is high time to sound the alarm.

C. Independency

Considerable as was the spread of the mission churches by 1950 across the continent, it was far from including the whole of Christian life for – unhappy as most missionaries undoubtedly were to admit it – there had also developed a large and clearly enduring body of churches wholly outside any mission connection: in 1950 the independent churches were a familiar part of the religious scene in many areas of Africa and Bengt Sundkler's pioneering study *Bantu Prophets in South Africa* had been published just two years previously. Here as in other fields of thought the Swedish Lutheran missiologist had pointed with learning and prophetic sensitivity to an area of Christian life which, hitherto, had been largely ignored by writers but which in coming years was to receive an ever increasing measure of attention.[95]

In general it was some of the oldest areas of sustained Protestant missionary work which by 1950 had become the home of the most marked independency: South Africa, the West African coast, the Congo basin, central Kenya. Already independency had its own lengthy history and its dead figures of prophetic and spiritual power whose stature grew rather than diminished with the passing of time: Chilembwe of Nyasaland, founder of the Providence Industrial Mission, whose strange uprising and beheading of William Jervis Livingstone in January 1915 had become for his fellow countrymen a symbol of defiant liberation at once political and religious; Wade Harris, the formidable Liberian prophet of the Ivory Coast who in 1913 and 1914 carried out what was probably the most remarkable single evangelical campaign Africa has ever witnessed, and then returned home to die in relative obscurity in 1929; Isaiah Shembe, the intensely magnetic Zulu healer and hymn writer of genius, founder of the Church of the AmaNazaretha, had died in 1935; Moses Orimolade, the Nigerian originator of the praying societies of Cherubim and Seraphim, well known as Baba Aladura, had died in 1933. The churches such men had founded, often almost accidentally, survived the deaths of their founders and, despite ups and downs of fortune, mostly grew and stabilised themselves with the years.

While there have probably been few years in the twentieth century, if any at all, in which some new movement did not arise, there would seem to have been three main waves, each with its own general character. The first dates from the last years of the nineteenth century and the first of the twentieth and produced in both Nigeria and South Africa the earlier members of the group of churches often known generically as 'African' or 'Ethiopian'. The movement here came from well inside the still small Christian community and was led by men, ordained or lay, already of some weight within the community. It was a protest against white domination in the mission churches, the moral impossibility of the promotion of blacks above a certain level – indeed a certain tendency in West Africa to demote Africans as the white missionary force increased. Such churches retained nearly all the characteristics of the body from which they had seceded, while in some cases tolerating polygamy more openly than did the missions – at least among the laity. While the principal churches of this type have expanded considerably in the years since their foundation and have also often succumbed to further internal schisms, they have not on the whole been as fast growing as either the missions or later independent groups.

From 1910 to the early 1930s one can point to a second and rather different wave of new beginnings – the 'spirit' churches: Zionists in South Africa, Aladura in Nigeria, and comparable prophetic and healing churches in Rhodesia and elsewhere. These tended to be far more in the nature of a popular, and even populist, movement, drawing their members from former Christians and non-Christians alike; they seldom began as a clear schism within a mission church; they emerged rather as the following of a prophet or group of prophets – the latter being men and women who had acquired a personal position on account of their prayer, healing or preaching activities within an existing church, but who clearly did not belong very closely to its hierarchy or regular ministry and sooner or later came adrift of it. The whole ethos of these spirit churches – their way of praying, their preoccupations, their type of organisation – was profoundly different from that of the main missions, though they undoubtedly learnt much both from elements in regular mission practice, Protestant and Catholic, and from a number of western missionary individuals or missionary fringe groups. In Central, South and West Africa some of the most significant roots of churches which have now long seemed wholly 'independent' and African can be securely traced to the work of one or another white missionary representing some such body as the American 'Christian Catholic Apostolic Church in Zion' of John Alexander Dowie, the Watch Tower Bible and Tract Society, 'Faith Tabernacle', a group in Philadelphia, or the British 'Apostolic Church'. The history of African independency could not be written without the names of such as Joseph Booth and Petrus Le Roux.[96] Nevertheless the quite limited and often seemingly somewhat unsuccessful activities of such people, while they explain the genesis of many names, ideas and practices within the independent churches, cannot explain them as a cultural whole nor their vast expansion which developed under African initiative, generally after any link with a white led church has been severed.

A third wave was just beginning in the late 1940s. It was not, perhaps, in character so different from that which preceded it, although there was to be less in the way of the individual charismatic giant and more of a multiplication of small groups, combined, of course, with major growth and

68

institutionalisation within some of the older movements. There was a growing state of unsettlement throughout the continent linked with the World War and rapid urbanisation; while political parties were multiplying they could as yet seldom mobilise the lower strata of society very effectively. The ever-widening spread of Christian ideas combined with the general absence of Africanisation in the leadership of the main churches provided a fertile field for new religious movements.

While one cannot avoid using group names to some extent, it would be mistaken to draw too clear a contrast and division between just two groups of independent churches – the so-called 'Ethiopian' upon the one hand and 'Zionist' upon the other. It is not only that essentially, while these names are often employed by those concerned themselves, they are as categories an external, white imposition – and one chiefly belonging to Southern Africa. It is rather that there is such a rich spectrum of diversity and that any consistent categorisation is either too complex to fulfil its purpose or simply misleading in being based on a too selective approach to the characteristic forms of church life. Furthermore, the primary internal purpose of these names is an evocatory one, and it is not at all clear that they evoke very different visions: Zion is of course Jerusalem, but it is a Jerusalem somehow realised here in Africa, and what is Ethiopia but *par excellence* such a Zion?

These movements are not to be seen, purely or even primarily, as a reaction against missionary Christianity. Most of them did not begin in conscious schism from an existing missionary church, and most of their members had never been full members of the latter. In some cases they emerged because there was no mission church in a particular area rather than because there was: the mission churches had still neither the resources nor the flexibility to respond to all the desires to become Christian now bursting forth in hundreds of unexpected localities. It could be claimed indeed that the ideal *locus* for independency was an area sufficiently close to missionary activity for the seed to have been sown – expectations raised, new ideas unleased – but not close enough for it to have been harvested, given the limitations in missionary personnel and the tight disciplinary requirements (lengthy probation and a heavy list of social prohibitions) which so often excluded from baptism those eager to receive it. If entrance to the kingdom was finally to be withheld by those who first proclaimed its arrival, the way in might very well be found through other doors.

The motivation of independency must then be investigated positively (in what it offered) rather than negatively (in what it rejected), but this positive rationale can be found in a number of very different, though not necessarily contradictory, contexts. There is, first, the context of the Protestant tradition: for a very large part these movements should be classified as falling well within this vast segment of Christian experience – be it Evangelical (e.g. low church Anglican or Methodist) or Pentecostal. The nature of the Protestant tradition, particularly in its nineteenth-century form, was already in Europe a very fissiparous one: there were at one moment nine different Presbyterian churches in Scotland and the Methodists who broke with the Church of England in the late eighteenth century were soon themselves divided into six or seven different groups. It would be naive to ask why African Methodists or Presbyterians proved prone to establish churches of their own, while African Roman Catholics so seldom did so, when it is obvious that such a pattern of behaviour was almost encouraged by the inner dynamics of one tradition, while it was almost the ultimate sin in the other. But it was particularly in parts of Africa where there was already a multiplication of Protestant missions close together, not strikingly dissimilar yet out of communion with one another, that African independency emerged as an initiative quite in conformity with the underlying realities of the ecclesiastical tradition they had entered into. There would, moreover, appear to have been in most places a greater cultural, social and even religious tolerance in regard to African tradition on the part of Catholics than on that of Protestants.[97]

While in some countries social and political discrimination certainly encouraged Africans to seek a church which would truly be a place of their own, where they were not second-class members, the relevant discrimination was probably less that of the general order of society and far more that which missionaries and white church members themselves practised within the religious context – in regard to seating arrangements in church, the salary and promotion of ministers, the courtesies of social contact between people of different races within a common congregation. Coupled with this was the sheer authoritarianism which was a marked characteristic of much missionary practice and in which Africans found themselves uniformly at the receiving end, deprived of scope for leadership or initiative.

There are indeed, within the phenomenon of conversion to independency, elements of reaction against missionary Christianity, just as there are elements of pressing the latter to a conclusion beyond what the missionaries themselves could countenance: thus it could emerge from the impact of an emotional revivalist programme deliberately initiated by Keswick minded missionaries, or from missionaries harping on 'freedom' as a Christian and Protestant ideal but never in fact tolerating much in the way of free behaviour on the part of their African disciples and even ministers, or simply from taking parts of the Bible more literally than did the particular missionaries who had here introduced it as the final religious norm. Still more important, however, was a positive search for values or the treatment of needs not much regarded in the parent churches. The values were those of traditional society and of traditional religion, but they were also, frequently enough, values or practices somehow recognised and sanctioned within the complex diversity of the Bible – either the Old or the New Testament – as they were not in the teaching of the missionaries. Revelation through dreams and visions, complex rituals, the separation between clean and unclean animals, the practice of polygamy, the descent of the spirit of God upon prophets – in many such things there was something of a natural alliance of the Old Testament and African traditional religion against missionary Christianity. The Protestant missionary sedulously presented a book to his converts, but he did not really expect them to imitate all its contents, any more than he did so himself – he had somehow overlooked, as essentially irrelevant, a great deal of what is actually in the Bible; thus he denounced polygamy without mincing his words, though his converts could find it apparently sanctioned within the very work to which he appealed as ultimate earthly authority, and the same was true for much else. He could thus be caught in a position of apparent inconsistency as against dissenting Christians, which the Catholic missionary, who rarely offered his converts a Bible and had anyway set up a clearly different source of authority behind his teaching, more often avoided.

It is important to note that the problem did not only concern the Old Testament. In the New as well the apocalyptic and eschatological teaching, the interpretation of dreams, miraculous healings and the expulsion of devils, even the sharp denunciation of the pharisees were all elements of great importance in the original text but which most missionaries undoubtedly thought more or less irrelevant to the current situation; they were bewildered when some of their converts selected their material so differently.

In the field of ritual too, much 'low church' Protestant missionary life offered little else than a void to replace the intricate network of ritual and sacrifice and protective amulet of traditional religion – a whole complex symbolic structure of rite, the use of space and time, of colour and particular objects, which had been so central to the previous religious experience of most Africans. Here the more liturgically minded Catholics, Anglo Catholics and Lutherans could offer a positive replacing pattern of worship. Such apparently little things as the liturgical colour of vestments, the use of blest water and medals could provide some sort of structural continuity with what had gone before – just as the Catholic stress upon guardian angels and prayers for the dead rather naturally replaced or intermingled with a world of spirits and ancestors. In these areas, it is not surprising that many independent churches, while emerging from a Protestant ecclesiastical background and emphatically denouncing the continued use of 'pagan' practices (so often indulged in surreptitiously by mission church members) in fact veered towards a more 'high church' pattern of ritual without in the least veering away from the 'Protestant' appeal to the Bible page.[98]

Decisively important in this context was often the sacrality of a chosen

71

place. There was certainly much recognition of this in traditional religion but there was almost none in Protestant missionary Christianity and less than might be expected in Catholic missionary practice – though here the blessing of churches and establishment of pilgrimage centres did certainly fulfil a felt need. But much of the Old Testament is quite intensely preoccupied with the assertion of a single sacred place, the holy city of Jerusalem. Psalm upon psalm evokes the joys of Zion. Missionaries who had read their psalters for years seem none the less bewildered at the African response to the symbol of the holy city and the consequent need for its re-enactment and ritual celebration. No theme is more vital to African independency. There was no missionary equivalent to Isaiah Shembe's poignantly beautiful hymns of Ekuphakameni, the mountain of the Nazarites, yet nothing was more biblically based.[99]

> We stand before thee
> O beautiful hen.
> Thou dost not love
> Jerusalem alone.
>
> O love us and hatch us
> Wondrous Hen!
> We dwell in thy kingdom,
> Our Hen of Heaven.
>
> O Lord, bring it forth,
> This Ekuphakameni,
> Just as a hen
> Loveth her chickens.

The quest of the independent church was the quest for a ritual, a belief and a realised community in and through which immediate human needs, social, psychological and physical could be appropriately met. Too many such needs had hardly been met at all in a meaningful way by the mission churches. Prayer for healing became the central activity of the spiritual churches in West, Central and Southern Africa. While the missionary approach of scientific medicine was only partially rejected, it had reached far too few people and excluded too many problems to fulfil the needs of the common man. Rituals of healing were among the most important of those in traditional society, and the most characteristic motivation of the new Christian movements in Africa was not an explicitly political rejection of colonialism or of colonial churches, nor any once and for all commitment to the millenium – though both were present at times – but the establishment of accessible rites of healing with a Christian reference and within a caring community by gifted and spiritual individuals claiming an initiative effectively denied them in the older churches.

There was within the religious tradition of many African peoples some

72

room for the prophet and much for the diviner.[100] The Zionist prophets who from the revelation accorded them in visions and dreams proclaimed a message of prayer and healing out of which the new churches grew, reflected in their role the immediate precedents of African religion far more than those of Christianity; but here too the confirmatory validation is to be found in the pages of the Bible, both Old and New Testaments. A prophetic tradition is not by nature a continuous one; it is something to be re-activated in times of social crisis and it was in circumstances of quite particular social uncertainty that a wide response to the prophetic voice was most likely to be forthcoming: the imposition of colonial regulations when political resistance was impossible, an influenza epidemic, the outbreak of world war, the apparently irresistible loss of ancestral lands to incoming white settlers – all such occasions were prone to trigger off a popular movement of 'liberation' through healing, social withdrawal or celestial discovery as proclaimed by a prophet with power.

There is no one way of assessing the 'Christian' character of these many different movements, nor their relationship to traditional religion: in few was Christ not explicitly central and, allowing for an understandable ambiguity, in only a handful have the founders been elevated to a comparable level or even identified with Christ.[101] Many of the movements which have taken over some of the concerns of traditional society most completely – concerns over witchcraft and sickness of all sorts – are also the most emphatically opposed to every expression of traditional religion which they condemn as 'paganism' with a forthrightness few mission churches could rival. Their cycle of prayer and visions, fasting and faith healing, white robes and pilgrimages to sacred mountains, may seem very different from most missionary Christianity, yet it can be argued that it is at least as faithful to the Bible as a whole. However, these are wide generalisations and differences between the movements in question have been so vast that it is wiser to turn to a consideration of particular examples.

Nowhere were independent churches more plentiful in 1950 than in South Africa (something like a thousand separate bodies comprising about 10 per cent of the black population), above all in Zululand. No major people in Africa had been so harshly treated as the Zulus – their very power had brought upon them a political and economic fate harsher than that of their neighbours, Swazi, Sotho and Xhosa. It is not altogether surprising if it was from this people that have come the most numerous, most creative, but also some of the most escapist of modern African religious movements, many of which began within a few years of the last Zulu Rebellion of 1906. But the Zulu response – if more frenetic and quantitatively the largest – was not different in kind from that of neighbouring peoples and the 'Ethiopian' and 'Zionist' movements of Southern Africa can in no way be limited to a single

73

people. There have been Swazi prophets and apostles in Zululand, just as there have been Sotho prophets in Swaziland, and Zulu prophets on the Rand.

By 1950 the movement, while far from having reached its zenith numerically, was already both vast and well established, directed in many churches by leaders of a second generation. In the older groups there was already a noticeable consolidation of tradition to balance the role of initiative, though this did not prevent the constant eruption of new schisms within almost every group – largely over questions of leadership and succession to it; there was nevertheless an increasing concern with place and property, with the training of ministers and with the attainment of some sort of public recognition by government.

The older 'Ethiopian' tradition was represented in 1950 by such government recognised churches as the African Congregational Church and the Bantu Methodist Church of South Africa among others. Widely established, with an urban rather than a rural mentality, they appealed to the more literate and to people able to express a sense of underprivilege in the social and political as well as the religious field. While the leadership of such churches, aware of how precarious their status remained, was generally cautious about much involvement in political protest – which came far more from the black elite within the mission churches – there was a sympathy here and a sense of shared purpose, much less marked between black nationalism and Zionists. In general, among the very poor in town or country – and most black South Africans must be so numbered – the 'Ethiopian' pattern of church life was waning before the 'Zionist' with its stronger rural roots, its direct response to the traditional needs of the people, its maximisation of aspects of the Christian tradition which belonged more to the early church and less to the ethos of post-Reformation Europe. 'Ethiopian' is in fact an oddly misleading name for what has been characterised as ecclesiastical Ethiopianism, because it is not a Protestant name at all, but in itself is already evocative of quite other things.[102] It is both symbolically African (proto-African or pan-African, one might say) and it can actually be found in the Bible. 'Where can you find the name of Dutch Reformed in the Bible?' or 'Methodist'? This was no idle question but a very serious one. You have given us the Bible, then to the Bible we shall go. The names of 'Zion' and 'Ethiopia' were most undoubtedly there. Names are important, particularly in Africa, and a church which called itself the 'Apostolic in Jerusalem Church in Zion of South Africa' might feel that nothing of importance had been left out, though another group would decide that 'Holy Cross Catholic Apostolic Church in Zion' attained a better balance.

The vast multiplicity of Zionism, originally emanating from 'Zion City, Illinois,' but expanding and altering phenomenally in and after the 1920s under the leadership of men like Daniel Nkonyane and Paolo Mabilitsa, was without doubt the central force within South African independency. Admittedly the name itself is not acceptable to all the churches which share its characteristic ethos and appeal, and there are bodies such as Shembe's Amanazaretha which all Zionists would deny to be part of the movement, though they have so much in common. But here as elsewhere a second generation was tending by 1950 to offer in the older groups a somewhat more restrained leadership than that of the earliest days. Philip Mabilitsa, head of the Christian Apostolic Church of Zion in South Africa since the death of his father Paolo in 1943, was a B.Sc. of Fort Hare; John Galilee Shembe, who had succeeded his father Isaiah with some reluctance in 1935, was a B.A. Their mode of authority and life style was more systematic, more controlled, more consonant with traditional orthodoxies, less personally decisive than that of their fathers.[103]

Three men who had died in 1949 may help us to catch something of the strange variety of this complex and irrepressible movement of the spirit. Timothy Cekwane had founded the Church of the Light long before in 1910, in response to the great sign of Halley's Comet. A small church with a splendid Zion in the Drakensburgs at Ekukhanyeni, where all meet together for a week of liturgical festival every August, its central symbols are blood and the broom with which God purifies the world. Their red garments distinguish them from the white of most Zionists, and as red is a dangerous colour in traditional Zulu religious symbolism as elsewhere, it sets them strongly apart, as does their deep preoccupation with purification and with avoidance of contamination by non-members.

Still more withdrawn and spiritually elitist was the little church of George Khambule for which he had composed the most intricate and often moving liturgies, a complex totality of words, music, dress and station. It had all been revealed to him across his 'heavenly telephone'. He had none of the ability of Shembe or Nkonyane to move, heal and organise thousands. His 'congregation of All Saints' was, on the contrary, a minute convent church withdrawn into a world of its own heavenly converse and – though it survived its founder's death for a little while – is now wholly extinct.

Ma Nku, the vigorous, outgoing, immensely popular healer and prophetess head of St John's Apostolic Church at Evaton near Johannesburg was quite a different sort of person: powerful, ebullient, one of those African women who can lead thousands and exercise authority as one born to it. Yet she was still a woman, and a woman prophetess needs a man to be bishop and administrator of the church. Unfortunately her husband, Bishop Nku, died in a railway accident in 1949 and though her son, Bishop Johannes Nku, was brought up to take his place, the loss was a serious one and years later she would come into painful and disastrous conflict with the man, more of an outsider, who was finally elected Archbishop in 'her' church.

Ma Nku was a Sotho and if the Sotho plunged less avidly into Zionism than did the Zulu, they too had shared in the movement from its early developments, as had other peoples. Ignatius Lekganyane was a Pedi who had been converted by an early Sotho Zionist, Eduard Lion, who in turn had been a disciple of the white South African Zionist, Edgar Mahon. Lion established a 'Zion City' in Basutoland in 1917 and though its appeal to the inhabitants of Basutoland was decidedly limited, or perhaps just because it was so limited, he came to refer to himself in the letterhead of his correspondence as 'General Overseer of the World'. The influence of his disciple, Lekganyane, was really to go much further: he set up a Zion Christian Church near Pietersburg in the northern Transvaal in 1925 and, though for many years it would remain just one more small group, this was destined in later times to grow into the largest of all South African independent churches and a power in the land. The immediate significance of Transvaal Zionism for us is that it was the springboard for a quick leap to the north. Rhodesian workers at Pietersburg and on the Rand soon joined it, among them David Masuka and Samuel Mutendi, two men who were to become leading prophets and bishops in their own country. They returned to preach in southeast Rhodesia, at first in collaboration but then in churches of their own. Mutendi indeed remained loyal to Lekganyane all his life and made regular visits to Pietersburg until the latter's death, but in practice his church like Masuka's was soon autonomous.[104]

The districts of Rhodesia around Fort Victoria became from this time fertile soil for the emergence of a multitude of 'Zionist', 'Apostolic' and 'Ethiopian' churches. In this part of Africa the spirit churches undoubtedly took priority as regards weight of numbers and in their impact upon society over the Ethiopians; among them Samuel Mutendi, who established his healing city of Mount Moriah on the model of Lekganyane's Moriah, became in some sort a father figure for the whole movement of independency, a master healer with pastoral authority exercised continuously for over fifty years from the 1920s to the 1970s. He could even be called in on occasion to consecrate an 'Ethiopian' bishop.[105] For a while at least the possession of a clear line of succession in authority from South African master Zionists and even from Dowie in America, thus linking one as it could seem with the original Zion in Jerusalem, had its importance. Here as elsewhere there was recurrent tension within a church between the claims deriving directly from personal charisma and the loyalty of a local congregation to its immediate prophet or pastor upon the one hand, the attempt to maintain authority, succession and a wider unity upon the other. Sooner or later the former tended to prevail over the latter, but the personal authority of a founder was usually sufficient to limit secessions within his own life time. Death could bring division. Thus David Masuka, really the first Zionist preacher in Rhodesia and head of the Zion Apostolic Church in South Africa, died in 1950 and was succeeded by his son of the same name who was, however, unable to maintain his hold on the majority of his father's 'Zionists of the Cord'; even in the home district of Bikita a senior bishop, Makamba, who felt that his years of cooperation with the father entitled him by right to the leadership, carried a majority of the congregations into his own Zion Apostolic Church, perhaps 5,000 people; Bishop Sharara did much the same for smaller numbers in Buhera and Bishop Kudzerema in Dewure. The young David Masuka was left with the legitimacy of his father's succession but only some 2,000 church members.[106]

For the most part these churches of the Fort Victoria area did not spread with comparable weight to other parts of Rhodesia, the great exceptions here being two most remarkable churches of 'Apostles', both founded in 1932 by two 'John the Baptists'. The Vapostori, the Apostles of Johane Maranke, were already by 1950 the most numerous independent body in Southern Rhodesia and had penetrated across the Zambesi beyond its northern borders. Maranke's call had come in July 1932 on the road from Umtali to his home. Near Mt Nyengwe he was suddenly conscious of a powerful light and a voice saying to him: 'You are John the Baptist, an Apostle. Now go and do my work! Go to every country and preach and convert people! Tell them not to commit adultery, not to steal and not to become angry. Baptise people and keep the Sabbath day'.[107] Maranke's conversion experience can be paralleled by many another, but out of it grew a particularly strong and evangelistic church. While having much in common with Zionists, it belonged to the subtly different 'Apostolic' tradition which avoided preoccupation with a single sacred city and tended to develop a more coherent ministerial organisation and greater evangelistic outreach, but also a harder sense of its own frontiers and of the profound difference beween members and non-members.

Johane Masowe had similarly experienced conversion and call in 1932.[108] His previous name had been 'Shoniwa'; it was during an illness that he received from voices his new name of 'John'. 'Masowe' means 'Wilderness' and that became his second name when after responding to the call he went there to pray: John of the Wilderness was what he now become and ever after remained. His preaching like Maranke's quickly drew its crowds and its believers, and it seems at the start to have included a potentially more political dimension than that of the Zionists in its response to the oppressed state of his fellow Shona. But the message he proclaimed was one of withdrawal from all European things – even at first from acquiring Bibles, though he had one himself from the start. Bibles, schools, employment, all alike were to be rejected; as the government grew more alarmed Masowe withdrew into a state of near permanent concealment, a life of wandering almost entirely outside Mashonaland. While the majority of his Apostles doubtless remained in eastern Rhodesia, the inner core of the church faithfully followed Baba Johane – first to Bulawayo and then right across the

Transvaal to settle in Port Elizabeth in the eastern Cape. By 1950 they were well known there as the Korsten Basketmakers, a closed and highly industrious religious community of Shona, the Apostolic Sabbath Church of God. From their origins in depressed rural Rhodesian society they had come in twenty years not only thousands of miles but also to an internally evolved way of life characterised by semi-industrialisation: they were effectively marketing their goods over a wide area – not only baskets but tinware and furniture.

By 1950 the Vapostori had reached Nyasaland. Decades earlier the spread of independent churches in that country had been considerable but by now, though quite a number continued to exist and to grow quietly, independency was in fact hardly a major ecclesiastical phenomenon. What there was could be classed as 'Ethiopian'.[109] Among these were the African National Church and the Church of the Black People, both secessions from among the Livingstonia elite (see page 47). Next door, in Northern Rhodesia, there was in 1950 still less strictly independent activity, its role being filled in part at least by the African Methodist Episcopal Church and the Jehovah's Witnesses, both of which while retaining their American links flourished here more than in any other African country.

The absence of independency was still more marked in Tanganyika and Uganda. The former had remained singularly free of churches founded within its own borders though the African National Church and the Last Church of God and his Christ had come across the Nyasaland frontier to establish small congregations among the Nyakyusa.[110] In Uganda there had once been a massive breakaway from the CMS among the Baganda in 1914, led by a county chief named Joswa Kate Mugema, together with Malaki Musajjakawa and, for a time, the still more famed chief and war leader, the great Kakunguru; it had focused its protest upon use by Christians of any medicine whatsoever. By 1950 its leaders were dead, it had dwindled to a small, ageing, obstinate group of people, still able to set about building a memorial church in brick to their founder yet well on the road towards extinction.[111]

In eastern Africa it was only in Kenya that in 1950 churches were to be found in any way comparable in vigour and number with those of South Africa, Swaziland or Rhodesia. It was at the end of the 1920s that independency really burst upon Kenya just as it did upon south-east Rhodesia, but here there is less evidence of any direct connection with outside influences. Rather, internal tension within the mission churches combined with growing unease at the political condition of the colony and the scale of European settlement to produce a series of movements, both in the central province among the Kikuyu and in the west among the Luyia and the Luo.[112]

Here as in so many places the distinction between the 'Ethiopian' type and the 'spirit' type of church is clearly manifest, and the churches which first grew large in Kikuyu country were of the former kind: the African Independent Pentecostal Church and the African Orthodox Church. They were nationalist, strongly interested in schooling, but unwilling to have it controlled and limited by white people. Their membership, at least initially, came largely from the mission churches from which they had separated at the time of the bitter conflict over female circumcision. By 1950 the Kikuyu Independent Schools Association linked with the African Independent Pentecostal Church had some 60,000 pupils in its schools, while the Kikuyu Karing'a Educational Association, linked with the African Orthodox Church which – like Spartas in Uganda – had obtained priests ordained by the black South African Archbishop Alexander, had rather fewer. These two had been joined in 1947 by a third, the African Christian Church and Schools, a major break from the Africa Inland Mission. These groups were close to the heart of the more coherent side of Kikuyu unrest, but around them by the late 1940s were several other movements of one sort and another. The Arathi or prophets were nearer the margins of society – the poorest, least educated of classes, their leaders not men who had any sustained experience of mission church or school. A movement of withdrawal, of rejection of western dress, medicine and education, they had the Bible together with a massive structure of rules of ritual uncleanness, partly derived from Kikuyu tradition and partly from the Old Testament, to establish their identity and apartness. By 1947 a chief could write that these 'People of God', the Arathi, had indeed 'become people of a separate kind'.[113]

Kikuyu society was torn apart in those years in ways too deep fully to understand and in its agony it had become the forum for simultaneous movements of rival ritual intensity: the 'Revival' within the Protestant mission churches reached its highest peak in the same years, as did the directly political resurgence lead by Kenyatta; both the Arathi and the 'Ethiopian' churches with their attendant schools stood somewhere between the two as a new wave of young white ex-servicemen came out unheedingly to settle and the country as a whole lurched forward towards emergency and civil war.

The Kikuyu were not the only people in Kenya to have turned significantly by 1950 towards independency. The African Brotherhood Church had been founded in 1945 among the Kamba, most of its early members having formerly been in the Africa Inland Mission. Its catechism, hymns and organisation were drawn from that or from the Salvation Army. In 1950 it established its own school of divinity for the training of ministers. An increasingly well-organised church which has grown steadily in size but has not many non-Kamba among its members, it presents one fairly normative pattern of the 'non-charismatic', 'Ethiopian' approach to independency.

The African Israel Church Nineveh was founded three years earlier, in

1942, by Zakayo Kivuli in western Kenya among the Luyia; the mission background here was Pentecostal and Friends. The African Israel Church Nineveh's integrating and reinterpreting of these two strands has produced the interesting case of a partially modernising spirit church. It has much in common with the Zionists of South Africa – the spirit possession, the constant singing and dancing, the special white clothes, the holy centre of Nineveh where the faithful gather together at Christmas, the charismatic and paternal figure of the founder and high priest. The Israelis are greatly preoccupied with the confession of sins and have developed a highly complex doctrine about sins and their bodily location which includes various physical avoidances. Yet at the same time, unlike many churches profoundly concerned with cleanliness in this form, they have in no way sought a systematic withdrawal from the modern sector of life. They do not reject western medicine, they do not allow polygamists to be pastors, they encourage every aspect of community development, they keep neat records of the church and its membership. If the Arathi represented a Christian community almost wholly within the traditional sector of society, uneducated and unstructured in western terms, shaped by the experience of the spirit and the frontiers of ritual avoidance, and if the African Brotherhood Church and the African Independent Pentecostal Church represented an almost clear commitment to a mission model of church with its catechism, schools and organised evangelism, the African Israel Church Nineveh stood for a type of Christian life at once more consciously independent, less withdrawn than the one and less competitive than the other.

By 1950 there were many other independent churches in Kenya besides; all in all they manifested a fragmentation of leadership and of sense of direction certainly reflective of the inner fragmentation within both the Kenyan missionary world itself and the wider society.

The West African coast was the first home and indigenous breeding ground for the mission churches in the nineteenth century; in the twentieth century it has fulfilled much the same function for the independent churches. Between the Ivory Coast and Calabar they have flourished as nowhere else except South Africa. Like the mission churches their bases have been very close to the coast itself. Only in Yorubaland were they, in 1950, numerous very far inland. Though so different in other ways, as regards independency Yorubaland might be seen as the Zululand of the West; here a multiplicity of thriving churches have emerged from the late nineteenth century onward, and within Yorubaland, Lagos. It was here that in and after the 1890s the 'African' churches were founded as precise withdrawals from the Baptist, Anglican and Methodist churches: the United Native African Church and the African Church established by leading members of the mission churches did not innovate in the fields of doctrine and ritual, but their members did do so in the wider relationship of church and society, church and culture.[114] Beginning as a protest movement over rigid white control of the church, they developed for some years as significant vehicles for socio-religious adaptation, made possible by the confidence of the original Lagos congregations but quickly spreading out over Yorubaland.

By the 1920s, over-restrained perhaps by the degree of western religious structure they had inherited but without the resources of the western churches, the impetus of these churches was on the wane. The religious initiative, as in South Africa, would be increasingly taken over by new 'spiritual' churches, here named generically aladura, the people of prayer.

The growth of spiritual churches depends upon a different pattern of ministry from that of the 'African' or 'Ethiopian': a more intensely personal, prophetic one. Yet it may be that one of the roots of the prophetism which swept across so many parts of Africa in those years was no other than the mission church's catechist, run just a little wild. It was the catechist with his limited training and simple message but great authority who really carried the mission church into the bush in the first decades of the twentieth century; in many a case the new prophet seems but old catechist writ large, so confident in his calling that he came adrift from his missionary sponsors. Such a one was the great Harris, a Liberian of Methodist and Episcopalian background who erupted upon the Ivory Coast and the Gold Coast in 1913 and 1914.[115] He was the first of Africa's major Christian prophets and no one else ever made quite so vast an impact in so short a time. Yet what Harris did in 1914, with his powerful message of the Bible, the One God, baptism, healing in faith, the utter rejection of fetishes, countless other prophets were to do in their lesser way in the coming years. Harris was deported from the Ivory Coast before the end of 1914 and was never to return there, but he had permanently altered the religious character of the coastal areas and established a religious tradition which was to flow on both into what was later to become the Harrist Church and into Catholicism and Methodism. It is striking how when, in the 1930s, the prophet Boto Adai began to preach in the Ivory Coast, not only his message but even his personal appearance was modelled quite remarkably upon that of Harris – the white robe and head band, the black cross bands over the chest, the cross in hand, the bowl and the Bible, all were precisely the same.[116] The imprint of the founding fathers in Christian prophetism could be as decisive as that of the most powerful of the early missionaries: they established a model which would remain in some sense definitive for many decades.

To the east of the Ivory Coast new churches were springing up in the Gold Coast as well, though in this period their spread remained rather limited.[117] That of the Twelve Apostles began with two people converted by Harris during his brief stay in their country. One of the best known was the Musama Disco Christo Church (The Army of the Cross of Christ) whose founder was the Prophet Jemisemiham Jehu-Appiah. He had been a Methodist catechist whose call by an angel with a Bible in his hand (lying open at chapter 10 of the Book of Acts) had happened in that widely important year for African independency, 1919. His ministry of healing and revelation continued for a while within the Methodist Church but the inevitable severance came in 1923 following which the Musama Disco Christo developed on its own around the sacred city of Mozano where his followers settled down and where a complex ecclesiastical hierarchy and ritual was devised, based upon the customs of the old Fanti court, to surround the clearly kingly role of Appiah himself, King Jehu Akaboha I. He had died in September 1948 and been succeeded by his son Matapoly, whose birth in 1924 just at the inauguration of the church had been seen as miraculous and the fulfilment of prophecy.

If the Musama Disco Christo dates back to the 1920s, the Prophet Wovenu's Apostolic Revelation Society, whose following was not Fanti but Ewe and his sacred city at Tadzewu, dates only from the mid-1940s, breaking forth from the Ewe Presbyterian Church as Appiah had done from the Methodists. But these and other such churches were all rather small in size in 1950. So too was Christianisme Céleste (The Celestial Church of Christ) which had been founded in Dahomey in 1947 in the old town of Porto Novo by a carpenter, Samuel Oshofa; twenty-five years later it would have become one of the best organised and most dynamic churches in West Africa.

Porto Novo is close on the border of Yorubaland, and it was undoubtedly here in Western Nigeria that the praying or prophetic churches, aladura as they were locally known, were in 1950 most numerous in their following, experienced in their leadership, influential upon society as a whole. Far more than any movement in the Gold Coast or indeed in almost any other country outside South Africa and Swaziland Yoruba aladura was at the centre rather than the periphery of its society. It too dated from the 1920s when the Cherubim and Seraphim Society emerged under the leadership of old Baba Aladura, Moses Orimolade, and the fifteen-year-old girl Abiodun Akinsowon; but the greatest movement of expansion came in 1930 when Joseph Babalola began to preach his revival mission at Ilesha. The impact of Babalola can only be compared with that of Harris or Kimbangu, but in this case government tolerated the new enthusiasm and if many of the converts joined, or returned to, the Protestant mission churches many others entered one or another of the main branches into which aladura was now growing – Babalola's own Christ Apostolic Church (previously known as Faith Tabernacle), the Cherubim and Seraphim, or Josiah Oshitelu's Church of the Lord (Aladura).[118]

In none of these churches was there the concern to have a sacred city apart, so characteristic of similar movements elsewhere in Africa. In part this is because they represent what one may call the 'apostolic' rather than the 'Zionist' thread within the Christian experience; in part it may also be because, while elsewhere the appeal of the spiritual church was particularly to an oppressed, marginalised or at least bewildered group of peasants and shanty town dwellers, aladura seemed to grow instead out of the most confident strata of urban life in a rather free and consistently confident society. Aladura was a movement of Christian revival – a challenge to the compromising mediocrity of mission church life, not unlike that of 'Revival' in East Africa; it was a movement of unequivocal rejection of paganism – no bonfires of the sacred things of ancient religion have been more confident, uncompromising and stunningly decisive than Babalola's; it was a movement in quest of spiritual things – prayer and health and holiness through prayer; its members bore no very precise secular message for the wider society in which they were and remained willing participants; it was neither consistently anti-colonialist nor strongly millennialist; it was not even unambiguously anti-missionary. On the contrary, a genuine connection with a foreign missionary body had twice been sought by its central group and its coherence with Protestant missionary Christianity went so far – in the case of the Christ Apostolic Church – as a consistent rejection of polygamy.

By 1950 the latter church, established by that name in 1941 after a final division from the British Apostolic Church which had been called in to help years earlier, was the largest independent body in West Africa. Joseph Babalola, the ex-steamroller driver, was its General Evangelist – one of the most responsible, persevering and pastoral of prophets; behind him as President of the Church was the still more unusual figure of Isaac B. Akinyele, a former clerk turned successful farmer. A childhood Anglican – his brother A. B. Akinyele was to become the first Anglican bishop of Ibadan – I. B. Akinyele was the writer of numerous religious pamphlets, consistently rejected all western medicine in his personal life, and was soon to become ruler, Olubadan, of the great city of Ibadan and would be knighted by Queen Elizabeth II. In the figure of Oba Sir I. B. Akinyele aladura stood in the 1950s at the very heart of Yoruba life, civil and religious.

The lower Congo had a cultural unity extending across Belgian, French and Portuguese colonial territory reflecting the old kingdom of the Bakongo; the tradition of Simon Kimbangu remained alive in all three. In the French Congo north of the river, however, the dominant influence by 1950 was that of André Matswa, who had founded a friendly society, the Amicale, in 1926 among Congolese in Paris and had become the political hero of the people around Brazzaville. Over the years a total confrontation had developed between the Amicale upon the one hand, which really meant the whole Lari people, and the French administration upon the other. Matswa was in his own time in no way a religious figure but a proto-nationalist; he made his plans in a Paris café and died in 1942 in a colonial prison. His followers calmly refused to accept the latter fact as true; their hopes remained fixed upon him as those of the Kikuyu were soon to be upon Kenyatta, and in his lengthening absence his power was continually magnified. At the general election in 1945 and again in 1951 Matswa easily topped the poll; but already the movement had turned mysteriously from a political to a religious expectation, and from the pursuit of modernisation to one of almost passive withdrawal while awaiting the return of Matswa, whether it be from France or from Heaven. Thus, out of the long frustration of a secular 'friendly society' was born yet one more church, this one wholly preoccupied with the second coming of its saviour:

> O Sovereign Father Matswa,
> Where are you, where are you?
> Where have they hidden you?
> O Sovereign Father Matswa,
> Return, return to deliver us.[119]

French colonial government had usually been more tolerant of religious independency than had the Belgian, and from about 1950 the Matsouan Church was free to organise itself. Across the river this was not the case and the followers of Kimbangu and of Mpadi had still to worship in secret (see page 32). In the Belgian Congo all such churches were proscribed and their leaders imprisoned or exiled. There was a simple consistency in Belgian colonial paternalism which found it impossible to believe that any initiative which came from the black man could possibly be for his own good. If occasionally a more tolerant attitude in the religious field had been proposed by officials in the administration, it could never long survive the opposition of Catholic ecclesiastical authority. And so the popular history of Zaire from the 1920s to the 1950s was one of a confused series of illegal movements, some more religious, some more political, each largely submerged, each associated with the name of one or more of the almost mythical heroes – Kimbangu, Matswa, Mpadi. Around 1950 the Kimbanguists often called themselves 'Malemba' meaning 'softly', because they had to work softly, in such clandestinity, that they hardly dared to breathe the name of Kimbangu. Thus one night in 1946 one might have detected a little group of new Malemba proceeding into the forest near Mapangu (formerly Brabanta in the central Congo) for their 'baptism of fire'. They carried white garments, and in the forest they found a great fire already lit and around it a group of believers. One of these read Matthew 3. 5–6 on the confession of sins and then each went aside to confess his sin, sorcery above all, to two people. All then donned their white garments and another elder read from Acts 19 on the baptism Paul administered to twelve men at Ephesus when the Holy

Spirit descended upon them.[120] For such groups and such a tradition the laws of the state had little cogency.

But they had all too much cogency in the life of the man who had, in his way, begun it all. In 1950 Simon Kimbangu was still alive, if now near to death, a prisoner at Elizabethville as he had been ever since 1921.[121] What he thought as he looked back across all those years on his six brief months of prophetic ministry, one will never know. A follower of the Baptist mission, he had preached the gospel of the One God, commanded the people to abandon their *minkisi* (fetishes), to give up polygamy and dancing, and he had cured the sick, praying over them. He had been listened to as no missionary in the lower Congo had ever been; prophets had relayed or distorted his message across a thousand villages, the missionaries had been greatly alarmed, the colonial authorities no less so. But he had done no harm to any man, his reported teaching was singularly pacific, and when he stood on trial in chains in October before Comandant de Rossi the sentence of death imposed on him was far from reflecting in gravity the vague charges and hypothetical evidence brought against him. On the petition of the Baptist missionaries King Albert commuted his sentence to one of penal servitude for life. Of the decades that followed we know little. He was never permitted a visit from any member of his family or Protestant pastor. 'His conduct was of an exemplary calm' reported an official and in later life he was placed in the prison kitchen. 'He seemed very effaced, very humble. A ladle in one hand, he raised the lid of the soup tureen with the other', remarked a passing visitor. 'He had nothing of the superman'.[122] Yet here too, as with St Alphonsus Rodriguez, was it not perhaps the case that God, in the words of Hopkins,

> Could crowd career with conquest while there went
> Those years and years by of world without event.

At least, as his disciples remark, if Jesus had thirty years of hidden life before his ministry, Kimbangu had them after. He died very calmly in hospital on the afternoon of Friday, 12 October 1951.[123]

2
1951–1958

A. Church and State

I

The 1950s were Ghana's decade. Despite its small size and limited population – or perhaps, indeed, because of them – the Gold Coast was able to take the political lead in black Africa and exercise an influence out of all proportion to its size so that 'Gold Coastism' was soon being emulated or denounced all up and down the continent. This was due before all else to the vigorous mind and personal magnetism of Kwame Nkrumah whom Cabral was later to describe as 'the strategist of genius in the struggle against classical colonialism'. The overwhelming victory of his party the CPP, at the elections of February 1951, while he was still in prison, brought him at once the position of Leader of Government Business. Yet for the next few years this radical theorist of pan-African liberation played a pragmatic, almost a quiet, game with the British authorities as he brought his country to independence. By 1954 he had an all-African cabinet of ministers and on 6 March 1957 the Gold Coast became independent as Ghana: surely one of the most significant dates in modern African history. Its example would quickly prove irresistible right across the centre of the continent.

Nkrumah was a highly articulate philosopher of action, the standard bearer of African renaissance. No one else at the time could so incarnate in a single life the cultural and political aspirations of the whole continent. Where Senghor placed culture first, Nkrumah placed politics: 'Seek ye first the political kingdom' he brashly proclaimed, making use of that evangelical language which undergirded so much African nationalism. In this he expressed the priorities of the new elite in almost every country, but culture was on the move as well. The year 1951 was also that in which Cyprian Ekwensi, to be hailed as the father of the Nigerian novel, wrote *People of the City* while on a ship sailing to England. It was published in 1954, being preceded by Amos Tutuola's *Palm Wine Drunkard*. The Cameroonian Mongo Beti's *Le Pauvre Christ de Bomba* appeared in 1956, the same year as Camara Laye's *The Splendour of the King*. Modern West African literature had arrived.

86

Political changes in the north of the continent, even if less potent symbolically than those in Ghana, would also quickly throw their shadow south. Libya's independence in 1951 affected its neighbours Tunisia and Egypt. In July 1952 General Neguib forced the King of Egypt to abdicate and less than two years later Nasser overthrew Neguib. The consequence was a sharp move forward on the road of effective anti-imperialism. Britain read the writing on the wall and agreed to withdraw from the Canal Zone. In January 1956 the Sudan became independent, finally refusing the union which Egypt had wished to thrust upon it. Here a major mutiny of southern troops against their northern officers the previous August had already indicated that the relationship between north and south was likely to prove a volcanic issue, but for the time the northern controlled government embarked, heedless, upon a line of policy almost wholly uncongenial to the southern third of the population.

In Tunisia and Morocco, meanwhile, growing unrest had forced the French from one concession to another so that by 1956 both stood upon the verge of independence, while Algeria – where French interests were vastly greater and the French immigrant population stood at nearly one million – was beginning to explode into civil war.

The most tense political crisis in black Africa in these years was that of Kenya faced with the Kikuyu revolutionary movement of Mau Mau, which erupted into the consciousness of the wider world during 1952. A state of emergency was declared after the murder of Chief Waruhiu in October. By October 1955, three years later, when the fighting was almost over, 479 members of the security forces had been lost and 1,292 loyalists killed, but 6,741 members of Mau Mau had died. These were the official figures of government. Tens of thousands of Kikuyu had been placed in detention camps. Jomo Kenyatta, by far the ablest black politician in the country, a man whose long overseas experience, academic confidence and enigmatic utterances infuriated the white settlers, was tried for 'managing' the revolt, convicted on questionable evidence and sentenced to imprisonment in April 1953. He was not to be freed until 1961.

At the time and for years afterwards most Europeans were not prepared to admit that this fierce and prolonged revolt was basically to be explained in terms of a deep and justifiable embitterment of Kikuyu peasants desperately short of land while faced with the sight of the wide European-owned farms of the White Highlands, their own ancestral heritage. Consequently all sorts of strange explanations in terms of a diseased collective psychology had to be produced and believed. In fact it was a nationalist movement focused upon the land issue aggravated by wider colour discrimination; it was a revolt of Kikuyu peasantry possessing the moral support of a large part of the population. But it was a true civil war as well as being a colonial revolt. There was a genuine Kikuyu resistance – from the more prosperous farmers; from men

87

who had loyally cooperated with the British authorities for years and did not intend to stop now; from devout Christians shocked by the appeal to traditional values and ruthless methods of Mau Mau. Mau Mau was a movement of tribal desperation, backed above all by the landless, the poor, the young. In military terms it was decisively crushed, but only after a remarkably long struggle, and in its wake the vision of a white-ruled dominion of East Africa was seen to be but an empty dream fading before the relentless pressure of a black nationalism which could take the form of a rural *Jacquerie* one year, a politically orientated urban trade unionism another.[1]

Next door in Uganda an outwardly rather peaceful state of affairs was suddenly rent apart by the exiling of the Kabaka Mutesa of Buganda in November 1953. The subtle politics of the Baganda have long been almost too difficult for even sympathetic outsiders really to understand, and certainly the Governor, Sir Andrew Cohen, with his brand of somewhat authoritarian liberalism found the enigmatic Ganda hankering after separatism baffling enough. His hasty exiling of a young but reactionary monarch united conservatives and progressives against him, but the settlement engineered through the good offices of the Australian historian Sir Keith Hancock which permitted Mutesa's triumphal return in 1955 involved the latter's formal acceptance of the role of a constitutional monarch, which was to create as many problems as it resolved.

These events had the most complex religious aspects. The political establishment of Buganda – Kabaka and chiefs – had long been an officially Christian one with a marked Protestant dominance. Ever since the Catholic–Protestant civil war sixty years previously a careful, suspicious balance had been maintained between the two Christian groups. While the Kabaka and most of his ministers were Protestant, the Catholics held some important chieftainships and were now considerably the more numerous group. While deeply loyal to the Kabaka, they felt discriminated against. The Kabaka's exile precipitated a considerable traditionalist reaction and a general reshuffle of religious and political forces. The Archpriest Reuben Spartas, recently released from prison, was never more popular. Thousands of people, mostly Christian, flocked to a new shrine of the old god of war, Kibuuka, whose young priest, Kiganira, was the son of a devout Catholic catechist. Cohen's action was endangering the whole religious state of the country, but as the Protestant Church was more identified with the British government, it came in for more of the blame. It was, then, important ecclesiastically that the Kabaka should be quickly restored and, when he was, the Rev. John Taylor of the CMS came in his entourage. If Kibuuka had been appealed to in Buganda, Lambeth had been appealed to in England. In the meantime the Catholics had discovered a new possibility for political initiative. Of the twelve members of the Buganda Constitutional

Committee which worked with Hancock three were, surprisingly enough, Catholic priests: Bishop Kiwanuka and two others. Together with Matayo Mugwanya, the leading Catholic layman and Chief Justice of Buganda, they cooperated with a new group of more progressive Protestants to carry through the 'constitutional monarchy' plan. This, they hoped, would not only bring back the Kabaka and halt the anti-Christian reaction, it would also provide a way whereby the Catholics might get their fair share of political power. It did not work out like that. The people, both Catholic and Protestant, who had elaborated the settlement were quickly edged out and in the new government of 1955 four out of six ministers were neo-traditionalist Protestants and only one a Catholic. A consequence the very next year was the founding by the Catholics of the Democratic Party with Mugwanya as its president – not only to challenge the new 'communism' of Congress but also the Protestant–traditionalist alliance favoured by the Kabaka.[2]

Further south one major advance in white power was achieved in these years. If setting a black Gold Coast fairly firmly on the way to independence was one of the last achievements of the Labour government in Britain, establishing a white-ruled Central African Federation was one of the first achievements of the Conservatives after returning to power late in 1951. It was done despite the overwhelming opposition of the African population of both Nyasaland and Northern Rhodesia. In January 1953 federation was unanimously recommended at a constitutional conference in London from which every African representative had withdrawn himself. Despite some measures of protection for black interests, this could only be judged 'a plain victory for the European settlers'.[3] The same month an assembly at Bukavu in the Congo of the 'Congress for the Development of Civilization in Africa' had been attempting to bring into being a wider effective 'white front' with representatives from the Congo, Rhodesia, Kenya and elsewhere. Parliament at Westminster quickly endorsed the report of the London Conference and by July the Royal Assent had been given to a bill setting up the new Federation.

African opposition, however, had not lessened, ineffectual as it seemed at the time. In March Harry Nkumbula, Congress leader in Northern Rhodesia, publicly burned seven copies of the white paper in the presence of a number of chiefs and a large crowd after singing the hymn *O God our Help in Ages Past*. The month the Royal Assent was given Kaunda was elected secretary of a defeated but not defeatist Congress. In Nyasaland the old Chief Gomani, the Ngoni Paramount, who had used his authority to urge non-violent resistance to federation, was arrested in May, rescued by his people and then taken briefly into Mozambique in the company of the irrepressible Michael Scott.[4]

If one takes one's stand for a moment some three years later to survey

89

Africa from the viewpoint of the rather quiet early months of 1956, things might not look on the surface so different from five years earlier. What was perhaps most characteristic of 1956 was the widespread use of terms like 'partnership', 'non-racialism', 'Belgian–Congolese community' and the like – such phrases expressed very much the current orthodoxy though nowhere in reality the current practice. Over most of black Africa white rule was still well enough entrenched. The Sudan had become independent on 1 January of that year, Morocco was to follow a few months later and Tunisia in 1957. In the Gold Coast Nkrumah had to pass the hurdle of one more general election in the face of increasing regional opposition from Ashanti and the north, but there could not be much doubt that independence was about to arrive. In Nigeria regional disagreement had been far more potent in holding back constitutional progress – the north continued to fear the domination of a more developed south and to stave off the day of self-government. In French West Africa, the Belgian Congo and Portuguese Africa these years had brought little or no significant constitutional change. In Uganda the Kabaka had returned and with him a measure of quiet. In Kenya Mau Mau was defeated but a new wave of black nationalist power had not yet built up and Tom Mboya, its destined leader, was in fact away studying in Oxford. In Tanganyika TANU had been founded in 1954 with Julius Nyerere, a Catholic school-teacher, as its first president but it had not hitherto got very far. In Central Africa the federation had pulled away to a good start, African opposition had faltered and its Governor-General, Lord Llewellyn, could comfortably declare in July 1956 that 'Mine is an easy job, because the Federation of Rhodesia and Nyasaland is a happy and prosperous country'.[5]

Nigeria's comparatively cautious constitutional advance during the 1950s was not a consequence of political torpor. At least in the south its parties were active enough: 'Wealth for All, Education for All, Health for All, Freedom for All. Vote for the Action Group' urged one of the most powerful ones, led by Chief Awolowo of the western region, during 1955.[6] Yet the other giant of black Africa, the Belgian Congo, had still hardly stirred from sleep. Following the Belgian election of 1954 and the defeat of the Catholic party, the key ministry of the colonies was for the first time out of the conservative Catholic hands and a liberal governor, M. Petillon, was making many administrative reforms. Yet there had been little suggestion upon the white side or the black that the days of Belgian rule were now severely numbered. Early in 1956, greatly daring, A. Van Bilsen published 'Un plan de trente ans pour l'emancipation politique de l'Afrique Belge'.[7] For the most part Belgians had simply refused to admit that the Congo could have a political future of its own in the forseeable future though phrases such as the 'Belgian–Congolese community' were now becoming fashionable, so many found it very shocking for a responsible person to propose that within a mere thirty years the country should be independent. The immediate African

90

response was one of almost incredulous welcome for anything so quick! Yet Van Bilsen had opened a Pandora's Box for the Europeans: once raised the issue was there for good. Kasavwbu had been elected president of ABAKO in May 1954; the latter now quickly developed into a Bakongo political party, publishing a manifesto in August 1956.

By this time too in French west and equatorial Africa the system whereby the various territories were moderately integrated into metropolitan France, returning a certain number of delegates to the National Assembly and the Council of the Republic, was proving less and less satisfactory. The novelty had worn off while the numerical inadequacy of the representatives in relation to population was stark. A condition of semi-autonomy was granted the different territories by the *loi-cadre* of June 1956. In March 1955 Senghor, the purest flower of the ideal of French–African union, could still write: 'What I fear is that in the future, under the fatal pressure of African liberation, we might be induced to leave the French orbit. We must stay not only in the French Union but in the French Republic'.[8] Since 1948 he had been a member of the inter-racial group of deputies who called themselves Indépendants d'Outre Mer, led by Dr Louis Aujoulat. Aujoulat had been a Catholic lay missionary and founder of the organisation called Ad Lucem. A deputy for the Cameroon (from 1951 for a wholly black constituency) and a minister in many French cabinets, his grouping was in loose alliance with the MRP, the French post-war Christian Democratic party whose policy of opposition to the break up of the empire it shared while pressing for reforms within the 'French Community'.

In the Cameroon itself Aujoulat, his allies in the Bloc Démocratique du Cameroun and other more moderate parties, had for long enjoyed very much less extensive support – at least in the more developed south-west – than the strongly nationalist Union des Populations du Cameroun (UPC) founded by Reuben Um Nyobe. The conflict between the colonial administration and Cameroonian nationalism came to a head in 1955 with the banning of the UPC and the latter's subsequent turning to guerrilla warfare. A situation developed not unlike that in central Kenya a little earlier. This forced both the administration and the more moderate parties to adopt more and more of the UPC programme in an attempt to undercut (fairly successfully) its support. In May 1957 André-Marie Mbida, a former seminarian and one-time ally of Aujoulat, became prime minister in the first African government.

The ideals of French–African alliance to which Senghor and Aujoulat had paid service for so many years were appearing increasingly unrealistic at the strictly constitutional level. Senghor and his perennial rival, Houphouet of the Ivory Coast – both in a way already clearly conservative – were now not the people who made the running. That was being done, not only in north Africa through the independence of Tunisia and Morocco and the colonial war in Algeria, but also by the radical trade unionist Sekou Touré in Guinea and by the UPC leaders in the Cameroon. The complex structure of French rule in Africa was breaking down upon every side.

If in mid-1956 there remained some overall appearances of colonial stability, this was soon to change. The November invasion of Suez by Britain and France – the last major attempt to assert the dominance of imperial power over nationalism – hastened by its failure the emergence of a new order. The Macmillan era of genial disengagement was about to begin. By 1958 the picture was a very different one. General Massu's mini coup in Algeria in May, intended to ensure the maintenance of the French presence there, not only brought de Gaulle back to power but also the entire question of French Africa's future to a head. Before the end of the year each territory had had to choose whether to remain within the French Union or not, and though at the moment only Sekou Touré's Guinea voted to leave with full independence, each country now became effectively self-governing. That same month, October 1958, in the Congo a radical new party was established, the Mouvement National Congolais, with Patrice Lumumba as its president, while in London a Nigerian constitutional conference settled for independence by October 1960. In Kenya, if a new constitutional formula devised earlier in the year still left the white settlers in a very privileged position, there were now sixteen Africans in the Legislative Assembly led by Mboya. Though Kenyatta was still in prison and destined to remain in detention for another three years, the African members had publicly declared that he and he alone was the true leader of the people. In Tanganyika Nyerere was now the unquestioned spokesman of the nation. There had been a first national election this year for thirty members of the Legislative Council – a third African, a third Asian, a third European. Unrealistic as this division must seem in a country with so tiny a proportion of non-Africans, it mattered relatively little as all those elected had received TANU support.

Finally, in Central Africa any prospect of stable government and racial harmony within an increasingly liberal federation was already almost smashed. In Southern Rhodesia the Prime Minister, the former missionary Garfield Todd, had proved too genuinely anxious to promote African advancement for the tastes of his white electorate and was replaced early in the year. At the same time in the northern territories African opposition to a white-dominated federal government was growing apace with the return of Dr Hastings Banda to Nyasaland in July 1958, after decades of absence in America, Britain and Ghana, to lead the nationalist forces into battle.

North of the Zambezi, then, while the constitutional form of the black political resurgence varied greatly from country to country, by the close of 1958 these differences might be seen to matter rather little. The common direction and pace of the movement were now clear enough. In the Federation the immediate upshot of conflict between black power and white was nevertheless still an open question, while to the south of it the direction of political advance had been all the other way. In South Africa the nationalist government had pursued apartheid with a carefully systematic and conscientious ruthlessness which may well command admiration of a sort. In 1954 the aged Dr Malan was succeeded as premier by Advokat Strydom. With Malan nationalist policy was still tinged with some slight moderation and spirit of compromise; with his successor this wholly disappeared. More than anyone else before or after him the mild-mannered Strydom stood simply and unashamedly for *baaskap*, white supremacy. A somewhat insignificant person in appearance, he was regularly outshone by his Minister for Native Affairs, Dr Verwoerd, the architect of 'Bantustans', who in September 1958 succeeded him as premier. Three months later on at the nationalist ritual festival of 16 December, Verwoerd outlined his fundamental ideological position, without ambiguity: 'We are standing like a Luther at the time of the Reformation, back against the wall . . . Never in history, at least not in the history of the past 2000 years, was the position of whitedom (*blankdom*) in danger to such an extent as now'.[9] The aim to which he had committed himself was no less than the survival of 'everything which has been built up since the days of Christ . . . for the salvation of mankind'.

These were the years in which the coloured voters in the Cape were at last removed after five years of struggle from the common roll. They were the years of the Bantu Education Act which ended financial help from the government for church schools for black people so that Africans should in future be educated only in accordance with the educational philosophy of Verwoerd. They were the years in which a massive redistribution of population began in accordance with the Group Areas Act, removing tens of thousands of black, coloured and Indian people from their old homes, now judged too close to white residential areas.

Politically the nationalists grew stronger with every election, their white rivals of the United Party holding a steadily smaller proportion of the seats in parliament. While a new white-led opposition of considerable ability appeared with the foundation of the Liberal Party, by Alan Paton and a group of like-minded people, its numerical support was insignificant. There remained, however, a vocal black opposition in those years – stronger and more purposeful, indeed, than it had ever been before. The African National Congress, led by Albert Luthuli, was still very ready to cooperate with all other racial groups in opposition and this cooperation culminated in 1955 in the 'Congress of the People' which drew up a 'Freedom Charter' proposing a comprehensive alternative to apartheid. 'South Africa belongs to all who live in it, black and white, and no government can justly claim authority unless it is based on the will of all the people'. The Freedom Charter was too inter-racial for some, too socialist for others. The Pan-Africanist Congress, led by Robert Sobukwe, was to break with Luthuli and the African National Congress on these grounds a couple of years later. But for the government the Freedom Charter was communism and it was revolution. In December of the following year 156 people of all races were arrested one morning and the great treason trial was begun. Luthuli himself, Z. K. Matthews, Oliver Tambo, all the cream of the opposition leadership suddenly found itself, perhaps not unexpectedly, facing the gravest charges. For almost five years the trial lingered on until in March 1961 the last men were acquitted; the government had failed to prove a single charge. Yet the Treason Trial marks in many ways a political watershed for South Africa. By the time it was over Sharpeville had happened and any constitutional non-white political opposition had effectively ceased to exist.

The year 1958 ended with Verwoerd and Nkrumah, the white messiah and the black, both in the zenith of their careers. All across Africa the lines were forming. That December the All-African Peoples Conference met in Accra, Dr Nkrumah's latest tactical tool for Pan African liberation. Tom Mboya was its chairman and there were 500 delegates from every part of the continent. Patrice Lumumba was here from the Congo, Holden Roberto from Angola, Kamuza Banda from Nyasaland, and Michael Scott represented Chief Hosea of the Hereros. 'We meet here in Africa' declared Mboya, 'to announce African unity and solidarity, to tell the colonial nations – your time is past, Africa must be free'.[10] It was a moment of great optimism, of the walls of the colonial Jericho being about to tumble before the trumpet blast of the captains of nationalism.

II

At no time were relations better in Africa between the imperial governments and the major churches than during these final years of colonialism. There were now in most places a harmony of outlook and a degree of close practical cooperation, at least in the educational and medical fields, such as had rarely been achieved. Only in South Africa and in the Sudan was there a real diminution in cooperation. In Kenya, undoubtedly, there were church remonstrances about army brutality and in Central Africa there were some ecclesiastical doubts (if too few) about the wisdom of imposing federation, but by and large there was a steady mutual confidence, even where previously this had been somewhat lacking. In British Africa relations between the Catholic Church and the colonial authority had greatly warmed, particularly during Archbishop David Mathew's seven-year tenure of the Apostolic Delegation to East and West Africa; in the Belgian Congo Protestants were now receiving a fairer deal; in French Africa little remained in government of the old suspicious anti-clericalism.

The coming of independence to the Sudan was followed in 1957 by the nationalisation of all mission schools in the south. 'The Catholic Church cannot but reassert and defend her right to possess her own schools' declared the Catholic bishops, most of them Italian, but to no avail – the Catholic schools went the same way as the Protestant. If this was very much part of the deepening crisis of confidence within the country separating north and south, it was also indicative of the way things were likely to go sooner or later in many another independent country. Indeed that same year the administration of the Eastern Region of Nigeria, now self-governing, was attempting to take over mission schools, but it failed to do so in face of the strong opposition mounted in that very Christian area.

The general attitude of the new class of African political leaders towards the churches was an ambiguous one. On the one side many of them had been educated at mission schools or in theological colleges and had retained affectionate memories, perhaps a friendly relationship, with one or another missionary. Some had subsequently been employed by the missions, or belonged by family to the central core of church society. A few – notably the Catholics Youlou and Boganda, and the Methodist Sithole – had actually been ordained. Their common stock of political ideas – about democratic government, the rights of the individual, and so forth – had come to them as likely as not in markedly Christian garb. On the other hand, they frequently had cause to resent the authoritarianism of missionaries, both inside schools and afterwards: a considerable inability to show respect for the more forceful products of their own educational institutions. If they had studied abroad, it was quite possibly in anti-religious circles. In comparison with their new university mentors, the Christian missionary in the African countryside appeared only too easily as but half-educated, an out-dated expression of western ways. It seemed at times that he could be respected neither for his African sympathies, which if real were kept well hidden from what he liked to call an *évolué*, nor for his European standing which could seem to newly opened African eyes low if not comical. It was felt too that many missionaries had willingly shared in the practice of a colour bar – if only on train or golf course – and had closed their eyes too often to other colonial injustice.[11]

There was, understandably, some tendency for political opposition to be linked either with a revival of traditional religion or with membership of an independent church. In Buganda, when the Kabaka was deported amid great popular indignation, many people stopped going to church and resorted instead to the shrines of the ancient gods. If strong mission-church Christians tended to take a pro-government line in opposition to Mau Mau in Kenya or (to a lesser extent) over federation in Central Africa,[12] political opponents of colonial government naturally looked elsewhere for a source of spiritual validation. So the Afro-American AME (African Methodist Episcopal) Church tended in these years to become the spiritual home of

Northern Rhodesian nationalism and Kenneth Kaunda joined it for a time.[13] The exuberant Dr Azikiwe even established his own church – the National Church of Nigeria and the Cameroons – which in November 1952 officially canonised both him and the late Herbert Macaulay. Next day the *West African Pilot* appeared with the headline 'Zik and Macaulay Take Their Place Among the Saints'.[14]

Such connections seldom lasted long or found much political favour. Only perhaps in Swaziland was an enduring and significant alliance established between the growing nationalism – here a strongly traditionalist kind – and Christian independency: a number of thriving Zionist churches.[15] In most countries the new elite took the mission churches, their outlook and language, very much for granted. Dr Nkrumah was certainly not a regular mission-minded Christian, but he found it perfectly in keeping to broadcast to the nation on the first Christmas Eve of Ghana's independence beginning 'As we in this country gather around the family circle to celebrate once again the birthday of Our Lord and Saviour'.[16]

For many nationalist leaders of the 1950s, despite their impatience with the majority of white Christians, Christianity itself remained a principal source of their motivation. So Eduardo Mondlane, by now in the United States, could demand at a conference in 1952 with the fiery Christian conviction of a young man: 'Can the Church do anything to alleviate the political problems in Africa? What does the Christian ethic say about these things? What did Christ mean when he said that he was coming to set free those who were bound?'[17] He would ask himself such questions many times in the years to come. By the mid-1950s in both the French and English-speaking world there was a strong intellectual anti-colonialism among Africans which simply took Christianity for granted and used it to judge the white man's political deeds. An example among many is the Declaration of the Catholic Students of Black Africa in France of April 1956, affirming the Christian duty of decolonisation and deeply regretting the complicity of some Catholics in resisting the ending of the colonial system.[18] Of course for many missionaries such statements were little short of communism.

It was, perhaps, the Zulu Albert Luthuli who can most honourably and properly bear the *persona* of the black political Christianity of the 1950s. A profoundly sincere, tolerant, moderate and humorous gentleman, he led his people through horribly difficult and ever darkening years with careful wisdom and complete integrity. As an expression of his Christian conscience one may ponder his comment upon the burning down of churches during the East London riots of 1952.

When a church is burnt down, some whites say, 'But a *church* – I simply cannot understand it.' Others say, 'There, you see! They even burn down churches, because they are barbarians!' But how far is it not tragically true that these churches have become distorted symbols? How far do they stand for an ethic which the whites have brought, preached, and refused to practise? 'You close your eyes obediently to pray,' goes the saying, and 'when you open them the whites have taken your land and interfered with your women.'

How far do these churches represent something alien from the spirit of Christ, a sort of patronising social service? Do not many Christian ministers talk down to us instead of coming down (if that is the direction) among us, as Christ did and does? African people bear these things long and patiently, but we are aware of them.

White paternalist Christianity – as though the whites had invented the Christian Faith – estranges my people from Christ. Hypocrisy, double standards, and the identification of white skins with Christianity, do the same. For myself, for very many of us, nothing short of apostasy would budge us. We know Christianity for what it is, we know it is not a white preserve, we know that many whites – and Africans for that matter – are inferior exponents of what they profess. The Faith of Christ persists in spite of them.[19]

The large majority of white missionaries in the 1950s were, as they always had been, somewhat apolitical. They did not question that religion and politics were very different things and their mission related to the former. They accepted the legitimacy of a benevolent colonialism; they accepted too the legitimacy of a movement towards self-government but greatly hoped it would not come too fast; they welcomed the increased subsidies most governments were now offering the missions for schools and hospitals. In practice they deeply distrusted the rise of political parties and were inclined to see 'communism' – a vague but abusive word – under every bed. Existing government was good enough and should not be challenged, at least in public.

There were, indeed, churchmen who took up a line which can only be described as one of bitter hostility to current African political aspirations, who consistently described blacks as savages and publicly defended a colour-bar. Such a one, a sad example, was old Walter Carey, formerly Anglican Bishop of Bloemfontein in South Africa – writing in Kenya in the stress of the crisis of 1952 what he called 'Christian Common Sense on Mau Mau and the Colour-Bar'. In this he repeated, page after page, that 'the real issue' is 'how to turn primitives into educated people, or savages into civilized men and women. And it's here that two hundred years are wanted at least'. 'I want these Africans to be educated: but it must be education by christian teachers, in christian principles, and in a christian atmosphere. Otherwise you will create more clever savages. I wouldn't touch that sort of education with a barge-pole'.[20]

Carey represented one missionary extreme as Michael Scott – whom he inevitably attacked – represented another. Michael Scott had his followers, people like Guy and Molly Clutton-Brock who in 1949 had gone to Rhodesia on his advice and were gallantly struggling all through these years to build up on church land an inter-racial agricultural commune called Saint Faith's Farm.[21] Then there were the Scottish Presbyterian missionaries in

Nyasaland battling for the African cause against an imposed federation.[22] But such were few indeed compared with the many who certainly shared Carey's general viewpoint and even way of speaking. Probably, however, still more common was a sort of apathy which quietly turned aside from political to ecclesiastical issues. Gonville ffrench-Beytagh was Dean of Salisbury Cathedral in the late 1950s and has remarked how 'in the Anglican Church at least we spent hours and hours working on the canons of the new province and things of this kind while the Federation for which the province was created fell apart around us'.[23]

One must, nevertheless, note a growing concern in some missionary circles with a more sophisticated approach to social and political issues, and among a lively minority strong support for a rapid, but peaceful, advance to independence. John Taylor's popular paperback *Christianity and Politics in Africa*, published in 1957, represents this point of view, one deeply influenced by the Michael Scotts and Trevor Huddlestons but less maverick. It draws together the strands of a new approach strongly anti-racialist, which had established itself among progressive Christians in the preceding years. It was much what P. Maydieu and P. Michel had been saying in Paris, Canon Collins and the Africa Bureau in London: Christians must get off the colonialist barricades at once and, instead, lead the anti-colonial crusade; by doing so they can still greatly affect its character and methods.

The Conservative government in Britain and the Gaullist in France were somehow convinced by these arguments. Both countries had extricated themselves none too painlessly from Asian and middle-eastern possessions and now proved open to rather easy conviction that a generous response to black African nationalist demands would combine profit with piety. In Britain in particular the government, the churches and the liberal lobby were working together from a common rather optimistic philosophy of decolonisation and with a fair measure of agreement over the desirable tempo. It need not be doubted that church thinking contributed its share to the rather peaceful way in which the British, French and Belgian empires in Africa in fact ended during the next few years. As a young Christian academic historian wrote at this time: 'The question, as a missionary with experience of the Communist victory in China points out, is not "Will there be a Revolution?" but "Who will *lead* the Revolution?" It is *my* hope that in Africa the Church will prove strong enough to lead the revolution'.[24]

Once all this was seen to be so, some churchmen felt one had better take positive steps to ensure that the right political parties did emerge led by sound Christians. They should be fostered not just tolerated. As the 1950s advanced a number of such political parties or movements appeared in various countries of Africa with a fairly strong religious inspiration. They stressed the virtues of western democracy, racial partnership and harmony, and were firmly anti-communist. Their roots were Catholic rather than

Protestant, their model the Christian Democrat parties of continental Europe. One such was the Capricorn Africa Society which was founded in Rhodesia and spread as far as Kenya. Its chief exponent was an English Catholic, Major David Stirling, and it had the enthusiastic support from England of the veteran missionary statesman, J. H. Oldham, now in his late seventies. An inter-territorial political movement, calling for a common voting roll and the elimination of racial discrimination, it acquired some real significance in the mid years of the decade. Essentially, however, it came too late and its position was by then a non-viable one – far too liberal to gain any appreciable portion of the settler vote, far too much of a white-led and anti-populist movement to hold the confidence of the rising tide of black nationalism. The politician who most clearly showed this attitude of mind was Garfield Todd, a former Protestant missionary, Prime Minister of Southern Rhodesia from 1956 to 1958 – the most liberal moment of Rhodesia's history; his discomfiture – quick rejection by the white electorate as his moderately advanced views were recognised – was probably inevitable.

The position of the groups in French Africa linked together in Aujoulat's Indépendants d'Outre Mer had not been dissimilar in inspiration, though operating through the very different medium of French constitutional structures. The period around 1956 and 1957 was the time in which this type of approach was being advocated most enthusiastically, at least in English-speaking Africa; 1956 was the year of the much publicised Capricorn convention at Salima in Nyasaland and of the launching of the Democratic Party in Uganda; 1957 saw the emergence of plans for what became the Basotho National Party in Basutoland. Aujoulat's own political career had now passed its zenith: his 'black heart' could no longer make up for his white skin, but it was the year in which he completed writing his enthusiastic and inspiring book *Aujourd'hui l'Afrique*.[25] There can be no doubt that there was wide missionary encouragement behind all this; it was linked with ecclesiastical condemnations of communism with which the local 'Congress' or other nationalist party was often identified, both in church newspapers and by formal statements from the bishops. The many attacks on communism, for example, in *Le Cameroun Catholique* cannot be separated either from the bishops' condemnation of Um Nyobe's UPC in April 1955 or from the activities of Dr Aujoulat's rival Bloc Démocratique du Cameroun.[26] Equally, in its early stages, the Democratic Party in Uganda owed very much to the support of Catholic Action: many people passed very easily from one to the other while Fr Tourigny, the National Director of Catholic Action in 1956, could write of the rival Uganda National Congress 'the religious authorities strongly disapprove of the adhesion of Catholics to the Congress' and declare of the DP that it had been 'received with enthusiasm in all Catholic quarters'.[27] In the coming years some of these movements quietly fizzled out, others became serious and independent parties, generally to the right of the political spectrum, but with decreasing ecclesiastical links.

There were undoubtedly ecclesiastical leaders and thinkers who feared the implications and consequences of such an institutionalisation of a Christian political view in opposition to other nationalist parties. They preferred to offer general political guidance and to cultivate wherever possible good relations with politicians irrespective of party. They did not wish to alienate the hardline nationalists. Thus the Protestant Church in Cameroon had far more sympathy for the UPC. This was not only a common Protestant viewpoint, consonant with normal British and American experience; it was shared by a number of the more far-sighted Catholic bishops, notably Joseph Blomjous of Mwanza. In several countries the Roman Catholic hierarchy published significant pastoral letters on the evolution of society during those years, and if such documents seem more cautious than the pronouncements of some individuals in other communions, it may be remembered that they carried more weight in coming from a whole bench of bishops and in providing guidelines which would actually be implemented by many church workers. Already in 1951 Mgr Sigismondi, the rather open-minded Apostolic Delegate to the Congo had declared that 'Black people expect from the Church visible evidence of its social doctrine'.[28] The most impressive of the pastoral letters was probably that of the Tanganyikan bishops entitled *Africans and the Christian Way of Life* and dated 11 July 1953. It was a very sensible statement about politics, education and economics in relation to the development of Tanganyika issued a year prior to the foundation of TANU. Largely the work of Bishop Blomjous, its signatures included that of the first African bishop of the country, Laurean Rugambwa, appointed the previous year.[29]

Although Tanganyika was economically and politically one of the more backward countries of Africa, a basis for sound church–state relations was thus being laid at this time which would endure for many years. If the pastoral was one expression of this, the friendship between Dick Walsh, the White Father Education Secretary of the Catholic Church, and Julius Nyerere was another. Fr Walsh's support not only for Nyerere's studies in Edinburgh but also for his early political activity while a teacher at St Mary's, Pugu, proved to be as far-sighted as it was beneficial and Nyerere did not forget it.

The Mau Mau crisis had such a special character and its religious aspects were so considerable that it requires more particular consideration. That central Kenya had for many years before 1952 been in an increasingly disturbed state is not questionable. Kikuyu society had been a melting pot for new religious and political movements including a large number of independent Christian churches. While these churches were not behind Mau

Mau, which appealed only too explicitly to the 'God of Kikuyu and Mumbi' and to a new version of ancient practices, particularly oath-taking, yet the deep distrust of European churches which was one factor responsible for their rapid growth was closely akin to the still deeper distrust of European settlers and officials which exploded in Mau Mau. Religious and political rebellion were here intertwined. Thus Bildad Kaggia could help found the 'Friends of the Holy Spirit' Church, popularly known as the Dini ya Kaggia, in the 1940s and help organise Mau Mau in the 1950s. Looking back on his more religious period Kaggia later wrote: 'We compared the clergy and the whole hierarchy of the "Mzungu" (European) Church to the Pharisees of old, those who outwardly professed godliness but were ungodly inside'.[30] In fact if Kaggia soon lost interest in this church despite the forcefulness which gave it his name for good, the church itself seemed to have sensed danger in such a hot and closely political line; during the emergency it held firmly to a 'non-aligned' position.

The mission churches had no sympathy for either independent church or Mau Mau; they quickly came to identify the latter with the very devil and the battle against it was seen in strongly religious terms. This could be the view of both white and black. Faced with some horrible and well-publicised atrocities and with its deliberate appeal to the pre-Christian past, no other view seemed possible. While the large majority of ordinary church members probably sympathised with much in Mau Mau or at least took its oaths out of fear, a nucleus of committed church members stood out utterly against it. Inevitably they became its principal victims, for their very existence prevented a united front of Kikuyu against the white man without which the movement could not be successful. If Mau Mau produced what was basically a nationalist anti-colonial war and a poor man's anti-settler landowner war, it also produced a straight civil war, Kikuyu against Kikuyu, and a religious war polarising non-Christian and Christian motifs upon opposing sides.

Harry Thuku, the nationalist hero of many decades, was now a strong loyalist. Founder of the Young Kikuyu Association in 1921, he had subsequently been in detention for years. It was Thuku whom Kenyatta succeeded in 1947 as president of the Kenya African Union. He then settled down in retirement as a prosperous farmer in Kambui, an elder of the Presbyterian Church, and a very good friend of the murdered Senior Chief Waruhiu. For such men Mau Mau made no sense. 'For myself I opposed Mau Mau quite openly; I did not care what they did to me', wrote Thuku many years later, 'My reasons for hating Mau Mau were first, that they killed innocent women and children – sometimes pregnant women. Then they killed Mr. Leakey of Nyeri, by burying him upside down. Also there was the massacre at Lari. But the Mau Mau did not get a hold of this area for Waruhiu had been here, and Magugu, Wanyoike and I all spoke quite openly about Mau Mau to our people'.[31] The Christian lead was taken by men of the calibre of Warahiu and

101

Thuku, closely allied to clergy such as Wanyoike Kamawe of the Presbyterian Church and Obadiah Kariuki, the Anglican rural dean and later bishop. They were supported by a tiny handful of resolute villagers, many of whom had been active in the Revival movement. Alone in their little huts they were defenceless against the night attack and the story of many of these simple Kikuyu martyrs, resolutely refusing to take the oaths in face of torture and death, is an intensely moving one.[32] The key element in the Mau Mau oath was blood – goat's blood or the blood of the oath-taker himself, while a key motif in the spirituality of the Revival was the blood of Christ whereby they were saved and which they received in communion: 'I have drunk the Blood of Christ, how then can I take your blood of goats?' was a frequent reply of the Kikuyu martyrs: one blood brotherhood against another, one sense of certainty and purpose against another.

White Christians were in far less danger and were not likely to be troubled by any conflict within the family or sense of divided loyalty. For most of them, at least initially, here was a simple case of evil to be combated, and the explanation of how it had come about was either directly diabolical or in terms of some collective psychological aberration on the part of the Kikuyu people. Christianity and government had never seemed so close together: each made use of the other. The independent schools, long disliked by missionaries, were blamed and closed. Denunciations flowed out from pulpits as from District Officers and when, in a more positive manner, the device of the cleansing ceremony was created to rehabilitate Kikuyu who had taken the oath, church ministers carried out such services with enthusiasm.

Before long, however, differing attitudes began to appear in church circles. If, undoubtedly, there were African Christians with strong Mau Mau sympathies, there were white Christians like Bishop Carey whose generalised condemnation of the savagery of the black people was wildly unrestrained. Already, early in 1953, the Anglican Church Missionary Society felt compelled to denounce his published articles.[33] Furthermore, missionaries soon began to realise that there was grave brutality on the part of the security forces as well, coupled with frequent harassment even of the most loyal blacks. In January 1953 Canon Bewes, the African Secretary of the CMS and an old Kenyan hand, visited the country bearing Kikuyu Christians a message from the Archbishop of Canterbury. On returning to London he created an uproar by alleging police brutality against suspects, and over the next years some churchmen played a major part in challenging the ruthlessness of the army and police reaction. At the same time they began to speak out more about the underlying problems – the 'White Highlands' policy and racial discrimination – which were behind the bitterness. When early in 1955 the CMS, which bravely took the lead in so much of this, published a manifesto *Kenya – Time for Action*, calling for major

102

changes in policy, even its own, more cautious bishop on the spot, Leonard Beecher, declared himself 'bewildered and embarrassed'.[34] A full-time secretary to the Kenya Christian Council, Stanley Morrison, was appointed whose task it was to galvanise the churches to face together the real problems of the country in the aftermath of Mau Mau. When in 1957 a new Christian newspaper, *Rock*, was launched to give a lead in the social and political field, though at first cautiously enough, it soon came under fire from settler circles as 'communist'.

In August 1957 Bishop Kariuki visited Jomo Kenyatta far away in detention at Lokitaung. Both had married daughters of old chief Koinange. Kenyatta received him kindly, they prayed together and Kenyatta asked to keep the Bible Kariuki had brought with him. His religious and irenic response to Kariuki's visit was different indeed from the image of 'the evil genius' with 'the witch-doctor's eyes' which much European and missionary propaganda long continued to depict.[35] The new Kenya would emerge from both sides of the Mau Mau divide. The assistant editor of *Rock*, John Kamau, had only just been released from detention and would later become General Secretary of the National Christian Council. The church like the nation would have to learn how to reconcile the two sides of a civil war, and it would be able to do so the better because of the common bonds of kinship, political aspiration, and even religious sincerity.

The decision of the South African government to establish its own system of 'Bantu Education', withdrawing all support from church schools, produced what was probably the most important single issue in church–state relations in South Africa in the 1950s.[36] It represented a sharp repudiation of many years of educational cooperation and it could be expected to produce a more united church opposition than any other aspect of nationalist policy. Yet while this opposition was indeed there, it failed to agree upon any common policy in face of the challenge, and in fact three different lines were followed. The large majority made their protest and then did what the government wanted; that is to say they leased their schools to the state and abandoned all control of them. This was Archbishop Clayton's policy, followed by all Anglican dioceses except that of Johannesburg, and by most Methodists, Presbyterians and others. There were two alternatives: one was to refuse to hand them over, but to close them instead as the church had not the money to run them independently; the other was to maintain them in existence and find the money somehow. The Anglican diocese of Johannesburg, under the leadership of Bishop Reeves and encouraged by Father Huddleston, chose the former; the Roman Catholic Church chose the latter. So did the governors of Adams College, the famous Natal school founded by the American Board of Mission in Boston. Most other church leaders were simply not prepared to attempt the financial struggle to which these decided to commit

103

themselves. All three lines had their pros and cons. For his part Clayton declared 'I am haunted by the fear that if the number of school buildings available is greatly reduced by refusal of the missions to lease any of their buildings, the result will be the throwing of large numbers of children upon the streets. . . . Even a rotten system of education is better than that.' To which Reeves replied 'I dare not take the risk that buildings which have been erected by the money and labour of church people may be used to indoctrinate children with a racial ideology . . .' The Catholic bishops for their part, relying upon a stronger group commitment to the support of 'Catholic mission schools' and rather greater likelihood of considerable overseas financial support, issued a pastoral letter in November 1954 appealing for sacrifice from all and simply refusing to 'yield on principle'. However while the government registered most of the Catholic schools as private and so permitted them to continue, it found pretexts for liquidating Adams College: such a breeding ground of free men could not be suffered to survive.[37]

So Lovedale and Adams College, which both dated back more than a century, and many another church school lost their character or were closed entirely, and the white Protestant churches lost one of their most important and creative links with African people. And what of the Catholic schools? The bishops raised £750,000 in two years and yet many schools had still to be closed in the coming decade. By July 1959 the pupils in Catholic schools had dropped from 112,000 to 93,000, the loss being greatest at the secondary level, yet in 1972 there were still 391 Catholic schools with 80,000 pupils, though by then many people were coming to doubt whether the financial burden could be borne much longer. Was the long struggle worth while? It is hard to say, but it is at least probable that the best Catholic secondary schools, such as Mariannhill, were in the 1960s by their very survival fulfilling something of the national role played earlier by various Protestant schools: they were producing the elite of a new African leadership. If this be the case, the decision of the Catholic bishops may have justified itself in a way well beyond their own intentions at the time. But it could not compensate for the loss of so much else. Lovedale would be followed in 1959 by the university college of Fort Hare, taken over and radically altered by the government. What had been for decades the Mecca of forward-looking Africans of every tribe and nation in southern Africa, one of the Church's most creative and respected contributions to the continent, was now to be restricted to the Xhosa and to be subjected to an essentially different educational philosophy. Professor Z. K. Matthews, now its acting-Principal, and Dr M'timkhulu resigned in protest. Z. K. was within two years of retirement and by doing so lost all his pension rights.[38] As much as anything the rape of Fort Hare marked the end of an epoch.

The greatest book to come out of the African church in the 1950s was, without much doubt, Trevor Huddleston's *Naught for your Comfort*.[39] Its message rings down the years with gospel clarity – a searing condemnation in the unmitigated light of the love of God for the structured inhumanity of South African society and apartheid policy as seen at work in the slums of Johannesburg. Huddleston shared with Clayton, Scott, Reeves and (later) ffrench-Beytagh the strengths of a high Anglican Catholic tradition: incarnational and sacramental. With all but Reeves he shared the role of a celibate – a role which can free a man for a more challenging stance than the married minister may be able to exhibit. Closer to ordinary African society than any of the others, Huddleston remained very English, a steady rather paternalist pastor in Sophiatown who – despite his critics – never went very far into any form of organised political action. His only weapons were, as he reminded one, 'my mind, my tongue and my pen'.[40] His writing moved countless hearts across the world and infuriated his opponents because of its spiritual power, its sheer quality, its un-nuanced but compelling handling of the individual event. It infuriated more pragmatic churchmen at least as much as secular politicians.

Clayton contrived Huddleston's return to Britain at the end of 1955 but his inspiration remained. Just a few months later a young Methodist missionary arrived at Cape Town bound for Northern Rhodesia, clutching a book beneath his arm. The book was *Naught for your Comfort*. Its bearer was Colin Morris.[41] Meanwhile Ambrose Reeves, the Bishop of Johannesburg, was to continue the struggle with no less vigour but in a rather different style: less prophetic fire, but more committee work, more collaboration with African leaders and – as was fitting for the bishop of the largest city in the country – on a rather wider front.

The reaction of the government to *Naught for your Comfort*, published when Huddleston was already back in England, had been to close down his old school of Christ the King, Sophiatown. 'The Minister's action seems so petty' declared Clayton, no admirer of Huddleston's hot and well-publicised tactics. The archbishop himself was soon to enter his last crisis. The Treason Trial was about to begin and Clayton joined Reeves in sponsoring the Defence Fund. In the meantime a clause in a proposed new law, the Native Laws Amendment Act, would be able to make segregation obligatory even within church buildings: it would become an offence in certain circumstances to admit blacks to a white man's church. In the words of the nationalist paper *Die Transvaler*: 'As long as liberalistic bishops and canons, professors, students and politicians can freely attend church and hold meetings and socials together with non-Europeans, apartheid will be infringed in its marrow. It is high time for this to end'.[42] Here at last the leaders of almost all the main churches were prepared to make a stand, despite Verwoerd's passionate remonstrance 'It has nothing to do with the working of the Church. It has nothing to do with the freedom of religion and it has nothing to do with the sovereignty of the Church.'[43] Clayton, in his bones a high Tory and now over seventy and about to retire, yet knew that on this there should be no compromise come what may. As Archbishop of Cape Town and Metropolitan he wrote to Strydom the last of many writings.

Dear Mr. Prime Minister, . . . We recognise the great gravity of disobedience to the law of the land. We believe that obedience to secular authority, even in matters about which we differ in opinion, is a command laid upon us by God. But we are commanded to render unto Caesar the things which be Caesar's, and to God the things that are God's . . . It is because we believe this that we feel bound to state that if the Bill were to become law in its present form we should ourselves be unable to obey it or to counsel our clergy and people to do so.

Having written this, Ash Wednesday 1957, Clayton took Reeves by the arm and said, 'Reeves, I don't want to go to prison. But I'll go if I have to'. The next day he was dead. At his funeral the government was wholly unrepresented but in the coming months the church clause was somewhat modified and, even so, has hardly been applied.[44]

In the 1950s the main thrust of public ecclesiastical opposition to the implementation of apartheid undoubtedly came from a small group of Anglican clerics: this was really part of a wider pattern of Anglican initiative in the continent. The last decade of the British Raj was also the last decade of that spirited and imaginative, if also frequently *de haut en bas*, leadership which the wider church owed to Anglicans. The age of Clayton, Reeves, Huddleston and Scott, was also the age of Max Warren, John Collins, Charles Raven and John Taylor. The weakness of such leadership, even when that of a bishop, tended to be its individuality, the lack of reliable institutional or parochial support, though this weakness was largely overcome in the case of a Clayton or a Warren.

The pattern of Catholic leadership at the time was clearly different: dull, somewhat impersonal but fairly steadily consistent. The stand of the bishops over schools was followed up with a strong wider statement issued from Pretoria in July 1957: 'The white man makes himself the agent of God's will and the interpreter of His providence in assigning the range and determining the bounds of non-white development. One trembles at the blasphemy of thus attributing to God the offences against charity and justice that are apartheid's necessary accompaniment.' Again, the bishops urged South Africans 'to consider carefully what apartheid means: its evil and anti-christian character, the injustice that flows from it, the resentment and bitterness it arouses, the harvest of disaster that it must produce . . .'. Nevertheless it urged 'counsels of moderation' and 'gradual change' rather than revolution. To Catholics themselves the bishops had this to say: 'The practice of segregation, though officially not recognised in our churches, characterises nevertheless many of our church societies, our schools, seminaries, convents, hospitals and the social life of our people. In the light of Christ's teaching this cannot be tolerated for ever. We are hypocrites if we condemn apartheid in South African society and condone it in our own institutions'.[45] Sadly, these sentiments remained little more than words. It can be asked what sustained effort the bishops made, then or for many years, to eliminate the ecclesiastical 'practice of segregation' whose existence so considerably undermined, in the Catholic as in other churches, the credibility at least in black eyes, of public condemnation of apartheid policy.

While it would be exaggerated to speak of unanimity in the ecclesiastical approach to the things that belong to Caesar in the closing years of the 1950s – increasingly benign years as regards the colonial system, increasingly tense years in South Africa – there was probably nevertheless (outside the Catholic Church in the Portuguese territories and the Dutch Reformed Churches in South Africa) a greater measure of consensus in political outlook from the more vocal and senior church leadership across the continent than could be found in either earlier or later periods. It was the consensus of a moderate liberalism which willingly accepted the general structures of a secular state and the coming of independence where it was on the way, while expressing a measure of reasoned criticism of racial discrimination where white rule still firmly prevailed. The last thing church leadership was looking for anywhere in 1958 was some sort of confrontation with government – though the thrust of South African policies was making that increasingly difficult to avoid – but it was less anxious than previously to be closely identified either. It wanted to be able to look forward to long years of harmonious cooperation. In the meantime its personnel had not notably changed: within the main churches its senior leadership remained almost entirely white, and while it was accepted that this would now have to alter, there was still little sense of urgency as the last hours of the Indian summer of the *ancien régime* ticked not uncomfortably away.

B. The historic churches

The 1950s could well be judged the last great missionary era in Africa's history. Through the greater part of it missionaries continued to hold the senior posts in all the larger churches; they grew ever more numerous[46] and with the financial support of most governments their influence upon the wider society through the major institutions they directed was at least as considerable as it had ever been. Moreover, the churches they presided over were almost breaking at the seams, so rapid numerically was their growth at this time. It is probable that the number of members of the mission churches more or less doubled in the course of the decade. This happened through a number of different processes. On the one hand there was an immense increase in the number of mission-controlled primary schools whose members almost automatically became church members at one stage or another; then there was the natural tendency in some rather strongly Christianised areas for older people who had hitherto stood apart to decide to throw in their lot with the new society and become at least catechumens. Further, in Rwanda, Burundi and elsewhere there were mass movements of conversion in process. But beyond all this there was a strong missionary advance in these years into areas where hitherto little work had been done. The most important of these areas comprised the sudanic belt – the northern districts of the Ivory Coast, Gold Coast, Togo, Dahomey, Nigeria and the Cameroons; northern Uganda, northern Kenya and southern Ethiopia as well as the southern Sudan. In some of these territories, such as the southern Sudan, missionaries had been present for a long time; but in many of them this presence was extremely slight previous to 1950.

In West Africa it was striking how little the old established Protestant churches of the coast had penetrated into the northern parts of each country. Here there had been some Catholic work as also a certain Baptist, Pentecostal and other Protestant fundamentalist presence: the Assemblies of God and the Sudan Interior Mission in particular. One of the most important features of the history of the 1950s was the advance of these two groups, Catholics and fundamentalists, in the sudanic zone. Thus where the Catholics had but two prefectures (Kaduna and Jos) in the northern province of Nigeria in 1950, they had by 1959 an archdiocese of Kaduna, the dioceses of Jos, Lokoja, and Makurdi, and the three prefectures of Sokot, Yola and Maiduguri. What had been a mere handful of SMA and Holy Ghost Fathers had been immensely reinforced both from their own societies and from two newly arrived groups – American Dominicans in Sokoto and Irish Augustinians in Maiduguri. The same sort of thing was happening in all the neighbouring countries.

It was also happening on the Protestant side through the work of the Sudan Interior Mission, the Sudan United Mission, the Assemblies of God and the Danish Lutherans.[47] The growth in the number of American missionaries in Africa meant above all a growth in the sudanic belt. The impact of this missionary redeployment was considerable, even though it was clearly very much of a white impact but the desire of these districts to catch up educationally with the southern parts of their countries before the arrival of political independence made them give a warmer welcome to new missionary initiatives than might have been anticipated. On the Protestant side, however, the general lack of continuity between southern and northern Christianity remained a serious weakness; only in the Catholic church did southern immigrants make some significant contribution to evangelisation in the far more Islamic north. The degree of Islamisation of these vast areas of course varied enormously – almost 100 per cent around Kano, very slight in much of northern Ghana. In Upper Volta the White Fathers and the Assemblies of God had been present for many years and both had already acquired real local roots. Here the direction of advance was southwards rather than northwards and one of the most interesting mass conversion movements of this period was that of the Dagarti people of the extreme north-west of Ghana into the Catholic Church. By the end of the decade both here and in the neighbouring areas of Upper Volta an indigenous rural Catholicism was starting to thrive under White Father encouragement very different from the old established and far more urban based religion of the coast.

It was an age in which the quality of church institutions was being improved very considerably, partly because of far more ecumenical cooperation between Protestants and partly through government financing. There was still, however, next to no cooperation across the Catholic–Protestant divide. Secondary schools and teacher training colleges were enhancing their buildings, their science equipment and their libraries; they were raising their standards as well as their numbers as they were drawn more and more into the orbit of the new universities. So excited indeed could Catholic missionaries become with the challenge of higher education and so anxious were they to control it, if possible, at every level, that their dreams were now of a number of Catholic universities. In the Congo Lovanium was emerging under the tutelage of the Catholic University of Louvain and in Basutoland the Canadian Oblates of Mary Immaculate had set up the little university college of Pius XII at Roma. In eastern Nigeria and Uganda there were unrealised dreams of a similar kind. If the Catholic bishops could 'own and control' schools in Nigeria with more than 900,000 pupils which were 'managed' by priests and nuns who thus had 'more than thirty thousand

Catholic teachers on their pay roll',[48] why should they not have a university too? There was a risky unreality about the missionary educational euphoria of the time, especially upon the Catholic side, a reluctance to acknowledge how dependent this house of cards was upon government goodwill.

While the main Protestant churches also greatly expanded their schools in these years, concentrating perhaps rather more than the Catholics upon the quality of the very top school and less upon the quantity of the middle level ones, they were certainly ahead in the attention they paid to a wider range of cultural phenomena and institutions. One important concern here was the development of an African hymnody.[49] A second was radio. Radio ELWA in Liberia and Radio Voice of the Gospel in Addis Ababa, both to become very considerable ventures covering between them most of Africa, were the fruit of these years. A third was the production of literature. The old Protestant concern with the translation of the scriptures was widened to embrace a variety of booklets and newspapers of all sorts, produced for instance by the East Africa Literature Bureau or by the extensive Librairie Evangelique au Congo (LECO) at Leopoldville set up by the Congo Protestant Council together with a large number of mission bodies.[50] But all across the continent institutions, conferences and commissions for Christian Literature were now the order of the day. The immediate force behind such moves was generally a national Christian council of which by 1955 there were fourteen in Africa.

There was, too, a growing, though still hardly universal, realisation within the churches of the urgent need to increase very greatly the number of ordained African ministers, as also the academic quality of their training. The latter need was much more a Protestant than a Catholic one since Catholic standards for ordination had always been high, if unadapted, while the Protestant standards had generally been adapted, but rather low. There was still a striking difference between the large academically qualified staff to be found in almost every Catholic major seminary and the single man who might be found running a Protestant theological college with the help of his wife and some part-time assistance.[51] But on both sides standards were rising, and the character of the courses provided was, to some extent at least, under public scrutiny. In many cases the only practical way to raise standards was by wider cooperation – between different churches on the Protestant side, between different religious orders (often quite as difficult an enterprise) upon the Catholic. Thus Presbyterians and Methodists had run a small joint theological college in Kumasi since 1943 and there were other such ventures.[52] The 1950s brought with them the ideal of the large 'United College', but it often took years to realise. As an ideal it was linked with the development of departments of theology or of religious studies in the new universities. The university colleges at both Accra and Ibadan had such departments from the start; their personnel was largely derived from the

Protestant missions – for instance the Methodist S. G. Williamson simply moved across in 1950 from being Principal of Trinity College, Kumasi, to the Department of Theology at Legon, where he was joined by C. G. Baeta. The role of such departments would be increasingly important within the life of the churches themselves, both through the diplomas they offered the seminary trained minister and through the growth within them of an academically respected nucleus of ordained leaders who could find therein an independent but recognised institutional base.

In East Africa a university department of religious studies would only come in the 1960s – a reflection of the weaker Protestant presence on that side of the continent – but a United Theological College for Anglicans, Methodists and Presbyterians was established in 1955 at Limuru in Kenya. However, some of the best colleges continued one-denominational, such as the Lutheran Makumira in Tanganyika.

An impression of the overall quantitative growth of the ministry can be gauged from the figures in Table 1. They are doubtless not quite complete for either Protestants or Catholics, but they provide a reliable general picture.[53]

Table 1. *Ministers in training 1958–9*

	Protestant	Catholic
Sudan	20	45
Kenya	20	43
Uganda	60	142
Tanganyika	99	176
Federation of Central Africa	104	80
Southern Africa	276	35
Portuguese Africa	44	85
Belgian Africa	96	539
Nigeria	135	154
English speaking W. Africa, excluding Nigeria	50	51
French West and Central Africa	74	196
	978	1,546

Courses in Protestant seminaries were generally three of four years in length, those in Catholic seminaries at least seven; moreover, the number of 'drop-outs', not reaching ordination, was certainly far larger in the latter. This number of students seems to have produced rather over 150 Protestant ordinations a year and 100 Catholic. What these figures emphasise is the continuing location of Protestant strength in South Africa and Nigeria, while the main Catholic centres were to be found in the Congo, parts of French West Africa, Uganda and Tanganyika. The Catholic figure for Portuguese Africa relates only to Angola; there was not, it seems, a single Catholic senior

111

seminarian in Mozambique at this time; Protestant churches, however, had twenty-six men in training in Mozambique. Apart from South Africa the Protestant numbers remained clearly very inadequate. On the Catholic side the same was true for all but a handful of dioceses. Only nine dioceses had more than twenty-five students and six of these were in the small area between Bukavu in the eastern Congo and Kampala, Uganda. The other three were Peramiho in southern Tanganyika and Onitsha and Owerri in Nigeria: an indication of the rapid growth taking place in Igboland.

With few exceptions the churches faced the end of the 1950s and the advent of political independence with an extremely small ordained native leadership. All in all it would just suffice in most places to ensure their credibility in face of the coming challenge to 'Africanise', but in many a case when the missionary Mother Hubbard eventually went to her cupboard to get 'a black bishop', the cupboard would prove all too bare of men with experience and education.

While these years were seldom ones of the transfer of ecclesiastical authority from white to black in the major churches, they were ones in which the local church was formally established with its own juridical autonomy, equivalent to that of its European parents. Thus an Anglican 'Province' was set up in West Africa in 1951, in Central Africa in 1955 though not in East Africa until 1960 and 1961; at these dates the local dioceses ceased to be under the metropolitan jurisdiction of the Archbishop of Canterbury. Similarly in the Catholic Church hierarchies were established in British West Africa in 1950, in South Africa in 1951, in East Africa in 1953, in French Africa in 1955, and in Belgian only in 1959. By this change 'Vicariates' became dioceses or archdioceses, but they remained subject to the curial congregation of Propaganda Fide, and the real effect was rather slight. In 1955 the first All-Africa Lutheran Conference met by Mount Kilimanjaro in Tanganyika and provided a considerable spur for the further organisation of the Lutheran churches. The juridical autonomy of local Protestant churches had in some cases already been established; for instance that of the Presbyterian Church of East Africa in 1943 and that of the Gold Coast in 1950. In other cases it dates from these years. Thus three West African churches which obtained juridical independence in 1956–7 were the Evangelical Churches of West Africa (derived from the Sudan Interior Mission, mostly situated in northern Nigeria), the Tiv Nungo u Kristu (from a South African Reformed mission), also in northern Nigeria, and the Evangelical Church of the Cameroon. In such cases the change did normally bring with it the effective commencement of black responsibility for church leadership, but in the Anglican and Cátholic cases this was not so. Although Archbishop Fisher consecrated four African Bishops in Namirembe Cathedral, Uganda, in May 1955, there was still no black Anglican diocesan bishop in East

Africa at the beginning of 1960, and no black bishop at all in Central and Southern Africa. By then there were seven assistant bishops in Eastern Africa (four in Uganda); only in Nigeria were there diocesans – in Lagos, Ibadan, Ondo-Benin and the Niger Delta.

In the Catholic Church progress was also very slow in this field, but there was some. Joseph Kiwanuka had been consecrated in Rome by Pope Pius XII in 1939; he remained the solitary black Catholic bishop on the continent until 1951 when he was joined by two exarchs in Ethiopia and by Laurean Rugambwa, the bishop of Rutabo – the corner of Tanganyika bordering upon Uganda and upon Kiwanuka's diocese. In the next seven years, up to the end of 1958 and of Pius XII's reign, nineteen more were appointed. One of these simply replaced the earlier exarch of Eritrea, Ghebre Jacob. Of the remaining eighteen nine were auxiliaries. The nine others who were given effective authority over a part of the church again indicate some of the areas of the greatest Catholic strength. They included Bigirumwami of Nyundo in Rwanda; Mabathoana of Leribe, Basutoland; Mongo of Douala, Cameroon; Yougbaré of Koupela, Upper Volta; Chitsulo of Dedza, Nyasaland; and Msakila of Karema (Ufipa), Tanganyika. This brought to eleven out of over two hundred Latin dioceses and vicariates the number ruled by an African. It is striking that in the Congo at the beginning of 1959 there was still no black diocesan bishop and only a single auxiliary (Kimbondo in Kisantu), though there were now more than three hundred African priests in the country.

A well-informed observer of the African church had this to say in 1956: 'The white missionary, immensely important as his contribution will be for many years yet, is becoming visibly the stop-gap holding down some essential place in the total organisation until an African is ready to fill it. But the village catechist and teacher is still today the corner-stone of the African Church.'[54] This observation was certainly true, yet it could also be misleading. On the one hand many missionary societies still showed very little sense of being now no more than a stop-gap: the Universities' Mission to Central Africa, for instance, would be celebrating their centenary with some solemnity the following year. While they had much to thank God for, it did not apparently produce any qualms that they had not a single African bishop within the four countries where they were working.[55] The number of white missionaries was still growing fast in some churches and while the number of African ministers was certainly growing too, the growth – as we have seen – was rather inadequate. Even in those areas where a larger number of ordinations was now forthcoming, the position was often hardly less serious because they tended too to be the churches or dioceses with a rapidly escalating multitude of adherents. Above all, it was still unusual to find a church or diocese seriously planning the training of clergy to take over the most senior, as also the more technical, of the posts held by missionaries. Certainly the

113

official stress here was more often on the 'for many years yet' rather than on the 'stop-gap' aspect of things.

Perhaps more curious was the position in regard to the lower, more localised ministries. The numerical growth of the churches and therefore of the number of rural congregations was proving phenomenal and the gap between them and the ordained clergy, whether white or black, was in general steadily increasing: the latter just could not visit so many congregations so often. Hence the absolute need for 'the corner-stone of the African Church' – the village catechist and teacher. Of this there can be no doubt. But whereas 'the village catechist and teacher' had in previous ages been a single person, he had now split rather sharply in half. The catechist was having less and less to do with government recognised schools, the teacher was a young man formed in a teacher-training college and being called back regularly for government sponsored refresher courses. The former was elderly and clearly a church person, the second was young with a rather ambiguous role. The teacher-training colleges and schools were indeed being increasingly shouldered by governments now really interested in the development of a national education system. What is curious about the 1950s is that the churches, Protestant and Catholic, were so blind to the logic of this situation. They had come to concentrate their attention upon the teacher taking it for granted that the catechist was an institution of the past which would now simply fade away.[56] The old catechist training schools had been closed or turned into teacher-training colleges. It is hard to find a Catholic catechist training centre at work in the early 1950s. Church authorities seemed to have the greatest confidence in the primary school teachers as church representatives in the villages, yet it was already becoming clear that the teachers themselves were increasingly uneasy with any church role and frequently refused to lead services or have any special responsibilities outside their scholastic ones. In fact the catechists, ageing, poorly trained or hardly paid as they mostly were, remained as indispensable as ever from the viewpoint of any specifically church activity: the taking of a service, the teaching of catechumens, the visitation of the sick.

They seldom, however, continued to provide a dynamic core to the church's life. This was often done instead in a far more fully lay way, through associations, frequently female associations. There are many different sources of influence here, but one of the most important would seem to be the Methodist, both in the south and the west. In South Africa the Methodist was the largest black church, and it was from here with its 'class' organisation that the inspiration for the Manyano of South Africa, the Rukwadzano of Rhodesia, most derived.[57] Other organisations, such as the Anglican Mothers' Union, have played a similar role. While undoubtedly such lay associations go back a good deal further, it would seem to be the case that it was in the 1950s that in many places they emerged in full confidence to provide something not far short of the central core of public Christian life. The earliest membership of most Christian churches in Africa had been predominantly male. It would be fascinating were it possible to check the growth in female participation, but one has the impression that the 1950s witnessed something of a breakthrough on this side. From then on the majority of active members of a congregation might well be women, and there is a growing sense that Christianity and the church belong to them – the men being far more likely to become permanently excommunicated for reasons of polygamy. Again, the increase in migrant labour in many parts left the women as the staple members of the local congregation. While the female associations did not in any way take over responsibility for the general running of the church and its official ministry, they did become increasingly decisive for its vitality, its fund raising and its growth.

While the Catholic Church was traditionally far less given to encouraging an active lay and female role, things were changing here too. The new concern for the Lay Apostolate and Catholic Action was making itself felt in Africa[58] and the most popular form of it at the time seemed to be that of the Dublin-based Legion of Mary. Though by no means intended only for women, the Legion was certainly proving popular among them and it was spreading everywhere. Thus where there were seven *praesidia* in Kasama diocese, Northern Rhodesia, in 1946, there were 134 in 1962 with well over 2,000 active members.[59] In Calabar diocese, Nigeria, there were 45 *praesidia* in 1939, 68 in 1952, but 148 in 1957.

'Where do you think we get the strength to persevere? It is in our Manyanos.'[60] The Manyanos of Johannesburg might not appear as a progressive force. Groups of women with their characteristic uniforms meeting regularly on Thursdays to 'preach' and pray together, to pour out their woes, seek comfort, collect money, were a source more of irritation than of congratulation to the clergy: they were largely independent of them and indeed could easily resent any male clerical presence. They had little to show, except financially, for all their attendances. To a large extent the spirit of the Manyanos, with their concentration upon the small praying community, the confession of problems and failings, their emotional even ecstatic prayer, was the spirit of the independent churches – and indeed there were Manyanos inside the independent churches as in all the white-led churches. Their experience had certainly a good deal in common with that of Revival in East Africa, though its spirituality was clearly far less evangelical. To understand what was happening here it should really be seen at one and the same time in a context of female reaction to male dominance, of lay to clerical dominance, and of black to white dominance. Where the new female collectivity was accepted on its own terms and the requisite adjustment made on the part of the dominant, it could bring enduring strength to the church; to the extent that it was resisted by the powers that be who insisted on turning it into their own channels, it could simply go dead while its members, or many of them, slipped away to more understanding churches. The impression is that all in all at the end of the 1950s the Methodist Church in South Africa was able to hold and be strengthened by Manyano but that increasingly the Anglican Church found it hard to do so and suffered accordingly: its type of high church clericalist tradition, coupled with a large and dominant white membership, would seem to have stood it in bad stead here as in much else. There were important exceptions to this – the outstanding charismatic figure of the Transkei in the 1950s was an Anglican woman, Mrs Paul. While her following was not all Anglican, she received some recognition from the bishop and never withdrew from the church. The position might be easier here than in most dioceses in the absence of any considerable white population.[61] But in general the Anglican Church was finding itself able neither to promote Africans within its hierarchy nor to leave them sufficiently free to do their own thing on their own. While in this it was much like the Catholic Church in South Africa, the consequences could be more serious for it, because hitherto it had been so very much more important a church and Africans had come to expect a lot of it. Moreover the Catholics had in a sense staked their own future, and not unwisely, on clinging to the schools, while the Anglican educational withdrawal was bound over the years to present for a church with such heavy white leadership and attachment to white affluence an increasing problem of black relevance.

In one way and another all the mission churches in the 1950s were faced with frequently agonising tensions, and where the question of schism and withdrawal was not directly put it always could be. Manyano, the Order of Ethiopia, Revival, Jamaa, a League of the Sacred Heart, the Legion of Mary, all these things could flourish within the Church, but if confidence were lost between black and white (or, as could so easily be the case, between the one black man – priest or bishop – who had the ear of the white man, and other black men) and a rather heavy hand imposed, all could lead too to a bid for independence. The history of the mission churches in these years is to a significant extent the history of mounting independency, but for each movement which actually broke surface there were many others at work, as capable of bringing a mission church new strength and a deeper measure of Africanisation as of provoking another debilitating disruption. In several instances the latter was probably only avoided by a prudent establishment of autonomy. The case of the Evangelical Church of the Cameroon is an interesting one. Here was an important and growing Christian community, the fruit of work by the Basel and Paris mission societies. In 1953 there erupted a major conflict, L'Affaire de Bamoun, between a missionary, Henri Martin, and a leading pastor, Josue Muishe, in which more and more people became involved.[62] Muishe was accused of 'immeasurable pride' and of involvement in local politics. Here as elsewhere the unwritten agenda of the dispute would seem to have been the question of which group of men was finally to control the church and its priorities, and it was exactly contemporaneous with the political conflict between the French administration and the UPC. It was a situation which for a time seemed insoluble and could certainly have brought schism had not the white leadership suddenly realised that essentially its time was now past. The quarrel had revealed the basic need for an altered power structure if the black leadership was not to be irrevocably alienated and in March 1957 the Church received its full autonomy from mission control, just two months before the first black government took power. The Evangelical Church of the Cameroon was to become one of the strongest of mission-based Protestant churches and the Cameroon would be noted as a country with little independency.

One of the most original developments of this period was undoubtedly the emergence of the Jamaa of the Flemish Franciscan, Placide Tempels. After some years of enforced sojourn in Belgium he had returned to Katanga, to the mining town of Kolwezi, where soon began to develop around this strange prophetic figure a major religious movement.[63] In *Bantu Philosophy* Tempels had appeared to challenge the underlying assumptions of much mission work and particularly of the hard, rather authoritarian form Catholicism often took in the Belgian Congo: it gave so much but in a highly organised, paternalistic manner which implied that one always knew what was best for 'the African' but without every knowing *him*, for he was – or should become – a *tabula rasa* on which Christianity and civilisation would be kindly but firmly drawn. No, said Tempels, Africans have their own deep concepts and a living Christian faith can only be arrived at through a personal encounter which fully respects the ways of thinking of those concerned.

Jamaa (family) grew as a non-organised series of cells out of the personal contacts of Baba Placide and the miners of Katanga. There was a deliberate refusal of the model of a preconstituted message, of any organisation with some sort of constitution, of anything indeed but the experience of 'Love' out of which the spiritual family, Jamaa, would be formed. The enemies of love were identified as isolationism and a sense of superiority. Love is found supremely in marriage, and the regular members of Jamaa are married couples – a Baba and a Mama who can themselves generate new spiritual children but have first to generate each other: the husband is Baba to his wife, the wife Mama to her husband. Christ and Mary were seen as the model relationship, the perfect Baba and Mama, and the movement would later be accused both of suggesting an intolerable relationship between them and of sexualising the whole of Christian life. These were aberrations. What seems clear is that the spiritual model of Jamaa was the opposite pole from that

117

most commonly associated with the Catholic Church in the colonial Congo; as such, and coming when it did, it was welcomed by some missionaries as well as by many Africans. Though Tempels himself and other priests could have a deep personal influence through the movement, it was as such a profoundly non-clerical affair: once it had begun, the priest was marginal to it. Its coherence and lines of influence lay elsewhere. Nevertheless, while Fr Tempels remained on the scene, this was doubtless not fully evident.

If the 1950s was an age of secessions, as was to a considerable extent the case, this should not be seen simply as an indication that 'independence' was now in the air on every side, nor that the mission churches had all in all failed to justify themselves in the eyes of Africans. It must equally be seen within the context of the very great success and growth which was undoubtedly theirs too. Doubtless the growth was too fast and in some ways unbalanced; doubtless there were failures of policy and of individual understanding on the part of the missionaries which might have been avoided, and doubtless the sense that colonial walls might soon be crumbling in an almost magical way encouraged the thought that missionary walls should crumble too and a golden age of God's kingdom in Africa could shortly arrive. But the very considerable secessions of the mid- and late-1950s only make sense within churches which had grown remarkably well, and which in fact survived the secessions to grow a great deal more. It is easy in Kenya to concentrate one's attention on the Anglican priest who marches out bravely to found his own Church of Christ in Africa, Mathew Ajuoga, but in the long run the priest who stays in will certainly prove a great deal more influential, Festo Olang'. If the Lumpa Church swept almost all before it in north central Zambia in the mid-1950s, in the long run the hardy opposition of Fr Kakokota and of Bemba Legion of Mary activists would prove as significant. Certainly by the mid-1960s it is they who would be left in possession of the field. They had, of course, behind them a host of White Fathers while Lumpa crashed when it came into head-on conflict with Kaunda's UNIP. But Lumpa had lost most of its support before that, while the White Fathers could have done little without a core of Bemba Catholics whom Lenshina had failed to win over. The attention of research workers has been too much fixed all across the continent upon the one side to disregard or belittle the strength and values of the other. The mission churches of the later 1950s were certainly faced by an increasingly severe challenge on several fronts, and that challenge would on occasion appear almost overwhelming; but it cannot be questioned that they responded with vigour, not only (a little slowly) on the level of control and leadership, and (a good deal faster) on the level of increased educational aspirations and a new political activism, but also in many places on that of the straight religious needs of the mass of men and women in local congregations. Revival, Jamaa, the Legion of Mary and Manyano were all in their different ways popular vehicles for evangelism, prayer and moral commitment suitably at work within the mission churches of the 1950s.

It was not a period of creative thinking in Catholic mission circles. The guidelines here were the papal encyclicals *Evangelii Praecones* of 1951 and *Fidei Donum* of 1957. The main message of these documents was the simple one of the need for more local priests and more missionaries. There was nothing very startling here nor in any other missionary literature. All the more startling then was the sudden emergence of a black clerical voice with a sharp message of its own. Around 1954 and 1955 there was a remarkable group of young black priests studying in Rome: Alexis Kagame from Rwanda, Vincent Mulago from Bukavu in the Congo, Robert Sastre and Bernardin Gantin from Dahomey, Joaquim Pinto de Andrade from Angola, Robert Dosseh from Togo, Jean Zoa from Cameroon. From their Roman Association of St Augustine began to appear articles on all sorts of subjects and such as to prove very alarming in some missionary circles. A movement of Young Turks, in fact, had quite unexpectedly arrived. Joined by friends in Paris they produced in 1956 *Des prêtres noirs s'interrogent*, a book of wide-ranging and hard-hitting essays which was to have a very considerable impact. The same year Kagame's thesis, *La philosophie bantu-rwandaise de l'être*, was published in Brussels.[64] Here was an articulate African response to Tempels and the beginning of a debate on the nature of African religion and the proper relationship of Christianity to it which would soon, if belatedly, become a central Catholic preoccupation. Rome, meanwhile, made no attempt whatever to suppress her Young Turks; on the contrary, many of them were clearly destined for early promotion to the most senior ecclesiastical positions.

The concerns of the *prêtres noirs* would not, perhaps, have appeared so novel within the Protestant world. Here in some circles there was a longer tradition of open discussion about African traditional religion and missionary adaptation, encouraged particularly by the Le Zoute Conference of 1926, though there was also in many other circles a far greater practical intransigence than could be encountered among Catholics. The lead on this side was now being taken in Ghana, whose University Department of Theology was flourishing and where the Christian Council had sponsored a conference the year before on 'Christianity and African culture' in which Dr Busia had appealed to the church to 'come to grips with traditional practices, and with the world view that these beliefs and practices imply'.[65] But there were still few African theologians to undertake the hard thinking and research such a task must involve.

Two conferences which took place in West Africa in 1958 sum up between them the changing pattern of thought and of ecclesiastical contact; it was indeed the great year for conferences in West Africa. In January the All

Africa Church Conference was held at Ibadan under the chairmanship of Sir Francis Ibiam.[66] It was the first major Pan-African Christian gathering and from it grew the All Africa Conference of Churches which would provide Protestant Christianity with a symbol of unity and something of a common sense of direction. Hitherto the wider links of the African churches had been almost entirely with the home base of their particular mission society. The construction of inter-African and inter-denominational relationships would not however prove easy, particularly across the strangely deep divide of the major European languages.

A few months later the final assembly of the International Missionary Council (before its amalgamation with the WCC) took place in Ghana. It was for the old Protestant missionary bodies something of the end of the road. The churches of the third world were becoming independent and the old missionary relationship which so clearly involved a status of dependence must inevitably end. What role would there now be for missionaries? The future was none too clear but having chosen to meet in newly independent Ghana the IMC could hardly not recognise that, if there was here a great new beginning, there was also a sad farewell. The leading missionary theorist present, Professor Freytag, dwelt gently but firmly on this theme to make of his paper little less than an appeal for 'fewer and fewer missionaries'. 'Who would want to impede the development of Churches which in some degree depends on the absence of missionaries?'[67] For many Freytag's view was, without doubt, quite unacceptable but that it could be stated so clearly and with such authority was a pointer towards the rapidity with which the more thoughtful ecclesiastical leadership would now respond to greatly altered times.

C. Independency

It is probable that, all in all, the 1950s were the greatest decade for ecclesiastical independency in Africa: an age of expansion, of consolidation, of an increasingly self-aware confidence, of expectation of things to come – things in fact of which many are as yet unrealised. If the mission churches too were growing fast, their sense of direction and ethos had changed rather little in response to the quickly mounting waves of nationalism and cultural consciousness. In country after country the colonial system was manifestly weakening, yet African initiatives and ambitions still found all too little room for manoeuvre within missionary controlled structures and were turned increasingly into other channels. Some of these channels were political but in few countries was any large scale political mobilisation of the common people achieved before the final years of the decade, and it seems likely that much of the mounting frustration found its expression in religious independency. Almost everywhere numbers grew rather rapidly, and if there had been 800 independent churches in South Africa in 1948, there were 2,200 by 1960. Some countries such as Tanzania and Uganda continued to be substantially unaffected but elsewhere there was an ever-increasing volume both of separate bodies and of the total number of adherents. This meant both growth in what was already there and some major new beginnings. Thus in Rhodesia, if the Zionists and the Apostles had dominated the scene hitherto, the 1950s saw a rapid and significant growth in two Ethiopian-type churches – the Chibarirwe and the Topia,[68] thus demonstrating that if in one country the historic trend within independency could be to start Ethiopian and then pass to Zionist, in another it could be quite the opposite. Again, in Northern Rhodesia, where there had been rather little full independency hitherto, the 1950s saw the emergence of the major church of Alice Lenshina, as well as the small but fascinating congregation of the Children of the Sacred Heart. In Western Kenya, furthermore, this decade witnessed the largest clergy-led schism ever to take place within an African mission church.

It was an age, one might say, of religious women – of Alice Lenshina and Mai Chaza and Mariam Ragot; of Ma Nku and Ma Mbele in South Africa, of Captain Abiodun in western Nigeria – either new arrivals or now at the peak of their influence. It was an age of the internationalisation of some of the larger churches; Cherubim and Seraphim had arrived in Accra; the Church of the Lord (Aladura) was spreading in Sierra Leone, Liberia and the Gold Coast due to the efforts of Apostles Oduwole and Adejobi;[69] the Vapostori of Johane Maranke had reached Katanga and even the central Congolese

121

city of Luluabourg.[70] It was an age in which impressive buildings and the ownership of schools were becoming a practical possibility for at least a few independent churches; for example, the Christ Apostolic Church in Yoruba-land could open a modern school at Efon Alaye in 1952, a teacher-training college in 1955 and a Bible training college in 1956.[71] There were in many countries by the mid-1950s churches which government and public opinion could hardly fail to notice, to respect and to cooperate with. Until the Mau Mau emergency began in Kenya such was the position in regard to the two quite considerable school networks linked there with independent churches. With the explosion of Mau Mau, however, these were judged to be a seedbed of sedition and late in 1953 all such schools were closed – though some were later re-opened under the District Education Board. Here was a situation of colonial conflict where independent churches of an 'Ethiopian' type were naturally inclined to sympathise to some extent with the political rebels. Nevertheless it should be noted that the recently formed 'African Christian Church and Schools' took a more firmly pro-government line than almost any mission church in Kikuyuland.

Advance in formal education was usually preceded by a less easily measurable economic advance. It is likely that the members of many an independent church had tended over the years to work harder and to prosper rather more than their neighbours; hence, while in most countries their educational level was far lower on average than that of the followers of the mission churches, their level of economic prosperity could be as high.[72] It was natural, furthermore, that the fruits of this prosperity should begin to appear in the bricks and mortar of church-owned building and in a widening concern for educational advancement.

One wholly astonishing example of economic advance was that of the Holy Apostles Community at Aiyetoro above a Nigerian coastal lagoon.[73] A dissident group of Cherubim and Seraphim, they had moved to Aiyetoro as a body in 1947 and decided the next year to live a fully communal existence. Out of this decision grew one of the most remarkable religious and secular experiments of modern times. From a simple group of huts built on stilts in the water grew an ever more complex set of buildings, domestic and indus-trial, all joined meticulously by well-constructed walks – the main street (or bridge) was at first a quarter-of-a-mile long, later a mile, and (by 1954) twelve feet wide. From being an almost outcast band of uneducated fisher-men in the 1940s, united in a closed community by their particular brand of Christian faith, they became in a few years a highly industrialised little city with a great diversification of skills. The one comparable group was that of Johane Masowe's Apostles developing in much the same way and at the same time in Korsten, Port Elizabeth[74] (each settled down in 1947 after persecution and migration; each had got so far as to install its own electric plant by 1953!) The Aiyetoro Apostles soon began to shine in every trade, particularly boat building; their first big launch, the 'Aiyetoro Community Enterprise' was completed in 1954, the same year in which their almost unbelievable seven-mile canal through mangrove swamp to the sea was widened to forty foot. In June 1959 a new £20,000 power station to supply electricity was switched on – paid for out of the profits of their fishing industry. The 1950s were indeed the great years of Aiyetoro, 'the Happy City', ruled by its first Oba, Ethiopia Ojagbohun Peter, a man who combined great spiritual wisdom and pastoral concern with immense resourcefulness and business acumen. Never perhaps has the sheer worldly advantage of hard work, a religious commitment and quasi-monastic existence been so quickly and decisively demonstrated. However, we should not misinterpret this. The industrial and financial success of Aiyetoro has been such that some observers have wished to identify it as essentially a 'nonreligious' community, but it is very doubtful whether such a view could possibly be justified either in regard to its theoretical presuppositions or in regard to Aiyetoro's own understanding of its collective purpose and achievement, at least in its earlier years: for those involved in it, the whole communist–capitalist way of life, its carefully constructed social relations and its material production were rather an expression of 'the new order which will be the universal practice in Christ's Kingdom'.[75]

The 1950s witnessed a more positive attitude on the part of many independent churches towards government and public order. It is hard to generalise here, but on the whole the longer a church lasts the more likely it appears to be that it will value public order and seek the recognition, and indeed approval, of the state. Where independent churches were in conflict with the state, it was either that they were very new or that the state had for *a priori* reasons systematically proscribed them, or again that the order of the state itself was about to change and that one or another church was in conscious sympathy with the movements working for political revolution or independence. The independent churches of the 1950s had, then, at least some degree of political horizon. In South Africa it seldom went beyond the aspiration to be officially recognised, for such purposes as the registration of marriages or the purchase of communion wine: 'I want to be near the Government' said the Reverend Majola in 1958.[76] For the most part the churches of Zionist, Apostolic or Pentecostal inspiration were only too anxious to fit into the structure of apartheid society, if they could do so with a little dignity. Yet in fact only eleven churches were ever recognised by the South African state, so insensitive in its dealings even with those black men most anxious to conform with its basic, if mysterious, demands.

One of the most impressive figures in South African independency in the 1950s was undoubtedly that of Job Chiliza, founder of the African Gospel Church, one of the privileged eleven. Not a Zionist, though he had formerly been one and still had much in common with them, a splendid preacher and efficient administrator, he represented that 'Apostolic' thread which cannot properly be described in South Africa or elsewhere as either 'Ethiopian' or 'Zionist' or 'prophet-healer'. 'May they all be one' (John 17. 21) was his favourite Bible verse, he applied it – not as most modern churchmen would tend to do to the uniting of different churches – but to the races, the true ecumenical problem of South Africa: 'Africans and Europeans must be one, and love one another. That is the mind of God.' Once in Pretoria in the corridor of a government department he had caught sight of the great Verwoerd himself: 'I shall die satisfied to have seen the face of Dr. Verwoerd.'[77] But 98 per cent of church leaders had their humble pleas for government recognition for ever disregarded. They never saw that face.

Elsewhere in Africa aspirations for an improved political status might venture considerably higher. The mounting size and confidence of ecclesiastical independency by the late 1950s came at the same time as a wider revolution in political consciousness marked either by a far more general and vocalised sense of disillusionment with white rule – as in the Federation of Central Africa – or the expectation of approaching independence. Whichever was the case there was a tendency for the two movements to support one another at least locally, and to the popular mind one or other independent church might seem for a while to represent something not far short of a 'national religion'. It seems probable that the considerable growth of the hitherto tiny African Congregational Church (called *Chibarirwe* 'Our very own') in the Southern Rhodesia of the late 1950s owed a good deal to popular disillusionment in the mid-years of the Federation; in the same years Lumpa in Northern Rhodesia was making still greater headway, and that at a moment when specifically political black power was at a low ebb.

The contemporaneous emergence of an institutional Kimbanguist church in the lower Congo could benefit from a still stronger claim to being the national religion, as could that of the Matsouan Church north of the river. Again, in the Ivory Coast, the Harrist Church grew particularly in these years, benefiting from a sympathetic relationship with Houphouet's increasingly dominant Rassemblement démocratique Africain, its public ceremonies patronised by friendly government officials. Harrism seemed to represent during the mid-1950s, in the eyes of many ordinary people in the coastal part of the country, a 'national religion'.[78] These were natural developments, for the most part not over encouraged by senior black political leadership, which retained its own fairly firm links with the mission churches – Azikiwe's short-lived National Church of Nigeria and the Cameroons was an exception here. In general, however, the highly fissiparous character of most of these movements soon revealed itself as a major political disadvantage, together with the rather restricted geographical base of almost any particular one: the very strength of their grass roots origins, the multiplicity of revelations, the charismatic character of the authority structure, all meant that their national vocation reflected more a period of adversity and political leaderlessness than one of efficient mobilisation for a workable new secular order. Once victory was certain the political parties would tend to pull away from these religious allies and repair their bridges with the older, more established bodies.

No other single development in this period was as striking as that of the Lumpa Church of Alice Mulenga Lenshina among the Bemba of Northern Rhodesia (Zambia). It began, as so many others, with the personal spiritual experience of a woman who, in 1953, believed herself to have died after a serious illness but to have been sent back to earth by God with a special mission: 'Send her back. Her time has not yet come.'[79] At almost the same time another woman, Mai Chaza in Southern Rhodesia, had a very similar experience. Lenshina was a Presbyterian, worshipping at their mission of Lubwa in the Chinsali district; Mai Chaza was a Methodist; each continued for a while within their former church with some sort of special spiritual ministry, but in each case the internal logic of the movement with its own developing clientele and altered pattern of loyalties and behaviour made a break inevitable, and each established her own church in the course of 1955.[80]

Lenshina's church drew together three strands of experience: missionary Christianity, the witchcraft eradication movements which have been such a feature from time to time of twentieth-century Central African history, and the profound black frustration with the political situation in the early years of the Federation. The new church drew in fact from many sources of inspiration and tradition. If its primary ecclesiastical roots were Presbyterian, Petros, the husband of Alice, had formerly been a Catholic and Alice's 'new name' of 'Lenshina' was no other than an Africanisation of the Latin *Regina*, Queen. Fr Peyton's world-wide Rosary campaign had just been making its impact locally.[81] There can be no doubt, too, that Christian millenialism, so widely sown in Central Africa by Watch Tower literature, was a strong influence with the Lumpa Church as it had been with earlier movements such as those of Kamwana and Tomo Nyirenda.[82] Either Alice herself or someone close to her had a genius for the composing of Bemba hymns, and the quick conquest of Lumpa over the mission churches certainly owed much to the superiority of Lenshina's hymns over the stiff translations used in other churches. The very meaning of 'Lumpa' seems to be 'that which excels' and by late 1956 the Presbyterian and Catholic churches in the area seemed almost deserted while pilgrims were arriving at Alice's home of Kasomo at the rate of a thousand a week.

Those of Lenshina's followers who came from the Copperbelt continued, on their return, to share in the general life of society, but in the Bemba countryside a segregated Lumpa community was constituting itself with whole villages completely committed to her ways – to that enthralling hymn singing and the fierce rejection of pagan practices, sorcery, beer drinking, polygamy: it was a new and cleansed society awaiting the coming of God. In the meantime a great brick and pillared church, the cathedral of Lumpa, was being built at Kasomo, the longest church in the whole district. It was modelled on the Catholic procathedral at Ilondola, but was just that much larger. It was completed and opened in November 1958, the moment of Lumpa's greatest appeal but also the beginning of its decline. The pillar at Kasomo built as a perch upon which Christ could now descend remained unoccupied. The greater the promises, the greater for many the disillusion, and Lumpa was soon upon the point of turning from a mass movement and an almost tribal church into being a threatened minority of true believers isolated within their stockaded villages. They were the steadfast ones who had read the Bemba words carved in stone above the great west door at Kasomo and did not doubt that in Lenshina's Church they had found their fulfilment: 'Come unto me all ye that labour and are heavy laden, and I will give you rest.'

The spiritual history of Northern Rhodesia is a particularly complex and difficult one; this is linked both with the relative weakness of the efforts of the main mission churches, Catholic and Protestant, and with the very wide range of influences which made some significant impact. The age of Lumpa was also the great age of the expansion of Jehovah's Witnesses – by now a very orderly hard-working group of people – and of the African Methodist Episcopal Church which came nearest to offering a spiritual home at this time to the young nationalist leadership. A far smaller church than any of these was that of the Bana BaMutima, the Children of the Sacred Heart, whose leader was Emilio Mulolani, a former Catholic seminarian, catechist and teacher.[83] He had founded the 'League of the Sacred Heart' as a temperance group combining a number of typical Catholic motifs of the 1950s – devotion to the Sacred Heart, Fr Peyton's catchword 'the family that prays together stays together', and something of a Franciscan preoccupation with love and simplicity (there were Franciscan missionaries on the Copperbelt). While the bishops welcomed this at first, they soon grew worried by Mulolani's visions and the long emotional night services, and he was forbidden to teach in diocese after diocese. Mulolani struggled to remain a Catholic and even went as far as Mombasa to appeal to the Apostolic Delegate, and one wonders whether in this case if the church authorities had been more sympathetic a break need ever have come. But they weren't and it did, so that by July 1958 Emilio had to say to his followers, 'We are and will always remain Catholics, but not Roman Catholics. From now on our Church will be called the Catholic Church of the Sacred Heart.' Many of his disciples never fully separated themselves from Roman Catholicism; those

126

who did set about establishing their own village settlements – Namfumu and Mutima. A characteristic mission practice has been the segregation of the sexes in church, one probably in harmony with most traditional African ideas; Mulolani had criticised this already on the basis of Fr Peyton's principle. Now on their own, their Franciscan concern with love led to its uninhibited manifestation on an inter-sexual plane, the assertion of 'innocence' and the practice of mixed bathing in the nude to bring down on them the condemnation of society and take Mulolani to prison. In this the movement is strangely similar in spirit to that of Jamaa, over the border in the Congo. The Children of the Sacred Heart never grew very numerous but they represent a characteristically Catholic form of independency, both in origins and in spirituality, and are interesting in part just because there have been so few independent churches of Catholic inspiration.

Rather, but not wholly, different was the far larger movement of Kuhama ('separation'), taking place at just the same time within the Anglican Church in western Kenya.[84] In 1954 Max Warren wrote of the East African 'Revival' movement that 'From the first the Revival has remained faithful to the conviction that its vocation lies within the Church.'[85] Hardly had the General Secretary of the Church Missionary Society written this than Revival provoked a schism more considerable in scale than any other separation this century. Lumpa may well have taken more people away in all from existing churches, but not at one blow, and it certainly did not include senior clergy. Kuhama could mean separation of church from world, of Balokole (the Revived) from non-Balokole, or of black from white control. In fact Revival had proved continuously divisive within the Anglican Church of western Kenya ever since its arrival from Uganda at the end of the 1930s. One of its first local leaders, Ishmael Noo, had left in 1948 to form his own little church, preoccupied, rather like Mulolani, with the sexual freedom which true Christian love requires. The rest of the movement then began to be called the Joremo, 'the people of the blood', on account of their insistence upon the blood of Christ, a key Revival motif, but the Anglican Church was soon split anew in a bitter dispute whose roots seem to have been, at least in part, tribal: the new Luyia assistant bishop, Festo Olang' (appointed in 1955), found himself in conflict with most of the Luo clergy who had formed themselves into a subgroup or counter group named the Johera, 'those who love', under the leadership of Mathew Ajuoga. The lay-inspired talk of a Kuhama of 'Revived' from non-revived had triggered off a more clerically inspired counter Kuhama of withdrawal from the Anglican church itself. Within a couple of years the break between Ajuoga's group and the Anglican Church was complete so that 1958 saw the beginning of a major new body of a straight 'Ethiopian' kind, the Church of Christ in Africa (registered by the government, 8 January 1958), which carried with it at least seven ordained Anglican priests and some 16,000 of the faithful. Ajuoga, initially its 'chairman', soon became its bishop. The inherent sectarianism of revival seemed here to combine with episcopal authoritarianism and an element of tribalism to produce a break which all the same might well not have happened at any other time than the 1950s. It is curious that the appointment of an African bishop – Olang' – actually helped to precipitate a conflict between authority and black clergy, but much the same thing has been known elsewhere: a lack of inter-racial and inter-tribal confidence was brought to the surface by the appointment of a single individual to high authority and, in the general tension which marked church life in many quarters at the time, no way out short of schism could be found. It is to be noted that within two years several of Ajuoga's fellow priests had parted from him to establish yet another body, the Holy Trinity Church in Africa.

Just below the surface there were similar rumblings in many other places – for instance the Catholic dioceses of Mbarara in Uganda and Kumasi, Ghana, though prolonged public conflict was just avoided. If Kuhama, 'separation', was the key word in what was happening in western Kenya, it is no less symbolic for a much wider range of developments in the mid-1950s: Ajuoga's 'People of love' were separating themselves in a rather Anglican manner, just as Mulolani's people of love were separating themselves in a rather Catholic fashion, while Lenshina's Presbyterians were separating themselves more decisively than almost anyone else and in a manner peculiarly their own. And on the other side of the continent in the Ivory Coast those of Harris' followers in certain villages – Abia-Niambo, Mbadon Cocody and Abobo-Te – who had for forty years refused to be integrated into either the Catholic or the Methodist church suddenly surfaced in a church of their own. The 'Harrist Church', a body with an institution, buildings, a written catechism really emerged with the synod of August 1955. A catechism was printed the next year.[86] In the Belgian Congo Kimbangu's followers, who had suffered far more severe persecution than had those of Harris, were doing just the same: after three-and-a-half decades of persecution and clandestinity, in which many had publicly professed membership of one or other of the mission churches, they too were now publicly separating themselves.

The death of the prophet in prison in 1951 certainly in no way diminished the strength of the movement bearing his name. On the contrary: there were soon reports that he had risen again and visited his at first incredulous disciples still banished in the detention camps of the eastern Congo. When they at length recognised him and believed, he preached to them from Leviticus 25. 10: 'You will declare this fiftieth year sacred and proclaim the liberation of all the inhabitants of the land. This is to be a jubilee for you; each of you will return to his ancestral home, each to his own clan.'[87] The long years of exile and persecution were indeed nearly at an end and a new generation was taking over the leadership of the movement determined to win it both freedom and honour. It seems that it was from about 1954 that Joseph Diangienda, Kimbangu's youngest son, a well-educated and competent government official, really assumed a directive role. He had become the esteemed secretary of M. Peigneux, the governor of the Kasai. The relationship of Diangienda in these years both with the Colonial Government and with the still persecuted Kimbanguist faithful remains one of the most mysterious phases in the history of the movement.[88] He was supported by his two brothers, his mother, and various older stalwarts such as Emmanuel Bamba, who had been with Kimbangu in prison at Elizabethville. Closely working with Diangienda was another young man, Lucien Luntadila, a former Catholic seminarian. Members of the new elite, and far from revolutionary, they had as their primary aim to demonstrate the non-subversive character of the Kimbanguist movement and so gain legal toleration from the new, more liberal-minded, Governor-General, Petillon.

The second immediate objective was to draw together the wholly unorganised network of Kimbanguist believers into a recognisable and independent body, inevitably separate – as hitherto the Kimbanguists never had been – from the mission churches. In retrospect they would blame the Protestant churches for driving them out, and certainly neither the Protestant nor the Catholic leadership could suddenly adjust to the emergence of a large Kimbanguist segment within their faithful. But essentially the separation would seem to have been due to the sheer fact of a considerable body of people being already secretly tied together by a religious tradition and shared experience quite foreign to that officially characteristic of the mission churches. Kimbanguism had evolved far too far for it to exist now other than on its own.

These developments were only possible with a gradual relaxation in the government's attitude to African religious movements. Hitherto they had all been illegal. By the mid-1950s, however, Petillon was trying to bring about a change, being pressed to this both by a carefully organised Kimbanguist campaign in Leopoldville and by increasing criticism inside Belgium. In December 1957 he finally ordered a major revision of policy in a letter to the Provincial Governors.[89] It was – in the long unhappy history of Belgian colonialism and the Kimbanguist movement – the moment of 'historic compromise', though full legal recognition would still not come for two years. The triple task of Diangienda and Luntadila in those years was to obtain that recognition, to establish a coherent doctrine and organisation of their own, and to ensure that all those who considered themselves to be Kimbanguists were brought together into what was now to be no longer a movement but a church. In regard to the first and second aims they proved outstandingly successful, but for the third their achievement would be more partial. While the 'Église du Jesus Christ sur la terre par le prophète Simon Kimbangu' (EJCSK) would be by far the largest of Kimbanguist bodies, it would still be but one of many, surrounded by other smaller groups with varying doctrines.

It was in the catechism of July 1957, written by Luntadila, that the church's basic position was first defined (just one year later than the Harrist catechism). In answer to question one, it was asserted that 'Tata Simon Kimbangu is the envoy of Our Lord Jesus Christ.' The main events of his birth, ministry, miracles, first helpers and trial, as remembered by the collective tradition and the prophet's widow, were then recorded. Finally, 'after being sent to Upper Congo by the government, Tata Simon Kimbangu died and rose again and is with us in the spirit'. 'Tata Simon Kimbangu is not God, but in every age God chooses one man from each race to enlighten his people.'[90] In the course of 1958 the constitution of the new church was established and in December an application was made for civil personality with Joseph Diangienda appointed indefinitely as its legal representative. At the same time it asserted its 'exclusively spiritual role' removed from all political tendencies. Thus, well before the absolute end of the colonial era – in that intermediate moment when the old order was irretrievably slipping away but the new not yet arrived and when the mission churches had still hardly begun to orientate themselves imaginatively to the coming face of things – the Kimbanguist Église had emerged, separate, institutionally minded from the start, earnestly wrestling with the relationship between Tata Simon and the Christian gospel. It would soon be the largest and best organised independent church on the whole continent.

By the end of 1958 Lenshina in Northern Rhodesia, Ajuoga in Kenya and Diangienda in the Congo were all leading quite large churches, consisting predominantly of Christians who had two or three years previously been members of a mission. There was a hard note of separation in the air, of confidence lost and found, of patience exhausted, of Rubicons crossed. If missionary statesmen at the time were well informed, they could hardly but have shuddered as they contemplated the half-empty churches and the ease with which tens of thousands of their faithful could be borne away in country after country into some new religious allegiance. Was this but the beginning of the fall, an inevitable concomitant of the withering of colonialism?

3

1959–1966

A. Church and State

I

The first week of 1959 saw a major riot in Leopoldville with several hundred deaths, which rocked the Congo and precipitated it at a blow into the frontline of change. Feeding on urban unemployment, the volatile new parties had suddenly posed a challenge to Belgium which no one had the heart to resist for long with any vigour. The French and British examples could not safely be ignored any more: just across the river in Brazzaville that amiably flamboyant priest-politician, Fulbert Youlou, was already prime minister. A complex Congolese political world had suddenly emerged, wholly inexperienced, wholly resolved on acquiring power with the minimum of delay. On one side stood Joseph Kasavubu of A B A K O, a former seminarian, appealing for the revival of the ancient tribal kingdom of the Congo within a weak federation, a charismatic figure into whom – according to lower Congo rumour of 1959 – Simon Kimbangu's own spirit had 'entered'.[1] Next year when, just before independence, Kimbangu's body was solemnly brought back from Elizabethville, Kasavubu would be there at the ceremony. On the other side stood Patrice Lumumba of the Mouvement National Congolais, committed to a non-tribal nationalism and a unitary state, the electrifying demagogue of the new society. Lumumba's return from the Accra Conference heightened the tension which produced the January riots, signalling the start of eighteen months of frenetic political activity: party-making, constitution-making, government-making for the greatest state of Central Africa.

The following month Dr Banda's return from the same meeting had a similar effect in Nyasaland: 'To Hell with federation,' he cried, 'Let us fill their prisons with our thousands, singing Hallelujah.'[2] Wide disturbances were followed by the inevitable arrests not only in Nyasaland but also in Rhodesia. Banda was to be in prison for the rest of the year and Kenneth Kaunda for most of it. In Southern Rhodesia Robert Chikerema, George Nyandoro and hundreds of other people, including Guy Clutton Brock, were arrested. In these lands there still remained a stubborn resolve to retain both the Federation and white rule. Elsewhere what remained of the European imperial will was quickly weakening. The brutal death of eleven Mau Mau detainees at Hola Camp in Kenya in March produced uproar in Britain and significantly contributed to the growing British resolve to withdraw honourably but rather fast. De Gaulle's 1958 plan for autonomous states within a federal community, to which all French Africa except Guinea had voted 'Yes', never even began to become a reality: the federal structure hardly went beyond paper, and autonomy – hardly gained – changed in 1960 to full legal independence.

It is well to remember that it was the most eminently respectable of senior European statesmen – Charles de Gaulle and Harold Macmillan – who presided over this rapid winding up of empire. They could see no practical alternative. The British Prime Minister expressed his conviction of the inevitability of change in a famous speech to both Houses of the Union Parliament in Cape Town in January 1960: 'The most striking of all the impressions I have formed since I left London a month ago is of the strength of African national consciousness. In different places it may take different forms, but it is happening everywhere. The wind of change is blowing through the continent.'

Without doubt 1960 was the year of Africa: the year in which sixty-nine people were shot at Sharpeville in March by the South African police. The year in which the Congo became independent in June and at once dissolved into anarchy. The year in which Africa's other – and greatest – giant, Nigeria, became most peacefully independent in October. The year in which by September France could sponsor the admission to the United Nations of twelve independent black African republics from Senegal to Congo (Brazzaville).

The following years would see the process move speedily eastwards and southwards: Tanganyika in 1961; Rwanda, Burundi and Uganda in 1962; Kenya in 1963. That year two further significant events took place: the Central African Federation was dissolved by the British Conservative government belatedly recognising the overwhelming opposition to it from the African population of its northern constituents. This left Malawi and Zambia to become independent in 1964. In May 1963 the Organisation of African Unity was established in Addis Ababa: the symbol of the new order that had now arrived all across the middle of the continent. These early years of the 1960s may well be seen, despite the troubles of the Congo and elsewhere, as a golden spring of independent Africa. And that is how it certainly felt at the time. Here was a new era presided over by the venerable imperial figure of Haile Selassie and the brilliantly successful philosopher-politician, Kwame Nkrumah. Universities were springing up on every side. Nigeria alone now possessed five – Nsukka, Lagos, Zaria and Ife had already joined Ibadan. Scholars, novelists, poets were beginning to appear and to be

132

hailed in many lands. Wole Soyinka, Chinua Achebe, James Ngugi, new names were being published every year. It was an age of exciting promise, of exhilarating opportunity, of immediate achievement – the voice of Africa was actually being listened to, whether in the pages of its writers or in the halls of the United Nations.

White rule, it must be admitted, had tumbled remarkably easily before the wind of change, owing perhaps to the underlying western assumption that if the transition was a peaceful and happy one, the new rulers would be favourable to the West, economic and cultural ties would continue and grow, Russia would be effectively cold shouldered; while if independence had to be fought for, then nationalism would almost inevitably take an anti-western and 'communist' form. With Zambia's independence in October 1964 black rule had reached the Zambezi and the whole political map of Africa had changed almost unbelievably from what could have been anticipated only ten years earlier when Mau Mau was being struck down and Sir Roy Welensky's Federation of Central Africa embarked upon with enthusiasm.

If the overall impression of the early 1960s is one of a peaceful transfer to black rule in an orderly and even democratic manner, with no less than two general elections per state normally included in the British model at least, there were some serious exceptions to this. In Cameroon the protracted war in the south-west between the radical nationalist UPC and the government (formerly French, later conservative Union Camerounaise, led by Ahmadou Ahidjo from the Moslem north) grew more not less bitter with the approach of independence, bringing with it the murder of four Catholic missionaries and two Protestant pastors. In fact Ahidjo had achieved both the UPC's original aims – independence and reunification – and the continuing conflict came to acquire a more regional or tribal character.[3] And that was the pattern elsewhere as well.

In Rwanda independence was both preceded and followed by intertribal conflict, between the hitherto dominant Tutsi overlords and the Hutu proletariat comprising well over 80 per cent of the population. While both the Belgian government and the Catholic Church had previously strongly upheld the Tutsi primacy, in the late 1950s both altered course and began instead to foster Hutu aspirations. Sensing this, and feeling the winds from the Congo next door, the neo-traditionalists around the throne began to bid for a quick independence before their power would be shorn in the name of democracy, to the advantage of the Hutu. It was not to be. What began as a village *jacquerie* in November 1959 with the burning down of Tutsi homes quickly developed with Belgian connivance into a major social and political revolution involving the abolition of the monarch in 1961 and the establishment of a republic presided over by the astute former secretary to the archbishop, Grégoire Kayibanda. Thousands of Tutsi fled into exile – to Uganda and Burundi, from whence they attempted several counter-

133

revolutions, ineffectual and disastrous. On each occasion the reprisals of the Hutu against the Tutsi who had remained within the country grew more terrible and indiscriminate. The worst of these was in December 1963 when at least 5,000 and probably 10,000 people died in the most appalling massacres independent Africa had yet known.

In the Sudan the policy of the government to force the south into the mould of the north and to extinguish the widespread southern desire for regional autonomy, if not independence, grew far sharper after the army take-over of November 1958. From 1960 the aim of Islamisation was quite open – at least in the actions of certain local officials, most notably Ali Baldo, the governor of Equatoria Province. Southern political leaders, mostly Christian, escaped across the border to Uganda and three years later, in September 1963, rebellion which had smouldered since the 1955 mutiny broke into flame with the formation of the Anyanya, the military wing of the southern movement.

Early in 1964 all foreign Christian missionaries were expelled from the south (272 Catholics, 28 Protestants). The worsening situation helped to bring about a return to civilian rule in Khartoum in October and a short respite. There was an unsuccessful round-table conference between north and south a few months later, but by the middle of 1965 things were worse than ever. The Christian elite in the southern towns were ruthlessly attacked and there were massacres in Juba and Wau in July. Christian institutions such as Bishop Gwynne College, the Anglican seminary, were literally levelled to the ground, and most of the local clergy, Catholic and Protestant, fled the country to Zaire or Uganda together with some 300,000 other refugees. From then on there was unbroken civil war: the government held the towns but the Anyanya almost all the countryside, and so it was to remain for many years.[4]

This was not primarily a religious war and for long most Christians in both Europe and Africa were decidedly hesitant, probably over-hesitant, to give the southern Sudanese much overt, or even covert, encouragement. Faced with the far greater technical resources of the north theirs seemed a hopeless cause and no African government could easily countenance yet another attempt at what looked like secession. The southern Sudanese went for education to Uganda and Zaire and were soon filling up Ugandan theological colleges as well as schools, but they obtained little else. Their great resource was the sheer size of the south but it would be years before the strength of the Anyanya was taken very seriously. In the meantime Christianity increasingly gave a sense of coherence to the southern resistance – a sense hardly experienced previously. 'We the children of Mary will kill the Arabs' they sang in their dances,[5] and the churches spread more rapidly across the southern bush in the absence of the missionaries than they had ever done in their presence.

134

The breakdown in the Congo (Zaire) was far better publicised. It began immediately after independence in June 1960 and lasted for years. It was a consequence of a number of things – the almost complete administrative and political unpreparedness of the Congolese to rule themselves (there was, for instance, at independence not a single black commissioned officer in the military *force publique*, which promptly mutinied); the vast size of the country with its rather thin population and poor communications made unified government difficult at the best of times: no adequate work had gone into relating the whole and the parts in a viable manner; the pressures of international 'cold war' politics and the entry of Russia as a major power into African affairs. Not surprisingly the rich and remote Katanga quickly headed for independence on its own under Moise Tshombe with much covert support both from former colonial interests and from Roy Welensky over the border. The brilliant but wildly unbalanced Lumumba, prime minister at independence, was edged out, arrested, and murdered to become the leading martyr-saint of millenialist nationalism and the mythology of international leftism. The United Nations were called in, prevented Katanga's secession, but otherwise could do little to impede the political and economic disintegration of the country.

Governments came and went, still claiming some sort of democratic authentication, until in 1964 the whole eastern part of the country centred upon Stanleyville (now Kisangani) as also the Kwilu district in the west came quite adrift, mostly falling for a while under some degree of erratic control from a revolutionary counter-government set up with support from communist states in Kisangani by Gbenye and other representatives of the Lumumbist tradition.[6] In the extensive massacres which followed in some places (by no means the first in the Congo since independence) 109 foreign missionaries met their deaths, though this was not the policy of rebel leaders such as Gbenye and Soumialot, and the Congolese army committed about as many atrocities against common people as did the rebels.[7] Gbenye was dislodged from Kisangani in November with mercenary assistance and a Belgian–American air operation, but the overall political confusion continued until in November 1965 General Mobutu, already the power behind the throne and the recipient of Belgian–American confidence, finally sent President Kasavubu and the politicians packing and set about reconstituting ruthlessly but fairly coherently an ordered, centralised and stable state.

In the meantime the churches had done much to carry the country across the breakdown in administration. They had, of course, themselves suffered enormously in the anarchy, being at times even a principal target for attack. Some local priests had drifted off into politics; many missionaries had left; others had been killed. The attacks on Catholic missions reflect the extraordinarily powerful position the church had occupied in the Congo until then, and the overbearing manner in which missionaries had often behaved. 'You are as wicked as a priest' (*Tu es aussi méchant qu'un père*) was a common saying in some parts of the country. Attacks were not directed against all missionaries indiscriminately; some at least were deliberately directed at priests who had provided good cause to be hated.[8] The power of the church was recognised and feared. It could be threatened on occasion, soothed on occasion, but not ignored. Already in October 1959 Antoine Gizenga – himself a former seminarian – had written a letter to priests declaring 'You should fear the vengeance of public opinion, for it is terrible. The first victims of the troubles of 4 January 1959 at Leopoldville, and of other troubles, were unfortunately priests and nuns. Doesn't this make you think?'[9] In fact many priests, black and white, were highly respected and during the rebellion some were carefully protected because they were known to be doing good work.[10] As a whole deep resentments against the Catholic Church, which had for so long so powerfully made use of colonial privilege, were only to be expected, and from this point of view the explosions of 1964 were unlikely to be the end of the story.

Nevertheless the structures of the church frequently proved more tenacious than those of the state and in many up-country areas their presence alone ensured the survival of basic services. Furthermore at the centre the Catholic Church performed a crucially important task in keeping the university of Lovanium at Kinshasa running during the most difficult years at a very high standard of academic performance if in economic and political conditions all its own. The number of Congolese with higher education was as a consequence very different in 1966 from what it had been in 1960. Probably no other university on the continent had so greatly expanded during those years.

It was not difficult at this time for the white-ruled south to point the finger at the Congo when it wanted a reason to justify its refusal to allow the wind of change to blow south of the Zambezi: anarchy and a whiff of communism. From the end of 1964 the continent was divided clearly enough into two sections. North of the Zambezi the logic of black nationalism had everywhere prevailed, but in the Republic of South Africa, Rhodesia, Angola and Mozambique white rule remained as seemingly firm as ever. The governments of Pretoria, Salisbury and Lisbon had no intention whatsoever of changing course, nor was there anything to compel them to do so. In 1960 the old black constitutional opposition in South Africa came to its end. The winds of black nationalism had indeed been blowing as far south as the Republic. Their authentic representative was now less the revered Luthuli of the African National Congress with its multi-racial allies than Robert Mangaliso Sobukwe, President of the Pan-Africanist Congress, the true southern counterpart to Nkrumah or Lumumba. It was the PAC which engineered the campaign against the Pass Laws (whereby every African over sixteen is required to carry with him a 'reference book') of which the Sharpeville demonstration on 21 March was part. The crowd was large but not violent. Suddenly the police began firing into them, 69 people were killed and 180 wounded within forty seconds.

The Sharpeville massacre electrified the world. Nine days later 30,000 Africans marched to the centre of Cape Town: a massive but peaceful challenge to the corridors of power. That same day, 30 March, the government declared a state of emergency; hundreds of arrests followed and in April both the African National Congress and PAC were banned for ever. Organised legal African opposition was at an end in South Africa and over the next years the structures of oppression grew steadily more formidable. From 1962 a list of more than one hundred persons was issued whose speeches or writings might in no way be published. Besides many whites, it included Luthuli, Oliver Tambo, Nelson Mandela, Walter Sisulu, and many of the same people were subjected to house arrest. In these circumstances it was inevitable that some people should turn, logically if futilely, to illegal resistance and the planning of sabotage. It took the form of an organisation named Umkonto we Sizwe (Spear of the Nation), led by Mandela, previously Luthuli's right-hand man in the African National Congress. 'Government violence can do only one thing and that is to breed counter-violence,' declared Mandela in 1962.[11] In the 'Rivonia' trial two years later this too was brought to an end when Mandela, Sisulu and others were sentenced to life imprisonment for attempted sabotage. Neither constitutional nor unconstitutional resistance was a practicable option for Africans any more. The black voice within the Republic was – for a while – effectively silenced: Z. K. Matthews, Oliver Tambo and many others were now in exile; the rest of the older leadership was on Robben Island or under house arrest. The South African government at least was not allowing the case for white rule to go by default. In 1964, the year of the Rivonia trial, Verwoerd summed things up as follows:

The tragedy of the present time is that in this crucial stage of present-day history, the white race is not playing the role which it is called upon to play and which only the white race is competent to fulfil . . . Is not our role to stand for the one thing which means our salvation here but with which it will also be possible to save the world, and with which Europe will be able to save itself, namely the preservation of the white man and his state?[12]

Throughout southern Africa a rough but reliable political alliance was being forged as the Republic, Portugal and Rhodesia began to pull together despite the undoubted differences in their legal systems, cultural ethos and religious tradition. In Angola as elsewhere nationalist feeling had been mounting steadily during the 1950s, but 1960 saw the start of a new pattern. In June Dr Agostinho Neto, who had returned from Portugal only a few months before, was arrested in Luanda and deported to Cape Verde. A qualified black doctor as well as a taciturn leader of the newly formed MPLA, he was already famous among his own people and a week later a large demonstration in his home district of Catete called for his release. It was met by a volley of bullets in which twenty to forty people were killed.[13] Small in comparison with many subsequent massacres, that of Catete had nevertheless the significance of a new beginning. Coming just three months after Sharpeville and at the moment of Congolese independence, it marked only too emphatically the choice that Portugal had made. Six months later, in February 1961, there were riots in Luanda attempting the release of political prisoners. They were unsuccessful but produced a violent white reaction in which hundreds of people undoubtedly died. In March there was a wider uprising in the north of the country. The incipient Angolan national-ist movement was already split sharply in two and while the MPLA, a determinedly inter-tribal movement of Marxist inspiration led by coloured intellectuals and such men as Neto, was behind the Luanda riots, it was Holden Roberto's UPA which produced the war in the north in which many atrocities were committed upon both sides. This was a predominantly Bakongo movement, not so distant from Kasavubu's ABAKO over the border, though at the time Roberto too was seeking for a wider inter-tribal support. Dr Salazar took over the Ministry of Defence in this emergency – the first serious threat to Portuguese rule in Africa for fifty years – and announced on television the 'nation's determination' to remain in Africa to 'defend Western and Christian civilisation'.[14] The rebellion was ruthlessly crushed, hundreds of thousands of Angolans fled to the Congo, and it would be some years before any serious challenge was mounted again to Portugal in Africa.

If the break up of the Federation brought independence to Zambia and Malawi it brought no good to the black cause in Rhodesia. The crucial switch here was at the general election of December 1962 when Sir Edgar White-head, Garfield Todd's successor as prime minister, was defeated by the Rhodesian Front. Whitehead, a tough intellectual and a far more profes-sional man of government than Todd, had remained sincerely committed to the aim of racial partnership and had already gone some way over the last two years in breaking down the legal colour-bar. His 1961 constitution brought Africans into the Legislature for the first time. Such measures were too late and too cautious to win back black confidence. Whitehead could not anyway go nearly fast enough for the nationalists, Nkomo and Sithole, in that heyday of black triumph across the continent, while he had already gone too far for most of his European electorate. So he repressed the one only to be rejected by the other. The Rhodesian Front stood unabashed for white supremacy.

In Rhodesia, as in Angola, there was already a disastrous division among black nationalists between two conflicting parties, ZAPU and ZANU, and the leaders of both were soon in detention or exile. When Ian Smith made his Unilateral Declaration of Independence in November 1965 there was effectively no one to say him nay. Rhodesians had, he told the world, 'struck a blow for the preservation of justice, civilisation and christianity'.[15]

Thus by the close of 1964 white rule in these southern countries seemed to have coped successfully with the wave of black nationalist enthusiasm that had flooded across the continent in the preceding years. Thus far and no further, they had said. Indeed not for many years had the African voice been so muffled from the Zambezi to the Cape. And yet already a new challenge had begun to emerge, little as its seriousness was recognised at the time. Mozambique was in many ways one of the most backward parts of the continent. It certainly had no striking recent record of African political activity. Yet here too resistance was now to develop – more effectively indeed than anywhere else. On 25 June 1962 the Mozambique Liberation Front (Frelimo) was formed by exiles in Dar es Salaam with Eduardo Mondlane, just returned from the United States and a job in the UN, as its first president. Two years later, September 1964, it began a guerrilla war in the north of Mozambique and the Achilles' heel of southern Africa was about to be revealed.

The year 1966 marked the end of an era. It saw the independence of Botswana and Lesotho and so (apart from Swaziland) a process which began with Ghana in 1957 was now concluded. It had been an age of heroes and ideologues, if of easily formulated and quickly tarnished ideals. But it was now over. Even its masterly counter-hero, Dr Verwoerd, was to die, struck down by an assassin, before the year was over: the man who had dominated South African politics for fifteen years by the sheer power of moral conviction, an architectonic capacity for racialist social theory, an uncompromising administrative ruthlessness. Now he was gone, to be succeeded by the hard pragmatist, John Vorster.

All across the continent the features of the early independence period were fading, a certain semi-democratic optimism being replaced in country after country by military or dictatorial government – frequently as the only apparent alternative to political chaos. In the southern Sudan there was now civil war; in the Congo General Mobutu had declared military rule in a resolve to bring to an end years of chronic anarchy. In Malawi Dr Banda had expelled or imprisoned many of the people who had worked with him to gain independence, and was revealing himself as a man increasingly impatient of any thought processes but his own. The man who had destroyed the Federation was now to make of Malawi a mental backwater reflecting his own image: British middle-class morality of the 1930s somehow wedded to the one-party state. In Uganda early in the year Obote arrested five of his leading colleagues in the middle of a cabinet session and drove the Kabaka from his palace and the country. The very first week of 1966 Colonel Bokassa had taken over in the Central African Republic.[16] A few weeks later, to the world's distress, a coup in Nigeria by junior Igbo officers brought the death of its gentle prime minister, Sir Abu Baka Tafawa Balewa, together with the premiers of the northern and western provinces. Over the next few months the greatest state of Africa lurched ever nearer to complete political disaster as east and north pulled apart. In October there were large-scale massacres of Igbos in the north and the stage was set for secession or civil war.

Balewa's death in January was followed by Nkrumah's deposition in February to the rejoicing of his own people and the bewilderment of much of the rest of the continent. He had grown increasingly dictatorial at home, a mental victim of his own self-projected image, while his party had grown both corrupt and inefficient, yet his rule never had the quality of brutal tyranny about it which several other countries were soon to experience. His political passing indicated only too well the fragility of power, of even the ablest and most far-sighted politician: how easily the acclaimed hero of one year could become the feared and isolated autocrat of another, and then how easily a few army officers could engineer his overthrow. If the tone of 1961 was incredibly different from that of 1956, the quality of 1966 was hardly less different again: the struggle for independence seemed quickly twisted into a sordid power game, dutifully cheered by a disillusioned and powerless populace. The faces of the rulers were black where formerly they had been white, but the deeper social, political and economic structures created by colonialism had clearly outlived the passing of empire – structures which differentiated profoundly between dominating elites and dominated masses. Indeed the changes which had taken place, so loudly trumpeted, seemed now in many countries to have done little but accentuate the inherent immorality of the underlying system by increasing the scale of personal corruption and diminishing the mechanisms of accountability. The campaign for political independence had been sold to the common man as the road to something little short of an economic and social millenium. That glittering prize was now found to be reserved to the small minority who could move into government jobs and settler farms, play ball with international capitalism, and become with every year that passed more alienated from the common man, whose smile turned slowly sour in the bewilderment consequent upon so great, if inevitable, a deception.

II

The political stance of ecclesiastical leadership in a time of rapid governmental change is inevitably a delicate one, but perhaps still more delicate – and potentially disastrous – is its position in a period of the more or less successful repression of popular movements. It was easier for the churches in west and east Africa to chart a new course across the coming of political independence while retaining their integrity than for those in central and southern Africa to weigh with honour the claims of white and black members, government and congress, in these years when there was a steady hardening of position on the part of well entrenched minority governments.

It might have seemed least difficult within the northern territories of the Federation where African opposition to the latter was overwhelming and the final say in government remained in London. Colin Morris might be unusual enough and unpopular enough with his Copperbelt neighbours for favouring the nationalist cause while a minister of a white Methodist Church in Chingola, but he and his like had powerful support back in Britain as well as the comforting feeling that the wider tide was moving almost irresistibly in a way they approved of. The most influential church in Nyasaland had traditionally been the Presbyterian; for no other part of Africa did the Church of Scotland feel so responsible. In 1959 the General Assembly was expressing itself more forthrightly than ever against the Federation – Lord Macleod being the Church of Scotland's outspoken Moderator that year – while in Nyasaland its daughter, the Church of Central Africa, Presbyterian, was almost as committed in opposition as Banda's Congress. The same year the Catholic bishops of the Federation, instigated by the far-sighted Pailloux of Fort Rosebery, complained to the prime minister of the 'disparity between the ideal of partnership and its practice'.[17]

In general, however, the mission churches tended to share the white man's fear of the growth of African political movements and to take the government's case very much for granted. The friendship of Colin Morris could be most valuable for Kaunda personally but at the time such links were not so significant for Kaunda's party, UNIP. In the early 1960s UNIP supporters often attacked mission property, as did ZANU and ZAPU supporters further south, and nationalist leaders all across the Federation had grown increasingly embittered with churches that practised racial segregation even in worship and only on the rarest occasions came out in criticism of government or settlers.[18]

The mission churches had bred the nationalist leaders here as everywhere: Kaunda and Banda had been Presbyterians (if both subsequently changed to the African Methodist Episcopal Church for a while); in Southern Rhodesia Nkomo had been a Methodist lay preacher, Sithole a Methodist minister, Nyandoro an Anglican, Chikerema and Mugabe Catholics. Many of these men started their adult lives as enthusiastic church members, but these links were either weakened or wholly broken – partly, doubtless, because of a simple change of concern in their lives, but partly because the mission churches showed themselves for the most part intensely suspicious of black political activity as being an ungrateful, dangerous and unnecessary response to the white man's tutelage.

Only one or two men, such as Morris and Bishop Ralph Dodge of the Methodist Episcopal Church, really managed to keep the lines of communication open. The white Christian most successful in doing so had been a layman: Guy Clutton-Brock. St Faith's Farm had been through the 1950s a Christian cooperative where partnership really was experienced as a reality. It did not survive 1959. Clutton-Brock had moved on to other fields, leaving the very competent John Mutasa as manager of the farm. St Faith's was on Anglican mission land and aroused suspicion, not only because of its inter-racial achievement and relatively radical politics – Clutton-Brock was one of the only white members of Congress, Herbert Chitepo a welcome visitor – but also because of its ecclesiastical openness, a certain unformulated but practised ecumenicity which could seem equally scandalous. Father Arthur Lewis had been appointed Anglican priest-in-charge at St Faith's in September 1958. A man of long missionary experience and sacerdotalist Anglo-Catholic views, who had served Africans devotedly for many years but was temperamentally incapable of listening to them, he found St Faith's a disturbing place. In the course of the next year the inter-racial farming commune was destroyed by the Diocesan Standing Committee and the priest-in-charge determined to re-establish a 'proper' mission and the total authority of its priest in place of that of a 'village committee'. This was not simply a conflict over race relations but also one over two contrasting models for church and society. For the new brooms at St Faith's a free-thinking English liberal like Clutton-Brock's colleague Ralph Ibbott was quite as unacceptable a part of the community as a lay black manager. And both had to go. 'The Church has failed to fulfil its promises' commented John Mutasa sadly.[19] The institutional grounds for African loss of confidence in the missionary church were seldom more cogently revealed.

If the official Anglican Church in Rhodesia moved steadily nearer the settler position during these years, the Catholic and Methodist churches moved almost equally steadily towards a public championing of African interests. The coming of U D I brought with it an increasingly sharp sense of confrontation. Bishop Dodge was deported the same year, to be replaced in due course by an African – Abel Muzorewa. The Catholic bishops, representing by far the largest church in the country, now took up the mantle of political prophecy with mounting clarity and forcefulness: 'Vast numbers of people of Rhodesia are bitterly opposed to the unilateral declaration of independence' they declared in *A plea for peace* dated the first Sunday of Advent 1965.

They are particularly angered that it should be stated publicly that this action was taken in the name of preserving Christian civilisation in this country. It is simply quite untrue to say that they have consented by their silence. Their silence is the silence of fear, of disappointment, of hopelessness. It is a dangerous silence; dangerous for the Church, for all of us. It comes as no surprise, therefore, that many are saying, 'So this is Christian civilisation! This is what Christianity is! The preservation of privilege for the few and well-to-do, and the neglect of the many who have nothing.'[20]

To the west of Rhodesia there was no comparably forthright Catholic voice in that, at least nominally, far more Catholic country, Angola. Here too these were years of apparently successful repression of the African voice. The abortive Angolan rebellions of 1961 and the hardening triangular conflict between Portugal, MPLA and FNLA (as Roberto's movement may be named, though UPA or GRAE refer to essentially the same thing) had considerable religious implications. The Portuguese had always feared Protestant missionary organisations as at least potentially seditious – by the nature of the case British and American missionaries could hardly contribute to the policy of 'Portugalisation' very convincingly; they brought instead a greater sympathy with democracy and African nationalism than Catholic missionaries usually evinced. Not unnaturally, then, a considerable proportion of the nationalist elite were drawn from the Protestant elite, though this was less true of MPLA than of FNLA. The latter's leadership was overwhelmingly northern and Baptist, though Roberto did endeavour to get beyond both of these frontiers. Dr Neto was the son of a Methodist minister and had himself as a boy acted for a while as Bishop Ralph Dodge's personal secretary. He had gone to Lisbon to study on a Methodist scholarship.[21] Several of the Loanda and Mbundu leaders of the MPLA had a Methodist background; but others, naturally enough, were Catholics and some had studied in a seminary. Mario de Andrade was probably the most influential of MPLA's founders; his brother Joaquim Pinto de Andrade was a Catholic priest and chancellor of Loanda archdiocese. He was one of a number of priests caught up in the nationalist movement, and one of the many Angolans arrested in June 1960. He was subsequently detained in Portugal for many years.[22]

The Catholic Church was, nevertheless, very clearly identified with Portuguese rule as the Methodist and Baptist Churches were not, and it was noticeable that while many Catholic missions were attacked by the insurgents, Protestant missions were left untouched. In the repression the pattern was inevitably reversed and more than reversed. Almost all Protestant missionaries were expelled, their property was destroyed or closed – even the Methodist clinic in Loanda was burnt by a white mob – and at least eight African Methodist pastors were killed either by armed white civilians or soldiers. If Angolan nationalism was arraigned internationally by Portugal as a communist plot, it was arraigned locally as a Protestant one. While essentially it was neither, there was of course a pinch of truth in both views, and during the 1960s it was to a large extent British Baptists and American Methodists who endeavoured to convince the western world how repressive

Portuguese rule in Africa really was, while Catholics continued to provide many of Portugal's most reliable apologists.

That great sage of modern Christendom, Bishop Bell of Chichester, remarked 'Johannesburg is the second most important see in the Anglican Communion.' Ambrose Reeves was bishop there from 1949 to 1961.[23] In his latter years he not only denounced government policy in general in the strongest terms ('It is flagrantly immoral to attempt to maintain white supremacy in a racially mixed society'), he also took on a more precise political role than any other bishop of any communion before or since. He had become indeed a sort of majordomo of liberal opposition to government policy. Archbishop Joost de Blank of Cape Town could condemn apartheid sternly enough and so could the Catholic bishops and the Methodist Conference, but only Bishop Reeves was willing to get down to the hard grind of endless committee work in cooperation with black politicians, Marxist lawyers and progressive businessmen over such practically vital but complex secular issues as the bus boycott, mass evictions, the provision of financial aid to the accused in the Treason Trial, the publication of the facts about Sharpeville. He brought unlikely people together; he made multi-racial opposition respectable without making it toothless. He had become apartheid's most efficient opponent. In the wave of arrests that followed Sharpeville Reeves heard, on 1 April 1960, that he too was likely to be arrested; after consulting various diocesan officials he decided to escape to Swaziland to avoid being silenced. From there he proceeded to England. Almost certainly Reeves' flight to Swaziland was a major error of judgement which gravely weakened his moral authority and from which he never really recovered. Some of his white clergy now endeavoured to persuade him to resign. They claimed he was over-involved in political causes and, as a consequence, neglecting his ecclesiastical responsibilities. 'There has been a growing feeling,' the diocesan chancellor wrote to him, 'that the amount of time and attention given by you, ostensibly as Bishop of Johannesburg, to extra-ecclesiastical affairs, has left you with less and less time for the people and problems of the Church.'[24] Reeves rejected this appeal, returned to South Africa in September and was promptly deported. The deportation of a senior bishop with no charges made against him was surely an event of major and disgraceful significance, and the church made its proper protest. Yet many were quietly relieved and Reeves' South African career was at an end. The Anglican Church in South Africa would never again attempt so sturdy an opposition to the powers that be or so clear-sighted a resistance to social injustice.

1960 was the year of Sharpeville and of the deportation of Bishop Reeves. It was also the year of the Cottesloe Consultation, in some ways about the most significant church meeting ever to be held in South Africa. Shocked by

Sharpeville, the churches were more ready than they had ever been previously to examine their relationship to society and race relations, and this included the Dutch Reformed Churches. It was agreed that each of the South African member bodies of the World Council of Churches should send ten delegates to a consultation at Cottesloe near Johannesburg in December, sponsored by the WCC. Three Dutch Reformed Churches participated in this. There had been a growing unease with apartheid on the part of a Dutch Reformed minority for some years associated in particular with the name of Dr B. B. Keet, Professor at the theological seminary of Stellenbosch. Already in 1953 he had declared to the horror of many church members that 'there is only one apartheid known to scripture, and that is separation from sin, not from our fellow human beings, least of all from our brethren in Christ.'[25] Immediately prior to the Cottesloe Consultation eleven theologians of the Dutch Reformed tradition published a symposium entitled *Delayed Action* which presented for the first time a major challenge from within this most influential of South African Christian groups to the philosophy underlying the policy of the government. Dr Keet was one of the writers and Professor Geyser who held the chair of New Testament Theology at the University of Pretoria another. The resolutions of the Cottesloe Consultation which followed, while not the most remarkable in themselves, were extremely remarkable in appearing with the backing of most of the Dutch Reformed delegates. Never had there been so serious a seeming rapprochement between the two white Protestant traditions in South Africa in finding a social and racial policy. It was not to last. The Cottesloe Resolutions were almost immediately repudiated by the various Dutch Reformed synods involved, who then went even further in withdrawing from the WCC altogether and turning to the persecution of those of their members who had dared confront government policy in the name of the gospel.

The chief victim was to be Professor Geyser of the Nederduitsch Hervormde Kerk who was forced to resign from his university chair, found guilty of heresy, and had his ministry in the church terminated. On the last count he appealed to the Supreme Court which set the Synodical Commission's findings aside so that Geyser could be reinstated as a minister. He had by then moved to a post at the University of Witwatersrand.

The leadership of this small but high-powered group of Dutch Reformed Christians who challenged the whole theological and moral underpinning of South African racialism fell increasingly to Dr Beyers Naudé, who was at the time vice-chairman of the Transvaal Synod of the Nederduits Gereformeerde Kerk. He had taken a leading part in the Cottesloe Consultation. A member of the Broederbond, a theological graduate of Stellenbosch, already one of the most influential ministers of the Nederduits Gereformeerde Kerk, he had come slowly over the years in the depths of his Christian conviction to a realisation of the enormity of social injustice in his

145

country and the vastly added enormity of its justification on religious grounds by his own church. Naudé and the timid words of Cottesloe represented a far graver challenge to the upholders of apartheid than did Ambrose Reeves. The latter was a foreigner, an Englishman; his very attacks on the system could be used to reinforce the nationalist sense of grievance and Afrikaner church–state unity which were the greatest bulwarks of apartheid. Beyers Naudé was undermining just those bulwarks, his voice unmistakably Calvinist and Afrikaner, speaking with a Christian seriousness the like of which is very rarely met and taking up, at the ultimate level of conscience, not only the issue of racial openness but also that of ecclesiastical openness, of the obligation to ecumenicity – both alike unacceptable in a world view dominated by selection and segregation.

The point of no return in Naudé's life was April 1961 when the Synod of the Nederduits Gereformeerde Kerk had worked itself into a fury of repudiation of the Cottesloe Resolutions and expected its delegates to express their regret at passing them or at least to withdraw into silence. Naudé refused to do so.

I had to decide – would I because of pressure, political pressure and other pressures which were being exercised, give in and accept, or would I stand by my convictions which over a period of years had become rooted in me as firm and holy Christian convictions. I decided on the latter course and put it clearly to the Synod that with all respect which I have for the highest assembly of my Church, in obedience to God and my conscience I could not see my way clear to giving way on a single one of these resolutions, because I was convinced that those resolutions were in accordance with the truth of the Gospel.[26]

Two years later, in August 1963, the Christian Institute was founded in Johannesburg as an ecumenical group of Christians concerned to bring about reconciliation within South Africa and to relate the gospel to daily existence. In November Naudé became its first director and as a consequence his status as an ordained minister of the church was taken from him to his deep regret. In the coming years the Christian Institute was to prove by far the most powerful and effective Christian witness to justice in the country. Before leaving his ministry Beyers Naudé preached a final sermon to his congregation at Aasvoëlkop in Johannesburg on the text of Acts 5. 29 'We must obey God rather than men.' 'Oh, my Church, I call this morning in all sincerity from my soul – awake before it is too late. Stand up and give the hand of Christian brotherhood to all who sincerely stretch out the hand to you. There is still time, but the time is short, very short.'[27]

The range of Christian reaction to government policy may be exemplified by three events of 1964. First, the much respected Catholic Archbishop of Bloemfontein, William Whelan, came out with a sudden defence of apartheid which conflicted with numerous previous statements of the Catholic bishops and with increasingly forthright anti-apartheid utterances of Archbishop Hurley of Durban.[28] His statement reflected the views of the very small group of people anxious to build bridges between the Catholic Church and the main Afrikaner tradition; elsewhere it caused much dismay and undoubtedly introduced a new element of uncertainty into the church's position, adding new ground for the disillusionment of black Christians with white leadership.

Secondly, in December 1964, a young man, Hugh Lewin, was sentenced to seven years in prison after pleading guilty to being an active member of a revolutionary group. A convinced Christian, the son of a priest and a disciple of Trevor Huddleston, he had reluctantly come to the conclusion that at least some measure of violence was necessary if the violence of white oppression was to be overthrown. He had joined a group committed to 'symbolic' violence – blowing up power pylons and the like. It did not get far. Most of the group were not Christians and while Lewin's decision to join them, his arrest and heavy sentence seemed at the time of rather minor significance, they were pointers to what was soon, and inevitably to become a decisively dividing issue: that of Christian support for revolutionary violence. It was an issue which, at the time of Lewin's gesture, the churches were wholly refusing even to acknowledge.

Finally, one other incident of 1964, the story of a far milder clerical response to black misery and its failure, is worth recalling as somehow expressive of the ecclesiastical and social world within which Whelan and Hurley, Ambrose Reeves, Hugh Lewin and Beyers Naudé had to take their decisions.[29] The Reverend D. P. Anderson, a Congregationalist minister in a white Johannesburg suburb, Florida Park, had organised services for Africans, mostly house servants, in his church. He was informed by the police that this must cease on the instructions of the town council because local residents had complained that Africans attending a two-hour Sunday afternoon service in their area would cause property values to drop. Mr Anderson protested that there were about 25,000 Africans in the area, and, except for a few 'garage services', no facilities for worship for them whatsoever (any more than there were any recreational facilities). The police kindly permitted Mr Anderson to hold one final service in which he could tell the people that there would be no more.

III

The coming of political independence to most of black Africa brought a far slighter immediate shift in church–state relations than might have been anticipated. Even where there had been considerable tension in the previous years between nationalist movements and the missions, for instance in central Kenya or Northern Rhodesia (Zambia), this faded away easily enough in the light of independence once achieved. The main Protestant

147

churches mostly Africanised their leadership very promptly in these years and if the Catholic Church did so more slowly, it too soon had an adequate number of native born archbishops and bishops to indicate its full participation in the new political era. African statesmen seldom pressed for more in the first years. While a white political establishment gave way to a black one, in most countries the religious ethos surrounding government, at least superficially, did not change at all strikingly. The same cathedrals were used for the same type of public services graced, as previously, by figures of state. If such services tended to be more ecumenical than previously, this was not only due to an African preference, but also to an almost universal change in ecclesiastical atmosphere differentiating the 1960s from the 1950s. There was too, understandably, some diminution in Anglican influence in former British territories as a far smaller proportion of Africans than of Englishmen have any Anglican affiliation and the Anglican communion had been filling a role related more to its position in England than to that which it had acquired within African society.

Only in one or two rather exceptional cases, predominantly Muslim countries such as Sekou Touré's Guinea and Sudan, was there an almost immediate deterioration of relationship from the rather rosy atmosphere of the preceding years. Elsewhere institutional advantages and personal propensities combined to ease the churches' road across the watershed of independence. Their major contributions in the fields of education and medicine were still required. While few African politicians were willing to contemplate an indefinite ecclesiastical control of these areas, they were equally reluctant to embark on major changes at once. There were more important political and administrative positions over which they had first to establish sure control. Moreover they looked in the early years for major educational expansion despite their limited resources and it was clear that the missions could still prove cheap and reliable partners in development while remaining open to fairly easy removal later on.

The new governments could not but be conscious of the great power which the missionary churches exercised in many up-country areas; if this was a possible threat, it was also something to be benignly harnessed within the new endeavour rather than hastily outlawed. Nor was this so difficult. If some smaller churches stood rather coldly aloof from new secular developments, for the most part the churches were only too glad to be allowed to bless and participate in it all – even to bow and scrape on occasion. They were delighted to find that nationalist politicians on coming to power were far indeed from being communists; they responded with profound gratitude and a real anxiety to help serve the new political order. Such a piece as the pre-independence Pastoral Letter of the Tanganyikan Catholic bishops of Christmas 1960, *Unity and Freedom in the New Tanganyika*, was a model of advice for which the politicians could only be grateful themselves. Centred

148

around the concept of 'pluralism' it might seem more characteristic of the post-conciliar Catholic thinking of the later 1960s, though that very emphasis might have gone down a good deal less well at a later date in the Tanzania of a one-party state. It was in its time noticeably different from the very much more heavy-handed production of the hierarchy of the Congo (Zaire) in 1961 with its central stress upon the rather dated conception of 'Catholic Action'.[30]

Church–state relations do not only concern mission churches and one of the major developments in these years was the fundamentally altered relationship in the Congo (Zaire) between the 'Church of Jesus Christ on earth through the Prophet Simon Kimbangu' and the state. It was only in 1959 after nearly forty years of intermittent persecution that the Belgian colonial authorities finally granted full legal recognition and freedom to the Kimbanguists. Christmas that year was the first they had openly celebrated together without fear. The coinciding of the swift march to independence with the liberation of Kimbanguism inevitably produced some intermingling of the two processes and contributed, at least temporarily, to emphasising the public and nationalist import of the Église. There was for a time much sympathy between ABAKO and the Kimbanguist leadership. Charles Kisolokele, the eldest son of Kimbangu, was one of ABAKO's most prominent members and a cabinet minister in the first government after independence. Kimbangu's body had been triumphantly translated from Elizabethville to the holy city of N'Kamba only three months before independence, in April 1960, and Kasavubu had taken part in the ceremony. There was even talk of the Église becoming the state church of the Congo. This was in fact clearly unrealistic as its support was very limited in many parts of the country and even in its home areas it remained a minority. More prudently, across the uncertain political history of the subsequent years, Joseph Diangienda led it to a firmly apolitical position unallied with any party and undesirous of recognition beyond that of being one of the three main churches in the country.

Others, however, reacted differently, and the intertwining of religious and political protest is a major theme in the tangled Zairean story of those years. Charles Kisolokele was not by any means rare in being committed within both fields. The formal politics of the early years of independence, expressed in secular western terms, was often only a thin top layer in an amalgam of which some of the most vital and forceful elements were religious sects and movements of one sort and another – some more Christian, some more within the sector of traditional religion – which had existed for many decades in a semi-clandestine manner but were now to enjoy a veritable field-day, stimulated in particular by the disillusionment of the aftermath of independence. If one major strand of clandestine religious independency had surfaced within the increasingly structured and respectable community of the Kimbanguist Église, other strands took very different directions.

Here are some of the remarks made by village people attending a semi-religious meeting with Catholic links in Kwilu in 1962: 'Before Independence, we dreamed that it would bring us masses of marvellous things. All of that was to descend upon us from the sky . . . Deliverance and Salvation. But here it is more than two years later that we have been waiting and nothing has come . . . On the contrary our life is more difficult; we are more poor than before.'[31] The vast upsurge of unrest in Zaire in 1964 was at once regional dissatisfaction with the incapacity of complacent Leopoldville politicians to cope with many of the country's most basic requirements, a remarshalling of the more radical 'Lumumbist' nationalist forces, and a popular explosion of something almost millenarian – at times more secular in its aspirations, at times overtly religious or magical. Mulele, leader of the Kwilu uprising, might have imagined himself a Marxist; he quickly became a messianic and magical figure and far across the country people who had never once seen him confidently chanted *Mai Mulele* (water of Mulele) as they swept into battle.

At Kisangani in the bloody first weeks after it had been captured by the rebels in August 1964 it was Alphonse Kingis, a Kitawalan pastor, who half ruled the town and whose youth-gangs were responsible for something of a massacre of unreliable intellectuals. He was himself assassinated a little later.[32] The area had long been known as a stronghold of Kitawala.[33] Emmanuel Bamba, a better known figure, had been at one time one of the leading figures in the Kimbanguist Église and even the young Diangienda's patron. Imprisoned in Elizabethville, he had actually met Kimbangu a little before his death and been greatly moved. In 1960, the year of independence, Bamba, like Kisolokele, was active both in the Kimbanguist revival and in ABAKO. Two years later he quarrelled with Diangienda and founded his own church Le Salut de Jésus Christ par le témoin Simon Kimbangu. By 1966 he was also one of Mobutu's cabinet ministers, quarrelled with him, joined an attempted coup d'état and died before a firing squad.[34] The restlessness of one form of religious independency and its interaction with politics, strikingly illustrated in Bamba's life, were commonplace in the Congo of the early 1960s, but far more rare elsewhere – though the Lumpa war in Zambia was taking place at the same time as the strange régime of Kingis in Kisangani. Churches which desired to survive, however, soon realised that it was safer to embrace the political neutralism and moderation so sedulously pursued by Diangienda.

The mission school education and personal friendships with churchmen of many of the leaders of this era were a factor of considerable importance for the secure status and new orientation of the main churches. In English-speaking Africa a small number of elite Protestant schools such as Alliance

High School in Kenya, King's College Budo in Uganda, Livingstonia in Nyasaland and Mfantsipim in Ghana proved to be the seedbeds of the new leadership – Protestant out of all proportion to the overall proportion of each country. Over half of Kenyatta's first cabinet were old boys of Alliance. In French-speaking Africa there was, equally, a strong Catholic background behind a majority of the leaders of the independence era. Some had even been priests, like Youlou of the Congo–Brazzaville and the very gifted Boganda of the Central African Republic, who was killed in an air crash just before independence; others, like Senghor, Kasavubu and Kayibanda had been partly educated in a seminary; a number among them were one-time Catholic Action activists. Some like Houphouet-Boigny were simply Catholics by allegiance. As a whole they provided the core of the more conservative political leadership in French-speaking Africa as represented, for instance, in the so-called 'Brazzaville Group' of states in 1960.

While the religion of some of these men was mainly the expression of an educational fact – the near impossibility of securing any non-ecclesiastically orientated secondary education in colonial times – or of a social attitude, for others it was an enduring and important element of personal commitment. The religious philosophy of Senghor, the Protestant humanist ethic of Kaunda, the radical Catholicism of Nyerere, are things that they have contributed back to the church rather than any mere matter of colouring to their political formation. Much here is a matter of personal genius but much too could depend on the individual friendships which they formed as struggling politicians with churchmen of imagination and courage. As Tshekedi Khama came to his premature death in June 1959 his old friend Michael Scott was praying by his bedside and to Scott's prayers Tshekedi added a firm *Amen*.[35] When Carey Francis, the old headmaster of Alliance, died in Nairobi in July 1966, Oginga Odinga, Tom Mboya, Charles Njonjo and Ronald Ngala, tough political rivals as they were, united to act as pall bearers.[36] If political Africa was so little alienated from the churches in these years not a little was due to the bridging efforts of such men as Scott and Francis.

Once an independent state got into its stride, however, points of friction were likely to emerge. If Ghana led the way to independence in the late 1950s, it was also leading the way in church–state confrontation some six years afterwards. The main issues have reappeared since in country after country. One was the control of schools;[37] a second was the move away from liberal democracy and the respect of personal rights it enshrines to a one-party state, government control of the press, the development of ideologically controlled youth movements, and the preventive detention of opponents; a third was the personal glorification of the leader – adopting the old African custom of multiplying praise names – even the tendency to build round him a religious mystique which drew on Christian terminology

151

and inevitably became something of a state religion at the expense of any other.

By 1962 there was some tension in Ghana relating to most of these areas, the lead upon the churches' side being taken by the Christian Council, by the Anglican Bishop Roseveare – who was deported for a while – and by the Catholic Archbishop Amissah. The churches objected to the famous inscription on Nkrumah's statue 'Seek ye first the political kingdom and all other things will be added unto it' as a disrespectful reference to Matthew 6. 33, to some of Nkrumah's titles and to the indoctrination of the 'Young Pioneers' in a 'godless' manner. Senior church leadership undoubtedly found its natural links with the opposition rather than with Nkrumah's Convention Peoples Party. Dr Busia had to retreat into exile and Dr Danquah – the country's most distinguished intellectual of the older generation as well as being a courageous politician – died in prison. In return the CPP criticised the 'divisive and disruptive' influence of the churches and their tendency to protect 'counter-revolutionary' elements. Yet while there was tension between the two, there was never a sustained conflict. Church leaders were considerably relieved when Nkrumah fell but it must be said that they had much less to complain of than would many a hard-tried bishop in other parts of the continent over the next decade.[38]

In few countries were the churches so intricately involved in the political processes around independence as in Uganda and especially Buganda; the colonial–nationalist argument had there to be worked out within the context of two others which often appeared to be even more important and divisive – the old Catholic–Protestant tension and Buganda's own traditional sense of identity versus the concern for modernity and a wider Ugandan unity. By 1961 these three interlocking issues had produced three fairly clearly defined political positions: first, that of the Kabaka and his supporters organised within a movement calling itself 'Kabaka Yekka' (The King Alone) – neotraditionalist, fearful of independence within a unitary Uganda, predominantly Protestant in leadership as the court of Buganda had long been; secondly, the Uganda Peoples' Congress, led by Milton Obote, the principal political coalition outside Buganda, committed to a modern unitary state, again dominantly Protestant (it represented both the traditional establishments in most parts of the country other than Buganda and the fashionable nationalism); thirdly, the Democratic Party now led by Benedicto Kiwanuka, a lawyer from the Catholic heartland of Buddu (Masaka). In origin a party of Catholic Baganda with strong clerical support, it had developed in five years into a genuinely independent national party including some prominent Protestants who appreciated its moderate progressive attitudes and were sick of the traditionalist clique which dominated the government not only of Buganda but of many other districts and so perpetuated Catholic resentments. While this remained a genuinely three-

152

cornered contest the DP did unexpectedly well: it was the only one of the three whose support really crossed the divide between Buganda and the rest of the country. Aided by a Kabaka Yekka boycott of the general elections, Benedicto became the country's first chief minister in July 1961. This posed a threat both to Congress and to the Kabaka, who engineered a somewhat curious alliance which dished the DP and brought the country to independence with Obote as Prime Minister. The Kabaka preferred as premier a Protestant from the north – who could not compete, he felt, for the loyalty of his own people – to a Catholic Muganda and a commoner, whose influence with the Baganda was likely to grow with the months. As it was, Kabaka Yekka swept Buganda – village Catholics as much as Protestants and Muslims – leaving the DP stripped to its Catholic Action stalwarts.[39]

While fate remained still in the balance Archbishop Joseph Kiwanuka addressed to his people a Pastoral Letter on church and state in November 1961. It constituted, as he saw it, an earnest appeal to return to the genuine principles of a constitutional monarchy as agreed upon in the Namirembe Conference of 1954 whereby the monarchy was theoretically taken out of politics. Keep away from Kabaka Yekka was his advice: 'If the king still mixes up in politics the kingship is on the way to digging its own grave.'[40] The moral authority of the archbishop – who had now been a bishop for over twenty years and was a man of great experience and firmness of mind – was vast, but the king was in no mood to listen to the archbishop's advice. The latter was conveniently abroad when the letter was published and in a rage the Kabaka flung Monsignor Ssebayiga, parish priest of Rubaga cathedral, into prison – from where the Kabaka's ministers speedily rescued him. The disagreement was complete, the Kabaka won the day, overturned Benedicto and effectively placed his kingdom in the rather less sympathetic hands of Milton Obote. The alliance between Kabaka Yekka and the UPC quickly broke down after independence; the Kabaka was wholly outmanoeuvred and finally fled the country – pausing somewhat ironically for a breather after escaping from his palace at the cathedral clergy house of Rubaga.[41] Meanwhile Obote had quarrelled as well with many of his old Protestant allies in Congress and had them detained at almost the same moment as he ousted the Kabaka. A curious consequence was that by 1966 the Catholic–Protestant political divide of so many years had largely disappeared inside the wider collapse of traditional institutions and multi-party politics. A rump of the DP led by Benedicto struggled bravely on for a while but Obote's party and government had ceased to have any recognisable colouring and in fact his most reliable supports were now Basil Bataringaya and Felix Onama, erstwhile militants of Catholic Action.

What happened in major key in Uganda happened in a more minor key in many other countries: prior to independence denominational rivalries – often linked to the old-boy networks of particular schools – had some

153

noticeable importance; in the aftermath of independence the significance of this almost everywhere quickly diminished, though Lesotho was an exception in which the Catholic–Protestant divide remained politically sensitive through to the 1970s.

Just west of Uganda the drama of another ancient monarchy's demise had been played out in a far more bloody manner. Rwanda's situation was in some ways closely comparable to Buganda's, yet profoundly different too.[42] When Archbishop Kiwanuka gave his advice to Kabaka Mutesa to stop digging the grave of the monarchy, the kingship in Rwanda had just been abolished and Mwami Kigeri sent into exile. Of this Mutesa was well aware. Kigeri had not had to face Mutesa's problem – his kingdom could arrive at independence on its own, not as a segment of a larger state; but Mutesa had not Kigeri's problem – the monarchy's identification with an ethnic aristocracy, alienated from the large majority of the population. Nevertheless both had opted heavily for neo-traditionalist régimes in the face of challenges from parties claiming the legitimisation of democracy and responding to a sense of grievance on the part of an under-privileged majority: the DP and PARMEHUTU, the one representing an upsurge of Catholics, the other of Hutu. In each case the new party had the strong approval of the Catholic archbishop – Kiwanuka and Perraudin of Kabgaye. Here the resemblance ceases. The British in Uganda were not prepared to back the DP against the Kabaka as the Belgian authorities in Rwanda were prepared to favour PARMEHUTU against the Mwami; still more important the Kabaka could count on the obedience of the majority of his subjects as the Mwami could not – Catholic grievances were trivial in comparison with those of the Hutu. The finally decisive criterion of loyalty among the masses proved to be ethnic–traditional rather than religious.

In past decades the White Fathers in Rwanda, like the Belgian government, had taken the Tutsi ascendancy for granted and even cultivated it. At independence the large majority of African priests were Tutsi and so were two out of the three local bishops – Bigirumwami of Nyundo and Gahamanyi of Butare. But in the course of the 1950s the majority of missionaries, led by Archbishop Perraudin, had become convinced of the deep injustice and latent danger of the whole Rwandese social order and had set themselves instead to encourage Hutu advancement. For a couple of years from 1954 the young and highly articulate Hutu leader Grégoire Kayibanda was editor of the church paper *Kimanyateka*. A protegé of Perraudin, trained in the ethos of the *Young Christian Workers* (Jocists), Kayibanda was soon to launch PARMEHUTU.

By 1959 Perraudin was seen as the most dangerous enemy of Tutsi hegemony. By this time the smaller Protestant Church (CMS founded) was regarded as pro-Tutsi, as were the majority of local priests, while the dominant Catholic missionary body was behind PARMEHUTU. In this

154

largely Christian country many of the victims of atrocities upon both sides were church members, just as were many of their perpetrators. The Tutsi Anglican Pastor and Balokole leader, Yona Kanamuzeyi, was just one of many who went to their deaths in December 1963, but not many possessed, as he did, the serene faith to go singing to their butchery. The worst massacres of that month were in the prefecture of Gikongoro. It was perhaps not wholly unrelated that this was within the diocese of Bishop Gahamanyi whose brother Michel Kayihura was the ablest of the leaders in exile. Church and state were here inextricably mixed.

By 1966, however, they had begun to pull apart: the control of the schools was already an issue, *Kimanyateka* would soon ironically have to cease publication – too freely spoken to survive in Kayibanda's increasingly mono-form state; and even Perraudin would be blamed for protecting and favouring the interests of the remaining Tutsi. If one now attempts some comparison between Rwanda, Uganda and Ghana, it appears that Kayibanda and PARMEHUTU came to power with a good deal of church support, Obote and UPC with some church (at least Catholic) opposition, Nkrumah and the CPP with next to neither. But the final pattern in the three cases was markedly similar – neither the support nor the opposition seemed to matter very much once power was attained. The ruling party in each case set about generating and communicating its own ideology, tussling at times with the churches but never engaging in a major confrontation. The churches for their part grew increasingly cautious about any intervention within the political arena.

In the aftermath of Nkrumah's fall in 1966 the interim government of Ghana, the National Liberation Council, convened a Ceremony of Rededication at Christiansborg Castle to which it was returning the executive seat of government. The ceremony was intended to indicate the spiritual values affirmed by the new order. While ministers of various churches participated, the chief part was taken by C. K. N. Wovenu, leader and prophet of the Apostolic Revelation Society, whose holy city is at Tadzewu in the Trans-Volta region. This invitation surprised and upset the more established churches and Professor Baeta of the Religious Studies Department of the University of Ghana wrote to Lieutenant General Ankrah to express their misgivings.[43] This little incident might suggest the budding forth of some sort of spiritual alliance between government and one or another independent church to the seeming detriment of the older churches, but it must be said that such is in fact far from being characteristic of the period. Even in the Congo (Zaire) a national role for the Kimbanguist church failed to materialise; elsewhere individual independent churches almost always remained too small for a feasible working relationship to be formed with the state, even if this were desired upon either side – which was almost never the case. They continued to coalesce far less easily with government than did the

155

main mission churches. While Ndabaningi Sithole might well propose the ideal of a fairly non-denominational African Christianity at one with the continent's own spiritual traditions, the 'Mudzimu Christian',[44] it was unlikely that this would take institutional form in a particular independent church, at least in a way agreeable to the pragmatic post-independence politician. In practice any 'Mudzimu Christian' church seemed more likely to clash than to collaborate with the government of an independent state – though not usually with the almost suicidal determination displayed by the Lumpa Church in 1964.[45]

In principle the Lumpa Church had always possessed as strong a will to withdraw into otherworldliness as could be found anywhere in the long history of 'fuga mundi': 'Do not look for the things of this world' had been Alice Lenshina's constant refrain. But the consistent application of a ruthless otherworldliness by a whole group of people is only too likely to have revolutionary here and now consequences. The Lumpa vision of life was forcing its members to withdraw from the wider community into purely Lumpa villages up and down Bembaland and inevitably such villages, holding to their own view of things, became simply foreign to the regular body politic. They were becoming, in fact, a body politic of their own: a sort of independent theocratic peasant state. By 1959 – probably the year of the movement's greatest numerical strength – local chiefs around Chinsali, the real stronghold of the movement, were finding themselves almost powerless to enforce the law inside the Lumpa community. But at that moment the attention of the colonial authorities was concentrated upon the challenge of UNIP and the evolution of the Lumpa Church passed almost unnoticed.

While Lumpa and the anti-Federation nationalism had grown up cheek by jowl in the mid-1950s, and for a while Lumpa even looked a bit like the nationalists' own church, they now fell – inevitably, on the internal logic of each movement – profoundly apart. Lumpa had grown best in the years in which the Federation had appeared most successful and black nationalism most ineffectual. Their real objectives were simply too different and as from 1960 the nationalist movement went from strength to strength under the new leadership of Kaunda and UNIP, successfully mobilising an ever larger proportion of the population, the followers of Lenshina both declined in number and withdrew into a profound spiritual, and then physical isolation. In its home base of the Chinsali district its support declined within months from 70 per cent of the population to 10 per cent. In 1962 and 1963 UNIP made its peace both with the institutions of government, which it was soon to take over, and with the mission churches. Everyone was invited, indeed more or less required, to participate in the new state, a UNIP state, which was about to be created. But Lumpa was quite unable to do this and the aggressive isolation of its own stockaded villages was now sharply revealed.

Lumpa members would not carry party cards; Lumpa children would not be sent to school – they would be educated by God – and this at a time when UNIP was backing a big educational drive.

All through 1963 there were incidents in which Lumpa churches were burnt and Lumpa militants raided their antagonists in retaliation. Effort after effort at reconciliation and the peaceful disbanding of Lumpa villages proved unavailing. Kaunda himself came several times to Chinsali to talk with Lenshina. For him the impending tragedy was a particularly poignant one. He and Alice had sat together on the school benches of Lubwa; his elder brother Robert was one of her staunchest supporters; even his mother had for a time been her follower. Her great church of Kasomo, the Sioni of Lumpa, stood only five miles away from his childhood home and the Presbyterian mission of Lubwa which had somehow sparked off so much of the spiritual vitality of modern Zambia – not only Kaunda and Lenshina, but Simon Kapwepwe, Kaunda's main political ally and then most dangerous opponent, and John Membe, brightest light of the African Methodist Episcopal Church.

But now it was too late. There was a terrifyingly uncompromising commitment within the Lumpa villages, perhaps even a thirsting for martyrdom, and in July 1964 catastrophe ensued. The conflict escalated into pitched battles when the police were ordered to bring the segregated Lumpa villages to an end. Within their stockades Lenshina's followers were resolved to meet force with force and they went down fighting at place after place. At Kasomo itself 85 people were killed. The last battle was fought only two weeks before the country's independence in October. In all over 700 people had died. Alice herself and her husband were taken into custody and the church was banned.

The conflict here can be paralleled rather closely by the less bloody one five years earlier in Congo (Brazzaville), also at the moment of independence, between the government of the Abbé Youlou and the Matsovan Church: it too refused to vote, to pay taxes, to possess identity cards – to participate in fact in the modern state. Ironical as it must seem, the religious disciples and even original companions of the Congo's first great moderniser now refused any truck at all with such worldly enterprises. Instead they awaited Matswa's return. For them the new wave of politicians appeared not as Matswa's successors but as traitors to his name.[46] In each case was revealed the incompatibility between the simple imperatives of a starkly millenialist or other-worldly religion and those of a nationalist party bent upon the hasty mobilisation of a whole nation for this-worldly ends. Nevertheless the head-on bloody conflict in Zambia would hardly have happened had it not been for the curious intertwining of the history of the two movements and the inability of the Lumpa leadership, already set upon a course of community withdrawal, to adjust even minimally to the sudden

157

ascendancy of its former half-allies, the UNIP organisers in the villages. The speed with which in Lusaka the world of Welensky had been replaced by that of Kaunda was paid for not in white blood but in that of confused peasants hailing from villages around his childhood home.

B. The historic churches

I

On 29 June 1959 the Abuna Basilios became the first Patriarch of Ethiopia, and the Orthodox Church in that country ceased finally to be in any way dependent upon the Coptic Patriarchate of Alexandria. Indeed the status of Ethiopia and its official church was now such that the relationship could begin to be reversed: at least the Ethiopian Chruch could take a wider lead, guaranteed as it seemed to be of a degree of governmental backing which the Coptic Church could not possess. In 1965 the emperor was able to preside at a conference in Addis Ababa of representatives of many branches of 'non-Chalcedonian' Orthodoxy: Egyptian Copt, Syrian and Indian Jacobites, Armenians and, of course, Ethiopians.

These dates stand for peaks in the modern resurgence of Ethiopian Christianity. They symbolise too the wider reversal of ecclesiastical relationships characteristic of these years across the continent, as of a reaffirmed harmony between church and state. Everywhere the juridical autonomy of the local church was being peacefully established at the same time as the highest positions of leadership were taken over by local people. Thus, to take three examples from among the oldest and most respected Protestant churches of Africa, in April 1960 the Synod of Mansimou established the full autonomy of the Protestant Church of the Congo (Brazzaville) from the Svenska Missions Forbundet (the SMF).[47] In 1961 the Methodist Church of Ghana became fully autonomous with its own conference. In 1963 the Evangelical Lutheran Church in Tanzania came into formal being. Of course, in all these cases there had for many years been local synods with a considerable measure of practical autonomy. Nevertheless either the missionary society or the 'home' church had retained certain basic rights and powers of veto and this tended to give the missionary members of the local synod a commanding position. Thus the Methodist churches of West Africa until that date had remained subject to the British Methodist Conference whose authority was mediated via the Methodist Missionary Society.[48] For some years there had been negotiations as to how to change this and it had been proposed that the Methodist churches throughout West Africa, in Gambia, Sierra Leone, Ghana and Nigeria should form a single 'Conference of West Africa'. This was indeed provisionally agreed upon in 1955 but it soon became clear that it was a missionary project with little African support – at least from the larger churches. One reason for establishing full local autonomy was claimed to be so as to make local reunion schemes with other denominations easier: Ghanaian Methodists might be held back from full

159

unity with other Ghanaian Christians by being tied juridically to some wider international group with which their rank and file, at least, could hardly identify.

In somewhat the same way the establishment of a national Protestant Church of the Congo in Congo Brazzaville brought with it, inevitably, a greater distancing from the Protestant church across the river in Congo (Kinshasa), founded by the same mission and with which, hitherto, it had been practically one church. In the Tanzanian case, however, 1963 brought a fuller unity with no such drawbacks. Until then there had been seven Lutheran 'churches' in the country, although they worked closely together in federation. Moreover, until recently, there had also been a distinct Lutheran Mission Council. From 1959 the latter's functions had been transferred to the federation. At the level of personnel each of the churches had its bishop or president and until 1959 all had been missionaries. In that year Stefano Moshi became president of the northern diocese, and over the next ten years all these positions were Africanised.[49]

Almost everywhere in these years the dominant and prevailing aim was the establishment of the national, uni-denominational church, to which the 'mission' should now be somehow subject. While the achievement of autonomy itself was a relatively easy acquirement, the relationships of the resultant body with the missionary society and with other neighbouring Protestant bodies could prove far more tricky issues. In some cases missionaries wisely handed over their property and responsibilities from the start to the new church, and acted subsequently in dependence upon it; in other cases this was not found possible, certain things were reserved and an uneasy 'partnership' was attempted between two more or less autonomous groups. In the latter cases the leadership of the young church could soon be frustrated to discover how limited its property, financial resources and qualified personnel were in comparison with those of the 'mission'.

The lengthy, formative, and frequently painful shift in ecclesiastical responsibilities from white to black which characterised these years hardly affected the largest heartland of Protestant Christianity in Africa: the South. Indeed the great paradox of it all was that just as the church was coming of age, it had to get on functionally severed from its chief branch. The severance was not, of course, complete, but in experience it was very considerable. While the churches of West and East had now to take on their own leadership, in the South the far larger number of Protestant Christians was still regarded as incapable of doing so. It is true that in 1964 for the first time the Methodist Church of South Africa elected a black president, Seth Mokitimi, but this remained much of an exception. The Anglican Church, above all, with its old and massive black membership in the south made very little attempt to adjust. In 1960 Alpheus Zulu was appointed a suffragan bishop of St John's and in 1966 he was elected Bishop of Zululand. For many years thereafter he would be the sole black Anglican bishop in the Union.

The development of a multitude of national denominational churches was not what the more imaginative missionaries had been hoping for in their last years of influence and control. On the contrary, the ecumenical movement had convinced them how unfortunate it had been that such a crowd of often rather small Protestant churches had been brought forth by a splintered missionary movement. The model of the Church of South India was now before them and many dearly hoped that in various parts of Africa similar entities could be engineered before it was too late. It must be said that this conversion to ecumenism was on the whole rather late in coming to the African scene; indeed until the close of the 1950s it is in general remarkable how little serious effort was made to unite different Protestant denominations and how slowly what negotiations there were progressed.[50] But now in a very changed atmosphere brought about by the growing influence of the World Council of Churches, the Lambeth Conference of 1958 and the advent of political independence, there was a major volte-face and schemes for African church unity were earnestly canvassed in Central, East and West Africa. In general it is clear that these were missionary schemes, the underlying motivation of which Africans little appreciated or entered into; the only major success achieved was in Zambia where white influence in the church remained particularly strong. Elsewhere the movement to unity diminished to the degree that Africanisation advanced.

Northern Rhodesia had a long history of unity negotiations.[51] The need here was indeed particularly clear for here there had been many Protestant missions and the churches they had brought into being were all rather small and regional. The Presbyterians of the north-east had united with the London Missionary Society and the African Copperbelt United Church in 1945, though this had partially separated the former from the united Presbyterian Church in Nyasaland to which they had hitherto belonged (its Dutch Reformed constituency was not prepared to be in union with ex-Congregationalists). They had further united with some white congregations on the Copperbelt to form in 1958 the United Church of Central Africa in Rhodesia (UCCAR) which still remained, however, quite a small church. In 1965, with the encouragement of Kaunda, a very considerable further step was taken. The UCCAR was joined by both Methodists and the Church of Barotseland to form the United Church of Zambia. The negotiations for this union had been hanging fire for years and there can be little doubt that it was the arrival of political independence which conquered the waverers and brought it into being. The negotiations had been mostly with the Methodists; the case of Barotseland is different and unusual. Here the Paris Evangelical Missionary Society had not favoured union; it was the new African church leadership which insisted, at quite short notice, on joining in. The UCZ

161

brought together Presbyterian, Congregationalist and Methodist traditions in what was certainly a wise, fairly broad-based, move to create a
middle-sized church. It did not, however, include all or even nearly all the
Protestants of Zambia, as neither the strong African Reformed Church
(from a Dutch Reformed mission) nor the AME joined it; nor did many
other smaller groups; nor did the Anglican Church. It came into being on a
crest of popular excitement at a moment when 'One Zambia, one nation'
was the great political cry. The Lumpa Church, Kaunda's peasant rival, had
been crushed six months before; political independence had arrived three
months before. Now on 16 January 1965 the ecclesiastical coping to the new
national edifice was unveiled. The inauguration day of the United Church of
Zambia at Mindolo Ecumenical Foundation seemed in some way the culminating moment, not just for some rather troublesome local unity negotiations but for Zambian nationalism, and – on a longer view – the whole
Protestant missionary movement in Central Africa. Not far away David
Livingstone had died at the village of Ilala. Here at Mindolo a range of
different Protestant traditions were uniting in a single church at the dawn of
a new political age with one of its leading statesmen to bless the proceedings.
Kenneth Kaunda read the lesson and Colin Morris preached the sermon. It
was all as it should be.

The UCZ, however, proved to be the exception, not the rule. For the
most part African Methodists preferred to retain the name of Methodist, as
did Anglicans the name of Anglican. Other schemes were discussed over
many years in East and West, only to be shelved when African Christians felt
confident enough to challenge the ecumenical orthodoxies. Those for East
Africa were dropped in 1967,[52] but the most striking story is that of
Nigeria.[53] Here a complex scheme of unity between Methodists, Anglicans
and Presbyterians was actually agreed upon in 1965. The new church, which
would have been by far the largest Protestant church in black Africa, was to
be inaugurated on 11 December, so that the same year would have seen the
achievement on different sides of Africa of two great enterprises for Christian unity. But if January 1965 represented the *élan* and the packaged
accomplishment of Africa's brief age of optimism, December 1965 would
represent instead the confused division of a longer, possibly more realistic,
certainly for the outsider less understandable, period of stress and strain.

It was only at the very last moment that the scheme fell through. The
minutes of the intended final meeting of the Inauguration Committee on 3
November record how 'A telegram was read from Rev. E. B. Idowu addressed to the Chairman calling for the postponement of the inauguration of
Church Union.'[54] Professor Idowu was voicing widespread unease among
many Nigerian Methodists in his characteristically forthright way. The
unease was not about doctrine and it was certainly not with the idea of
'taking episcopacy into one's system'. It was, rather, about property, about

162

liturgy, about personalities, and about the growing general lack of confidence inside the Nigeria of the mid-1960s. Despite attempts to salvage the scheme, the opposition was far too great and it quickly receded into the realm of impractical and unwanted things. Paper schemes for unity meant too little at the level of the local congregation with its concerns for its own identity, its own precise worshipping tradition, its own name. There was no participation here in that newly generated liberal ecumenical consciousness which was so increasingly decisive an ethos for the missionaries who had gently but resolutely fostered such plans.

Here as elsewhere what again became clear was that the basic structuring of the Protestant churches of Africa for a long time to come would be both national and denominational. Some wider links are certainly welcomed, but not if they imperil those two characteristics. The Revival movement in East Africa had always easily crossed denominational boundaries, and many of the church's new leaders came from this background – such as the Anglican Olang' or the Lutheran Kibira. Nor should new bonds which have been forged in these years be underestimated. They are, first of all, the national links of a Christian Council and its affiliated works. The first strong Christian Councils in black Africa were those of Ghana and Kenya, both with full-time secretaries from the 1950s; but the Councils were established in more and more countries, and they tended to draw into membership the larger of the independent churches, and to play an increasingly valuable role in sponsoring common activities, particularly in the fields of publishing, ministerial training and industrial mission, and in providing a channel for a united approach to government.[55] Without such Councils, furthermore, cooperation with the Catholic Church which was now becoming a real possibility, would have been extremely difficult to arrange. There is no tendency for African Christians to wish to withdraw from these. On the contrary. When in 1966 the Africa Inland Mission in Kenya voted to sever all connections with the Kenyan Christian Council because of its too open and liberal an ecumenical approach, it expected the Africa Inland Church to do the same. The church leaders, however, were clearly amazed by the proposal; they had no intention of withdrawing from the CCK and as a result the Africa Inland Mission did not do so either.[56] The characteristic African approach, in short, was proving rather less ecumenical than that of one wing of latterday missionaries but rather more so than that of another.[57] On the whole it appeared to be rejecting, almost instinctively, something of the polarisation that in the white world was developing on these issues during the 1960s. But certainly the fellowship and patronage of the World Council itself could be greatly valued as a most welcome step further for newly arrived autonomous churches. It gave them prestige together with an overseas point of reference and assistance other than that of the mission society they had hitherto depended upon. Sir Francis Ibiam was elected one of the six presidents of the

World Council at the New Delhi Assembly of 1961 and in the coming years it would sponsor or co-sponsor a number of important services for its African members.[58]

The most important new arrival of these years was undoubtedly that of the All Africa Conference of Churches, formally inaugurated with the Kampala Assembly of 1963. It would take some years really to establish its character and working viability and a second assembly would not be held until 1969 in Abidjan. The multiplicity as well as the poverty and fairly small size of many of its members were obvious factors inhibiting the establishment of an effective international and interdenominational organ of this sort. A further problem was the sharp language division between the English- and French-speaking groups. But perhaps the greatest difficulty was that it was of its nature and by its whole ethos a church development in response to the independence of black Africa, but the largest Protestant churches which could most naturally provide much of the leadership remained caught within white-ruled southern Africa. The most prominent African ecumenical figures, men like Z. K. Matthews and Donald M'Timkulu, were in fact exiles from South Africa with no longer a sure church constituency behind them. Inevitably there was a certain weakness in the direction they could provide.

The AACC secretariat was based for its early years at Mindolo Ecumenical Foundation in Kitwe. The 1960s were Mindolo's years. The Foundation had been established in 1958 as an interchurch centre for dialogue and social training, and was located beside an old ecumenical Copperbelt Church.[59] It now represented the brightest ecumenical ideals of the age. The mission churches had been notoriously weak in urban and industrial Africa and nowhere more so than on the Copperbelt. Mindolo was to be a shining attempt to pioneer a new model of mission and it received a great deal of overseas support. It certainly achieved much as a venue for dialogue and conferences both large and small, and its domestic women's training course had a solid character and wide-spread influence which some other of its activities may have lacked. But for a long time it remained a predominantly white operation and an extremely costly one. The local base of Zambian Protestantism, even with the United Church, did not prove a strong one from which to recruit staff and as the Zambezi border hardened between black- and white-ruled Africa, Mindolo appeared less usefully central. It is hardly surprising that the AACC moved away to Nairobi, increasingly Africa's communication centre, but its effectiveness would depend for a while very largely on the older West African coastal churches from which it now drew its general secretaries – the Ghanaian Sam Amissah and, a little later, the Liberian Burgess Carr.

These same churches were taking the lead at the academic and literary level. By the mid-1960s the university departments of religious studies in the west were all headed by African professors – Bolaji Idowu at Ibadan,

164

Christian Baeta in Accra and Harry Sawyerr in Freetown – and their writings were starting to build up a core of theological literature actually produced by Africans. One can think here of Idowu's *Olódùmarè* and of Baeta's *Prophetism in Ghana*, both published in 1962. They would be joined by John Mbiti of Kenya and occasionally even share ideas with French-speaking theologians from the Congo or Cameroon. Admittedly it was not a large group and Mbiti could declare firmly in 1967 that the church in Africa 'is a church without a theology, without theologians, and without theological concern',[60] but it was a beginning and one from which, optimistically, much was expected.

It would be a mistake in concentrating upon the new leadership to ignore the continued presence of the old. Missionaries continued in their thousands in all sorts of roles. Some were elder statesmen like Archbishop Beecher in Kenya who only retired in 1970; some were headmasters; many chaplains. While the older missionary societies were mostly by the mid-1960s trying hard to fill gaps only in a rather temporary manner and to diminish their overall presence, there was a steady increase in the number of missionaries from other more theologically conservative groups.[61] Thus the Sudan Interior Mission (admittedly not a new arrival) had in 1966 no fewer than 648 missionaries in Nigeria alone and 315 in Ethiopia. In many cases the coming of political independence was a signal to arrive not to withdraw. Thus about as many new missions (all of them American) began work in Ghana in the decade after independence as in the century before. This included Mennonites, Lutherans, the Christian Church, the Universal Christian Church, the Church of God, two groups called the Church of Christ, the Watchtower Church of the Delivering Christ and the United Pentecostal Church.[62] To take one other example, that of Uganda, where hitherto there had been a fairly simple missionary pattern, the Full Gospel Church arrived in 1959, the Conservative Baptists in 1961, and the Pentecostal Assemblies of God, the Elim Missionary Assemblies, and the Southern Baptists all in 1962, the year of independence.[63]

While in many cases these newly arrived missionary groups were small in numbers and made rather slight an impact, that was not by any means always the case if they chose their ground well. Thus the Southern Baptists and Pentecostal Assemblies of God concentrated with much success upon the Teso district of Uganda, a populous area but one in which the older churches were undeniably weak. Of course a body with an older history like the Sudan Interior Mission was mostly working from existing foundations and the expansion of its work in northern Nigeria and south-west Ethiopia was closely on a par with that of the Catholic Church at this time.

Whether through the activity of missionaries or of local evangelists or just the pressures of some sort of social necessity, the number of church adherents was in many places growing prodigiously in these years. In general, as is

165

understandable, this growth was especially in inland areas of recent evangel-isation. In Southern Africa the main Protestant churches were not now growing fast. On the contrary, both in South Africa and in Rhodesia the impression is rather that they were beginning to be a little squeezed between independents upon the one hand and Roman Catholics on the other, both of whom were undoubtedly increasing. Overall Protestant numbers were maintained or somewhat augmented by population growth which offset the effect of defections, but there was seldom any longer a large increase through conversions.[64]

North of the Zambezi the position was often very different. In almost all countries there was still a very large proportion of the population with no real commitment either to a Christian church or to Islam. It would seem to be the case that the political changes, which somehow brought almost everyone into the 'modern area' of society in a new way, stimulated rather than discouraged the inclination to seek membership in one or another church. The Africanisation of ecclesiastical leadership naturally done with a maximum of publicity, combined with the obvious public links which existed between many of the new national leaders and the churches, probably provided further encouragement. To these factors was added the extremely weighty practical one that in most countries the churches retained effective control of the school system all through the 1960s. The consequence of this for growth in church membership may well have been phenomenal. Political independence in most countries brought with it a new campaign for mass popular education and there was rapid institutional growth at both levels of primary and secondary schooling. In practice this could mean that the churches were simply provided with a more powerful and omnipresent lever than they had ever had before, and they would retain it in many places almost to the end of the decade, if not beyond. In some regions there were also more particular forces at work. Party political rivalry could be linked with church affiliation and the consequences of political campaigns at elec-tion time could be to press the masses, not only into one party or another, but also into the churches which provided them with a sort of zone of spiritual sympathy. This was certainly the case in Kigezi, western Uganda, during 1960–2 in the tense contest between the UPC with its Protestant sympathies and the DP with its Catholic ones.

It was in areas where evangelisation (and 'westernisation') had only begun to bite rather recently that the greatest growth was now reported. Northern Nigeria provides some of the most striking examples: the Evangelical Churches of West Africa (ECWA derived from the Sudan Interior Mission) had an average Sunday church attendance of 42,360 in 1961 and 202,000 in 1970; the Fellowship of the Churches of Christ in the Sudan (TEKAS, derived from the Sudan United Mission) saw its Sunday attendance rise from under 100,000 in 1958 to over one million in 1973;[65] the Tiv Nongo u

Kristu (from a Dutch Reformed Mission) had a regular Sunday attendance of 23,000 in 1957, 54,000 in 1962, 100,000 in 1964 and 143,000 in 1967.[66] The strength of all these churches lay in Nigeria's mid-northern belt, far less Muslim than had at one time been supposed, but now desperately anxious to catch up educationally and professionally on other parts of the country. Doubtless quite such rates of growth were abnormal even for these years but there were many places where much the same was happening. The Anglican diocese of Central Tanganyika (worked by the Australian CMS, more fundamentalist and less withdrawal-minded than most Anglicans) was one such example from the east, but there were few countries where at least one region was not witnessing in these years a literal explosion in the numbers of people committed to church membership. If the Lutheran Church in Tanzania advanced from 206,000 baptized members in 1955 to 413,000 in 1965, that probably represented a fairly average rate of growth.

The deep effect of this on the life of the church is not easy to define but it can hardly be over-estimated. Without any doubt the length and conditions for the catechumenate were greatly reduced in many places; the amount of instruction most new members were able to receive from ordained ministers or other more theologically qualified people was also very limited, for many it must have been none at all. Moreover, the post-baptism shape and structure of the local congregation altered. There were, of course, always more such congregations, each with a higher proportion of new members; there was also far less regular post-baptismal pastoral care by the ordained. There was in most churches no increase in the ordained comparable with that in members; moreover the very limited number of abler, better educated, African clergy were inevitably being drawn away from rural pastoral work into positions of church leadership and administration. None of these trends was wholly new. They had been going on for a long time but they were quickly accentuated in the conditions of the 1960s. The burden of congregational responsibility in all churches, Protestant, Anglican and Roman Catholic alike, was becoming always more a lay one. While the elemental liturgical and doctrinal order of a particular ecclesiastical tradition was faithfully adhered to and passed on, this was inevitably combined with much more supple patterns of morality, discipline and initiative than had been countenanced in an age when foreign missionaries were still effectively in control of churches with quite a limited number of congregations and adherents.

II

In October 1958 Pope Pius XII died and Pope John XXIII was elected. Within three months he had announced the calling of an ecumenical council. For the Catholic Church in Africa the vast internal revolution set in motion by Pope John more or less coincided with the political and cultural revolution of Independence. The effect of this was to be enormous. The immeasurable adjustment which a very rigid missionary church would have to undergo in the post-colonial situation was made far easier but also far more internally profound and spiritually worthwhile by the *aggiornamento* going on in the church everywhere. It was 'Africa's hour' but it was 'the church's hour' too, and their near coincidence proved fortunate. In an at times almost unbelievable way the most unbending of positions were indeed enthusiastically bent, and for a few years the dynamism of reform actually came from the top, rather than as a force opposed to and by the top.

Very little of this was apparent at the beginning of Pope John's reign though a deep sense of relief was almost immediately widespread; for the most part, however, the effects of the council would only reach Africa after the final session was over at the end of 1965. The bishops were with a few exceptions mentally quite unprepared for the conciliar themes and they had few advisers, moreover many of the missionary bishops were on the very point of retiring while the African bishops had hardly arrived. The deeper consequences of the council made themselves felt here, as elsewhere, in the second half of the 1960s rather than the first half. Nevertheless there were stirrings from the start, some of which indeed antedated the conciliar tide itself just as they did in Europe. The *African Ecclesiastical Review* (*AFER*) began to appear in January 1959 from Katigondo in Uganda and became almost at once the chief forum for clerical discussion all across English-speaking Africa.[67] If it was a younger sister to the *Revue du Clergé Africain* produced by the Jesuits at Mayidi in the Congo, it obtained a far larger diffusion and achieved a somewhat dialogical character very different from the magisterial manner of the great Fr Denis. There was already in the years before the Council actually began a clear loosening up in Catholic structures and attitudes, even if there were many topics discussed in later numbers of *AFER* which could hardly have been handled in the first year or two. The main preoccupations of the time were with the lay apostolate and catechetics together with a less widely shared but still growing sense of the need for liturgical reform and a measure of ecumenism. In *AFER*'s second number Bishop Blomjous of Mwanza, its principal patron and probably the most creative figure in the episcopate at that time, wrote on 'The Position of the African Layman in the Church'. It was his perennial preoccupation. A fat and homely Dutchman, with a cheroot in his mouth and a two-storied building by Lake Victoria constructed to contain his private library, he lived in a room in his seminary, the intellectual of the missionary church, the confidant alike of superior generals, African bishops and little known fundraisers in northern Europe. His most ambitious production in these years was the Social Training Centre at Nyegezi – a smaller, Catholic, East African version of Mindolo – and in August 1961 he hosted there a well attended and influential East African Lay Apostolate Meeting.[68] It was just before Tanganyika's independence while the final year of preparation for the Vatican Council was beginning. It was again a time of happy optimism in which black and white, clergy and laity could mingle and work together, confident and without tension. While Blomjous sat back in an evening cheerfully smoking his cheroot and the conference relaxed, his auxiliary Bishop Butibubage joined in the dancing and Bernadette Kunambi, later to be one of Nyerere's most trusted district commissioners, could lead off the singing:

> We never saw the bishop shine so bright
> Oh Mama in Nyegezi

Blomjous was one of a number of liberal white bishops – men like Moynagh of Calabar, Pailloux of Fort Rosebery and Hurley of Durban – who shone in these years carrying the church across rather quickly from one epoch to another.

Catechetics were a parallel concern, stimulated upon the one hand by the world-wide catechetical movement led by Fr Hofinger, upon the other by the sheer practical necessity to do something about the scope and quality of religion teaching in a quickly exploding church which boasted of scores of teacher-training colleges and thousands of schools and tens of thousands of teachers and catechists, but had given almost no thought hitherto to textbooks, curricula and methods other than the provision of the most old-fashioned catechism. The movement led up to the Pan-African Catechetical Study Week held at Katigondo in August 1964,[69] certainly the most important Catholic conference to be held in these years in Africa.

The need for liturgical and ecumenical revolutions was not yet so widely sensed though, as regards the former, some Africans at least were already strongly pointing out the need, not just for the full liturgical acceptance of the vernacular, but also for a quite new approach to African music, musical instruments, forms of chant and ritual symbols.[70] For ecumenism, Vincent Donovan's forthright appeal in the third issue of *AFER* entitled 'The Protestant–Catholic Scandal in Africa' might be bitterly resented in some quarters,[71] but would increasingly set the tone for the coming years. Where there had been a vast cold absence of human contact there would soon be a growing number of joint discussion groups and the replacement of hostility by the sense of a shared task. The first and strongest resolution of the Katigondo Catechetical Study Week was an earnest request to the bishops to work together with the Protestant authorities for the early production of adequate translations of the Scriptures.

If the wider pastoral lead was most clearly provided at this time by an East African group linked with *AFER*, the line of development was common to all, though – admittedly – the new winds began to blow in some quarters a good deal sooner than in others. In French-speaking West Africa a group somehow in continuity with the *Prêtres noirs* of the 1950s produced a lively volume entitled *Personalité Africaine et Catholicisme* at the threshold of the council. Englebert Mveng, Robert Sastre and their fellow writers were really asking the council, preoccupied as it seemed to be with the problems of the West, to take Africa seriously, at the depth of Africa's own spiritual needs. Meanwhile in the Congo, despite the spate of political crises, the Faculty of Theology at the University of Lovanium was developing by far the most professional school of its kind anywhere in Black Africa. A group of Louvain's ablest scholars was establishing a school with the most exigent standards, even if its cultural ethos was at first very decidedly Belgian rather than African: Louvain transplanted to Africa. Tharcisse Tshibangu's *Théologie positive et théologie spéculative*,[72] published in 1965, was incomparably the most serious piece of theological scholarship yet produced by an African. With Mulago and Tshibangu to join the New Testament scholar Cambier, the dogmatician Vanneste, the liturgist Luykx, the church historian Bontinck, Lovanium would endeavour to combine in its faculty of Theology the institutional effectiveness so characteristic of the Belgian Catholic tradition in the Congo with a new acceptance of African capacity and concerns.

The Catholic Church refused rather emphatically to be stampeded by the arrival of independence. Only in Togo had a black majority of bishops arrived by 1965 (3 – 1), elsewhere the greater part of the episcopate remained white until at least 1968. At the beginning of that year there were, for instance, still nine white bishops to two black in Kenya, and eight to one in Zambia. Even Tanzania, one of the most Africanised of churches, still had fourteen white bishops against nine Tanzanian.[73] Rome's main change here was at the archiepiscopal level. The policy, where practical, was to appoint a black archbishop to head the church and preside over what would still be a predominantly white episcopate. Thus the elderly Kiwanuka moved from Masaka to Kampala at the end of 1960 and Mabathoana was similarly moved to become archbishop in Basutoland in 1961. Elsewhere a number of much younger men were chosen from 1960 to 1962, among them Yago in the Ivory Coast, Zoungrana in Upper Volta, Gantin in Dahomey and Amissah in Ghana, all in 1960, Zoa in Cameroon in 1961, and in 1962 Dosseh in Togo and Thiandoum to replace Lefebvre in Dakar. A dozen or more African archbishops were soon providing a markedly new image for the church. At the same time, in lesser dioceses, where suitable African candidates were not available, new white bishops continued to be appointed as a matter of course.

While no country had more African priests than the Congo, in no country was there a greater reluctance to appoint them to the episcopate. The challenge to the church here was graver than almost anywhere; strong anti-clerical and anti-missionary sentiments were expressed in many of the disturbances both before and after independence and many mission stations were physically assaulted. However, despite the recognition by some that the most profound changes were required in ecclesiastical policy,[74] remarkably little was still forthcoming. The truly massive four-hundred-page *Actes*[75] of the Congolese Episcopate, meeting in Leopoldville in December 1961, shows all the professional care, but also all the heavy missionary clericalism, which had for so long characterised this church. One really wonders who was envisaged as the reader of these complex instructions. Certainly they provide as good a view as any of immediately pre-conciliar Catholic thinking. Of the thirty-seven archbishops, diocesan bishops and prefects taking part only four were African, of the six archbishops not one. It would require a further devastating national crisis to bring about the appointment of a black archbishop – Joseph Malula to Leopoldville in July 1964.

The Catholic missionary force had never been more numerous or more efficient. Numbers continued to rise greatly, probably reaching their highest point in 1966, after which they may have begun very slightly to diminish. They now stood at something like 12,000 priests,[76] 20,000 nuns, several thousand brothers, together with a large, almost uncountable number of lay auxiliaries. They were with few exceptions an almost incredibly disciplined, self-denying and increasingly highly qualified group of people. Priests and nuns stuck to their posts in the Congo through months of perilous anarchy, only leaving if and when they were given formal orders to do so. The various societies were cooperating together a good deal more easily than heretofore; they spanned countries and were, many of them, very international in membership. When men were forced out of one place, they could often be absorbed rather easily elsewhere, but for the most part their characteristic was that of stability. Old and young hung on regardless of change. Some would grumble at the supposed diminished efficiency of a new African bishop, but they served him as loyally as his predecessor and while, before he was appointed, there might have been African talk of the need for a missionary withdrawal, such talk seldom continued for long once he was in control. His overseas auxiliaries were too clearly an irreplaceable asset.

The missionary level of education and qualification had also risen considerably. While it could be fairly said that those Protestant missionary societies which did have mounting numbers were those which tended to appeal to the less educated, the Catholic position was now quite the reverse. From the 1950s all the main societies had worked consistently on the qualifications of their personnel and were sending out an increasing proportion of people with a degree or even two degrees. In the past the sisters running hospitals had often had very limited formal qualifications, now there were scores of doctors and trained nurses in their ranks, if never enough for their purposes. The sheer quality of the Catholic missionary army all up and down Africa in the mid-1960s is not something to be overlooked, and the influence it had, not just on the running of the church itself, but on the whole shaping of the education, medical and developmental programmes of the new states, was often immense.

The number of African priests remained small in comparison, not more than about 12 per cent of the total, and as previously they were concentrated in a small minority of dioceses. Despite the massive network of major and minor seminaries, priestly ordinations were running at not more than 150 a year all through the 1960s.[77] The Congolese proportion of the total was steadily falling, the Nigerian proportion rising; thus the three years 1959–61 saw 75 new Congolese priests and 22 Nigerian, but the triennium 1965–7 saw 57 Congolese and 76 Nigerian, and that of 1968–70 saw 50 Congolese ordinations and 66 Nigerian (despite the fact that most of these Nigerian priests were Igbo and the civil war was now on). In general, here, as in the Protestant churches, the abler young men had increasingly to be sent for further studies and were then quickly drawn into 'specialised' tasks (diocesan administration, seminaries, secondary schools); there were not many left for the regular run of the rural parishes, which remained as much as ever in the hands of missionaries, who had to cope with as great an increase as they had ever witnessed in the number of the faithful, as well as with their old institutional responsibilities in the area of schooling. Indeed here too their burden could still grow remorselessly. While in many countries the older Protestant churches were beginning to pull out, almost relieved, from their educational commitments, the Catholics were still busy increasing theirs. There was many a bishop in the 1960s keen on opening new secondary schools with inadequate buildings and staff, wherever he could obtain governmental permission.[78]

Nevertheless the more far-sighted leadership had long seen that the concentration upon seminaries for the clergy and schools for the laity could, if not further supplemented, lead to disaster. The fruits of the former were too sparse, the church's hold over the latter too shaky. The foreign missionary might be expelled any year and who would then provide even a minimum of organised ministry in most of rural Africa? Even if he stayed, effectively he was able to do less and less just because Catholics multiplied far faster than priests. While the priest–people ratio was growing most frightening in the great Catholic heartland around Lake Victoria, it was deteriorating everywhere. The reply of the 1960s was the resuscitation of the catechist.[79]

In this as in so much else Bishop Blomjous of Mwanza took the lead when he opened a new-style Catechist Training Centre at Bukumbi in 1957. In the next ten years a score or two of such centres were opened. The model was a two to four year course for married men, most having primary but not secondary schooling, there was generally a course for their wives as well and there was an emphasis not only upon doctrine and catechetical techniques

172

but also upon a wider range of skills useful for a rural community leader. As the new type of catechist multiplied, the question of how he was going to be paid soon emerged and it was recognised that it was unrealistic in most parts to imagine that a mission-parish could support more than one or two such people. For the most part they would have, then, to be 'part-time' and more or less self-supporting – unless, indeed, Rome or some other foreign agency could permanently subsidise catechists just as they subsidised so many other things. The danger and impracticability of this was widely recognised but here as on other matters there was still a strong Catholic tendency to look upon foreign money as the final way out of a problem.[80] The great majority of village churches (there might well be twenty or many more in a single mission-parish) could clearly not be provided with their own minister fully trained at the Catechist Training Centre level, and the development of short refresher courses for the older catechists often appeared as the more practical way of upgrading the rural ministry. Certainly in one way or another the revival of the catechist, apparently slowly dying in the early 1950s, can be seen as the single most significant feature of the Catholic ministerial pattern of the 1960s.

The second Vatican Council lasted a long time. Announced by Pope John in January 1959, it first met in October 1962 and concluded its fourth and final session under his successor Pope Paul in December 1965. To a real extent the anticipation and, still more, the working years of the Council inhibited major decisions locally until it was over. Thus, a little paradoxically, the most decisive years in modern Catholic history could also, away from Rome, be some of the less eventful. When they were over, the implementation of the 100,000 words of conciliar constitutions and decrees would have to begin.[81] While they were on, the bishops spent too much of the year in Rome to be noticeably active elsewhere! Of the bishops at the fourth session 311 (out of a total of 2,625) had come from Africa, of whom about sixty were black. It cannot be said that the African contribution was a major or decisive one,[82] but it was dignified and not insignificant, largely because the group was one of the best organized in the world, with an effective secretariat directed by Zoa on the French language side and Blomjous on the English. Blomjous (on the laity) and Hurley (on seminaries) had each a considerable personal part to play as members of commissions, but the most important speeches in plenary session were often made by Rugambwa as spokesman of all, or a large section of, the African group. The bishops of Africa did not provide any of the Council's major orientations; the thrust of their interventions was almost entirely practical and pastoral with the needs of their own churches in mind but with, perhaps, a certain reserve in pushing forward too much. In general they tended to be moderately progressive and positive, with their chief interventions coming in the discussions on ecumenism, the laity, mis-

173

sionary activity, and the church in the modern world; but some had decided reservations about the introduction of a married diaconate. At least the African contingent – unlike many of those from North America – were fluent in Latin themselves. While they appealed for the use of the vernacular for their people in the liturgy, Latin was not for them a clerical problem! Most of the new African bishops had studied in Rome and enjoyed it; their frustrations had often been very much more with missionaries hailing from other lands. There was, perhaps, less latent hostility towards the curia in this group than in most. And Rome itself noticed this. Hitherto a little nervous of the impact of nationalism, it now sensed that it had nothing to fear from the Africanisation of the hierarchy. On the contrary, it might well bring the papacy new support in tussles with liberal theologians and the more critical episcopates of northern Europe and North America. Africanisation need not involve, it seemed, de-Romanisation, for who could be more Roman-minded than Cardinals Rugambwa and Zoungrana, the new spokesmen of East and West?

C. Independency

As the structures of colonial Africa appeared to shake or crumble ever more palpably around 'Africa's year' of 1960, so did the independent religious movements thrive and multiply, whether in loose alliance with a political party, in competition and potential conflict, or simply as still the sole viable channels to 'be oneself'. The thirst for freedom and independence as it affected the common man was a spiritual and cultural phenomenon as much as a political one; it was not hard for it to take very varied, and even contradictory, forms. In one case the pursuit of the political kingdom might undermine much of the thrust towards religious independency, in another it might simply give the latter added force or, again, appeal to a quite different class of person. Moreover, once political independence was gained and – in the eyes of many – found wanting, the religious search might be renewed with all the more vigour. That is to say, if religious independency had been a recognisable phenomenon proper to a colonial situation in which political protest was partially or wholly suppressed, it could within a few years become instead a popular response to the new frustrations of a post-colonial situation. It is noticeable, for instance, that in the heyday of Nkrumah, the 1950s, religious independency did not by any means demonstrate the appeal in Ghana which it did at the time in many less politically advanced countries; but from about 1960 there is a striking outburst of small independent healing churches in southern Ghana. Whether this was a reaction of disillusionment with the fruits of the political kingdom or a sort of carrying across into the religious field of the political achievement, it is in evident contrast to patterns elsewhere.

1959 and the immediately following years were then undoubtedly ones of vitality and growth in the field of religious independency. The year 1959 was probably the moment of Lenshina's greatest following, some 100,000 people. In April 1960, just three months prior to political independence, Simon Kimbangu's body was returned in glory from Elizabethville to his own home, the holy city of N'Kamba. The South African census of the same year showed that membership of independent churches there had now passed 2,300,000 – 21 per cent of the African population and 31 per cent of the African Christian population. New movements were continuing to burst forth in many countries, notably South Africa, Kenya, Zaire, Ivory Coast and Ghana, while the mission church leadership was at long last becoming manifestly conscious that all this was not just a joke or the actions of a few malcontents but a major, continent-wide movement with a deep, if mysterious, logic of its own which the 'historic' churches could ignore only at their peril.

More than ever, however, it was becoming misleading to speak in terms of a single explicative logic or frame of reference for so many and varied movements. In some places they found their natural home in the country-side, but in others they appeared as primarily urban phenomena; in one country they catered for the poorest of the poor, in another for a new artisan elite; look one way and they appear to provide the African equivalent of a misty 'cargo-cult' for people profoundly unadjusted to a competitive environment and unable to get their feet onto the new political and educational bandwaggons, look another and find them innovating, progressive, the spiritual home of the successful shopkeeper and small farmer. By the 1960s independent churches, while lacking the massive capital, institutional plant, and full-time personnel which characterised the major mission churches, were in fact catering for about as wide a range of religious options as the latter. Nevertheless the balance remained very different. While they had – or some of them had – their sacred cities and their recognised schools to put against the heavily equipped mission stations and colleges of the older churches, their focal point remained the small congregation (very probably with no building at all) rather than the large centre, and their theme healing rather than schooling. It is probably not too much of an over-simplification to say that the commonest symbol and attraction for the ordinary man of a mission church up and down the continent was a school, of an independent church it was its healing power.

Increasingly even the 'Ethiopian-type' church while decidedly hesitant about river baptism and opposed to white flowing robes and noisy spirit-possessed congregations, found services of healing and even the assistance of a prophet a desirable asset. Nowhere was there a greater growth of churches than in Soweto, the black half of Johannesburg. There were now many hundreds of different churches present there, most them quite small (with less than 500 members each in all), unrecognised by the government, without any permanent church buildings of their own. Very many of them drew upon both the 'Ethiopian' and the 'Zionist' traditions. Such a one, decidedly on the Ethiopian side, was the Holy United Methodist Church of South Africa.[83] It was founded in 1963 by the Rev Macheke, who became its president. Previously he had been vice-president of the Free United Methodist Church which had earlier broken away from the Free Bantu Methodist Church, which had itself seceded from the Bantu Methodist Church which had left the white-led Methodist Church of South Africa in 1933. The Holy United became a body of some 400 people, mostly living in Soweto, and without buildings; its ministers adhere to the black colour of the western clerical tradition, its services follow the form of the Methodist prayerbook, it practises infant baptism by sprinkling, a quarterly holy communion, and insists upon monogamy and a civil wedding followed by a church service, while it prohibits drinking and smoking. Besides this appar-

176

ently conventional Methodist pattern of church life, it holds healing services carried out by women through prayer and the laying on of hands while the congregation dances round in a circle, and its president stood in hopes that a prophet would sooner or later be found to work within his church – he himself clearly had no such gifts. Nevertheless the healing services of a church such as the Holy United could not provide the same attraction as that generated by one whose power comes most clearly from the prophet-healer at its centre; its primary drawing power lies rather in being a small caring community with a helpful leader and a religious format which is somehow authenticated by the dominant culture of South Africa while relating to the immediate personal needs of a bewildered inhabitant of a vast, shapeless, anonymous new town.

The year 1963 was again the crucial date for a far more striking secession which took place in East Africa – that of the Maria Legio among Catholic Luo in western Kenya.[84] It was also the year of Kenya's independence. Numerous movements of religious independency had long been a characteristic element of the Kenyan scene, both among the Kikuyu in the centre of the country and among the Luo and other peoples in the west; but the year of political independence was to be also the date for the most numerous single new movement, and in some ways the most unexpected. For this was one whose origins were firmly within the Roman Catholic community – the only such movement, at least of any size, in East Africa and the largest in the whole continent. The leaders were Simeon Ondeto, an ex-catechist, and Gaudencia Aoko, a distraught young mother two of whose children had died on one day. The moment of origin of the Maria Legio was, it seems, the month these two spent together in April 1963. They then parted, Aoko to work in Central Nyanza and Ondeto in the south. While the former concentrated on mass baptisms, Ondeto set about building an institutional church with a hierarchy and a central headquarters on the sacred mountain of Got Kwer. By the end of 1964 the Legio may have had some 100,000 members and was developing a pattern of belief and worship which, while drawing heavily on its Catholic origins for vocabulary and symbols, looked increasingly similar to many churches whose roots were Protestant. While the original membership had largely come from Catholics or from people linked with the Catholic Church though still unbaptized, it drew its members and inspiration from many sides. Motifs of the Dublin-centred 'Legion of Mary' which had been so active in Kenya[85] were linked with the ritual retention of the Latin language (just about to be largely abandoned by the Catholic Church), titles such as 'Pope' and 'Cardinal', and a strong devotional concern with rosary and crucifix. 'We are still Catholics,' claimed Bishop Tobias Ayieta, 'although we don't have anything to do with the Roman Catholics, for we are Catholics in Africa and not Catholics in Rome.' Yet Maria Legio's preoccupation with deliverance from witchcraft, its healing services, its trances, prophecies and spirit possession, its avoidance of pork, smoking, drinking and dancing, its acceptance of polygamists, all suggest that its essential character is far from being decisively dependent on its Catholic origins. In many ways Maria Legio bears closest comparison with Lenshina's Lumpa. Each was a mass movement, without clerical leadership, erupting among the rural poor and spreading like wildfire among mission Christians and their neighbours amid the uncertainties of a period of political transition. Each urged withdrawal rather than acceptance of a new secular order. The Maria Legio had no time for the worldliness of schools and medicines any more than it had for the paraphernalia of African tradition. Prayer and not works was to be its concern.

The homeland of Maria Legio was the diocese of Kisii, but it soon spread to wherever the Luo were numerous – across the Tanzanian border in the district of North Mara and eastwards to Nairobi. It gained few non-Luo members. If it be asked why here and here alone the Catholic Church was the seed-ground for a major independent church, a few necessarily inadequate pointers towards an answer can be suggested. The number of nominal Catholics in the diocese of Kisii was particularly great in comparison with the number of priests: the 1963 statistics were 137,000 Catholics, 24,000 catechumens and 31 priests. That is to say, one priest for more than 5,000 people. Yet it was not a diocese in which new non-clerical patterns of ministry had been pioneered to cope with this practical breakdown of the customary Catholic structure. The emergence of unconventional leadership might be anticipated in such a state of vacuum where baptisms were very numerous but a regular ministry decidedly scarce. Secondly, there had already been a large number of independent churches among the Luo derived from Protestant missions. There must come a time when the power of example can draw not only Catholic individuals into Protestant derived churches but also produce new beginnings which are specifically Catholic. Thirdly, the moment of political independence could well be a precipitating factor within a situation which had for long been seething beneath the surface. Finally, there are aspects of the spirituality and small group organisation of the 'Legion of Mary' which naturally cohered with the sort of religious and social needs which are elsewhere met by independency, and this could well have provided the crucial lever which set the movement going – though in a direction which was soon characteristic, not at all of Dublin, but entirely of Africa.

If in the early 1960s Kenya was one area of continued new beginnings, Ghana was another. There had been a steady strand of independency in Ghana, including the Musama Disco Cristo Church since the 1920s and the Apostolic Revelation Society since the 1940s; yet all in all these were still in the mid-1950s neither numerous nor influential in the life of the country. It could be claimed that 1957, the year of independence, was the key date when this changed, and yet the impression remains that even then the growth in independency which followed was at first stimulated as much by external influences as by anything internal. A number of new small American missionary groups, fundamentalist and Pentecostal, entered Ghana in these years and while most made little lasting impression themselves, they stimulated some who joined them to set up similar churches of their own. Furthermore, there was a considerable Nigerian impact. A growing number of Yoruba coming to Ghana at this time brought their own churches with them so that Cherubim and Seraphim, the Church of the Lord (Aladura) and others were soon established up and down the country, recruiting further local members. Schisms quickly followed providing a number of native Ghanaian churches dependent upon the tradition of Aladura.

Probably the most substantial new Ghanaian church of this period was that founded by Charles Yeboa-Korie. Here too 1963 is the crucial date.[86] Its origins were fairly typical of many a small West Africa 'spiritual church'. Yeboa had been a Presbyterian; he was a young man in his early twenties who created round him a praying and healing circle. What began simply as a group quickly became a church with its own name and special claims. It was during one of his frequent fasts that Yeboa had a vision of a rich garden and a river flowing down on him. The river parted and over the garden was an inscription which read 'Eden Supreme Garden'. So it became the Eden Revival Church and later the Feden Church. The long night services of Eden with candles, water and incense, the exciting new hymns, the hand-clapping and dancing, the prayers of Yeboa over his patients – mostly women – all this was much like the services of many another little spiritual church – each as much a 'clinic' as a 'church'. But in the case of Eden this was greatly augmented from 1966 with a much wider range of churchly interests – a poultry farm, schools, a brass band and then a declared interest in large-scale evangelisation: 'Crossing Africa with Jesus' was the new motto. Yeboa had visited the United States and much of the new orientation stems from contact with American evangelical sects. Soon his church would be admitted to the Ghana Christian Council (the first independent church to be so) and would issue a formal credal statement. In all this Eden was illustrative of a wider tendency increasingly manifest by the later 1960s: the tendency of independent churches to re-acquire American or European links, to come very much closer in ethos to the smaller Protestant type of mission-founded church.

While this had been a common tendency, what is unusual in the case of Yeboa-Korie is the speed with which the whole process has happened. Nevertheless Eden remained a church whose focal point and major attraction was the hope of healing through the ministry of the strange, self-confident, almost mesmeric figure around whom it all centred.

The Congo (Zaire) was yet another part of Africa for which the early 1960s was a time of the most luxuriant multiplication of small sects.[87] Joseph

Diangienda and Lucien Luntadila had struggled hard from the mid-1950s to bring together all the streams of what can loosely be described as 'Kimbanguism' into the church they were founding, centred upon N'Kamba, Kimbangu's original village and the site of his miracles, to which the coffin containing his body, 'the ark of the covenant', was returned in April 1960. The possession of Kimbangu's body and the possession of N'Kamba were the two great strengths of the church of his sons, for almost everyone finally appealed back to Kimbangu with a unanimity which cannot but surprise. Even Simon Mpadi, himself a legendary figure in the long history of Congolese religious dissent, could only begin the apologia of his own church and mission with an account of the classic story of the work of Kimbangu while then going on to claim that 'the Prophet Simon Kimbangu confirmed entirely that the one who had been named by the father almighty was the Patriarch Mr Mpadi Simon-Pierre who is the great shepherd of Africa'.[88] Mpadi returned from prison in 1960, quite unwilling to be part of the Église of Diangienda, and established instead his own 'Church of the Blacks'. He was only one of many – if the most famous – who for one reason or another established their own little churches in the newly independent Congo. By 1966 some five hundred new churches had been founded, most of them exceedingly small. Some of these represented elements very close to the central Kimbanguist tradition – perhaps closer than Diangienda himself. Aged returned exiles who were unable to accept the leadership of the educated, urban young men who had never been in detention but now controlled the Église, formed little groups such as the Église du Christ sur la terre par ses Deux Témoins, Simon Kimbangu et Thomas Ntwalani. So one of the latter's founders, Thomas Duma, could declare, 'In 1921 I witnessed the dead rise, the blind recover their sight, the dumb speak in the name of Jesus'. He had been taken in the same boat as Kimbangu to the upper Congo. But a number of the survivors of that first age, Kimbangu's companions, did remain in the church of his sons – Pierre Ndangi, John Mayanga, Mikala Mandombe. They and N'Kamba itself and the prophet's earthly remains provided the basic ground of credibility and authentication for the new church, together with the deep African sense which has prevailed in church after church that spiritual authority passes from father to son. No other body could even begin to rival the EJCSK in its claims or its size, or – very probably – in the prudence of its leadership. While Diangienda set himself indefatigably to build up an ecclesiastical and educational organisation to rival that of the mission churches, his brother Dialungana Salomon presided over the holy city itself, its regular round of worship and pilgrimage. Based on N'Kamba, Africa's new Jerusalem, the appeal of Kimbangu's sons to their brother Bakongo was a weighty one:

We should follow the Scriptures, and the example of Jesus and the first believers, who never forgot that Jerusalem is the Promised City. But now many have bestowed prophethood upon themselves, and chosen pools for themselves, and set themselves up as the equals of Simon Kimbangu; and they dissuade others from going to Jerusalem, for they also have their holy cities, and their pools. But where in the Bible do you read about these cities and these pools? These are the Hills jealous of the Hill chosen by God, the New Jerusalem; and you know that God has rejected them.[89]

The religion of EJCSK was a highly disciplined, indeed puritanical one, firmly forbidding not only polygamy, but dancing, drinking, the eating of pork; it was emphatically non-violent, probably following in all these things the explicit position of the prophet. It was hardly any more a church of miracles, and only in a very restrained way, around the pool of N'Kamba, a church of healing; and it was a church whose claims about Kimbangu himself were increasingly careful. There could now be no doubt that for it the prophet was neither identified with, nor had he replaced, Jesus Christ; while Joseph Diangienda, its spiritual Head dressed in no special clothes, was an intensely hard-working and conscientious pastoral administrator, gravely authoritative but with rather little of the prophet about him.

The character of Simon Mpadi's church provided a striking contrast: a relaxed, flamboyant, jovial prophet, he appeared dressed in a rich red gown, with a crown on his head and a sceptre in his hand. His was a church of drums and dancing in which polygamy was in principle compulsory (a very unusual stipulation and hardly workable, at least for younger members), and where in the evening Mpadi would relate to the faithful stories of the great persecution, of the tribulations which he and Kimbangu had undergone, followed by the still more wonderful recital of his own fourteen resurrections. From Mpadi to Diangienda the Kimbanguist tradition was, indeed, a wide one.

The Église of Diangienda was to be found by 1966 in every province of Zaire, though its strongest presence remained undoubtedly around Matadi in the west. It was one of a score or so of independent churches which in various parts of Africa were by that date reaching a size, stability, and outreach not less than that of some of the more considerable Protestant mission-founded churches. The Christ Apostolic Church of Nigeria was certainly one of the most considerable of these. It had grown steadily and by 1966 had about 100,000 members and could survive without disruption the death of its major prophet, Babalola, in 1959 and that of its first president, Sir Isaac Akinyele, Olubadan of Ibadan for nine years, in 1964.

Another very considerable but not quite so stable a church did not so easily surmount the passing of its founder. Johane Maranke died in 1963.[90] No other Rhodesian church had spread so widely as his Apostles, the Vapostori, first throughout Rhodesia and then elsewhere. They entered Katanga, in the Belgian Congo, in 1952 and had reached Luluabourg (now Kananga) in Kasai by 1956.[91] This was Luba country, somewhat between the Kimbanguist world of western Congo and the Kitawala areas of the east, and the Vapostori soon became a solidly based little local community – some

181

5 per cent of the urban population, much the same as the number of Kimbanguists.[92] Ten years later there was a small Vapostori community even at Kinshasa, a group of Luba who had moved to the capital.[93] The maintenance of some sort of ecclesiastical unity within this community stretching among the poor from Rhodesia and Mozambique through Malawi and Zambia to some quite remote parts of Zaire was a difficult problem. The symbol and administrative instrument of unity evolved was the annual sacramental meal of the Passover, the Paseka – a sort of annual spiritual visit to Jerusalem for a church which did not stress a localised Jerusalem – which the founder or one of his close assistants endeavoured to celebrate in each main centre of the church. In fact Maranke was only able to enter Zaire to do this for the first time in 1963, just before his death. It was a memorable visit about which Zairean Apostles would sing for many years:

> The Congolese of the Kasii have intoned Hosanna
> At the arrival of John in Congo Kasai
> They have sung Hosanna to glorify God.[94]

While the maintenance of effective, or merely symbolic, inter-territorial links was undoubtedly a serious problem, the cause of the schism following Maranke's death did not lie here. It was, on the contrary, yet again the issue of whether a son or the elderly senior assistant of the founder is to succeed him. Maranke's closest confidant had certainly been his cousin Simon, but when it came to succession the family set Simon aside in favour of the founder's eldest son, Abero. This decision prevailed for the great majority of Vapostori though Simon's breakaway following, his own African Apostolic Church of St Simon and St Johane, was not inconsiderable. Doubtless rather little about such personal issues was communicated to remote congregations in Zambia and Zaire, and Abero was able to celebrate the Passover at six places in Zaire the following year.

If the Kimbanguist Église was without doubt the largest independent church in Africa by the mid-1960s, with at least half a million members, and the Vapostori probably the most extended, the largest in South Africa was now Edward Lekganyane's Zion Christian Church. It had been founded by his father, Enginasi, at Zion City Morija in the northern Transvaal.[95] Enginasi died in 1947 and since then the church had grown very large indeed; by the mid-1960s it counted some 200,000 members, a very powerful organisation and quite considerable possessions. Lekganyane's style of leadership was very much that of the chief, with his de luxe car, his bodyguard, and his secluded villa where he and his wives lived. Dressed in splendid uniform he can be seen in the photographs treasured by his followers above the title 'Edward Lekganyane, King – Chief – Messiah'. Lekganyane illustrates just one of the directions in which South African Zionism could turn over fifty years, a direction not unlike that of Mpadi in Zaire. One could contrast the history of the Zion Christian Church with that of the Amanazaretha of the Shembes in Natal. Isaiah Shembe was far more of a messiah than the first Lekganyane and spoke much less explicitly of Christ; but his son, Johannes Galilee Shembe, stressed the Christian character of his church far more, interpreting his father rather as did Joseph Diangienda his father Kimbangu. In the case of the ZCC the opposite happened and the son achieved not only great material and organisational success but orientated his church in a direction more personally messianic and less emphatically Christian.

Politically too the Zion Christian Church became a power in the land and besides the relief of its healing services and major pilgrimages, it was able to provide very poor people with some lasting sense of status, of belonging to a successful institution which they could publicly identify with and be proud of by the standards of this world. In its own particular, rather brash, way it reconciled the claims of the spirit with those of the present age, but that – after all – is what many a worldly church has done in every generation. If it was one of the least clearly Christian of Zionist churches, it was also the one that the South African government had favoured the most. It, at least, could feel the face of Verwoerd had shone upon it, and his Minister of Bantu Affairs, Dr De Wet Nel, actually visited Morija on Good Friday, 1965. Lekganyane presented him with a carved stick declaring in his address of welcome that it resembled the rod of Moses, for Dr Verwoerd's Minister of Bantu Affairs was indeed the new Moses who had led the African people and the Zion Christian Church out of bondage and into a land of freedom.

4
1967–1975

A. Church and State

I

The fifth of February 1967 marked a new beginning for Africa. It was the day of the publication by Julius Nyerere of the Arusha Declaration on Socialism and Self-Reliance, to be quickly followed by two further documents *Education for Self-Reliance* and *Socialism and Rural Development*. These together outlined the policy which Tanzania has consistently attempted to apply since then: a policy of rural socialism and village re-groupment; overall state control of the economy; a stress upon self-help, local or national, in preference to reliance upon the assistance of international agencies, whether capitalist or communist; deliberate restriction of affluence of the elite; the primacy of the interests of the masses, especially the rural masses; a working democracy structured upon a one-party pattern. They represented the most serious challenge yet made to independent Africa's flagrant failure hitherto to do other than perpetuate, and even considerably accentuate, the elitist structures of a divided society inherited from imperial days. They also represented Nyerere's personal thinking, faced by the poverty of Tanzania and the wider collapse of African political morale in the mid-1960s. The epoch of Nkrumah as the continent's prime guru was over and that of Nyerere had begun: far less flamboyant than Nkrumah, less ambitious in continental terms, more aware of the weakness of his own position, more realistically down to earth of the village where most Africans live and die.

Ujamaa has not been everywhere in Tanzania a popular policy, particularly not with the incipient capitalists of wealthier areas, and since the increasingly compulsory tone of its implementation after 1973. It could be that as a whole Nyerere's strategy will be judged less beneficial, more grievously maimed bureaucratically, than his apologists are willing to admit. But there can be no gainsaying its moral seriousness, the reality of the evils which it is designed to overcome and which are so manifestly rampant in many other African countries, Mwalimu's sustained commitment to a rather gentle, humane and personally non-acquisitive model of government, or the position of intellectual and moral leadership which he has attained not only in Africa but in the world: no African politician since Jan Smuts has achieved a comparable status within the international community.

Without the slightest doubt Tanzania's policies have been Nyerere's in a personal way that is true of the policies of very few governments, while Nyerere's vision has owed much to his own religion – a form of radical Catholicism. It is not for nothing that he lectures the bishops from the pages of the New Testament, draws their attention to the writings of Archbishop Helder Camara, or finds it worth his while to give a major address to the Maryknoll Sisters in New York. It may be that he is disappointed with the amount of practical support he has received from the churches. Nevertheless in few countries have relations between church and state been as good as in Tanzania, and the former has made it very clear that it fully endorses the Arusha principles. 'We can see very well,' the Catholic bishops declared in a joint pastoral, 'how closely it [the Arusha Declaration] agrees with the true spirit of Christ and the Church.'[1]

Tanzania is only one country of Africa and its policies have not been widely imitated elsewhere though Somalia followed a similar line from 1969 on. Nevertheless the Arusha Declaration and the ongoing policy of Tanzanian socialism has far more than a national significance: it has provided a moral flag for Africa in a period of coups, civil wars, brutal tyrannies and widescale aimlessness, and it has heralded a growing movement in the 1970s towards a far more strenuously socialist approach to the problems of society than was apparent in the decade of independence.

The wider immediate picture of 1967 was not that of a move towards socialism, but towards tough, dictatorial, often military, government as a rough and ready remedy for the growing strains and fissures of independent but also largely impotent, countries. The available resources of most African governments in the 1960s were very much more limited than had been anticipated, while their problems mounted menacingly. The western democratic constitutions and neutral civil service bestowed upon them as a birthday gift had no indigenous roots to speak of, and even the political parties which had been easily mobilised for the gaining of independence as easily withered when unsustained by any further high *raison d'être*. Each became only too easily a new expression of a regional, tribal or family promotion network, despite the high language and ritual demonstrations in the capital. Politics simply faded away in a sort of embittered derision – the banning of a multi-party system was followed only too naturally by the atrophying of the one party.

The very limited economic growth could hardly do more than attempt unsuccessfully to match the very rapid population growth, and a new stratification of black society – between the 5 per cent 'haves' and the 95 per cent 'have-nots' – became each year a little more glaring. The massive programmes for educational advance of the early optimistic years not only largely failed to achieve the target of providing most children with a significant degree of schooling, but could actually increase the wider social malaise by producing tens of thousands of half-educated youngsters for whom there was no work of a sort appropriate to the expectations the schooling had engendered. The general disillusionment with the failure of government to deliver the goods promised so facilely on the eve of independence turned to cynicism and hostility towards such groups as had apparently obtained a goodly measure of the loaves and fishes. One tribe or region might appear only too obviously to be now on top or on the way to getting there. Political and economic competition became a new and bitter expression of tribal or regional conflict.

At the same time the outside world, which had launched the new states with a smile in 1960, became increasingly uninterested in their needs except where its own profit or military strategy was involved. African political weakness encouraged both over-involvement of outside forces where something of profit was at stake such as Nigerian oil, and a weary disregard of the rest. Furthermore, there was the sheer pressure of technical breakdown growing year by year which explains much of the apparent chaos of the more up-country and backward areas in almost every state: the equipment installed at independence or shortly after was breaking down and there was a massive shortage of technicians to repair it, or of money to replace it. World inflation and the long drought in the Sahel compounded the problem of poor countries faced by 1975 with 50 per cent more people to feed, clothe and educate than they had had in 1960.

Faced with all this, 'left wing' or 'right wing' may appear at times as particularly meaningless categories to apply to government; nevertheless one may fairly distinguish between a minority which has seriously struggled with the colonialist inheritance of an elitist structure of society, whether or not out of a straight Marxist inspiration, and a majority which has wallowed in that inheritance. Class differentiation can take on a very strong regional overtone between favoured and neglected parts of the country, and many states have made some attempt to decentralise or otherwise counter the impression that the capital alone matters. In the long run, however, there has seemed little alternative short of anarchy to the uninhibited assertion in each country of a single authority, be its image that of army, party, or an all-wise father figure, 'the saviour of the country'. All in all it is perhaps surprising how many of the civilian leaders of the independence era were still ruling their countries at the end of 1975 – Ahidjo, Senghor and Houphouet-Boigny, Sekou Touré and Seretse Khama, Kenyatta and Nyerere, Kaunda and Banda. They remained, as a whole, Africa's more respected rulers.

Of course *force majeure* needs to be gilded and almost every government, however much it may start life with a straight military take-over, has felt the need to justify itself and its record by providing some form of ideological groundwork and doctrinal sense of direction. By the early 1970s this was taking two chief forms – one authenticity, the other Marxist socialism. The former opposes itself chiefly to the cultural imperialism of colonial times and insists upon a reassertion of African tradition in certain areas of life; it may coexist with heavy covert dependence on western capitalism and a 'right wing' position in international politics. The latter, which hardly appeared in Africa in the first years of independence outside Sekou Touré's Guinea, was spreading rapidly in the 1970s. While opposing the existing economic imperialism of western states in Africa, it is as critical of African tradition as of colonial structures. Its international links are with Russia, China and Cuba.

There are both military and civilian rulers in each category, and a trend towards totalitarianism – towards the elimination of all potential structures of opposition – runs right across the board. Hence, for this reason if for no other, both tend to come into conflict with the churches. The taking over of control of the national press, the disciplining of small but previously vociferous trade unions, the crushing of separatism, the humiliation of feudal chiefs – all this tends to leave the major churches as the only independent organisation of any weight in the country. The pattern has not been a universal one; Nigeria, in particular, remains much of an exception on account of its size, pluralistic ebullience, and a certain non-totalitarian pragmatism that successive central governments have evinced – but it is widely true. It is only the major churches which stand out, for the smaller ones have tended to go the way of other organisations – either banned or rather apolitically quiet. By the early 1970s quite a number of governments, notably that of Zaire, were somewhat ineffectually outlawing small independent churches just as many colonial governments had done in the past. They appeared both as possible fomenters of discontent and as being quite unable, on account of their small size, poverty and lack of overseas connections, to offer government anything very worthwhile in the way of cooperation or skilled but cheap personnel. Only the Kimbanguist Église in Zaire, the Aladura group of churches in Nigeria and some of the larger Kenyan bodies seem exempt from this predicament and these, in so far as they possess a political role, have one increasingly similar to that of the mission-connected churches. In general the political significance of the independent churches was far more slight in this period than in former ones, although they retained a potential (in government eyes a dangerous potential) for mobilising unrest among the very poor, whether urban or rural.

Overall relations between the state and the major churches remained decidedly good in a number of countries, particularly those in which the head of state was a convinced Christian. Zambia is a good example here. Kaunda has never developed an ideology or a practical policy which could severely alienate the churches; he trusts them but also expects their close cooperation. His regular six-monthly suppers with church leaders have given them a chance to approach him directly but the quid pro quo is that they never speak out publicly in criticism. The churches in fact have been gently harnessed to the ruling system and the Catholic Bishop Mutale even agreed to serve as a member of the commission for instituting a one-party state. Kaunda's very real Christian values and moderate policies, which make it possible for the churches to work with him so enthusiastically, are balanced by his acute sense of the realities of power. Without the intellectual original-ity or humour of Nyerere, Kaunda is something of his Protestant equivalent: glad to address the World Council of Churches at Uppsala or to open the All Africa Conference of Churches at Lusaka. A man of common sense and humanity (though his humanity did not extend to offering a refuge to the terribly persecuted Jehovah's Witnesses from Malawi), and very much a civilian, he is also a shrewd tactician who can use religious rhetoric and a gushing display of emotion in the pursuit of the most hard-headed of political objectives.

There are few countries where church leaders can expect so basically sympathetic an understanding as in Zambia or Tanzania. Almost every-where else they have had to watch their step increasingly warily. Young expatriates might cry out for the exercise of a 'prophetic voice' but senior churchmen knew only too well how easily they could overshoot their exer-cisable authority and disappear into the obscurity of exile or prison with next to no international outcry and the loss of whatever influence they had hitherto exerted. Yet despite a marked increase in tension church–state cooperation remained very considerable and while the state felt more and more the need to demonstrate rather loudly that it was the master, it also felt its own impotence and some reluctance to quarrel too irrevocably with its most reliable and understanding surviving friends. In these circumstances the churches have been able to retain in many countries both considerable institutional responsibilities and some ability to exercise a moderating or reconciling influence in moments of social and political crisis.

If there had been a widespread move to 'nationalise' Christian schools around 1960, it is probable that there would have been almost everywhere strong church resistance – particularly from Catholics – as was in fact the case in the Sudan and eastern Nigeria. But at that time few governments were anxious to do any such thing; when some ten years later the 'take-over' of schools did come in many countries, there was little conflict and in places church leaders actually encouraged it (for instance Bishop Trevor Huddles-ton in Tanzania). This was partly due to a recognition that the change was inevitable, that the church had no power to resist and should therefore yield with a good grace; but it was also due to a change in ecclesiastical priorities and attitudes whereby many churchmen had become genuinely convinced that the management of a vast school system was an undesirable burden bringing with it fewer and fewer religious benefits. A common philosophy about educational development shared by church and government underlay the take-over, a philosophy manifest in such works as Henry Makulu's *Education, development and nation-building in independent Africa.*[2] Hence the Kenya Education Act of 1968, the post civil-war nationalisation of schools in most states of Nigeria and similar developments in many other countries produced rather little friction between church and state. While in some places it did bring to an end any effective church activity in the educational field, outside specifically religious education, in many places there was more continuity than could be expected from the paper documents. This was particularly true in regard to Catholics – always more tenacious in this area than other groups – on account of their still considerable force of teaching sisters and brothers both indigenous and expatriate. Almost no government wished to be rid of such experienced and reliable teachers, but a continuity in personnel of this sort contributed considerably to a continuity in the ethos of important secondary schools.

In other fields too there has been much continued church–state partnership. Governments remained noticeably less anxious to take over rural church hospitals than rural schools, and the field of medicine has been one in which the institutional contribution of the churches throughout the period remained massive. Governments have also frequently encouraged the churches to launch out into new projects of small social development, the provision of urban hostels, as of schools for special categories of people, particularly the physically or mentally handicapped.

While ecclesiastical criticism of government policy, or even of the behaviour of middle level officials, almost inevitably produces strain, it remains the case that on many occasions churchmen have continued to provide something of a lead, even if they have come in as a result for, at best, a measure of passing abuse, at worst, exile, imprisonment or death. In Lesotho, politics in the early 1970s still retained a good deal of the denominational mould imparted in the 1950s; they were also highly affected by the country's proximity to South Africa. The post-independence government of Chief Leabua Jonathan and the National Party was predominantly Catholic in support and conservative in policy; it was also favoured by the government of South Africa. Its main rival, the African National Congress of Ntsu Mokhehle, was mainly Protestant, more radical, sympathetically linked to the black nationalist movements of South Africa. In 1970, when it appeared that Leabua would lose the elections, he declared a state of emergency, suspended the constitution and crushed the opposition. The press was stifled including the Protestant paper *Leselinyana* whose courageous editor, Seeiso Serutla, was imprisoned as were many of the political opposition. There can be little doubt that Leabua continued to enjoy the strong support of the core of the Catholic Canadian missionaries, but it seems clear also that the Sotho

189

Catholic clerical leadership had much less confidence in the wisdom of such a course. Archbishop Morapeli joined forcefully with the leaders of the other churches in expressing to the prime minister their dismay at the development of events.[3]

When in 1968 the Kenyan religious newspaper *Target*, whose editor was still an expatriate, bravely declared that the new party headquarters then under construction was a misuse of resources, all the churches hastily dissociated themselves from such a dangerous opinion. But when next year, under a Kenyan editor Henry Okullu, *Target* denounced the wave of Kikuyu oath-taking then in progress in an editorial headed 'Killing Our Unity', it did succeed in stirring the churches into adding their own protest, despite governmental condemnation of the editorial.[4]

When again, in February 1973 Archbishop Perraudin and the Catholic hierarchy of Rwanda protested against a new wave of anti-Tutsi violence, they were a move ahead of any public statement by the government in the same sense and Perraudin – in the past the great protagonist of the Hutu – was loudly denounced by some as a favourer of the Tutsi; but the Church's protest here as over the Kikuyu oathings was substantially accepted by the government.[5]

Time and again the difficulty is how to avoid the impression (or the reality) that the ecclesiastical voice is identifiable with that of a particular tribal or political group and can therefore be morally disregarded. The very fact that the political divide in Lesotho had a strongly denominational overtone made it easier for a Protestant paper's criticism of the actions of a Catholic prime minister to be somehow devalued. The close ties between the Presbyterian Church in Kenya with the political leadership of the Kikuyu, while other churches have a predominantly non-Kikuyu leadership, does not make it any easier for one church or another to speak out to the nation's conscience on vital issues which are closely linked with the Kikuyu political hegemony. When church leadership succeeds in speaking ecumenically (as it did in Lesotho in 1970, or as the Kenya Christian Council has managed to do) then this difficulty is to a great extent overcome – although it has to be admitted that inter-church statements seldom carry as much weight with rank and file church members as do purely denominational ones!

Mgr Albert Ndongmo, the Catholic Bishop of Nkongsamba in Cameroon, was condemned to death (though not executed) in January 1971 for countenancing the continued rebellion of the old UPC and allegedly participating in a bizarre plot by one Wambo to organise 'a spiritual coup d'etat' with the help of angels for the overthrow of the government. Ndongmo was a vigorous, somewhat naive man whose laudable attempts to reconcile the government with the rebels had drawn him into deeper waters than he realised. He denied ever taking Wambo seriously, but the ground of his disfavour with the government was undoubtedly the tribal resistance of the

Bamileke to the rule of Ahidjo. Bishop Ndongmo's fall is the more ironic in that, fifteen years earlier, the Catholic bishops of the Cameroon (then white) had been among the most inveterate opponents of the UPC.

There can be little doubt that Bishop Ndongmo was guilty of abetting the UPC rebellion. Another more distinguished churchman sentenced to prison the same month was probably guilty of nothing more than being an alternative source of authority, the representative of a wisdom other than that of a totalitarian government: it was Archbishop Tchidimbo of Conakry, arrested on Christmas Eve 1970 and sentenced to life imprisonment the next month on the charge of having taken part in a Portuguese attempt to overthrow Sekou Touré, a radical of the 1950s, one of the more ruthless and cruel of Africa's dictators by the 1970s.

In Guinea Sekou Touré faced the archbishop of what was locally a small church, though one with powerful international connections. In Zaire, the most Christian of black Africa's larger states, Mobutu was about to try conclusions with the archbishop of what was an extremely large and potent body. The Catholic Church in Zaire, despite a host of troubles of every sort throughout the 1960s, had remained both vast and very confident, with hundreds of local priests, thousands of missionaries,[6] many millions of adherents and a panoply of institutions. It was near inevitable that an increasingly dictatorial Mobutu should be resolved that the Catholic Church must be humbled, its wings clipped. The chosen context was the authenticity campaign officially launched in October 1971. The subsequent *Kulturkampf* between church and state in Zaire is one of the more significant episodes in modern African history.[7] Very comparable conflicts were taking place at much the same time in Togo, Dahomey (now Benin), Chad and elsewhere.

'We are now embarking on our cultural liberation,' declared Mobutu, 'the reconquest of our African, Zairian soul. We men of black skin have had imposed on us the mentality of quite a different race. We must become once more authentic Africans, authentic blacks, authentic Zairians.'[8] This appeal to 'authenticity' was employed as a unifying theme for the mobilisation of Zairians behind the government of Mobutu and for the humbling of the main institution which had hitherto remained somehow beyond the control of a state, which was becoming more and more intolerant of the least criticism or difference of opinion. While the Protestant and Kimbanguist churches also suffered (particularly in the later, more basic, stages of the *kulturkampf*), the chief assault of the government was undoubtedly directed against the Catholic Church, in practice because of its far greater power, in theory because its dependence on Rome introduced an inauthentic element into the country: 'I have never had trouble with the Protestants or with the Kimbanguists, because they never received directives from abroad.'[9]

The first open conflict came early in 1972. It concerned the introduction of the party's youth movement into all major and minor seminaries, the enforced conversion of Christian baptismal names into Zairian names, the nationalisation of the Catholic university of Lovanium and the closing down of various other church institutions. Under pressure from the Vatican anxious to appease Mobutu, Cardinal Malula went into temporary exile and was stripped of the National Order of the Leopard. In November all religious youth organisations were suppressed, to be followed in February 1973 by all thirty-one confessional newspapers and periodicals as well as the Catholic radio and television services. The bishops were forbidden even to meet.

There were three levels of conflict. The first was a personal one between Mobutu and Malula. The cardinal, a remarkable man, had been a person of influence already as a young priest in the early 1950s; he had been a bishop in the capital since a few months before independence and archbishop since 1964. He had now become the one and only alternative figure of major national authority. By 1972 the cardinal, whose outspoken remarks had already provoked the president on various previous occasions, had not only the almost complete support of his fellow bishops but may also have had strong backing from within the army.[10] There can be little doubt that this irked Mobutu considerably and he was resolved to cut Malula down to size. In this he was assisted by the Vatican and even, it seems, by the American and Belgian ambassadors, all most anxious to stave off a major confrontation which could conceivably have proved too much for Mobutu.

Beyond this was the institutional issue of the Catholic Church's position in the country and the deep resentment that decades of insensitive clerical power had produced in many a Zairian.[11] In 1971 there were still far more pupils in church schools than in the state network (1,849,484 primary children as against 414,602). The whole church structure from village to university looked too much like a state within a state; it constituted a challenge which could hardly be overlooked indefinitely. In no other country was government faced with a comparable ecclesiastical leviathan – and the scale of its power did much to produce the scale of the measures taken against it. But then we come to the third level – the particularly totalitarian character of the government party, the Mouvement Populaire de la Révolution, its developing ideology, and religious vocabulary. Small independent churches had already been proscribed; political opposition of one sort and another had been ruthlessly suppressed; now it was the turn of the major churches.

There was a respite in the first part of 1974. The bishops were permitted to meet and Cardinal Malula was even able to present a memorandum on their position to the president. They were starting to talk of dialogue, accepted all that had hitherto been imposed on them, and now set themselves to redirect their work within the new cultural and institutional context of authenticity. Hardly had this begun, however, than a new and unexpected wave of attack

192

swept over them. In June 1974 it was announced that Christmas would no longer be a holiday; the 25 June would be one instead. Next, all crucifixes and religious pictures were to be removed from every public place, including schools and hospitals, and every course of religious instruction, except the course on Mobutism, was to cease. The tone of government statements at this time took on a harsher tone:

> The missionaries, who came in the name of a certain Jewish child in order to make known a God who was no different from the one taught to us by our ancestors, have refused to recognise our right to teach God in the name of a son of our country (Mobutu) sent to us by our ancestors.[12]

Again,

> God has sent us a great prophet, our wondrous Mobutu Sese Seko. This prophet is shaking us out of our torpor. He has delivered us from our mental alienation. He is teaching us how to love each other. This prophet is our liberator, our messiah, the one who has come to make all things new in Zaire. Jesus is the prophet of the Hebrews. He is dead. Christ is no longer alive. He called himself God. Mobutu is not a god and he does not call himself God. He too will die but he is leading his people towards a better life. How can honour and veneration be refused to the one who has founded the new Church of Zaire? Our church is the Popular Movement of the Revolution.[13]

Behind the conflict over institutions there was now only too clearly a conflict about basic religious loyalty, about what it could mean to be a Christian in Mobutu's Zaire, but – as often happens – hardly were such issues formulated than they were shied away from. 'The radicalisation of the revolution' launched in December 1974 was undoubtedly influenced by Mobutu's visit to China; linked to Zaire's economic crisis and internal unrest, it might have taken him anywhere if it had really got under way. The church, it appeared, might make a convenient whipping boy to divert popular attention while many things were undertaken. A year later, however, Mobutu's increasingly grave position, challenged by the defeat of his Angolan allies, Holden Roberto and the FNLA, helped to bring about a change of direction and some rebuilding of bridges with the Church. The Chinese vision had faded rather fast. On 24 November 1975 Cardinal Malula was once more instated in the National Order of the Leopard, and fifteen months later the schools would be offered back to church management. In practice it was, perhaps, too difficult to do without the church: its supporters were too numerous, its expertise too valuable. The university might be nationalised but Bishop Tshibangu continued as its rector and in many lower institutions much the same thing happened. The church was learning to live with dictatorship on a basis of saying little and waiting for each storm to pass.

Some dictators might be still more difficult to live with than Mobutu. In Equatorial Guinea, whose less than half million population was two-thirds

Catholic, President Nguema, 'Great strength and only Miracle of Equatorial Guinea', according to the constitution, expelled the bishops and the missionaries and tortured or massacred the country's more prominent citizens with an almost unparalleled impartiality. No less than two-thirds of the members of the National Assembly set up in 1968 at the moment of independence had been sentenced to execution within the next few years, while a quarter of the total population is estimated to have fled the country. With all priests dead or in prison and the country's two cathedrals turned into warehouses, the church has been outlawed as nowhere else in Africa.[14]

What was happening in Uganda seemed at times little less horrific. General Amin came to power in a coup in January 1971, overthrowing Milton Obote. The style of his erratic and barbarous government was not at once apparent and many people who had disliked his predecessor's fairly gentle autocracy at first warmly welcomed the change. Obote had been most unpopular with the Baganda since the overthrow of the Kabaka in 1966. Amin solemnly received the Kabaka's body back from Britain. There was a splendid funeral in Namirembe Cathedral and Baganda Christian leaders waxed warm in support of the new ruler. The massacres which soon took place among his army opponents (or potential opponents) were largely overlooked. Benedicto Kiwanuka, in prison at the time of the coup, was made Chief Justice and for a time struck up a much publicised friendship with this jovial giant who was so quick to appeal to religion and to conscience. In September 1971 they sat down together to a luncheon party at the Grand Hotel in Rome with Cardinal Villot and Catholic missionary leaders, and a dozen Verona Fathers expelled from the north of Uganda by Obote were permitted to return. In the Anglican Church of Uganda the general set about mending the near schism which had broken out between the Buganda dioceses and the rest, for which purpose he called together a somewhat bizarre religious conference in Kabale.[15]

Equally unpredictable but far less amiable sides to his government soon, however, became uncomfortably apparent. People fell under suspicion and quickly disappeared until an atmosphere of terror was prevalent. The economy declined with the expulsion of the Asians and new scapegoats had to be found for the growing misfortune of the country. Amin, himself a Muslim, pushed the Muslim community forward, encouraging converts from Christianity to Islam to the further embitterment of the Christian majority. In September 1972 Benedicto was seized from his office and murdered; the next month the president announced plans to 'Ugandanize the churches' and in December fifty-five Catholic priests were expelled for not holding valid entry permits. Still more seriously, in wave after wave of assassinations many of the country's most distinguished citizens disappeared. Father Clement Kiggundu, the able and courageous editor of the Catholic daily *Munno*, was killed in his car in January 1973. In this situation, as in so many others, the

194

churches had little alternative but to endeavour to sit out each storm as calmly as possible.

The dictatorship of Dr Banda took far less startling and original forms. It was nevertheless remarkable in combining high sapiential claims and a rigidly puritan code of morals with all the machinery of a one-party state in which the slightest criticism could be punished with exile or detention. Here again the churches found it wise to adopt an increasingly low key. Even so the joint Christian Service Council, which had been doing much quiet good in various fields of social work, had to be dismantled in 1975. But it was the Jehovah's Witnesses who provided the regime's chief religious victims.

Witnesses await the imminent return of Christ to establish the Kingdom; in the meantime they see all governments as an expression of the power of Satan and, while willing to pay taxes and keep the peace, they refuse to participate further in political life – to join a party or vote, to sing the national anthem or salute the flag. It is not surprising that they are unpopular with governments, particularly young governments sensitive to any slight. In Africa Witnesses are most numerous in Zambia and Malawi and Nigeria; in most other countries they are very few.[16] Several independent governments have banned their activities but where they are not numerous they can fairly easily be overlooked.

In Zambia this was not so for their numbers have been very considerable both on the copperbelt and in Luapula province, and by 1967 they appeared to be offering UNIP and the state much the same sort of challenge provided by the Lumpa Church a few years earlier. They almost wholly lacked, however, the aggressiveness of Lenshina's followers. Nevertheless UNIP youth were soon hounding them in many places and during the latter part of 1968 forty-five Kingdom Halls were burnt down and much other damage done. Some Witnesses were killed and many more fled to the bush. At this point Kaunda stepped in, put a curb on the party hardliners and reasserted a very deliberate policy of tolerance. The Witnesses offered no real threat to good government; on the contrary their hard work and punctuality in tax paying were a noticeable asset, and their persecution was profoundly unjustified. Tension slowly diminished and, despite some subsequent conflicts at a fairly local level and the expulsion of foreign missionaries working with the Witnesses, Zambia adhered to its tolerance of an awkward group which would not toe the party line, except for its cruel refusal to provide an asylum for sorely pressed Witness refugees from Malawi in 1972 and again in 1975.

The attitude of the government of Malawi has been vastly less tolerant; first in 1967 and then almost continuously from 1972 the Witnesses were harried with mounting brutality by the Malawi Congress Party and its tough boys in the Youth League. They were denied legal protection, excluded from all employment, their homes were burnt, and dozens were murdered. After a vain attempt to find refuge in Zambia some 36,000 fled in 1973 to

195

Mozambique, where their apolitical attitudes were just what the Portuguese authorities liked to see in Africans and so they could settle undisturbed. The coming of independence changed all that. Frelimo had no time for small, intransigent apolitical churches and the Malawian refugees were forcibly repatriated in August 1975 to instant persecution.[17] The aim of the appalling bullying to which they were now again subjected was, in the words of the party manager, 'to make sure that each of them buys a Party Card. This is the only way ... we could show our appreciation to our Life Leader, the Ngwazi, for developing this country of Malawi.' It is notable that neither the Catholic, Presbyterian or Anglican Church thought it right to make public protest against these quite appalling procedures and yet, if the fate of the unfortunate Witnesses in Malawi reminds one, from some points of view, of that of Lenshina's disciples in Zambia a decade earlier, from another point of view it is not so dissimilar, on a very small scale, from what was happening institutionally to the Catholic Church in Zaire. Will the church, or will it not, 'buy a Party Card'? Whether great or small, any independent church is a potential threat to the new Leviathian and to whatever little *Duce* is here idolised.

The churches are faced with very special problems when a state breaks apart in open civil war. There were three instances of this which we need to consider during these years – those of the Sudan, Nigeria and Burundi. The war in the southern Sudan had dragged on for many years, the government controlling the main towns, the Anyanya most of the bush. While this was by no means a straight religious war, yet the leadership of the south was largely Christian in inspiration while that of Khartoum was almost wholly Muslim and the government's unification policy, to which the south so strongly objected, had so many Islamic overtones to it that Christianity had become increasingly a part in the southern right to be different for which they were fighting.

The former Catholic missionaries in the south had nearly all been Italian Verona Fathers and through the years there was continuous support for the southern cause in Italy; elsewhere there was little until Israel took up the matter quietly but forcefully for political reasons of its own. The main Protestant missionary society previously involved in the area, the CMS, tried for long to hold a rather neutral position. A massacre of some fifty Balokole (Protestant revivalists) in a little church just over the Zairian border in July 1970 and the eye-witness reports of survivors was one of the factors which helped to change this; from then on there was an increasingly vocal church and humanitarian lobby for the southern cause, but it had been long in coming. While it did some valuable work in getting medical supplies through from Uganda it was never a major factor in the war, as it had been in Nigeria. On the government side General Nimeiry had shown himself anxious to offer the south a new deal from the moment he came to power in May 1969. The long conflict drained the resources of a very poor country, the army was manifestly proving unable to achieve a military solution and after Nimeiry's break with Russia, the time was ripe for a major compromise. The Addis Ababa negotiations of February 1972 were assisted by Canon Burgess Carr of the All Africa Conference of Churches and led to a remarkably sincere reconciliation based on a wide measure of regional autonomy, but this was really made possible by the effective stalemate and a realistic recognition that neither side could wholly win.[18]

The Nigerian case was very different. The year 1967 began with a final fruitless meeting between Lt Colonel Gowon and Lt Colonel Ojukwu at Aburi in Ghana. By that time Ojukwu was set upon independence for eastern Nigeria and Gowon was immovable upon the basic issue of the country's unity. One of the most delicate and widespread problems of independent Africa was to be put to the arbitration of prolonged war: are the admittedly arbitrary boundaries of colonial times to be maintained inviolate or can various smaller areas claiming a historical or cultural identity of their own break away into independence? The claim of Biafra had been that of Katanga as of Buganda. Could the rest of Nigeria survive as a unity if the east were gone? And could such further balkanisation of the continent be anything but disastrous in face of the wider game of world power pressures? The claims of Biafra seemed strongest when viewed most apolitically in the context of their own consciousness and of the horrible massacres Igbos had suffered in other parts of the country during 1966, weakest when viewed politically in the light of the needs either of Nigeria or of Africa.

On the 30 May 1967 Ojukwu declared the independence of 'the Republic of Biafra' and in July the fighting began. After an initial brilliant Biafran offensive aimed at Lagos which took Benin in August but lost it in September, the federal forces slowly closed in, captured Enugu and – after a very long battle – Onitsha in March 1968. At that moment the war seemed nearly over. Instead it continued for nearly two more years as the Biafrans clung to their highly populated heartland around Umuahia and Owerri with fierce determination and a growing weight of international support (particularly French) feeding the enclave through an epic use of Uli air strip. Resistance only broke down in January 1970 after two-and-a-half years of continuous fighting.

There was something almost mystical about the Biafran endeavour; its fusion of hope and fear, the evolution of its national, cultural and religious consciousness across one thousand days, hovering anxiously between the dread of genocide and a near millenarian belief in the virtues of 'the Biafran Revolution' and the advent of a new Israel, half heaven half earth, among the hills and towns of Igboland. 'Holy Archangel Michael, defend us in battle' prayed Ojukwu in a midnight broadcast,[19] rescue us 'from Muslim

197

Hordes', 'from the clutches of Hausa–Fulani imperialism'[20] as Biafra purges itself of every trace of 'Nigerianism'.[21] He was supported by a splendid team. Cyprian Ekwensi and Chinua Achebe threw themselves into the work of the National Guidance Council conducting cultural seminars throughout the country, while Sir Louis Mbanefo and Dr Akanu (Sir Francis, until he repudiated the title on the grounds of Britain's support for Nigeria) Ibiam – twin pillars of Christian and professional respectability – presented the Biafran case to a sympathetic world.

The involvement of religion and the churches in the Nigerian civil war was so considerable and complex that it is hard to do justice to its many facets, particularly as it was vastly over-played in Biafran propaganda. In bringing about the conflict it was surely less important than in the Sudan, yet far from negligible: the sense of Christian identity of the Igbo and the increasingly aggressive pushing of Islam by the most powerful man in the country, the Sardauna of Sokoto, premier of the north, prior to his assassination in January 1966, were important factors in producing the crucial breakdown of confidence between the federal government and the east. There were millions of Christians upon the side of the Federation during the war and in no conceivable way can Gowon's government be justly dubbed a Muslim one (though it frequently was), but it must be said that the Christian Gowon had failed to exorcise the ghost of the Sardauna in the minds of Christian Igbos, terrified by the massacre their relatives had undergone in the north in May and October 1966. Ojukwu played incessantly upon this theme: 'Our Biafran ancestors remained immune from the Islamic contagion. From the middle years of the last century christianity was established in our land. In this way we came to be a predominantly Christian people. We came to stand out as a non-Muslim island in a raging Islamic sea.'[22] While the churches endeavoured time and again to exercise a ministry of reconciliation, this was rendered ineffectual by the pressures both of power and of mythology.

While there was little sympathy in eastern Nigeria before the war between the political and intellectual leadership on the one hand and the powerful Irish Catholic missionary body on the other, the experience of encirclement produced here a common interpretation of Biafra's predicament and a profound fusion of loyalty. Biafra became not only a self-consciously Christian but also (at least in the imagination of some) an almost Catholic country, whose self-understanding and public propaganda fell into a quite recognisable pattern of stereotypes with which Irish priests above all could feel as at home as a duck in water: David against Goliath, the little Christian island, the Muslim threat, British betrayal. Protestant missionaries found it far harder in their hearts to swallow an 'Alhaji Wilson' demonology.

The material needs of beleaguered Biafra were vast indeed, and they were effectively publicised to the world as few such needs in modern Africa have been. It was inevitable that the churches, as well as the International Red

Cross, should see this as a challenge and that the more hesitant should find it hard not to lose face if they failed to take the pace of the most committed. A wide series of church bodies, mostly coordinated in Joint Church Aid (JCA – sometimes nicknamed Jesus Christ Airlines), set about a humanitarian airlift on a scale which would have been unthinkable had there not been major political and economic interests also involved. While the achievement was remarkably ecumenical, it is not open to question that it was the Catholic *Caritas* and the Irish missionary lobby which kept up the pressure most uncompromisingly. The JCA made over 5,000 relief flights and seventeen of its pilots were killed.

While the purpose of this immense operation was charitable, it worked on both sides of the frontier, and was in principle neutral, it could not really be accepted in that way. It is not only that the supply of so much relief was having a significant political effect (at least in lengthening the war!) and that it is highly unlikely that the relief planes never carried weapons as well; it is not only that every appeal for a ceasefire from the church bodies concerned (such as the Vatican and the World Council of Churches) really presupposed the acceptance of the Biafran case for a separate national identity; it is that very many of the people most involved were quite uninhibitedly committed to the Biafran point of view and the rightness of the struggle for independence. This does not mean that it was wrong to give aid, but it has to be recognised that the giving of very substantial aid in a civil war is necessarily a political action. The natural response from the federal side was an increasingly bitter, often ill-informed denunciation of 'Humanitarianism'.

Christians were in a relatively small minority in northern and western Nigeria, though they provided much of the leadership in the federal government. It was, doubtless, a justified feeling that the very existence of Christians in Nigeria outside Igboland seemed to be almost ignored by the international ecclesiastical lobby which produced among some a veritable fury of reproach; thus Professor Idowu could describe the mild and saintly Anglican Archbishop Patterson as personally 'one of the tragedies of the Church in Africa . . . so bold in his diabolic machinations against the Church of God and against this country'.[23] Upon both sides Christians were caught up within a complex tissue of political, cultural and religious issues, national and international, which they were mostly unable to see through. It is the more commendable that there were doves remaining upon each side, and the more remarkable how quick and genuine the post-war reconciliation proved to be.

In some ways the much publicised intervention of missionaries was a help here: they could be and were made scapegoats for much that had happened, much more than they were really responsible for. The Irish priests who had committed themselves heart and body to the Biafran cause with a devotion which Igbos are unlikely to forget were rounded up and expelled ignomini-

199

ously, while Nigerian Christians upon each side found themselves, fortunately, able to forgive if not to forget. While it may be argued that government policy has been colder to the churches and their schools in the 1970s then it might otherwise have been, the fact is that within post-war Nigeria church–state relations have proved harmonious enough and that the nationalisation of schools is something which might well have taken place even earlier had it not been for the civil war.[24]

When Rwanda and Burundi became independent in 1962 the former was disturbed by repeated conflict between the Hutu and the Tutsi, while the latter appeared at first to enjoy a certain intertribal harmony.[25] In each country the Hutu were well over 80 per cent of the population, but in Burundi the division had been less sharp socially and there was much more intermarriage. As a consequence, while the clearly segregated Tutsi minority lost political power in Rwanda even before independence, in Burundi there was no immediate revolution and apparently no need for one. Despite tensions, not only between the two groups but also within the Tutsi, there were fair prospects that an increasingly non-tribal system of government would be established in which the majority could exercise its proper weight. Two of the prime ministers of the period – Pierre Ngendamdumwe and Joseph Bamina – were Hutu and in the general election of May 1965, 80 per cent of the seats were won by Hutu. The effect of this was disastrous. Real power remained in Tutsi hands; they saw the writing on the wall clearly enough if any form of democratic government continued and the consequence was a series of Tutsi reactions for long masked in one way or another. In this process the more moderate Tutsi of the north were increasingly ousted by a more uncompromising group whose strength lay around Bururi. A bloody repression of Hutu leaders in October 1965 (131 were executed including Bamina), was followed by the coups of 1966 which brought Captain Micombero to power and a steadily increasing polarisation of the country. By the beginning of the 1970s it was becoming clear that, in contrast to Rwanda, Burundi had developed as a black racialist state in which effective power was systematically monopolised by the small Tutsi minority.

On 29 April 1972 there was a sudden uprising of Hutu peasantry in the south responding to a refugee invasion from across the Tanzanian border. It was to some extent planned but most poorly organised. As a challenge to the central government it was a complete failure, but as a wild uprising involving the indiscriminate murder of opponents it rendered havoc in those parts of the country affected. Three to four thousand people were killed, among them apparently not more than a thousand Tutsi – for many Hutu were killed who refused to join in the revolution or who offered protection to fleeing Tutsi. The reaction of the government was one of violent and prolonged repression of the Hutu all over the country. It began with the

200

areas immediately involved and with political leaders, all the Hutu members of the cabinet included. Wholesale massacre of the Hutu continued day after day throughout May and much of June; in some places it had not ceased even in August. At least 100,000 and possibly 200,000 people were exterminated in this way – almost the whole elite of a small society. It was probably the only atrocity in recent African history which can without exaggeration be described as genocidal. While in many places the slaughter was quite indiscriminate, the victims were above all the educated – civil servants, professional people, teachers, nurses. Hutu society was to be systematically rendered once for all leaderless that it might continue as peasant serfs but no more. Nearly three hundred nurses and medical assistants thus perished, as did forty to fifty per cent of all the pupils of secondary schools. Of 4,580 Catholic catechists in the country, at least 2,100 were put to death; of 35 Anglican priests 15; of 138 Catholic priests 18 (but that was a high proportion of the number of Hutu priests). Among the dead was Father Michel Kayoya, a brilliant young Hutu author of two very beautiful and perceptive books. He was executed without trial on 17 May on a bridge above the Ruvubu and his body buried in a common grave with many thousands of others.

Burundi is statistically the most Christian, and the most Catholic, country of black Africa – the Catholic Church alone claims nearly 70 per cent of the population among its adherents. Throughout the repression the two Hutu bishops were under house arrest and the church's voice was expressed by Archbishop Makarakiza of Gitega and Bishop Ntuyahaga of Bujumbura, both Tutsi, though they spoke in the name of the whole hierarchy. Essentially, and lamentably, it was a voice which sanctioned and identified with that of the government. Time after time, in the weeks after 29 April, they spoke out to blame 'butchers' interfering from outside the country; they condemned people taking the law into their own hands but they deplored 'exaggerated rumours' about what was going on. Even on 12 August they could still say, 'It would be wrong to see the problem as a classical instance of internal politics, a conflict between Hutu and Tutsi. It is rather a diabolical plot to deceive the people in order to foster racial hatred . . . there are those who, under the pretext of protecting the little people, are grossly biassed in favour of one tribe.' At no point did the bishops criticise the actions of government or suggest that the Hutu uprising was a consequence of the intolerable injustice to which the majority in the country was being subjected. In the words of a confidential remonstrance sent by the superiors of the foreign missionaries in the country to the bishops: 'The Bahutu will never forgive the hierarchy for having allowed their most prominent people to be massacred without breathing a word.'

The tragedy of Burundi was in a way unique, yet it provides something of a horrific mirror in which to view the wider continent, some sort too of infernal parody of South Africa. If South Africa is arguably the most Christian country of the white world, Burundi is of the black. In each a racial minority of under 20 per cent ruthlessly controls the economic and political system of the country, reducing the 80 per cent to near serfdom. And in each the ecclesiastical leadership of major churches could be effectively encapsulated within the dominant elite. While lip service was regularly paid to the ideals of charity, reconciliation and justice, in hard terms this leadership proved wholly unable to do other than participate in the privilege of ethnic and class power, to challenge the underlying presuppositions and mechanisms of oppression. It cannot be said that throughout black (or white) Africa church leadership had uniformly followed so blinkered a line as it did in Burundi, but there is a very widespread and growing pattern of involvement of ecclesiastical authority with economic and political privilege. Church statements tend to be bromide at home, a ringing challenge to the Christian conscience abroad. The Christian witness that counts and costs, here as in the white south, is most often that of the individual: Michel Kayoya, Clement Kiggundu, Zedechias Manganhela. Such men are almost without protection. No international lobby proclaims their name as it does Beyers Naudé or Bishop Lamont. They rise and are cut down in the bloody tumult of the age as many a martyr has ploughed his lonely furrow across the murky frontiers of mankind's perennial barbarism.

II

Until at least the close of 1971 the impression of unchallenged white mastery throughout southern Africa established after Sharpeville remained overwhelming. Black political opposition had been successfully suppressed in South Africa and Rhodesia; economic sanctions had failed to break UDI and it seemed incontestable that Smith's calculated risk had succeeded brilliantly. Guerrilla attacks had made little impact – they were a subject of derision in white Rhodesian circles – and the British government was only too anxious to find any honourable way out of the impasse. While the application of apartheid rolled ruthlessly on within South Africa, Vorster was extending the 'outward' policy Verwoerd had begun of establishing friendly relations, through the offer of economic aid, with a number of black African countries, Lesotho and Malawi in particular. Thereby he further enlarged the network of power whose centre was Pretoria. Military links between South Africa, Rhodesia and Portugal had increased, and if the Portuguese were not managing their wars in Angola and Mozambique with startling success, they also did not appear to be anywhere near to losing them. In Angola indeed the liberation movements were clearly in some disarray, while since General Kaulza da Arriaga arrived in Mozambique in 1969 there had been a major reorganisation of the Portuguese defence strategy against Frelimo. The erection of a giant dam at Cabora Bassa on the middle Zambezi with international capital to supply electricity principally to the Rand became for friend and foe both proof and symbolic expression of a single variegated economic, political and military order based upon the principle of white supremacy and extending from Cape Town to the Zambezi.

The settlement proposals agreed upon between Sir Alec Douglas-Home and Ian Smith late in 1971 for ending the Rhodesian deadlock appeared likely to put the finishing touches to this picture, bringing a seal of constitutionality to the government in Salisbury. What else was there to do? Almost no well-informed observer at that time expected any significant change in the balance of power within the forseeable future. Black-ruled Africa was far too divided, poor and chaotic to challenge the white south, while internally its governments seemed firmly in control. And yet this whole picture was about to crumble stupendously.

While it can well be agreed that the Home–Smith proposals were in their content a betrayal of black interests by the British government, they nevertheless included the vital provision that they must be found acceptable to the majority of the African population. To gauge this the Pearce Commission arrived in Rhodesia in January 1972 and soon concluded that black majority opinion was dead against. A new body, the African National Council presided over by the Methodist Bishop Muzorewa, had hastily been formed to fight the proposals and the weight of support for the African National Council was unmistakable. In these circumstances the British government felt unable to go ahead with the settlement, so that the real if quite unanticipated effect of the whole exercise was to restore a public African voice and a large measure of confidence. On this issue at least they had won.

At the same time in neighbouring Mozambique Frelimo was making marked progress both in the far north and in the province of Tete.[26] The war was moving steadily south and east. By 1971 they were operating in force south of the Zambezi close to the Rhodesian border. By the end of 1972 the scale of Frelimo's presence all round the town of Tete provided the context for the appalling massacre by Portuguese army units of more than 400 villagers in Wiriyamu, Chawola and Juwau, only a few miles outside the town, on 16 December. A year later the war was approaching the port of Beira. Effectively the Portuguese army had lost control of half the country and knew it; at the same time the cruelty of its repressive response to the ever-growing support the people gave to Frelimo caused an international outcry and a major crisis with the Catholic Church. The Portuguese plight in the small West African colony of Guiné-Bissau was equally bad. It was the military situation in these two countries (Angola had ceased for a time to be a major worry) which was the basic factor behind the army coup in Lisbon in

203

April 1974, bringing an end to Caetano's government and fifty years of the Salazarist system.

The repercussions of the coup in southern Africa came thick and fast. While the provisional government of Spinola, or some of its members, still wished to temporise or at least spin out the process of decolonisation, this proved practically impossible. The situation had already deteriorated beyond remedy. The army was refusing to fight further and Portugal's African institutions were simply melting away. Guiné-Bissau's independence was recognised already in August; Mozambique became independent in June 1975 and Angola the following November. While P A I G C was able to take over Guiné-Bissau and Frelimo Mozambique through a peaceful governmental transfer, in Angola the division between three liberation movements – M P L A, F N L A and U N I T A – and the weakness of all three brought the country instead to disintegration and civil war. South Africa stepped in to assist Jonas Savimbi of U N I T A, while Mobutu was supporting Savimbi's half-ally, Holden Roberto of F N L A, and Russia and Cuba were backing their old friends the M P L A. If the latter held the capital of Loanda but neither the Bakongo area of the far north, nor the highly populated centre of the country around Nova Lisboa (Huambo) where U N I T A had strong links with the Ovimbundu, South African assistance proved to be the kiss of death for Savimbi and 1975 ended with M P L A pressing forward with its Cuban allies to decisive victory and the greatest humiliation South Africa had suffered for many years.

Meanwhile in Rhodesia Smith too had been forced to recognise the winds of change, at least so far as to release Nkomo, Sithole and other nationalist leaders from detention, and to begin a series of fruitless negotiations. As his determination not to accept any early transition to majority rule grew ever more obvious despite much pressure to be conciliatory from Vorster, Kaunda and almost every other part of the globe, the guerrilla war began again in earnest all down the long border with Mozambique. Rhodesia was in a state of near siege and its early conversion into a black-ruled Zimbabwe seemed by the end of 1975 to be next to inevitable.

South Africa alone had not been so immediately shaken by this startling series of events, but here too major change was now in the air and the 'Black Consciousness' movement was revitalising the African will to challenge white domination. Try as he might to protect his frontiers with a newly invigorated policy of 'Detente', Vorster could not prevent a vast psychological change coming over both blacks and whites in his country. The white power system all around him had manifestly broken down. His intervention in Angola had proved a fiasco; a radical black government was now ensconced just over the border in Maputo (formerly Lourenco Marques). The scene was inevitably set, even in the heart of white-ruled Africa, for a new and wholly unpredictable era of confrontation, reform or revolution.

The relentless struggle between the apartheid state, now directed by Vorster with a minimum of sensitivity and a maximum of realism, and a dissenting Christian minority continued throughout these years. The leadership here was taken less and less by church hierarchies. There was a steady drift among the latter particularly within the Anglican communion towards the safe and the apolitical, polite ecumenism and the new but not dangerous frontiers of pentecostalism. The only major figure who offered battle from the ranks of the hierarchy was Archbishop Denis Hurley of Durban. A born South African, a very young bishop already in 1950 and not an old one in 1975, he was a man of courage, of intellectual power, international reputation and liberal conscience. A zealous participant in the second Vatican Council, a President of the South African Institute of Race Relations and a highly vocal critic of government policy, Hurley became in many ways the natural successor to Archbishop Clayton. The 'Call to Conscience' which he and the Catholic hierarchy issued in February 1972 was probably the best spelt-out major statement on justice in South Africa to come at any time from any ecclesiastical source. It was indicative of the way that even in Protestant South Africa the Catholic Church was beginning to assume the mantle of political leadership. If Hurley was the guiding mind behind this, he suffered too from a weakness similar to that of Clayton – the intellectualism of the middle-class cleric, almost unable to cooperate intimately with black people or to apply liberal theory effectively even within his own diocese. He was less of a threat to the state than the angry and involved Franciscan, Cosmas Desmond, who so wholly identified with the most wretched of apartheid's victims suddenly removed from their little homes located in an area now designated white and dumped like rubbish in the wilderness. He described their ill-treatment with harrowing factuality in *The Discarded People* and was placed for his pains under rigid house arrest. The importance of Desmond lay in the clarity and moral power of his challenge to government policy over a specific issue, effectively this lasted a very short time; that of Hurley rested rather in the virtues of the long haul and in a capacity after periods of apparent ineffectiveness to return unexpectedly to the charge, with very considerable authority.

The most powerful theological assertion of the incompatibility between South African policy (indeed much that is central to the 'South African way of life') and Christianity is to be found in the *Message to the People of South Africa* published by its Council of Churches in September 1968.[27] Apartheid, it declared, involved 'a rejection of the central beliefs of the Christian Gospel'. To this Vorster replied in his own direct and unambiguous manner: 'Cut it out immediately, because the cloth that you are wearing will not protect you if you try to do this in South Africa.' The implications of this warning became very clear in the next few years. If bishops were becoming less willing to stick their necks out, a small but not inconsiderable minority of lower clergy was now more willing to do so than had been the case in the past. Some were associated with the theologically and politically radical group called the University Christian Movement; others were working with the Christian Institute of Beyers Naudé; some, like David Russell of King William's Town, were pretty much on their own. As a whole they represented a far more ecumenical and actively inter-racial group than anything that had appeared earlier in South African Christianity, and a major concern was to stimulate specifically African thinking and action – the Black Theology and Black Consciousness movements which were now gathering momentum.

The government's determination to break this whole development was provided with a congenial weapon to hand in the World Council of Churches grants to liberation movements for non-violent purposes which were first announced in 1970. The grants produced a heated controversy continuing for years not only in southern Africa but in churches throughout the world. For some people their justification was next to self-evident; for others they were clear proof that the World Council had been taken over by Marxist agitators or had, at least, wholly lost its way through an over-concern for the secular.[28] While the needs of bodies like Frelimo for money for medical and educational purposes cannot seriously be doubted, nor the practical value of the WCC grants – though their size was quite limited – the main point was a symbolic one: a public recognition by the church that the liberation movements had a right to be there, that is to say that black people had a right and a duty to take the amelioration of their conditions into their own hands even if – where they were denied constitutional methods of reform – this meant violent revolution.

From the viewpoint of the South African government the grants were an ideal instrument for dividing the sheep from the goats. The leadership in some churches, notably the Presbyterian and the Anglican, came out in strong condemnation of the grants,[29] so reinforcing their basic sense of where they finally stood, while more radical clergy who, like almost all Africans,[30] found themselves unable to do this, could now rather easily be proceeded against as crypto-Marxists threatening the security of the country. In 1971 the government set about systematically eliminating troublesome clerics while church leadership looked passively on. Between 1957 and 1967 there were twenty-five cases of church workers against whom the state had taken action (such as deportation, withdrawal of residence permit, refusal of passport, etc). From 1968 to 1972 there were eighty such cases, fifty of them being in 1971. It was the year in which Cosmas Desmond was banned and Dean ffrench-Beytagh of Johannesburg arrested and tried.[31] The result of this campaign was a very much more docile church in which for a while only one institution retained the will to do more than formally protest: the Christian Institute. It was forced to pursue an increasingly lonely course as a voice from the heart of Protestant South Africa and even from

Afrikanerdom (its growing links with Catholics did not alter that, though they added yet another ground for indictment).[32] The significant history of the church–state relations in these years came as a consequence to be focused upon the struggle of the state to crush the Institute, the last foyer of effective dissidence.

In 1972 a 'Commission of Inquiry into certain organisations' was set up, soon to be known by the name of its chairman as the 'Schlebusch Commission'. The organisations were the National Union of South African Students, the South African Institute of Race Relations, the University Christian Movement and the Christian Institute of Southern Africa. The UCM, a less cautious organisation than the Christian Institute, was anyway about to collapse from internal tension, and the other two bodies were not church-linked. While the attack upon them was also of importance, that which now developed upon the Christian Institute and its director, Beyers Naudé, had a special significance because of the meticulous care and theological precision with which Naudé consistently formulated his position. On account of the Commission's non-judicial character, its secretness and the apparent pre-judging of issues, Naudé refused to testify before it. For this he was brought to trial and convicted of breaking the law.[33] In 1975 the Commission finally declared the Institute guilty of supporting 'violent change' (despite the known pacifism of Naudé), that is to say of promoting the supposed aims of the WCC.

Effectively the Christian Institute was isolated and almost broken by these blows, its strength remaining little more than the single undaunted figure of Naudé. But just at the same time the Council of Churches of South Africa regained its sense of purpose with its Methodist secretary John Rees backed by the Dutch Reformed theologian David Bosch and the Lutheran Axel Berglund. It was appreciably strengthened in 1975 by the adhesion of the black Dutch Reformed 'Kerk in Africa'. Working more closely with the Catholic hierarchy than ever before, a wide new, more realistic and genuinely South African, less paternalistic or denominational, leadership was here being forged; but it could certainly not count on any large-scale ecclesiastical support.

In August 1974, at a meeting in St Peter's seminary, Hammanskraal, of the South African Council of Churches, the Rev. Douglas Bax proposed a resolution, seconded by Naudé, asking its member churches to invite their white members to consider the moral duty of conscientious objection.[34] It was a courageous counter move to the moral and patriotic emotionalism whipped up in reaction to the World Council grants and was bound to produce a further outcry. 'I want seriously to warn those who are playing with fire in this way,' declared the prime minister, 'to rethink before they burn their fingers irrevocably.' His brother, Dr J. D. Vorster, Moderator of the General Synod of the Nederduitse Gereformeerde Kerk, added that the

207

South African Council of Churches was 'playing into the hands of leftists', while Edward Knapp-Fisher, Anglican Bishop of Pretoria, rejecting the resolution said that 'to suggest that our society is so unjust that no one can be justified in taking up arms to defend the country seems to be ill-considered and unwarranted'. He was joined by leaders of the Presbyterian and Methodist Churches.

In October 1974 a new law came into force providing savage punishments for anyone encouraging conscientious objection to service under the Defence Act. Bill Burnett, Anglican Archbishop of Cape Town, and the Catholic bishops protested strongly if unavailingly against the bill. In the Hammanskraal resolution, as so often before, it was not just the government but still more the white churches which had been challenged – and precisely those churches which had so emphatically rejected the World Council grants on the grounds that violence is wrong: could they then recognise that white violence is wrong too?

By 1975 the Christian Institute, the Council of Churches and their few friends stood very isolated. If in the view of a very few white South Africans, very many black South Africans, and vast numbers of people abroad, Naudé stood for Christ and his opponents, from Vorster down, for most unchristian policies, this was simply not how the vast majority of white South African Christians – English-speaking or Afrikaans-speaking – saw the matter. For them South Africa was no worse than any other country, the Christian Institute was making mountains out of molehills, and if not communists they were the dupes of a communist view of the world. Vorster, on the other hand, was a statesman of integrity, a sound Christian with the Moderator of the chief church in the land as his brother. 'We cannot thank God enough for a Government which is aware of, and strives to fulfil, its christian duty,' declared the Chaplain General, the Rev. J. A. van Zyl in 1973.

Van Zyl was a member of the Dutch Reformed Church but the view of the majority of English-speaking churchmen was not significantly different. Their churches thrived within the upper echelons of apartheid society and were compromised at every turn by a deep mental and institutional collusion with its presuppositions and its mechanisms. Their protests against racial injustice were of marginal significance; their promotion of black men to positions of church authority little more than rural window dressing. With eleven diocesan bishops in the country the Anglican communion still had only one black one, in Zululand. Of some twenty-five Catholic diocesan bishops only two were black and they were newly appointed in Bantustan areas. For the rest the bishops lived elegantly in the more affluent of the white suburbs gently deploring the sins of the government and the blindness of their Dutch Reformed brethren. When in 1971 the boys of the white Anglican Diocesan College of Rondebosch voted by a large majority to admit the son of the Rev Clive McBride, a coloured priest of the diocese, the governing body could not agree. In 1970 five black Catholic priests declared in a bitter protest that 'the Roman Catholics pretend to condemn apartheid and yet, in practice, they cherish it'.[35] The elderly, cautious and highly experienced rector of St Peter's Hammanskraal, Fr Oswin Magrath, had to admit next year that for the majority of white priests in the country there is 'support of, or acceptance of, or at least compromise with, a state of vast injustice, and a basically schismatic tendency of refusal of full community with the majority of Catholics in the country'.[36] It was as true of the Catholic bishops as of the Catholic priests and it was the same in every church. The men who struggled to manifest the face of Christ condemning the massive barriers of oppression and brutality and the vast divide between the complacent affluence of white Christians and the crushing poverty of black Christians, were a mere handful. For the churches as a whole it is not unfair to end with the judgement of the Rev Theo Kotze, Director of the Christian Institute in Cape Town. With Beyers Naudé and Roelf Meyer he had signed the crucial statement on Divine or Civil obedience which brought them to trial. 'If blood runs in the streets of South Africa it will not be because the World Council of Churches has done something but because the churches in South Africa have done nothing.'

In Namibia (South West Africa), occupied by South Africa by reason of the original mandate of 1920 and subsequently partially incorporated into the Union in defiance of international opinion, conflict between the churches and the state has taken a direction of its own, especially since the International Court of Justice gave its opinion in June 1971 that South Africa's presence in Namibia is illegal. The country is ecclesiastically unique in Africa in that over half the black population are Lutherans, and this gives the African heads of the two churches concerned – Bishop Auala (of Ovamboland) and Moderator Gowaseb (of Windhoek) – a very special authority. The same month as the International Court's judgement they published a remarkable open letter to Vorster upon the injustices practised in the country and it is a measure of their importance that on 18 August Vorster actually consented to meet them together with other Lutheran Church leaders. No comparable encounter could take place in South Africa.[37]

The Lutherans have been more than backed up in their rejection of apartheid and all that goes with it by the far smaller Anglican diocese, whose clerical leadership has been mostly white and from outside the territory. Here alone the radically anti-racialist Anglican tradition of earlier years has been unequivocally maintained. As a consequence three of its bishops have been expelled – Robert Mize in 1968, Colin Winter in 1972 and Richard Wood in 1975; so have a very large proportion of its white personnel together with a number of Lutheran missionaries. In Namibia, on the other hand, Roman Catholics (apart from one fairly forthright pastoral letter of the Bishop of Windhoek in Lent 1972) have done little to give a lead. There can be little doubt that the government set itsclf quite deliberately to crush the independent voice of the Anglican Church in Namibia and that the latter received only the most subdued support from sister dioceses. Yet that voice was not silenced, due largely to the single-minded obstinacy and flair for publicity of Colin Winter, who continued as bishop of the diocese in exile. A disciple of Bell, Huddleston and Scott, he carried into the 1970s an Anglican voice strongest in the 1950s, but he combined it with the more radical politics of his own day in fully supporting Namibian nationalism.[38]

As Mozambique and Angola were constitutionally constituent parts of Portugal, the Catholic Church in them was regarded and treated as an extension of the church in Portugal. It was both greatly controlled and greatly privileged by the terms of the Concordat and Missionary Agreement of 1940. While the archbishops of Lourenco Marques had been unhesitating believers in 'the policy of amazing tenderness with which the State has treated this church' as Salazar described it,[39] Dom Sebastian Soares de Resende, the bishop of Beira – like Mgr Ferreira Gomes, the bishop of his home diocese in Porto – had been a tenacious, if inevitably cautious, critic and opponent. He had been bishop since the erection of the diocese in 1943 and there was no man who had greater stature in Mozambique. He had gathered round him a group of like-minded Portuguese priests and he consistently backed the foreign missionaries, particularly the White Fathers, whom he had invited into his diocese. His diocesan newspaper, the *Diario de Mozambique*, was the only more or less free paper in the country. In January 1967 he died; the Governor General attended his funeral but the censorship banned publication of the funeral oration.[40]

During the following years the offensive of Frelimo was making progress in the north and was receiving growing support from Africans throughout the country. To counter this the army was greatly reinforced while the activities of the PIDE (later DGS), the political police, grew more and more ruthless and ubiquitous. Inevitably the churches, and in particular the small number of African priests and the large number of non-Portuguese missionaries throughout the country, were forced to reconsider their position. Their catechists and teachers were being arrested, beaten, even killed on the slightest of pretexts,[41] so that missionaries who had come to the country with almost no political consciousness were pushed into recognising the anachronistic character of the Portuguese colonial system and its disastrous consequences for the church, and into protesting first against individual acts of injustice and later against the whole system. For the first few years of the war they remained almost surprisingly silent, despite the complete ravaging of the missions in the northern dioceses, but in 1968 a group of twenty priests from different societies addressed a letter to the bishops'

210

conference upon 'the necessity of facing foursquare the problem of the liberty of the church in Mozambique'.[42]

Until 1967 Mgr de Resende had somehow acted as a safety valve – a very senior bishop in whom the missionaries had confidence and who could speak out for African interests from the vantage point of high ecclesiastical authority. While the young bishop of Nampula, Mgr Manuel Vieira Pinto, soon adhered to the same line and in a more outspoken manner, he did not carry the same weight, and as the war advanced bringing with it more and more horrors the consequence was confrontation not only between a growing group of missionaries from several societies and the state, but also between the former and the hierarchy.

In Beira the new bishop, Dom Manuel Ferreira Cabral, followed a policy the very opposite to that of his predecessor, even selling the diocesan newspaper, hitherto so immensely respected by Africans, to its greatest enemies, a group of white businessmen of the extreme right wing, not unconnected with the D G S itself. Soon the diocese was in a state of extreme crisis, with heated demands for his resignation. In May 1971 the thirty-two White Fathers in the country, most of whom worked in Beira diocese, decided to withdraw as a group, unwilling to work further in a situation where they found such an intermingling of church and state. In the words of their Superior General Theo Van Asten, writing in Rome:

We wanted, we asked and for a long time we waited for the hierarchy to take a definite stand to dispel these ambiguities in face of injustice and brutality. Faced with a silence which we do not understand we feel in conscience that we have not the right to be accounted the accomplices of an official support which the bishops in this way seem to give to a régime which shrewdly uses the Church to consolidate and perpetuate in Africa an anachronistic situation, which in the long run is a dead end.[43]

When this unprecedented decision to withdraw was announced – causing something of an international sensation – the Fathers were expelled at forty-eight hours notice by the political police together with Mgr Duarte de Almeida, who had been Bishop de Resende's most trusted adviser and editor of the *Diario de Mozambique*.

At just this time the war was engulfing new areas in the province of Tete and two Spanish missionaries of the Burgos Society – Fathers Alfonso Valverde and Martin Hernandez – stationed at Mucumbura found more and more of their parishioners being murdered by the forces of the state as they wildly reacted to the incursions of Frelimo. The priests protested frequently, providing detailed evidence, both to the bishop and to the governor in Tete, but nothing was done. Finally they drew up a desperate appeal entitled *Mucumbura 1971 and the Rights of Man as recognised by Portugal in UNO*. Clear and unambiguous, it published names, dates and the precise unit of the Commandos responsible for the massacre of the villagers. It was signed on 28 November 1971 by the two priests and three nuns at Mucumbura. Its

211

attempted circulation produced the arrest of the priests on 2 January and their detention for nearly two years untried in the concentration camp of Machava at Lourenco Marques. The same week two Portuguese diocesan priests, Frs Joaquim Sampaio and Fernando Mendes, were also arrested in Beira for protesting in a sermon on World Peace Day against the barbarities that were going on. Held in prison for a year they were finally brought to trial and acquitted, only to be deported back to Portugal.[44]

In the course of 1972 the situation further deteriorated. In June a large number of Protestant leaders, particularly those of the Presbyterian Church, were suddenly rounded up and placed in Machava. Among them were their most senior pastors, men like Zedequias Manganhela, the sixty-year-old president of the synodal council, and Casimir Matie, vice-president of the synodal council, aged sixty-four. The government had always feared the political influence of the Protestant churches and many of Frelimo's leaders had in fact a Protestant background; now, with the security situation of the country near to breakdown, the D G S aimed a blitzkrieg at the Presbyterian Church from which Mondlane himself had come. Many were subjected to prolonged interrogation and beatings. On 11 December Manganhela was found hanged in his prison cell. Probably as a consequence of the embarrassment this event produced – the elderly pastor was well known in Swiss Protestant circles and an unlikely political agitator – most of the rest were released.

Only five days later a commando unit carried out what was possibly the largest single atrocity of the war – the massacre of Wiriyamu. A few survivors took refuge in the mission of San Pedro, on the outskirts of the town of Tete, run by two Spanish priests and an African, Domingos Ferrao. They resolved to draw up a report of what had happened in and around Wiriyamu that 16 December and present it to the bishops. The work was completed by 6 January, including a list of 180 victims, mostly women and children. The scale of the atrocity was such that the hierarchy felt bound to register a protest with the Governor General, which it did on 31 March. Neither the protest nor the non-committal reply were published at the time and few people even knew of their existence. Certainly it was not adequate response on the part of the church to one of the major atrocities of the twentieth century, and one carried out in the name of a government claiming high missionary and civilising purpose and most intimately linked with the Church. Yet it was extremely difficult for the missionaries to do more without episcopal cooperation; even to get copies of the report out of the country was not easy. Its publication in the London *Times* in July 1973 with the authorisation of the Superior General of the Burgos Fathers, just prior to a visit of Caetano, produced an international storm which severely damaged the reputation of his government and undoubtedly contributed to the crumbling of the Salazarist regime both in Portugal and in Africa[45] – somewhat as

212

the news of the Hola Camp massacre contributed to the crumbling of British rule in Kenya and My Lai to that of American intervention in Vietnam.

The protests of priests and nuns, not only about Wiriyamu but about the whole system of Portuguese colonialism, continued to multiply and so did the deportations. Finally in April 1974 the government expelled none less than the bishop of Nampula together with eleven Verona Fathers who had, with many others, signed a statement calling for the recognition of the justice of the aims of the liberation movement and an end to the Concordat.[46] Hardly a fortnight later Caetano's government fell and the political geography of southern Africa embarked upon a kaleidoscopic change. If it had not fallen, what would have happened next in the escalation of church–state confrontation it is impossible to say; what is certain is that the support of the church had long been a crucial pillar in the Portuguese colonial system and the bitter battle with a section within the church, plus the constant adverse international publicity which this produced, were significant factors in bringing about the fall. It is reasonably certain that the liberation movement would finally have won in any case, but the Lisbon coup might well not have come when it did had it not been for the ecclesiastical and international pressures which had been so considerably fuelled by a fairly small but very vigorous group of Catholic missionary priests.

While Frelimo appreciated the efforts which a minority of priests had made in the struggle for justice and while many of its ordinary members were devout church goers, the attitude of its leadership remained profoundly critical. Eduardo Mondlane had been assassinated in 1969 and his successor, Samora Machel, had imbibed a fairly doctrinaire Marxist critique of religion which was only too obviously applicable to much in the traditional Catholic role in Mozambique. Having come to power he had no intention of changing his tune. His message on Independence Day 25 June 1975, was a lengthy policy statement in which he scathingly berated the churches: 'Religion, and especially the Catholic Church, was a powerful factor in the cultural and human alienation of the Mozambican to make him a docile instrument and object of exploitation and smash any display of resistance in the name of the christian resignation.'[47] Church schools and comparable institutions were immediately nationalised and, while very few missionaries were forced to leave, many who had identified themselves with former policies naturally did so without delay. But it was the very small churches – such as the Church of the Nazarene, the Church of the Apostles in Mozambique, the Ethiopian Church of Portuguese Africa and, of course, the Witnesses – which most felt the early weight of Frelimo's hand. A number of missionaries expelled by the Portuguese authorities were able to return, including Bishop Pinto of Nampula, who was chosen to be chairman of the episcopal conference. Together with the new African archbishop of Maputo (formerly Lourenco Marques), the new Christian Council and the new African bishop of the

213

Anglican diocese, he had the task of somehow steering the churches through one of the most delicate situations they had experienced anywhere in Africa.[48] Nowhere else had the central ecclesiastical system been so closely identified with colonial oppression; nowhere had political change come more swiftly and nowhere was a new kind of society more vigorously pioneered. The leaders of the church were for the most part wholly unprepared for a change not merely in government but in the total pattern of social priorities and in the very substructure of the relationship between church and society.

In Angola the Catholic voice of protest had never been nearly so strong as in Mozambique (in part, perhaps, because the missionary body had been more predominantly Portuguese), while if the Protestant churches were more considerable here, their voice had largely been suppressed since the events of 1961. The Catholic bishops tried to adjust to the new situation with a cautious declaration issued in July 1974 but, despite the theoretically very high proportion of Angolans who are Catholic, Catholic influence on developments has been minimal throughout.[49] There were church sympathisers for all three parties in the civil war of 1975 but the decisive links here were probably more ethnic than anything else. MPLA, the most widely based of the contenders, had the mass of black Catholic sympathy as also that of Methodists in Loanda, but there was much Methodist support too for UNITA – particularly from the United States which had provided the Methodist mission in the past. FNLA had drawn much of its leadership over the years from Baptists in the north and the long years of exile in Zaire had tended to reinforce the Bakongo/FNLA/Baptist sense of identification. The massive return of several hundred thousand refugees from Zaire to Angola beginning towards the close of 1974 was at once a return of the Baptist Church and an establishment of FNLA domination. The FNLA defeat a year later was not followed by a new mass exodus. The people and the church remained, if apprehensive enough about their relationship with the new government of Dr Neto. For them, as for the churches throughout Angola and Mozambique, a new era was opening – exhilarating in that they had at last an Angolan and black government, alarming in that it seemed more influenced by a fairly doctrinaire Marxism than anything which had yet appeared on the African continent. Unlike the Catholic Church, so predominantly white and foreign in its ministry, the Baptists, like the Methodists in Angola and the Presbyterians in Mozambique, had at least the advantage of facing the new winds with an almost entirely indigenous ministry.

Across the Rhodesian border church–state relations had a very different ethos and past history from those of Mozambique; what is striking, nevertheless, is how by the 1970s they were taking on an increasingly similar pattern under the pressures of racial confrontation.

Up to about 1970 there was something of an ecclesiastical consensus in Rhodesia. Church leadership regularly criticised individual injustices or even major acts of policy such as UDI and it urged racial harmony, but it hardly questioned the basic presuppositions and structures of white political leadership, which indeed it paralleled within the church. While each church had its left and its right, Catholics, Anglicans, Methodists and the Christian Council all spoke at leadership level with much the same voice; and it was becoming a steadily clearer voice. The culmination of this process was the churches' response to the proposed new constitution in 1969, in many ways markedly more racialist and oppressive than that which it was to replace. The Catholic bishops declared in June that they had to 'reject and publicly condemn' it,[50] while Protestant leaders united to affirm that 'these proposals to entrench separation and discrimination are a direct contradiction of the New Testament'.[51] The white electorate nonetheless accepted the proposals by a vote of 73 per cent. As a consequence the Catholic bishops in a further Pastoral decided to renounce the 'honourable and fruitful tradition of understanding and cooperation which has hitherto existed between church and state in Rhodesia' because 'discriminating laws have . . . been enacted which are contrary to the christian faith'.[52]

It was at this point that the parting of the ways really came, not only between church and state but between the churches themselves and even within them. On one side all the churches, very much including the Catholic, had for decades largely accepted a racial discrimination within their own life on grounds of convenience, and this was supported by an overwhelming majority of the white laity and many of the clergy. The Rhodesia Front, full of church members and riding high with numerous political victories, was less and less inclined to be defied by the more liberal or radical section of the clergy; if the near silent African majority was growing increasingly alienated from both government and those churches which offered words but few deeds, white Christians were mustering the determination to bring their own church leadership into line – after all, they provided most of the church's financial support.

At this moment the issue of the World Council grants to liberation movements burst into prominence as a catalyst for polarisation. The radical Rhodesian Council of Churches, with a black majority, actually supported the grants, while the Anglican bishop of Mashonaland, Paul Burrough, strongly condemned them. The Bulawayo Council of Churches was forced to disband early in 1971 when it became clear that it no longer retained the support of a single English-speaking congregation.[53] The Anglican bishop of Matabeleland, Kenneth Skelton, who had just declared that 'Justice is more important than law and order' resigned under pressure in the middle of 1970 and left the country,[54] and from then on the Anglican leadership took a steadily more pro-white line: willing to take up individual injustices but not to question the basic constitutionality of Smith's government. Everywhere pockets of resistance were being eliminated. Thus the inter-racial agricultural community at Cold Comfort Farm, successor to St Faith's, was crushed at the end of 1970: the Clutton-Brocks were expelled from the country and Didymus Mutasa, the son of John Mutasa who had joined his father's friend in the new community, now joined many others of his race in detention.[55] Outspoken missionaries, such as Fr Traber, the editor of the influential Catholic vernacular newspaper *Moto*, were similarly deported. White Christians of all denominations, led by the Anglican priest Arthur Lewis, began denouncing the 'Marxist' influence in the World Council of Churches, and in church leadership both in Britain and Rhodesia.[56] The Catholic Chichester Club even requested the Pope to remove Bishop Lamont, the outspoken chairman of the episcopal conference, and a wider campaign in the press was mounted by Catholics against the bishops in general.[57]

At the same time the political situation was steadily deteriorating, while the guerrilla war had begun anew and in earnest. By 1975 it was clear that any sort of ecclesiastical common line had gone for good. Some black church leadership, headed by Bishop Muzorewa, tended towards more or less total identification with the liberation struggle; most white Protestant leadership had pulled back under pressure from its white pews to a fairly safe and wholly ineffectual position. The Catholic bishops, led by Bishop Lamont, had done neither. With far more considerable resources than any other church and less dependent on white society, they had stuck to their guns as the most forceful independent critics of government. Their clergy, predominantly foreign and wholly unmarried, tended to be far less identified with the settler population than, for instance, the mostly married Anglican priests who came out from England with wives and children and soon became part and parcel of white society (though English Jesuits, too, tended to identify far more in this way than did Spanish Burgos Fathers or Swiss Bethlehem Fathers). The very clericalism of the Catholic system rendered it rather less vulnerable to local settler pressures than that of other churches, so too did its strong consciousness of being one team with men working across the globe. By 1972 the new 'Justice and Peace Commission' spearheaded the critique of government brutality as the armed struggle gained momentum.[58] Their reports received the widest international publicity through the effective cooperation in London of the Catholic Institute for International Relations.[59] The staying power and systematic effectiveness of the Catholic Church once it had made up its mind to challenge racialism and injustice was becoming manifest here, just as it was in Mozambique.

All the same the overall achievement remained limited, both on account of the ambiguity of the church's own internal practice, and because of a basic inability of the bishops to face up to the inherent moral rights of a liberation movement challenging a ruthless and oppressive minority government which had refused for years all peaceful change.[60] They really had little meaningful advice to give Africans, while increasingly Africans were looking for deeds not words, for a major change of law not a well worded protest. When the African National Council was founded late in 1971 to fight the Home–Smith Settlement, Bishop Muzorewa of the fairly small United Methodist Church was chosen as its chairman. It was a sensible selection at a moment of national crisis when all the regular political leaders were either in detention or exile. Bishop Muzorewa demonstrated remarkable skill, patience and tenacity in holding the African National Council together over the next three years and in refusing to be intimidated or driven off course by the government. The position changed dramatically with the coup in Lisbon, the release of Joshua Nkomo and Ndabaningi Sithole, and the increasingly turbulent politics of 1975. Muzorewa found himself quite unable to hold the various groups together, moved for a while from Rhodesia into exile and became identified with a single section of the nationalist movement. It may be that his own political expertise was inadequate to grapple with the intricacies of the issues he had now to face; he had become one of a number of rival contenders for political power and in the process had sadly lost his original *raison d'etre* as a nationally acceptable bishop-in-politics in a time of emergency. However, his tenacious adherence to the goal of full political liberation (the establishment of black rule) with the minimum of violence may well be seen as the sanest stance for a Christian to take in what had become a desperately tricky and mountingly horrible situation.

The pitfalls of the church's involvement in the political field are here as manifest as the value of the role which Muzorewa bore during and well after the Pearce Commission. If there had been more senior black ecclesiastical leadership in the country, so much would not have been expected so impossibly from a single man. The range of options through Arthur Lewis and Paul Burrough to Donal Lamont and Abel Muzorewa – all intensely sincere men – demonstrates once more the complexities of theoretical model and practical priority confronting the churches at a time of acute ethnic confrontation and the breakdown of acceptable government.

III

By the end of 1975 it was clear enough that Africa and its churches were entering a new, unchartered sea and that many of the issues, supports and certainties they had lived with through the post-independence decade had now to be left behind. The hard frontier separating white-ruled from black-ruled Africa was no more. Mozambique and Angola had passed from one side of it to the other. The immediate future of Rhodesia and Namibia was a question mark. South Africa itself was only a few months from the Soweto riots. Here indeed the foundations had been shaken, but in black Africa the outlook was almost as unpredictable. Its political figurehead for so many years, the Emperor Haile Selassie, was no more and in Amin's Uganda Archbishop Luwum was about to be arrested and murdered. In Nigeria and Ghana, however, the military governments would be pressed to return to democratic and civilian government of a western kind. New winds could take the church in quite different directions: towards retreating into the catacombs in Sekou Touré's Guinea or Nguema's Equatorial Guinea, two singularly unhappy states, but towards resuming major institutional responsibilities in the field of education in other countries, where the value of ecclesiastical cooperation, efficiency and morale was increasingly recognised by governments with many headaches and few friends to turn to.

It is impossible to generalise in such conditions, still less to predict the future. But two major challenges of these years deserve to be underlined. The first is that of the new wave of radicalism. While what has been described as 'Africa's second independence' could take different forms, its general character has been largely determined by three things: first, the growing recognition that the governments of black Africa have done very little in the post-independence decade for the common man while the privileged position of a small minority has been steadily enhanced; secondly, the rather evident fact that the white-ruled south has been steadily abetted in deed if not in word by the western powers, at least until the Portuguese revolution of April 1974; thirdly, Marxist ideology.

While the churches felt rather little immediate effect from Africa's first independence, it is certain that the case must be quite different with the second, because unlike its predecessor it is concerned to alter underlying social structures – structures which the major churches have very much taken for granted. Even in Tanzania, where the 'second revolution' has come rather gently with some sort of continuity out of the first, the social gap between the Catholic Church's traditional structure based on the large mission station and the new world of Ujamaa has become increasingly apparent.

Hitherto organised Marxism had been a relatively secondary factor in most parts of the continent. For some years Somalia, Guinea and Congo (Brazzaville) were countries whose political attitude was characterised either by an alliance with Russia or China or by a definite profession of Marxism. They were not, however, very important countries, at least from the viewpoint of the church. Somalia was wholly Muslim and Guinea predominantly so. In the latter the small church had indeed been under painful pressure, but in the Congo, the most important of the three, a quite harmonious *modus vivendi* had been maintained, not unlike that of another socialistically orientated state, Tanzania.

The position throughout the continent changed sharply with the Lisbon coup of April 1974. The liberation movements of Portuguese Africa had become increasingly Marxist in attitude over the years – a natural, almost inevitable, consequence of Salazar's refusal to contemplate any acceptable political alternative to his own system. Without any free liberal lobby in Lisbon or a church able to condemn colonialism and countenance national-ists, the nationalist movement inevitably turned more and more commit-tedly to Marxist models and methods. The career of Eduardo Mondlane is an object lesson in the way things had to go, given the unyielding nature of the Portuguese régime. Marxism had in fact permeated the armed forces of Portugal very deeply as well. As a consequence the two years following Caetano's fall saw Guiné-Bissau, Mozambique and Angola taken over by liberation movements which were basically nationalist, but had been fed over the years with Marxist theory and supported most consistently by communist countries. The weakness of MPLA in Angola, faced with the continuing resistance of its rivals, UNITA and FNLA, made it dangerously dependent upon its Cuban and Russian allies, but it was soon clear that Frelimo in Mozambique, with far stronger popular backing and no history of heavy foreign dependence, was anxious to avoid any loss of national initia-tive and willing to take a relatively pragmatic approach to the restructuring of a desperately poor country left almost entirely without benefit from generations of colonialism.

All these movements were, at the level of their leadership, bitterly critical of the part played by Christianity, Catholicism above all, in the history of colonialism. They had swallowed whole the simplest Marxist critique of the role of religion and admittedly in the Portuguese system that role had often seemed verified well enough. At the same time they had been surprised and pleased by the emergence of left-wing Christian groups, predominantly missionary, which had brought them genuine assistance, and they had Chris-tian friends and backers in Nyerere and Kaunda. Like many other govern-ments, the new leaders of the old Portuguese colonies soon began to find that the churches could be useful assistants and tiresome enemies. Frelimo, with its profound concern for a genuine renewal of Mozambican society, its many Christian members, and the deeply African concern not to be manipulated by foreign powers, was certainly not simply the well rehearsed anti-communist's idea of a 'communist threat to the Church'. But it and its like were proof of the arrival of a world of ideological and political confronta-tion, not only in Portuguese-speaking Africa but far more widely, very different from that in which most of Africa had lived since the late 1950s, and it was unfortunately one for which – despite much writing on the wall – the churches were still largely unprepared.

The year 1974 saw, however, a still wider spread of the new Marxist radicalism – in Dahomey (renamed Benin) and, most important of all, Ethiopia. In neither case was it the Marxism of a party or of a popular revolution. It was rather the pragmatic Marxism of military rulers who sensed that military rule by itself was a discreditable option, at least for any length of time. A Marxist stance could justify the seizure and retention of power and constitute a lever for the obtaining of foreign support. The initial attraction of Marxism may here be explained in no deeper terms. The consequences, nonetheless, could be devastating. They certainly proved so in Ethiopia.

It was not, indeed, surprising that the aged emperor should finally be overthrown. Despite great shrewdness, total devotion to his national responsibilities as he saw them and an international aura, Haile Selassie had become more and more trapped in his old age within an arbitrary tyranny of his own devising upon which the veneer of liberal benevolence had grown very thin. His government had failed most disastrously to cope with a recent famine in the north-east, the country was now seething with discontent, and there were no clear plans for the succession. Unlike Franco's Spain, his Ethiopia still did not possess a solid middle class capable of ensuring political and economic continuity. An army coup d'etat swept away both emperor and the small aristocratic elite upon which he had relied. No contemporary polity was more individual than that of Ethiopia – a comity of crown, aristocracy and church, grounded in the old heartland of the kingdom but without deep roots or much love in the more recently acquired areas of the kingdom. For years the emperor had been fighting a secessionist movement in predominantly Muslim Eritrea in the north, while holding off Somalian claims to much of the equally Muslim and largely Somali east of the country. The new military junta, in sweeping away the institutions of the monarchy and so much that went with it, from the privileges of the Orthodox Church to the Lutheran-sponsored Radio Voice of the Gospel (now to become the Voice of the Revolution), swept away also almost all the meagre forces which naturally contended for the unity of Ethiopia within its modern boundaries. For years Ethiopia had been aligned with the USA, Somalia with the USSR. Now that the Ethiopian government had suddenly turned Marxist and appealed for Chinese and then Russian help, it proved a still more attractive ally for Moscow than its old friends in Mogadishu. The junta had reversed the emperor's policy in most things, but it could not do so on that of national unity and the national frontiers, consequently it had to go on fighting Eritrean and Somalian secession movements as well as 'counter-revolutionary' plots on the part of all those who deplored the wholesale destruction of the institutions of historic Ethiopia. The government's reaction grew increasingly brutal and bloody with waves of massacre of both high and low.

The Orthodox Church was quite unprepared to adjust to so vast a change of fortune. It had flourished with imperial favour without the slightest element of independence from governmental control. Its economic position had rested upon the land it had been granted and large additional subventions from the imperial purse. All this was now cut away, the patriarch was imprisoned, and the village priests with their ancient churches, their ikons, their long prayers and gentle ways were as lost in a spate of revolutionary Marxist verbiage as a butterfly caught in a hurricane. Nevertheless there were some signs of relief for a bewildered and beleaguered church. The government, faced with an ever greater threat of secession in the north and east, had inevitably to look around to salvage structures of national survival, even very traditional ones, and it soon appeared that among the more helpful could still be the Orthodox Church. There was, moreover, a handful of priests educated enough to begin to chart a new course for the church, and in this they were helped by the understanding friendship of the Moscow Patriarchate, which had lived so long with a comparable situation and which had already before the revolution established quite close links with the Patriarchate of Ethiopia.

At the same time as the new Marxist revolutionary wave was striking some of the churches of Africa, a new surge of Islamic political influence was overtaking them elsewhere. In no other continent were Muslims and Christians so extensively mixed as in Africa and on the whole they had learnt to live with each other amicably enough. Despite the civil wars of the Sudan, Chad and Nigeria, all of which had something of a religious dimension, these amicable relations had survived and even deepened since the coming of independence. Countries like Tanzania, Cameroon, Upper Volta and Senegal were examples of the building up of a mature political harmony between the two communities, despite considerable underlying opportunities of tension.

In the colonial era Islam had been at an apparent disadvantage, the colonial powers were 'Christian' and education was largely in the hands of Christian missionary agencies. Contact with the Islamic countries of the Middle East was largely discouraged. It is true that both the British and the French governments had done a good deal to balance this and had indeed been arguably over-protective in some parts, such as northern Nigeria, regarded as being Muslim when it could be the case that this was true of the chiefs in an area but of very few ordinary people. Independence brought changes here: the Christian churches could be more active in some traditional Muslim areas and even gain a number of converts – as in coastal Tanzania. On the other hand the vast educational imbalance in favour of Christians was at last beginning to be redressed and as a consequence the near Christian monopoly of the upper echelons of the new society was also broken. In countries such as Upper Volta, Sierra Leone and Nigeria, which had a mainly Christian intelligentsia but a far larger Muslim than Christian population, there was inevitably a fairly steady recession of Christian political influence.

The change in the balance was further affected by a rapid growth in

221

contact between black Muslims and the Middle East. By the 1970s nearly 50,000 Nigerians were going on pilgrimage to Mecca every year; the university of al-Azhar in Cairo was sending scholars to teach in many parts; and the Saudi Arabian government was widely providing financial support for Islamic institutions.[61] The oil revolution was bringing a large increase to Muslim funds just as Christian ones were feeling the wind. The advance of Muslim organisation in these years can be seen in many countries, as can a growth in numbers often comparable with the Christian growth and a penetration into areas where hitherto they had been very weak – such as Igboland. The establishment in 1973 of the new supreme Islamic Council for Nigeria was the indication of a new degree of coordination and collective purpose. Such developments can, of course, be fully paralleled on the Christian side but it is not surprising that the sudden sharp impact of oil money should in places have been felt by Christians as something of a threat.

Into this world, inherently volatile and in which religious divisions were often doubly sensitive in that they masked ethnic or regional ones, Colonel Gaddafy of Libya entered as a bull in a china shop with offers of money and Russian weapons to undergird a policy which might appear from such utterances as his anti-Christian diatribe of 23 March 1974 as little less than a crusade of Islamic political expansion. Gaddafy's policy was not, of course, backed by many other Islamic states – indeed his major political opponents in the Sudan and Egypt could certainly not welcome a line which increased his international influence and potential threat to themselves; moreover the rulers in black Africa who responded favourably to his overtures were not those upon whom most reliance could be placed. Idi Amin of Uganda, Muslim military dictator of a largely Christian country, was his most notable protégé. The erratic course of Amin's tyranny included a fairly strong element of Muslim assertiveness and Uganda was even taken as a Muslim state into the Islamic Summit Conference held at Lahore in February 1974.[62] It was indeed erratic enough and Muslim religious leaders were as unsafe as anyone else at the Field Marshal's hands; nevertheless almost all the key positions in his government fell to Muslims, conversions from Christianity to Islam were announced from time to time on the radio and relations between the two communities were inevitably deeply embittered.[63]

Elsewhere President Bokassa of the Central African Republic, another very unpredictable but rather more genial ruler, became a Muslim a little while before he became an emperor. He was followed in the former course, still more unexpectedly, by President Bongo of Gabon. There were few Muslims in Gabon and it is too early to say whether these conversions will have any long-term significance for Christianity, but in Africa today *cuius regio eius religio* is still a principle that can have some application and the seeming wave of Islamic political expansionism across central Africa, linked with the oil millions of the Middle East, could prove a not insignificant factor affecting the religious character of the continent.

It is too early to say. Church–state relations in the Africa of the mid-1970s have lost almost all predictability. With the plight of the once privileged Ethiopian Orthodox Church, with the murder of Cardinal Bayenda in Brazzaville and Archbishop Luwum in Kampala, with the conversion of Emperor Bokassa and President Bongo, with the effective pressure of the professional classes of Ghana on its military governors to return to civilian rule, with Mobutu's appeal to the churches to take back the schools he had so sharply confiscated, with riots in Soweto and the crumbling of white Rhodesia, it is no longer possible to chart a course or even list a limited number of likely alternatives. The storm has arrived and for a time at least the churches in many lands can but live with the faith they cherish which transcends politics but also with a pragmatism which may not wisely venture beyond the horizons of the next six months.

B. The historic churches

I

By the end of the 1960s the churches of Africa derived from the main Protestant missions were sailing full ahead; the harbour of their paternalist past was now well behind them; they were sturdy ships as they needed to be, for the storms they had to face could prove daunting. If in many countries there was an adequate measure of peace and security and rather harmonious relationships with government – and that was true of Kenya, Tanzania and Zambia, among others – elsewhere even an archbishop might have to take his life in both hands in the carrying out of his public duty. In general the new church leadership had developed a shrewd capacity to find the way through, combining a natural conservatism with the pragmatism necessary for the acceptance of quite major changes on occasion; yet the strength of the churches lay very much less than did that of many in other parts of the world in their institutions and their archbishops, and very much more in their ordinary membership. They could weather remarkably well, combining strain at the top with continued growth underneath.

While it is likely that the growth rates for almost all churches had fallen by 1970 on the figures of a few years earlier, considerable increase was still going on none the less in most places, particularly in the sudanic belt whose young but quickly maturing churches were now providing the core of the fundamentalist Association of Evangelicals of Africa and Madagascar. The general rapid rise in population – well over 3 per cent a year in most countries – continued to ensure church growth quite apart from any conversions. Reliable statistics, however, were becoming more and more difficult to obtain. Moreover, if the number of ministers was as inadequate as ever in comparison with that of the congregations, it too was now increasing a great deal faster than formerly. In most churches a striking characteristic of the period is the large rise in the number of candidates for the ministry. Whatever was the case in other parts of the world, in Africa the theological colleges were full to overflowing.

One cannot help having the impression that by the 1970s the foreign missionary had become, essentially, an irrelevance, or at least something vastly more marginal to African Christianity than he had ever been before. Certainly there were some influential survivals, father figures who had not yet gone. John Maund retired as Anglican bishop of Lesotho in January 1976 to be succeeded by Desmond Tutu; he had been bishop there since 1950 and can stand for many who were coming to the end of a long day's work. Some still continued: Donald Arden was a vigorous and respected

224

Archbishop of Central Africa from 1970 on, but north of the Zambezi he was an increasingly unusual figure. Two older missionaries with experience in the south had been called to office in Tanzania in the 1960s – Bengt Sundkler to be Lutheran Bishop of Bukoba and Trevor Huddleston Anglican Bishop of Masasi. Both made their mark, but both too had resigned in favour of an African successor before 1970. Even Colin Morris had left Zambia, sensing that it was one thing to be select chaplain to a revolutionary movement, rather another to bear the same role to a now dug-in political establishment. Essentially, white clerics had made their voice heard long enough; it was now time for the black.

Nevertheless Protestant missionaries were not absent in the 1970s; indeed their continued presence in quite large numbers provoked a much publicised appeal for a 'moratorium' – a complete halt in the sending of missionaries and money from European and North American churches to those of Africa. The concept of a 'moratorium' was not so far removed from the strategy proposed by Professor Freytag back in 1958; it had been suggested from time to time since then.[64] What was new was that it was now being urged by some African church leaders themselves, as it was by Asian and Caribbean leaders. John Gatu, General Secretary of the Presbyterian Church of East Africa, appealed for such a moratorium in 1971 at the Mission Festival at Milwaukee which produced consternation in many missionary circles in North America. In 1974 the AACC assembly at Lusaka declared that,

to enable the African Church to achieve the power of becoming a true instrument of liberating and reconciling the African people, as well as finding solutions to economic and social dependency, our option as a matter of policy has to be a Moratorium on external assistance in money and personnel. We recommend this option as the only potent means of becoming truly and authentically ourselves while remaining a respected and responsible part of the Universal Church.[65]

The presiding genius here was Burgess Carr, the AACC's General Secretary. As a matter of fact while the resolution was overwhelmingly passed, few of the church leaders present can have had any intention or desire to implement it very rigorously in their own case. The value of a little continued help from overseas was only too clear and the AACC itself, with some lack of consistency, went on to appeal for a very large sum indeed with which to build a new headquarters in Nairobi.

The total number of missionaries in Africa did not in fact alter greatly in these years but older trends continued to operate with a further rise in Evangelical North Americans. There were still some 2,000 British Protestant missionaries in Africa in the early 1970s, though the North American group was now nearly four times as numerous.[66]. The missionary force of the main 'historic churches' (Lutheran, Anglican, Methodist and Presbyterian) had already been declining numerically for many years. In this last decade this decline took a far sharper turn, prompted it would seem by rising costs and diminishing interest as much as by the appeals of the promoters of moratorium. For whatever reason, the facts are clear enough. In the world as a whole the Board of Missions of the United Methodist Church in North America maintained 1,415 missionaries in 1966 and only 788 in 1975; the same figure for the United Presbyterian Church declined from 1,088 to 438 and that for the Protestant Episcopal Church from 449 to 76. In the same years, nevertheless, other missionary agencies – Baptist, Adventist and Pentecostal – were increasing their numbers almost as dramatically. Thus the Southern Baptist Foreign Mission Board had 2,277 missionaries on its books in 1966 and 2,667 in 1975, while the Baptist Mid-Mission's total increased from 506 to 905. Thus in 1966 those two Baptist boards sponsored fewer foreign missionaries than did the Episcopalian, Methodist and Presbyterian boards; nine years later they were sponsoring almost three times as many as the latter.

In general it would appear to be the case that the more 'liberal' in theology and middle class in social ethos a church is the more its missionary commitment has been reduced; the more fundamentalist in belief and working class in membership, the more its missionary personnel has been maintained or even increased. Nevertheless there is more to it than that. Thus the Sudan Interior Mission, an old conservative evangelical body, also considerably reduced its personnel overseas in these years, from 1,196 to 699. A more restrictive government policy in its two chief areas of mission (Nigeria and Ethiopia) was doubtless a main factor here. Government restrictions affect a large and old-established body far more than a small, recently arrived group. The former cannot redeploy its personnel with the relative ease of the latter.

Nothing however has seemed able to arrest the numerical growth of the Southern Baptist missionary force. If its numbers in Nigeria were reduced from 247 to 131, they increased in Kenya from 60 to 110, in Rhodesia from 53 to 78, in Tanzania from 44 to 68, and they entered several new countries.

The countries which experienced a significant decline in North American Protestant missionary numbers in these years are shown in table 1.

Table 1. *Decline in Protestant missionary numbers*

	1966	*1975*
Ethiopia	703	519
Nigeria	1484	802
Tanzania	406	307
Uganda	94	28
Zaire	1,096	817

At the same time the increase is equally marked in another group, as shown in table 2.

Table 2. *Increase in Protestant missionary numbers*

	1966	1975
Botswana	8	86
Ivory Coast	143	211
Kenya	557	926
Niger	53	136
Rhodesia	402	533
South Africa[67]	435	595
Swaziland	63	149
Zambia	299	427

There is a clear tendency for the numbers to rise in white-ruled southern Africa or countries with a recognisably pro-western foreign policy, while they fall in countries with a markedly nationalist or socialist orientation. Nevertheless generalisations can be misleading: the overall decline in Tanzania was due to a church decision reducing over 200 American Lutherans to under 50; at the same time the number of Southern Baptists was mounting.

Kenya was certainly the Mecca in black Africa for western missionaries in these years. By 1975 it was host to nearly 1,000 Protestant North American missionaries belonging to some sixty different organisations, as well as 291 British and many other Europeans. Many of these groups were very small and recently arrived but one of the oldest in the country, the Africa Inland Mission, which arrived in 1895, continued to have by far the biggest number of personnel – 316 in place of the 176 it had maintained nine years before. It seems a little ironic that following John Gatu's 1971 Milwaukee appeal for a missionary moratorium there should be such prolific growth in foreign missionaries precisely in his own country – though not in his own denomination!

In general it remains true that the older and better established churches, with few exceptions, were Africanising hard in these years, at the same time reducing missionary personnel pretty drastically. The major foreign increases were mostly for newer and smaller churches, and it is probable that they have had a rather slight effect on the life and religion of the country. The foreign missionary who is not a welcomed auxiliary to an already well-established African church was likely to find himself in the 1970s in a far more marginal position than any a missionary in Africa had occupied for the last hundred years. Moreover, where a large mission remained, it could be faced with mounting tension if it attempted to maintain its own independent field of action. Thus the Africa Inland Mission endeavoured to keep its 'autonomy' from the Africa Inland Church in Kenya all through the 1960s, with the consequence of very strained relations. In June 1970 it wisely capitulated, at last handing over responsibility for all its works to its 'daughter' church.[68] The alternative could well have been schism.

227

In regard to American Baptist numbers, it is worth remarking that while the Baptist missionary formerly came from a church fairly low in the western social hierarchy and so less naturally 'imperialist' than the Anglican or the Presbyterian, or the Roman Catholic (in Portuguese and Belgian possessions), this has significantly altered in the last decades. Baptists were not numerically or socially a powerful community in any of the European colonial powers, but they are in the USA. The numerical increase of Baptist missionaries in Africa coincided with both the growth of American neo-colonial interest in Africa and the rise of Baptist social status in the USA. American Baptist missionaries were comparatively outsiders in colonial Africa; in the 1970s they are not only far more numerous, they are also natural religious representatives of the greatest western power concerned with the continent. They have, then, lost that objective status of disinterestedness and, perhaps, sympathy with the underdog which they previously possessed. In contrast Anglican or Methodist missionaries, now few, relatively poor and no longer entangled as formerly by their links with colonial powers, are in a better position to rediscover in themselves such qualities of disinterestedness and sympathy.

These were years in which the relative decline in significance of South African Protestantism became fully apparent. Its wider role of leadership in the continent was now clearly lost, even if this was not quite true of exceptional individuals like Manas Buthelezi and Beyers Naudé. Neither of these, however, achieved their position through membership of a major church, though Buthelezi as a Lutheran was not deprived of his church's support either – indeed his prominence was but one of a number of indications of an increasingly clear and weighty Lutheran voice. But that church, the Anglican, which had previously been most influential was now sagging the most conspicuously both in numbers and in an imaginative response to an admittedly fraught situation. Its discriminating clerical salary scales remained unchanged,[69] and having chosen not to keep its African schools but to keep its white bishops, and having then taken a strong line against the WCC grants but done little to back its bishops deported from Namibia, its appeal to the black majority was inevitably a diminishing one. Its expatriate priests were largely needed to help service white parishes and while its position remained very strong among the coloured people in its old strongholds of the Western Cape, elsewhere it was in decline. The non-white population of the country increased 39 per cent in the years 1960 to 1970, but Anglican non-whites increased by only 25 per cent which indicates a significant loss of membership. The census figures (in table 3) for the main churches show clearly how both Anglicans and Methodists failed to maintain their earlier impetus.

If the figures for the coloured population of the Western Cape were

Table 3. *Non-white Christians in South Africa*

	1946	1970
Anglicans	740,000	1,276,000
Methodists	1,093,000	1,794,000
Dutch Reformed	558,000	1,504,000
Catholics	372,000	1,539,000

excluded, the Anglican decline would be still more striking.

This decline was certainly not just a matter of statistics. It was still more one of leadership, though it may be that the former was in part an expression of the latter. The prophetic voice, so powerful in the past, was no longer heard from the episcopal bench but only from courageous, increasingly marginal, individuals: among priests David Russell, among laymen the economist Francis Wilson, editor of the *South African Outlook* and heir to the old free air of Lovedale.

Robert Selby Taylor, for ten years Archbishop of Cape Town, was not a prophetic figure. He had been consecrated long ago on Likoma Island in Lake Malawi as bishop for Northern Rhodesia, the very first missionary of the UMCA to be consecrated in Africa. The preacher at the service had been old Archdeacon Glossop who had arrived in Africa in 1893 and spent most of the time since on Likoma Island.[70] He belonged then to an old and honourable, if rather paternalistic, missionary tradition. From Northern Rhodesia he had been translated to Pretoria and Grahamstown and then, in 1964, to Cape Town. Wealthy, celibate, aloof, rather uninterested in social and political problems, he had found himself at home in South African society and, while devoted to black people, about whom he very possibly knew rather more than any of his predecessors, he was hardly one to alter a deep ecclesiastical drift to the ineffectual. He was succeeded by Bill Burnett of Grahamstown, but more significant than that election was the subsequent refusal of the white electors of the diocese of Grahamstown to listen to their black colleagues and choose Desmond Tutu, the one and only younger black priest of the Province with an international standing. It was maybe the moment, as much as any, when the old Church of the Province turned its face to the wall. Through all these years there had been one African upon the bench, the much-respected Bishop Zulu. He had certainly made his mark both in South Africa and at the World Council, but, sadly, his very moderation combined with his position as the sole black on a white bench to make of him, finally, the white man's black bishop. In 1975 Tutu was appointed Dean of Johannesburg – an imaginative response by the white bishop to the disastrous refusal of the electors of Grahamstown the previous year, though not an adequate one. The decisive question for the future of the historic churches in South Africa was now whether Desmond Tutu, Manas Buthelezi, Patrick Mkatshwa and a handful of other black clergy could somehow salvage ecclesiastical credibility in an age of black consciousness and in face of the unyielding 'whiteness' of the bulk of church leadership.

North of the Zambezi things were going very differently. In Uganda, where there was but one Anglican diocese in 1950, there were by the early 1970s thirteen (with three more on the way) and thirteen Ugandan bishops, led by the martyr-to-be Janani Luwum. Much the same was true for Anglicans in Nigeria, Kenya and Tanzania, and for many another church too. Of course there were not now thirteen times as many Anglicans in Uganda as there had been in 1950: the structures were changing as well as multiplying and the direction was towards smaller units and a more intimate and domestic leadership – intimate if often with a splash of titular triumphalism too! In 1975 the large Methodist Church of Nigeria suddenly took to itself bishops, archbishops and a life patriarch for good measure – the last being no other than the irrepressible Bolaji Idowu, who had however to relinquish his Ibadan professorship after becoming 'His Pre-eminence' in a five-hour-long ceremony which gave him his new symbol of authority, two golden keys. The pattern of ecclesiastical order could indeed alter unexpectedly, as when for two years Edmund John, the brother of Archbishop Sepeku, carried on an extraordinary ministry of healing and the driving out of devils in the Anglican church of eastern Tanzania. A catechist called by vision to this ministry, he swept the church into a pattern of excitement of a sort one would never have associated with the old Anglo-Catholic UMCA tradition. 'Such spirits will not be thrown out except by prayer and fasting' was a word of the Lord which he took to himself; his exertions wore him out and he died in June 1975. Emmanuel Milingo, Catholic Archbishop of Lusaka, was developing at much the same time into an almost equally enthusiastic healer and thrower out of spirits. The point here is that this sort of thing could now take place in a so-called former 'mission' church without the slightest tendency to separatism or even to a great sense of tension with its mission-inherited traditions. To some extent, of course, similar things were happening all over the world with the spread of Pentecostalism in non-Pentecostal churches under the aegis of the 'charismatic movement'. It was hitting white South Africans at much the same time.

Certainly in black Africa in these years there was a surprisingly natural drawing together of Christian traditions and experience in a way that brought new strength to the churches if, doubtless, problems too. Thus, to turn again to Anglican Tanzania, in missionary times there had been an extraordinarily deep divide between its very Anglo-Catholic UMCA dioceses and its very evangelical Australian CMS ones. Sharing between them was so minimal that it could seriously be said that the UMCA encouraged its Christians to go to Catholic churches when moving to a CMS area and the CMS encouraged its Christians to go Lutheran when living in a UMCA area. But with the establishment of Tanzanian bishops upon both sides, much of this seemed simply to fade away. The spikiness of neither party was quite carried across the colour line. A common sense of Anglican Christianity with its bishops, liturgy and the world-wide communion of Canterbury prevailed instead. And elsewhere much the same was happening. In Zaire, admittedly, under government pressure, the Protestant mission-founded churches, already loosely linked, became a single 'Church of Christ in Zaire'; but formal unity plans were also seriously advanced between Methodists and Presbyterians in Ghana. Here as elsewhere it had by the 1970s to be a clearly black decision. Apart from such precise proposals there was a growing sense of a common direction and identity symbolised by the adoption of the name 'Evangelical' together with the title of 'bishop'. Both were probably linked with a wide resurgence of Lutheran influence – noticeable from Ethiopia to South Africa.

All this does not mean that there were now no problems. There undoubtedly were. Anglicans in Uganda could be deeply divided, almost to the point of schism, for several years between the two Buganda dioceses and the rest over the institutional issue of making a separate diocese for the capital to be headed by the archbishop. It needed President Amin, in his early more apparently rosy days, to reconcile the two groups. Again, the Balokole of East Africa had fallen far from the great years of the revival, as of course movements of enthusiasm always do after a while.[71] An increasing measure of formalism, introversion and cliqueishness had sapped spiritual vitality until in 1970 they broke apart into two quarrelling groups, the 'Awakened' and the 'Non-Awakened'. Revival had, perhaps, reflected too many sides of the colonial world and the Protestantism of the 1930s to flourish in the very different society of the 1960s.

The late 1960s were the years of a first flowering of 'African Theology'. Harry Sawyerr, Idowu, Kwesi Dickson and John Mbiti set themselves to produce a theological literature for Africa, and the African churches certainly stood in need of it.[72] The central theme of this literature was the nature of the traditional religion of Africa and its relationship of continuity rather than discontinuity with Christian belief. While the point of view of its different proponents was far from identical, they were alike concerned to achieve a far more sympathetic understanding of the religious past than many missionaries had shown, and they were particularly interested in establishing, perhaps a little simplistically, that this past had been essentially monotheistic and essentially moral. These writers owed much to recent western scholarship and even to its 'missionary' wing (like Edwin Smith and Geoffrey Parrinder), but their books carried their own conviction and provided something of a theological and scholarly stiffening for the new African church which was important in the establishment of confidence; moreover as scholars they were available for consultation and lecturing both in Africa and beyond. Paradoxically enough, their greatest weakness may

231

come to be seen as one of over-belonging to the western academic world for all their appeal for Africanisation: too much the Cambridge or London scholar carrying on that tradition on a well-run African campus. There was also a limitation in theme: a few well-argued theses recur and they reflect the enlightenment of the last years of the colonial era rather than the increasingly baffling perplexities of the new age. It is not, all in all, surprising that 'African Theology' would come to be challenged, but also balanced, by a 'Black Theology' based in southern Africa and much more influenced by Afro-American Black Theology and Latin American 'Liberation Theology'. It is at least in embryo a theology of politics as well as a theology of religion. While concerned in part with the same sort of re-evaluation of the indigenous religious tradition, it was still more preoccupied with the liberation of today's oppressed innocents in the light of him who upon the cross was most innocent and most oppressed: Black Theology is a *theologia crucis* in a way that 'African Theology' has hitherto failed to be.[73]

Valid as a critique of African Theology may be, its appearance was one more sign that the African churches had come of age. The end of the 1960s and the early 1970s were a period in which the main stream of black Protestantism was well past the 'hand-over' stage in the transfer of responsibility; it was past the discovery that its South African elder brother churches were still so entangled in white supremacy and so weakened thereby that they could offer little to the rest of the continent except cries for help and some creative experiences in the margin; it was no longer being grievously bled by new waves of independency.

It had in the AACC an increasingly effective pan-African organ of cooperation. Nairobi had proved the right place for its headquarters surrounded by the many lively churches of Kenya. As a Protestant stronghold backed by the massive Anglican church in Uganda and the Lutheran in Tanzania, Kenya could now easily hold its own with the west coast. It had its own impressive spokesmen in men like John Gatu, Henry Okullu and the Methodist Bishop Imathiu, while the AACC had its forceful General Secretary, Burgess Carr. Most of the new church leadership had, inevitably, a fairly clear national character. Thus Bolaji Idowu in Nigeria was a dynamic academic and ecclesiastical politico whose chosen field was very much his own country from which he seldom cared to venture far. Carr and Mbiti, however, were exceptions to this. John Mbiti was Kenyan with an Africa Inland Mission background and a late conversion to Anglicanism. A gentle academic with a far weightier bibliography than anyone else, his work had kept him almost continuously outside of Kenya so that he possessed an international reputation as the leading African theologian but little of a home base. His acceptance of the Directorship of Bossey Ecumenical Institute in Geneva in 1972 further accentuated a certain remoteness from the hard realities of the African scene. Burgess Carr shared Mbiti's Genevan and ecumenical experience and his Anglican affiliation but he was otherwise a very different sort of person. A brash Liberian canon with striking political *savoir-faire* and endless energy, he had transformed the AACC from a rather weak association into a working instrument of ecclesiastical coopera-tion and political influence. Both its assembly at Lusaka in May 1974 with representatives of 112 member churches, and the fifth assembly of the World Council held in December of the following year in Nairobi owed much to Carr. More significantly they provided the formal public expression of the maturity which African Protestant Christianity had now attained, felicitous symbols of the end of a long march. When that December Presi-dent Kenyatta laid the foundation stone of the new AACC headquaters in Nairobi a whole epoch of African history might seem felicitously con-cluded: the LSE author intellectual of the 1930s, the nationalist demagogue of the 1950s, the man about whom church leaders had for years no good word to say, was now the benign father figure, with one brother-in-law an Anglican bishop, another a Catholic priest, blessing the Churches and en-treating them to do their duty.

Among the 750 delegates from member churches at Nairobi, 116 (one-seventh) were from Africa and this probably represents fairly enough the weight of contemporary African Christianity. They contributed enormously to the tone of the fifth assembly in a way that had never happened before, without of course becoming the dominant element. In the World Council of the mid-1970s there is no dominant element, which is maybe both its achievement and a source of puzzlement. Certainly for British churches which did tend to dominate ecclesiastically as well as politically in the recent past, it could be a bewildering condition. Delegates from such churches went, some of them, with teeth clenched to challenge some supposed third world take-over of the World Council and, in particular, to fight the leader-ship on the grants issue. These were churches without any past commit-ment to pacifism; on the contrary, they, as all the major churches of the West, had shown a long complacency with institutional violence. They had, too, strong ties with the more white-dominated of South Africa's churches.

The Nairobi assembly was not prepared in any way to go back on the 'Programme to Combat Racism'. The grants had, indeed, become more of a symbol than anything else: a symbol that Christianity was not what Malan and Verwoerd and Vorster and Smith had claimed it to be – a bastion in the fortress of white supremacy. And yet, in a remarkable way, this whole issue was all the same reduced in import and subsumed in a deeper vision in which the artificial contrasts which had been bandied about between 'horizontal' and 'vertical' approaches, or between 'liberal' and 'evangelical' almost faded away. Here the African contribution was not insignificant, and just because African Protestantism of almost any denominational brand is so devoutly

233

'evangelical' and yet so emphatically committed to the righting of racial injustice. In Nairobi it became almost unthinkable to assert some sort of 'evangelical' line which would withdraw support from the 'Programme to Combat Racism', and those who would have wished to do so mostly hung their heads.

This achievement was certainly no final solution to the World Council's role, nor even to the great practical problems of how to identify a genuine liberation movement – especially when there are several in bitter competition. Vast issues of every sort were inevitably left unresolved by Nairobi but it did provide something of an overcoming of the increasingly sterile polarisation of the post-Uppsala years, and this was won in a context of prayer. Here too the deciding contribution may well have been the African rather than the more self-conscious 'spirituality first' message of certain western delegates. The African churches, in their immense material poverty, are so manifestly prayerful – their services so long, so well attended, so absorbing. The most memorable moment at the AACC conference the year before may well have been the joyous, gloriously prolonged singing of the word *Amen*, a grateful *Amen* for the historic creed and the strange ways of God whereby in the years and the context of decolonisation it has been embraced by a non-European race on a scale and with a vigour unprecedented in all the ages of imperialism.

II

The Catholic experience in these years was partly similar and partly different, the main differences deriving from the aftermath of the second Vatican Council with its currents and cross-currents, from the heavier institutional structures and far larger continuing role of expatriates, and from a certain difference in timing.

The years 1966 to 1970 were ones of great optimism, intellectual vitality and creative reorganisation for Catholic Africa and its missionary societies. This atmosphere did not indeed extend everywhere; while it was widely shared in by both African priests and laity and by some missionary societies, there were many dioceses under complete missionary control where change came only grudgingly and by the letter of the rule. For while some of the societies working in Africa, notably the White Fathers during the generalate of Theo Van Asten, responded to post-conciliar renewal with great enthusiasm, there were others whose hearts were not in the business in the same way. The Council's underlying emphases had been upon a greater freedom in the church, an admitted pluralism, a turning away from the uniformity not only of the Latin language but also of the very monolithic conception of 'the Latin Church', dominant in Pius XII's reign, to the fostering of a 'communion of churches' in which the particular characteristics of a 'local church', relating to a local culture, were to be encouraged rather than eliminated. All this was as far away from the ultramontane presuppositions of many missionaries as it was from that of most of Rome's curial officials. Thus Archbishop Lefebvre, by this time General of the Holy Ghost Fathers, was upholding as conspicuously a 'traditionalist' line as was Van Asten a 'progressive' one – and these were still the two main missionary societies in Africa. The strains of the coming years, in Africa as much as in Europe, would often be basically between those who saw the Catholic Church as essentially a free fellowship of churches in communion with Rome governed by a truly collegial body of bishops, and those who saw it as the Roman Church, in which a few diversities could be permitted here and there but in which all important matters were to be settled in a uniform manner by the Pope with the advice of such officials and bishops as he chose to consult.

The documents of the council hinted at the one vision; canon law and papal practice continued to insist upon the other.

For the time being, however, most were at one in a massive programme of liturgical translation and revision. While the provision of vernacular texts to replace Latin ones for the mass and the sacraments was a world-wide exercise in these years, in Africa it coincided with the wider contemporary cultural thirst for Africanisation so that it assumed a deeper significance and was done with much greater enthusiasm. Moreover such translations often went with a real musical revolution. Here again it was largely a matter of happy coincidence. It had increasingly been realised that the failure of the churches to make use of African tunes and song forms and the imposition of narrowly translated western hymns with their tunes theoretically unchanged was a grave source of weakness in popular worship, while the strength of the independent churches often lay in their music. Indeed the Catholic revival in Northern Rhodesia (Zambia) following the triumphs of Lenshina had been intimately linked with a transformation of Catholic hymn singing based upon the example of Lenshina and of traditional Bemba music.[74] The same sort of thing was now happening in many parts of Africa, and, very probably, there was nothing else taking place in the Catholic Church quite as important as this musical revolution.[75]

It was linked, however, with much more – with a far greater concern with secular issues of social development, justice and peace; with the renewal of formal catechesis and the training of catechists; with a marked change in the balance of concern in regard to the rural church. Traditionally each diocese was made up of a number of 'mission stations', which were the centre of attention. It was now being recognised that far more important and truly central were the 'out-stations': the priests lived in the one, but the people in the other. The canonical parish, centred around the priest, mattered little in comparison with the 'sub-parish', re-christened in an almost mystical way the *communauté de base*. It was to this that people really belonged; it corresponded or should correspond to the small worshipping community of the independent church and a sound pastoral policy would concentrate upon making it – more or less priestless as it inevitably must be with the continued law of celibacy – as satisfactory and self-reliant a unit as possible, with its own liturgy, catechist, council and shared responsibilities.[76] The Catholic Church, curiously enough, was, at least in many places, endeavouring to adjust to being congregationalist – that is to say to being at local level almost entirely without priests.

Such problems could hardly have been approached at all without the foundation or development of a number of very active pastoral institutes and other similar centres – Gaba in Uganda, Bukumbi in Tanzania, Kinshasa, Cotody (Abidjan), Bodija (Ibadan), Yaoundé, and Lumku in South Africa. These institutes, at first staffed predominantly by expatriates, were the nerve centres for the new pastoral and missionary strategy with its deep anthropological and ecumenical dimensions and its presupposition that the teaching of Vatican II had to be taken very seriously indeed.

It was the age of 'experimentation' and of 'dialogue' in the Catholic Church and a wider and wider range of subjects was brought into question, two of the most important being the priesthood and marriage.[77] About both a lively debate developed as it became ever clearer that the church's canonical structures remained miles away from the realities of the African countryside and that the major needs of the missionary church had never really been stated at the council at all. Should there not be married priests, as in all other churches, drawn most probably from among the better trained catechists? Should not the church recognise the validity of 'customary marriage' and also accept some polygamous marriages, at least of those publicly contracted prior to baptism? While these questions and others were now openly debated in Catholic circles in a way that would have been unthinkable ten years earlier and while they undoubtedly related very closely to the most urgent pastoral needs, their theological and institutional implications proved too considerable for any immediate change of policy. In a number of African countries bishops asked Rome for permission to ordain married men in order 'to answer the most elementary pastoral needs'[78] but ever since his encyclical on the subject in 1967 Pope Paul had shown himself firmly opposed to any change of church law in this matter and with the years the attitude of Rome simply hardened. These were proposals which clearly went beyond the letter of Vatican II and the young African hierarchy, with so much on its mind already, was as a whole unwilling to press for further changes of great import, to some of which many of its members were personally profoundly opposed. Hence the lively debates of the late 1960s, for the most part initiated by a younger generation of missionaries, slowly subsided, though at the same time a very considerable structural shift in the church did take place by sheer force of necessity.

236

The general development of these years can best be reviewed under three heads: the African clergy, missionaries, the character of the local congregation. It is a striking fact that the number of ordinations throughout black Africa hardly increased throughout the 1960s while every other kind of professional group was multiplying so rapidly. Ordinations continued at about 150 a year. From the late 1960s, however, the number of major seminarians began to rise fast: 1,661, in 1960, 2,000 in 1967, 2,775 in 1971, 3,650 in 1974. Until 1960 by far the largest group had been that of Zaire, but numbers there fell in the following years and never fully recovered. Those of Nigeria, on the other hand, which had been low in the past, now mounted impressively, particularly after the civil war. Of the 1974 total over 800 were in Nigeria, mostly in the Igbo dioceses, and another 500 in Tanzania. In 1973 the number of ordinations rose for the first time over the 200 mark to 237, of which 84 were in Nigeria and 53 for the four Igbo dioceses of Enugu, Onitsha, Owerri and Umuahia.[79]

There may have been in all some 3,700 African priests in 1975 in well over 300 dioceses and prefectures. A good 2,000 of these were concentrated in some fifty dioceses – the old core of Catholic Africa somewhat enlarged. In each of these by the 1970s there were some forty local priests, still generally a minority among the clergy but sizeable enough to bear a wide range of responsibilities and guarantee a reasonable continuance of diocesan life regardless of a missionary presence. In the other 270 or so dioceses there was an average of not more than seven priests. But throughout black Africa there had been a major shift of ecclesiastical responsibility between 1968 and 1970. Until 1968 almost everywhere there was a clear majority of white bishops and beneath them the missionaries continued to hold most other key positions in all but a small minority of dioceses. From 1968 things changed remarkably sharply. Rome had evidently recognised that the position of a missionary bishop in most independent countries was too vulnerable and there was a spate of resignations and new appointments. If the first black archbishop was appointed in Zaire only in mid-1964, by the end of 1968 there was a black episcopal majority (24–22) in that country. Tanzania and Uganda followed in 1969, Cameroon in 1970, Nigeria in 1972.

The racial transformation of the Tanzanian episcopate, one in which the process began early and proceeded relatively steadily, is shown in table 4.

At the same time the African clergy tended to take over most of the more senior and public positions – those of Vicar General, cathedral administrator, seminary rector, secondary school headmaster, university

Table 4. *Number of bishops in Tanzania*

	Black	White
1960	6	14
1968	9	14
1975	19	5

chaplain, members of the national secretariat. When it is recalled that there were over 300 dioceses to provide for, it becomes clear that once these posts had been filled (sometimes by moving men from one diocese to another) there were very few African priests left (except in a handful of dioceses with higher numbers, and then chiefly the older men) for ordinary rural pastoral work, which remained perforce in the hands of missionaries and catechists. In many dioceses where a young African bishop was appointed about 1970 the almost complete absence of any African priests left him highly dependent upon the missionary clergy.

If the racial composition of the Catholic episcopate decisively changed in these years, there were at first observable changes too in its life style. The pre-Vatican II bishop in Africa was not only a white missionary, he was also a man who – if frequently authoritarian enough – seldom observed the formalities. He lived close to his fellow priests, often with no more than a room in the general clergy house beside his 'cathedral'. He had few perks as a bishop, seldom dressed up in special garb and might well be skilled in repairing the mission's landrovers. The post-Vatican II bishop was widely developing a rather different life style. The late 1960s saw the arrival of a crop of elegant 'bishops' houses', usually situated in an affluent area well away from any public church. This sort of thing, hitherto, had only existed in South Africa. While in some cases the new style was instituted by a white bishop, it was frequently associated with the appointment of the first black one. In Kenya, for instance, the palatial papal nunciature erected in Nairobi in the early 1960s was soon followed by stylish episcopal residences in Nairobi, Nyeri, Kisumu and Kisii. When in 1969 old Edgar Maranta was succeeded by Cardinal Rugambwa as Archbishop of Dar es Salaam, a man who had lived for forty years 'over the shop' – with the door of his bedroom in full sight of the crowd outside the cathedral – was replaced by a Prince of the Church residing in the comfortable seclusion of Oyster Bay. While some bishops resisted any change of this sort – the elderly and saintly Archbishop Mihayo of Tabora retained a way of life as simple as that of any of his predecessors – the tendency was clear all across the continent, from Oyster Bay to the splendid residence erected by the devout Biafran hawk Bishop Okoye in Enugu after the Nigerian civil war and his removal from Port Harcourt.

With the new style of residence went the Mercedes and an attraction for other prestige-building projects – such as Rugambwa's cathedral in Bukoba ('an elephant among goats' as another Tanzanian bishop irreverently described it) or the martyr's new shrine at Namugongo in Uganda. All Catholic bishops could count on some regular funds from abroad; a few could obtain from such as Cardinal Cushing of Boston very large sums indeed. Hitherto the standard of living of a bishop had hardly been different from that of his priests: if much higher than that of the rural masses, it was very simple by European standards. Bishops and priests now fell further apart. There was little, if any, foreign money for the normal clergy house. While priests continued in their old ways, they could feel ill at ease in the carpeted elegance of the new bishop's house and informal social contact between the two was as a consequence reduced. However, the poorer and more remote a rural diocese, the less likely it was that its bishop would adopt the new life style and the more probable that he would emerge rather as a more homely chiefly figure: powerful, clearly above the people but still close to them too, and simple in his ways apart from a little tinsel splendour for festivities.

As the number of African bishops multiplied in the 1970s, the practicability of a successful appeal for considerable funds from abroad greatly diminished for any but the privileged few. With the world economic crisis and the growing disarray of the African continent, bishops too in many a diocese had to be content with very little. A growing maturity and diversity appear in their attitudes. As a group they cease to project the rather Roman and canon law image of the previous decade. To pick out a few rather arbitrarily: Christopher Mwoleka of Rulenge, Nyerere's chief supporter among the Tanzanian bishops, settled into an Ujamaa village; Lucien Agboka of Abomey in Benin (Dahomey), a rough, untiring young man, could be found happily presiding in an old khaki cassock over an evening initiation of boys and girls into new Christian songs and dances, and was not much alarmed by a 'Marxist' government in the capital; Anselme Sanon, of Bobo-Dioulasso, was formerly rector of the major seminary of Kumi, author of *Tierce Église ma mere*, and one of the few recognisable theologians on the bench; Peter Dery of Wau (and later Tamale) in Ghana had been the first Christian among the Dagarti people and then their first priest, a linguist and a water diviner, a pastor incessantly burdened with the problems of others. Doubtless these men were exceptional, many of their colleagues being a lot less effectual and imaginative. But unusual bishops have not been so unusual in the Africa of the 1970s and certainly their role could prove a complex one calling for a wide range of religious and secular skills.

If the Catholic Church has continued to grow immensely in numbers in these years, to modernise quite efficiently, to initiate many new projects while maintaining its massive institutional structures for the most part intact, a large part of the explanation must be found in the survival of the missionary on a scale which may rank as one of the more surprising phenomena of these years. Almost everywhere the number of missionaries continued to grow until well into the 1960s, and since then it has only fallen sharply where, as in eastern Nigeria, there has been governmental compulsion. The figures shown in table 5 for expatriate priests in eastern Africa are not untypical of the general picture; those for nuns and brothers would show a rather wider decline.

The decrease in Tanzania and Uganda was more than balanced by a rise in the other three countries. Continent-wide this would not be true, but the overall decrease is certainly not enormous. If Tanzania's missionary force has declined a good deal in these years one must note that its 1961 figure was extremely high, and if Kenya increased its foreign priestly personnel by 231 in the decade following independence – a remarkable feat – it still did not reach Tanzania's figure. Moreover Tanzania had by then some 600 local priests against Kenya's 100.

Table 5. *Expatriate priests in eastern Africa*

	1961	1967	1973
Kenya	415	544	646
Malawi	206	226	242
Tanzania	900	876	794
Uganda	447	531	508
Zambia	289	352	381
Total	2,257	2,529	2,571

In most countries the total number of expatriate church workers remained two to three times that of expatriate priests. In South Africa, as against a Protestant total of 1,400 expatriate church workers, there were in 1975 5,800 Roman Catholics (many, of course, working among white people).[80] In Zaire in 1971 there were 2,500 foreign priests (against 600 Zairean), 560 foreign brothers (420 Zairean), and 3,100 foreign sisters (1,161 Zairean).[81]

Certainly by 1970 the Catholic missionary corps had passed its zenith. Recruiting in the main sending countries (France, Holland, Belgium, French Canada, and Ireland) had sharply fallen or even halted entirely, and many younger men were leaving the ranks. There were, it is true, new arrivals from countries which had hitherto provided little, such as Spain, Poland, Malta and even Central America, and Rome was in no way prepared to try the idea of a moratorium – nor was the leadership in most of the missionary societies. Nevertheless an adverse tide was now running strongly, not only politically but within the missionary movement itself and its traditional backers. It was perhaps only the wholesale expulsion from major areas such as Igboland and the Sudan which had enabled numbers to be kept up elsewhere as well as they had been. All in all the missionary decline was now running faster than the rise in local priests so that the combined number of priests was actually falling, whereas until 1970 it had steadily risen, and this despite a definite increase in African ordinations. The figures for the whole continent for five years are shown in table 6.[82] This indicates clearly enough the slackening impetus of the missionary movement. Nevertheless the survival into the 1970s of so many thousand missionary priests may in the context of wider African history be the more significant phenomenon.

The sheer tenacity of Catholic missionaries in these years, combined with a refreshing new flexibility in their ideas and work style, has probably been a

240

major factor in affecting the religious future of Africa.[83] One senses identifiable shifts in the ecclesiastical map. On the one side has been the steady growth in the sudanic belt where work mostly began so late. The striking development of the Catholic Church in south-west Ethiopia is a case in point. It is also a particularly interesting one on account of the simultaneous tendency to 'Ethiopianise' the Latin rite in Ethiopia. Since 1964 the 'Latins' have observed the Easter date of the Ethiopians and since 1969 they have used the Amharic 'Anaphora of the Apostles' instead of a western eucharistic prayer.[84] With the vernacular translation and adaptation of the Latin rite everywhere, it is possible in fact to overcome the old gulf between 'Latin' and 'Oriental' and to foresee the emergence of a continuum within the Catholic Church in Africa which includes a substantially Ethiopian segment, not wholly unlike the way in which in India the Syrian–Malabar tradition is increasingly permeating the western Latin tradition and spreading out of Travancore.

Table 6. *Decline in total number of priests (black and white)*

1970	17,142
1971	17,061
1972	17,043
1973	16,926
1974	16,428

In a different direction the Catholic Church has been tending towards a predominant position within some areas of old Protestant ascendancy where in 1950 its contribution still seemed very secondary. Ghana, Zambia, Malawi and even South Africa are all examples. In each of these it is probable that by 1975 the Catholic Church was the largest single church among Africans. Thus a scholar surveying the Ghanaian scene has remarked how 'the Catholic Church seems to be increasingly taking on the role of being Ghana's major church, vigorously expanding, and with its own distinctive style of indigenised life and liturgy'.[85] Much the same could be said of the other countries mentioned, except for South Africa where growth in numbers rather accentuated the deeply unhealthy state of the church illustrated by the way the number of black students for the priesthood was diminishing almost to vanishing point just as it was rising almost everywhere else on the continent. Here was a church overwhelmingly black in membership, overwhelmingly white in power.

A change in numerical balance between Protestant and Catholic is, however, not questionable. It would seem that the relative withdrawal of some of the main Protestant missionary bodies from the 1940s on, while their young churches were endowed with westernised church structures but very limited clerical resources, resulted in many cases in their not continuing to expand within their own heartlands quite comparably with the Catholics whose missionary personnel and expertise was now so much greater. Only in some of the oldest of the Protestant strongholds, such as the western Cape, Botswana, Sierra Leone, Liberia and western Nigeria, was the Catholic presence still notably weak in the 1970s. Kenya too remained a country where the Catholic Church did not thrive in the way that the Protestant churches were clearly doing, despite a large numerical growth.

This quite considerable shift in the Catholic–Protestant balance was not just one in numbers but in public leadership and a sense of confidence, intellectual and political. To be appreciated right it must be remembered that the frontier between Catholic and Protestant, so strong in the 1950s, had in many ways become distinctly blurred by the 1970s. New projects could now be almost automatically ecumenical, while many Catholic institutions opened their doors most willingly to members of other churches desiring to make use of their facilities. This was practicable because many attitudes which in the 1950s would have been characterised as distinctively Protestant and not Catholic were by the 1970s almost more a mark of Catholics than of Protestants. The Catholic communion, it might not unreasonably be claimed, was no longer a threat to the more enduring values of the Protestant tradition but rather their most likely upholder and disseminator.

All these advances, numerical and attitudinal, depended to a very considerable extent upon a foreign force of priests and nuns and so illustrated one very evident weakness within the Catholic system, but the old heartlands where the local clergy was strongest illustrated another. It was here that the number of the faithful had soared most strikingly, and as it did so the priests–people ratio grew rapidly worse. In many dioceses around the great lakes and elsewhere, there was now hardly one priest actually in pastoral work for 8,000 of the faithful. Mission stations formerly staffed by three men were now held by two or one; a few were even being closed. While the number of the baptized mounted unswervingly (if only because of the high birth rate), there was a slow erosion all through these years in rural priestly ministry. Faced with this the bishops were increasingly delegating powers of all kinds to catechists and local lay councils or movements. They and their advisers were fostering the idea of the 'basic Christian community' as almost advantageously priestless. Nevertheless there is no real alternative within the Catholic system to mass and ordained priest and the consequence of Rome's ruthless refusal to allow a new kind of priest was probably far more revolutionary than if it had granted the ordination of some catechists – the internal balance of the sacramental and the non-sacramental, the clerical and the lay was being altered a good deal more radically.

At the same time, whether on account of the shortage of priests and their pastoral care, or for other complex reasons, the proportion of the adult Catholic community permanently excluded from communion for marital reasons was mounting threateningly. The chief identifiable factor here was that of the church wedding, required for the validity of marriage by canon law.[86] Almost all across Africa the percentage of Christians celebrating their marriage in church before a priest was steadily diminishing from the 1950s on, and in the old Catholic areas around Lake Victoria it had fallen to about 25 per cent by the end of the 1960s. This meant that at least three-quarters of younger Catholics could be permanently excluded from the sacraments and their children regarded technically as illegitimate. Thus Masaka diocese in 1949 had a church population of 137,000 and 887 weddings; in 1969 it had one of 290,000 and 764 weddings. Tororo in eastern Uganda had 1,098 weddings in 1960 with 392,000 Catholics and 557 with 410,000 in 1969.[87] In old evangelised areas such as Buganda this process had already set in by the early 1940s; elsewhere it became a major phenomenon only in the 1950s or 1960s. Undoubtedly in most places the Catholic community had previously accepted the requirement of a church wedding and marriage rates were remarkably high for some years. But by the end of the 1960s the practice had decisively changed. A church wedding remained the norm for the new upper class, the educated elite, and also for the more devout families, especially those living in proximity to a mission or parish, but the mass of Catholic villagers were quietly opting out of it.

While the causes of this development were undoubtedly complex, it illustrates the deep distancing of the millions of the ordinary rural faithful from the tight structures of the Catholic institution. The figures shown in table 7 from the diocese of Morogoro in eastern Tanzania show just how steady the process could be.[88]

Table 7. *Diocese of Morogoro*

	Faithful	Marriages
1959	132,206	936
1961	140,267	847
1963	150,314	646
1965	161,108	585
1967	167,183	494

Clearly the cumulative effect on the proportion of all church members living in a union not recognised by the church is what is most important here. It is certain that since 1967 the position grew still more serious, and there was certainly little the diocesan authorities could do about it. The canonically valid celebration of marriage is bound to the presence of a priest, but priests are very seldom present in most of the places where people actually live: it is as simple as that. In Morogoro 1967 was to be followed by a particularly sharp decline in the number of its clergy. In that year it still had 88 priests: 25 Tanzanians and 63 expatriates (mostly Dutch Holy Ghost Fathers). By 1973 it had 73 priests: 36 Tanzanians and 37 expatriates. The profound real shifts in church life and commitment behind these dry statistics require much more study, but it is reasonably clear that the other side of the coin to the vast numerical growth of the Catholic community had been the speedy emergence (as in rural South America) of a Catholicism in which the mass, the priesthood and canonical marriage were all becoming peripheral.

There were certainly areas in which these trends were very much less manifest, east central Nigeria especially. In Igbo Catholicism in the mid-1960s the degree of conformity with church norms remained remarkably high[89] and here too a rise in ordinations was beginning to take place, unparalleled in scale elsewhere. Igboland was exemplifying a type of fervent clericalised Catholicism rather reminiscent of the Ireland from which its missionaries came, but the departure from the ranks of the clergy of its best-known priest writer, Bede Onuoha, showed too that patterns of rejection, clerical and lay, could build up here as in Europe. Indeed the phenomenon of anticlericalism was becoming a recognised element of Igbo life.

The enormous success of the Jamaa movement in Zaire in the 1960s must partly be understood against the wider background of tension between Catholic structure and Catholic community. It was only after Fr Tempels finally left Africa for Europe in 1962 that his ideas spread widely across a deeply disorientated Congo, particularly in Katanga and Kasai, bringing with them a striking spiritual revival within the church at an otherwise very difficult time. In a couple of years it had many thousands of members, to be found in every parish of the Kasai. Profoundly apolitical in character, the movement was equally fundamentally unclerical, so that if some priests welcomed it as a sign of the spirit and of popular response to the faith in a time of ecclesiastical depression, they could also feel deeply threatened by it – by its ability to spread from parish to parish and diocese to diocese without any clerical initiative or supervision, as well as by its use of sexual symbolism and its mysterious degrees of initiation. In the political chaos of 1964 the last white archbishop of Luluabourg could write about Jamaa with considerable enthusiasm[90] but increasingly, as the Zairean hierarchy was reconstituted with black faces in place of white but the same basic need to insist upon a clerically controlled church, the bishops grew suspicious and hostile. From mid-1966 the movement was forced more or less underground, the Flemish Franciscans who had encouraged it had to leave the country and at last in January 1973 the bishops published a very strong statement of condemnation.[91] In practice some bishops remained more tolerant than others and some Zairean priests remained in full sympathy.[92] What may surprise is how little sign there was of Jamaa actually breaking away to become a church of its own. Here if anywhere the Catholic aversion to independency was manifest. Jamaa was too much of a spiritual movement and too little of an institution of any kind to become even in rebellion an institutional church.

244

Moreover, while the Zairean bishops could publish their directives as they would, it is probable that they had a somewhat limited control over what actually took place in the religious life of a Katanga mining town or Kasai village: nowhere were Catholic numbers more vast, nowhere were ordinations more disappointing.

Elsewhere, particularly in Angola and Mozambique, church structures could be almost swept away by war or a wider political confusion. Thus nearly all the mission stations in the diocese of Porto Amelia in northern Mozambique were closed in the mid-1960s, but the Christians continued under the leadership of their catechists and the Legion of Mary to baptize, instruct one another and pray so that some 66,000 baptisms were performed in the next ten years.[93] With the fall of the Portuguese empire a large proportion of Catholic priests left the country altogether, while the small group of local clergy was quite unprepared for the changed situation, so that while the bishops were endeavouring to relate the church to the new and abrasive order, the divide between popular and institutional religion undoubtedly grew apace.

The evolution of Catholicism in these years did then take place at many levels, most of which we know as yet very little about. It is certainly easiest to outline that of the hierarchical leadership and the formulation of policy, remote as this might sometimes seem from the underlying realities, yet it was not unimportant. There was something of a tussle for leadership in these years. The first and obvious losers were the missionaries – whether it be the old-fashioned society superiors or the new post-conciliar enthusiasts. Lefebvre and Van Asten had both disappeared from the African scene by 1975 – Lefebvre to lead a European movement of Catholic traditionalists unwilling to accept the Vatican Council and in near-schism to the Pope himself, Van Asten to become a married layman, an executive of the Food and Agricultural Organisation. Another body of Europeans, however, was not so easily ousted and that was the nuncios. While Rome had been Africanising the episcopate, it had been building up a considerable network of nunciatures all across Africa in place of the four 'apostolic delegations' established forty years earlier. The nuncios were directly dependent upon the Secretariat of State whose powers in the latter years of Paul VI were greater than they had ever been previously. Many of the nuncios were personally very able men; they could help the African hierarchy with all sorts of political problems. Moreover the latter remained so deeply dependent upon Rome financially that it could not afford to reject Roman directives too emphatically. Rome's control of the church was thus substantially transferred from a network of superior generals to a network of nuncios, but it was not imperilled.

The African bishops themselves, however, were growing in strength – not only in number but in sense of purpose, and (unlike bishops in many other

245

parts of the world) they did not have to face much in the way of 'contestation' from their own theologians (there were still hardly any) or laity. It is true that the establishment in 1969 of SECAM, a body linking all the bishops of Africa, had proved of little significance. Pope Paul had visited Uganda in that year and the archbishops of the continent had assembled to greet him and meet among themselves as they had not been able to do since the end of the Vatican Council. Out of this came SECAM with a small secretariat in Accra. Various meetings followed at considerable expense but to little point – perhaps because they so largely lacked an adequate infrastructure of consultant theologians and ecclesiastical technocrats. Nevertheless the African contribution to the Synods of Bishops which Pope Paul called from time to time in this period was more impressive. It is true that the Synods themselves were not particularly successful or effective: they were little more than a Roman gesture to the principle of wider consultation from which nothing decisive was expected to come. Nevertheless the African bishops who were elected to attend them, new to the game of high ecclesiastical politics and less weary than their colleagues from elsewhere, took them seriously, prepared their interventions with care and made them with vigour so that the wider church was decidedly impressed. This was particularly true of the 1974 Synod on evangelisation. The men who were now taking the lead internationally were Thiandoum of Dakar (helped by his strong French connections), Malula of Kinshasa, Zoa of Yaoundé and Sangu of Mbeya in Tanzania, but they were backed and stimulated by some quite unconventional younger men such as Kalilombe of Lilongwe, Sarpong of Kumasi and Mwoleka of Rulenge. The African hierarchy of the 1970s was too large, too varied and too rich in talent to have a single mind or to reflect any longer, as had sometimes been suggested in earlier years, an almost Roman point of view. On the contrary it was becoming possible to imagine that the most vigorous challenge to the latter might soon derive from the bishops of Africa.

Their difficulties, however, were clearly legion. If they could claim to lead some of the most quickly growing churches in the world, they had also – many of them – to live within the most politically unstable situations. For priestly personnel and financial support they remained, with very few exceptions, profoundly dependent upon Rome, western Europe and North America. The Catholic Church in Africa was becoming a colossus unquestionably, but a colossus with feet of clay, over whose future a great question mark still rested. Its leadership had been fortunate in the rather favourable conditions which had existed in most countries during the post-independence decade and it had greatly benefited from those conditions in all sorts of ways. But its problems of personnel, structure and finance were as pressing as ever in 1975 and the basic issues of ministry and marriage could hardly be tackled while the rules of canon law were unchanged. No church remained more vulnerable to a government decision to exclude missionaries, while, quite apart from this eventuality, structure and community were falling further apart with each ensuing year. The bishops talked about fostering community, but they mostly found it too hard to accept when offered in the concrete form of either Jamaa or Ujamaa, spiritual or socialist. Could the African hierarchy break its canonical fetters and carry out a far more radical Africanisation of its institutions in the service of the community than anything yet attempted? Could it, highly clerical and western in its long training as it was, actually want to do so? And if it did, would the Catholic Church survive in a recognisable form? By 1975 the main Protestant churches of Africa had attained a certain measure of stability, something of a re-assimilated shape. For the Catholic Church this was not so. In a way its potential was greater, but so too its continued reliance upon missionaries and – almost more serious – its inevitable dependence upon Rome. And Rome in the 1970s was in a conservative and uncreative mood. In these circumstances the immediate future of Catholicism seemed less predictable than that of any other section of African Christianity.[94]

C. Independency

This was not the greatest period in the history of ecclesiastical independency though it possibly was in its historiography. The late 1960s, in particular, saw the publication of a series of major and highly influential works such as Harold Turner's *African Independent Church*, David Barrett's *Schism and Renewal in Africa*, John Peel's *Aladura*, and Welbourn and Ogot's *A Place to Feel at Home*. The following years would see a mass of studies, historical, sociological and theological, concerned with movements in every part of Africa. While this most helpfully made up for the relative neglect of earlier years, it somewhat obscured the fact that historically the zenith of the movement as a whole was already past, and it is difficult to point to any major new churches emerging in this period. It was rather a time for consolidation, for a greater concern with bricks and mortar, for writing the history of what happened, for jubilees such as the golden jubilee solemnised by the Kimbanguist Church, 6 April 1971, or that of the Eternal Sacred Order of Cherubim and Seraphim celebrated throughout Nigeria in September 1975.

It was also inevitably a period in which some of the last surviving leaders from independency's golden age passed away. One of these, perhaps the most mysterious of all the founding fathers, died in 1973. He was Johane Masowe: John of the wilderness.[95] His Apostles, the Vahosanna, the Shona basketmakers of Port Elizabeth, were finally expelled from South Africa back to Rhodesia in 1962. In Rhodesia they had no desire to stay, or at least to establish their headquarters, though many admittedly had never left their homeland. But they were looking for a freer and more missionary atmosphere; perhaps too a more essentially eschatological one. Jerusalem beckoned. While still in South Africa they had applied to the Israeli Consul for permission to move to Israel. It had not been granted, but if they could not go there at once, they could at least take that road, the road to the north. Consequently they settled on Zambia and selected Marrapodi, a suburb of Lusaka, as their new centre. Marrapodi quickly became another Korsten, a hive of industry, a village of tinsmiths, cabinet makers, basket weavers and car repairers. Masowe himself, however, went still further north and spent most of the 1960s secretly in Tanzania and Kenya planning the next stage in the exodus. He returned to Zambia to die at Ndola in September 1973, by which time the headquarters of the Apostles, the Ark of the Covenant, was in process of transference from Lusaka to Nairobi. Although he had not lived in Rhodesia for thirty years, Masowe's body was flown back there for burial in an altar-like structure on the top of Dandadzi hill at Gandanzara, near Rusape, where he was born and where he had preached and baptized at the start of his ministry. His tomb bears the simple inscription *Ngirosi ye Africa*, the Angel of Africa.

The church of this mysterious man is as unusual as its founder. It has spread as widely as the Apostles of Maranke, but in a very different way – almost entirely through the migration of its Shona members. It is unique or nearly unique in many ways: first, in its polity whereby its headquarters and leadership kept deliberately away from its base and recruitment centre in Shonaland; secondly, in the consistently hidden character of the life of the founder, present most of the time neither in Shonaland nor at the church's headquarters; thirdly, in his role as a baptist. Many prophets had claimed this title but in his church the founder alone was able to baptize (Lenshina had, at least for a while, claimed the same prerogative). What confirmation is for an episcopal church, baptism was in Masowe's, and far more: not only the supreme ritual occasion but probably the only time members would meet their almost mythical leader. His own journeys were chiefly designed in order to carry out this task in the many countries his Apostles now inhabited; towards the end of his life he was too ill to continue this and so for years no one was baptized. One of the hardest questions the Synod of his disciples had to decide a year after his death was whether baptism would ever be possible again. They decided that it would be.

The Masowe Apostles shared with the Nigerian community of Apostles at Aiyetoro the character of a totalitarian but industrially modernising society. But whereas Aiyetoro was a single home-based community, physically isolated from the rest of the world in its lagoon, the Vahosanna combined all this with both an extraordinarily peripatetic history and an equally remarkable liturgical and religious inventiveness which centred around a sort of convent of nuns, 'The Ark of the Covenant'. The Ark was a house of prayer marking the true centre of the church, first at Korsten, then at Marrapodi and now in Nairobi. It is here that the lengthy but profoundly restrained liturgy of the church is most notably celebrated, that the 'Hosanna mukuru' (the great Hosanna) is sung each day at sunrise and sunset. As Ark, 'this house' is both Noah's ark and ark of the covenant – the central symbol of a pilgrim journey, of salvation and divine presence.

As regarding the ark of virgins Father John declared that he had been advised by God to set it up for it is a covenant between God and his world. Adding, he said, that if the ark lasts up till the great and dreadful day of the Lord, the believers shall escape the destruction to come just as it was in the days of Noah when eight souls were rescued through the ark.[96]

Nairobi is not intended as a final home; it is seen rather as an approach to Ethiopia and the final homeland of Palestine: the gospel preached first in Shona on Mount Marimba will, one day, reach Jerusalem and so come home. A theology of the New Jerusalem which, with many a church, has simply canonised a new holy city as the centre of pilgrimage upon some mountain of Zululand or Zaire is here, instead, obstinately bent upon re-rooting it in its original geographic location.

By the 1970s the Aiyetoro community, having become extremely rich, seemed to be in a process at once of secularisation and of disintegration, in which its communal values were being replaced by more individualistic ones and its particular religious vision appeared almost lost.[97] It would be too early to say that the Vohosanna were in similar danger but the tensions in their strange community were certainly mounting and Masowe's death was followed by a disastrous schism in which many of the younger Apostles were separated from the Evangelists, the Sisters and the 'Loyalist' Synod which met in September 1974 in Rhodesia. They had at least to adjust to the predicament of being Vahosanna without Masowe, as the Vapostori had to be without Maranke, the Kimbanguists without Kimbangu, the Harrists without Harris and – very soon – the Amanazaretha without Shembe, father or son.

If the later 1960s, the years following the removal of the Ark from Korsten to Marrapodi, were an important and creative period of expansion for Masowe's Apostles, this was by no means universally true for African independency. New churches indeed continued to spring up in certain countries, notably, Ghana, Kenya and eastern Nigeria. The last is an interesting case and reflects the religious situation within the civil war and still more just after the civil war. Side by side with the main churches of Igboland small independent churches – which had long been numerous just to the south on the Calabar coast – now multiplied in a way they had never done before among the Igbos. Here, as in Ghana, such bodies have tended to be very small indeed – 'prayer houses' or 'clinics' – centres of a praying therapy, one might say, with a rather loose clientele, patronised often enough by people who continue in the long run to be active members of a mission-founded church. The contrast here may be becoming one between different types of religious activity rather than between separated 'churches' in a hard western sense.

No new church of any considerable size originated in these years. Indeed even the overall rate of numerical growth in membership of the pre-1965 decade does not seem to have been maintained. In South Africa, where that growth had been greatest, the segment of the black population belonging to independent churches appears to have become fixed at between 20 per cent and 25 per cent.[98] That of course, by no means excludes absolute growth in membership, relative to the considerable general growth of the African population. In a number of countries to the north the growth rate in membership of independent churches had certainly fallen below that of mission-founded churches. The strength of independency continued to derive above all from the large peripheries of society – the great bodies of people in both black- and white-ruled Africa more or less conscious of their alienation, their exclusion from the support network and avenues of advancement proper to the secular establishment and cultivated by the historic churches. For parts of West Africa – notably Southern Ghana and Southern Nigeria – this however was far from the whole story. Here independent churches were rather becoming the resort of a new social elite. It is essential to bear in mind that the continental diversity of spiritual situation had probably grown greater than ever before and also that where religious movements of any sort had taken root effectively in an earlier period they naturally continued while tending to expand the frontiers of their constituency. In this they did no more than conform to a law generally true of all churches in all ages.

Apart from the score of the most 'respectable', independent churches were by 1970 tending to fall under considerable government suspicion. Whatever sympathy black governments had initially felt for small churches established independently of white control, that sympathy had now disappeared. They were coming to be seen instead as uncontrollable, useless and potentially subversive: too many and too confused in their leadership to be controlled or even effectively registered; too small and too poor to cooperate in any worthwhile way with government plans; too much at home among the out of work, the dissatisfied proletariat, to be other than possible media for the articulation of subversive thoughts. The more autocratic a government, the less time for independency it would be likely to have. It is not surprising then that in May 1968 President Karume of Zanzibar warned people against 'the dangerous emergence of pseudo-religious sects in Africa aimed at fomenting internal strife in independent African countries', that the next month the Church of the Two Witnesses, Simon Kimbangu and Thomas Ntwalani was banned in Zaire with some other churches, and that in October of the same year even the Kenyan government outlawed, as its colonial predecessor had done, the Dini ya Msambwa, following this up with several more bannings the next year. Mobutu, Amin, Kaunda and other leaders were all soon to be banning various smaller churches. Doubtless such outlawings were often as ineffectual now as they had been in colonial times, and they could indeed contribute to the long-term survival of several of these bodies. What is clear is that, for the time being at least, independency had moved away from the centre of the social stage which it had a little earlier seemed to be approaching – so long, of course, as the score of churches already referred to are excluded from consideration.

To those we must now return. In 1969 the Kimbanguist Église of Joseph Diangienda was admitted to membership of the World Council of Churches: the best institutional criterion of ecclesiastical acceptability within contemporary non-Roman-Catholic Christianity. It had arrived and with its membership of perhaps a million faithful (claims of five million are certainly exaggerated), its considerable network of church buildings, schools and other institutions, it has at least as much claim to be there as many another church. With the Catholic Church and a union of Protestant mission-founded churches, it soon became one of only three churches to be recognised by the government of Zaire.

The EJCSK, while the biggest, stands for some twenty independent churches up and down Africa which have effectively entered into the category of a recognised Protestant church doing the sort of things which a mission-founded church is expected to do, while retaining a particular ethos and strong differentiating customs. The Christ Apostolic Church of Nigeria remained the clearest West African example but others are the Celestial Church of Christ, the Church of the Lord (Aladura) and the Feden Church. One of the most fast growing of such churches in the late 1960s in eastern Africa was the African Independent Pentecostal Church of Africa. Dating from the 1930s but suppressed at the time of Mau Mau, in the 1950s, it burst forth again in a rather political way with the arrival of Kenya's independence: thousands of official Presbyterians crossed back to the AIPCA which was soon claiming 100,000 members. This was, probably, the last example of what may be called the 'separation' phenomenon – in this case the re-emergence in the era of political independence of a suppressed independent tradition and its large-scale withdrawal from a mission-sponsored church. The AIPCA had an old tradition of concern with schools. Two other Kenyan bodies with a strongly educational emphasis also clearly consolidated themselves in these years. They were the African Brotherhood Church and the rather smaller African Christian Church and Schools (see p. 79). By 1975 the former had some 75,000 members and about a hundred clergy. Both had their roots in mass withdrawal from the Africa Inland Mission in the 1940s and both had now become members of the National Christian Council of Kenya, as had the African Israel Church Nineveh. Some of their ministers are now trained at St Paul's United Theological College in Limuru and further links have been forged with overseas mission churches. Thus the ACC and S has invited help from the Canadian Baptist Overseas Mission Board and received from it eight missionary assistants. A growing concern with schools, membership of a local council of churches, participation in ecumenical theological colleges, and new links with overseas missions – generally small mission-bodies, Evangelical, Baptist, Pentecostal, or the very helpful and disinterested Mennonites – these are four rather general characteristics of the more stable independent churches in these years. They go with a tendency to tone down their more eccentric customs, to produce doctrinal statements of unblemished Protestant orthodoxy, to introduce communion services where these were not formerly known, and in general to conform increasingly to one or another

252

model of the western ecclesiastical and clerical image. They also represent a trend back towards unity and inter-church cooperation hitherto little manifest.

While the flow of independency was initially, by its basic internal logic, one towards separation, multiplicity and diversity, there has in fact long been something of a counter-tendency, admittedly usually rather ineffective; this has been particularly true in South Africa where the fragmentation was greatest.[99] The African Ministers Independent Church Association goes back to 1934, and Bishop Dimba's Federation of Bantu Churches to 1943. In the 1950s among other ecumenical efforts a Zion Combination Churches in South Africa was founded by twenty-eight Zionist bodies. The purpose of such associations was to help one another in the field of government registration, in ministerial training and in various other areas where very small churches could not hope to cope on their own. The larger and better organised churches have seldom joined such federations of which the best known is AICA, the African Independent Churches Association.[100] This arose in 1965 with the encouragement and advice of Dr Beyers Naudé of the Christian Institute. Its primary purpose was to be the provision of theological education through short refresher courses, a correspondence course and even a theological seminary. AICA was for a while remarkably successful. Beginning with some 75 churches, by March 1969 it included 261 and two years later it counted over 400. They were predominantly small (though not the very smallest: its minimum conditions were five ministers or a congregation of 200), mostly on the Rand, and they covered the entire spectrum theologically. Their leadership had very little education, it was elderly, poor, and it found the greatest difficulty in coping with an organisation of the size and relative wealth that AICA acquired. The reasons for the wealth were the growing interest that independent churches inspired in Europe and the prestige of the Christian Institute. Through its assistance considerable sums of money were collected elsewhere for the running of AICA and the development of its courses and a small theological college was actually opened in 1970 at Alice beside the Federal Theological Seminary and Fort Hare.

The roles of President and General Secretary of AICA were inevitably very prestigious ones, far more so than that of head of a small church, and it was perhaps inevitable that bitter leadership disputes should soon develop. A failure to acquire or (still more) retain the leadership could bring with it the attempt to set up a rival organisation; this however could hardly succeed for long as such an association was pointless without money and what effectively held AICA together as it did was the considerable amount of foreign money providable to one body alone through the Christian Institute. In 1973 came collapse. The Institute had found it increasingly invidious to control the finances of the Association, particularly with an often sharply

divided Association in which defeated factions could denounce it for inter-
ference and in a wider atmosphere of mounting racial distrust and the
growth of the 'Black Consciousness' movement. The handing over of full
control of the finances in January 1973 was followed by increasing polarisation, financial mismanagement and within a matter of months complete
economic collapse. By December AICA seemed to have disintegrated – its
president deposed, its college and correspondence courses closed down. The
gap in purpose and model of organisation between the small and almost
moneyless independent church and the large, relatively wealthy, ecumenically
orientated Association was too great to be sustained: in retrospect it would seem
clear that it was only possible for so long as it was on account of the profound
moral prestige of Dr Naudé and his assistants which for some years made the
impossible seem practicable. This was not, however, to be the end. In a
humbler form, with new leadership and some help from the South African
Council of Churches, a new start was made in 1974. AICA collapsed, perhaps because its plans had been over-ambitious; it continued because the
need for it was irrefutable.

It is interesting that the humbler parallel women's organisation WAAIC,
which had far less money to spend, had far less bitter internal conflict and
survived AICA's collapse in 1973. The women had shown themselves
unwilling to allow AICA either to control their organisation or to divide it.
It is to be noted also that none of the larger churches ever joined AICA;
they did not stand in the same need of such an umbrella organisation and
they were probably wary of the Christian Institute's very bad image with
government.

At the moment of AICA's greatest apparent achievement in 1972 a
similar organisation was being set up under the same sort of enlightened
white Christian encouragement in Rhodesia. Established that year FAM-
BIDZANO was inspired by Martin Daneel for the same general purpose –
that of providing some theological education of a basically Protestant kind
for independent churches which could not possibly supply it on their own.
Both its success and its problems would soon resemble those of the older
body.

It could be argued that throughout Africa the academic study and
undoubted sympathy which white people – particularly the currently creative generation of ecumenically orientated Protestant missiologists – were
now demonstrating towards the independent churches was of its nature little
less than the kiss of death: a little financial assistance and the prestige of
entry into a local Council of Churches or even, conceivably the World
Council were baits – however honourably offered – to entice independent
leaders back towards 'orthodox' ways, the current norms of ecumenical
Protestantism. If Protestant missionaries had lost many of their converts by
schism of one sort or another in previous generations, their more enligh-

tened successors were now recovering them ten-fold. While this is to some extent true, it need not be seen as condemnable upon either side, and its effective extent should not be overstated. The complex process of loss and gain was in many ways an irreversible one and if the mission churches and their projects were now again influencing the independent bodies which had earlier cast loose from them, lines of influence were going the other way too: much which had been acquired in separation was being quietly incorporated by the older bodies. At the same time the size and diversity of the independent movement was such that the influence exerted on many of its members from outside was still little or none. If the E J C S K, the Christ Apostolic and the African Brotherhood Church were becoming rather recognisable and rightly respected members of the wider Protestant family, other quite large groups such as the Maranke Vapostori remained far more enigmatic. And beyond all these were the hundreds of very small churches whose rise and fall no historian could adequately assess. Many were natural occupants of the forgotten peripheries in an under-developed and under-educated society whose traditional religion had been hit too severely to sustain alone religious faith and hope in a hard and confusing world. It may be that in the wider view the larger, more coherent churches which we know more about are, for that very reason, the less significant. They are the minority, moving away from the peripheries towards the central areas and establishments of society already catered for by a plethora of ex-mission churches. The score of churches significant by size could finally prove insignificant; the thousands of the insignificant remain *ipso facto* significant. It could be. We really do not know.

One thing which does need to be remembered is that in 1975 large areas of Africa, including some very Christian areas, remained hardly touched by independency. Tanzania is the most obvious case from first to last, but that of Uganda over the twenty-six years of this study is hardly less striking. The traditional religions of Tanzania were not of a quite different kind from anywhere else; its inhabitants have experienced, as much as other parts, sudden religious, social and political upheavals – Maji Maji, witch eradication movements, religious revival. But none of these generated, to any significant degree, independent churches large or small. It is certainly the case that the forces which elsewhere created such bodies here operated to some extent at least within the mission-founded bodies, and it is probable that everywhere in Africa the difference between small local congregations, Catholic, Protestant, independent, is very much less than the theorist might suppose to be the case. Moreover even in countries most prone to independency there have always been an at least equal number of Christian Zulu, Luo, Yoruba or Kongo who – no less poor, no more educated for the most part – have preferred to retain membership of one of the 'historic' churches. Nevertheless the difference between the areas of major independency and those of minimal independency remains a striking one, and while cultural, political and economic factors are undoubtedly important in explaining this, it is hard to doubt that these finally achieve their relevance across their ecclesiastical impact and that the variations of independency have to be interpreted in religious and churchly terms – in the character of the mission or mission churches operating in a country, their purposes, methods and personnel, all this as affected not only by their own historic past and stated objectives, but by the quality of life of their founding fathers in a given area, by the degree of their overlap and inter-relationship, their policy towards both African culture and African advancement, by the degree to which their ethos and behaviour patterns were subtly controlled by those of local colonialism and its practice of racial discrimination, by the degree of genuine gospel freedom which they countenanced or encouraged within their walls. It could be that slightly different but comparable factors in the now existing major churches will be determinative of whether the future sees a further wave of religious independency appropriate to a politically 'independent' rather than a 'colonial' situation, or whether the time for this is now fairly definitively passed and there will be instead a steady stabilisation and institutionalisation of the more considerable bodies in existence, while the smaller ones either retreat into a reduced periphery or, in many cases, fade away entirely.

In Christian history it would be hard to find an epoch when no separate churches whatsoever came into existence, but there have clearly been a number of fairly short periods in which independency has been a major phenomenon followed in each case either by a reintegration of the new movements into the main stream (forcibly or by persuasion), or by their hardening each into a clearly established and institutionalised body of its own. The modern wave of African independency certainly reflects not only religious and ecclesiastical factors but also the dynamics of the colonial situation and the racial tensions which went with it. But the interaction between the main-line Christian church and its white representatives, religious rebellion and its black representatives, was made a good deal more complex by the influence of white 'independents' from North America and Europe. The challenge of the African charismatic and pentecostalist to the mission churches in the twentieth century cannot be isolated from a far wider challenge of the same type of person to the large established churches throughout the world. This challenge is usually also a class one. It is well known how throughout the Protestant (especially Anglo-Saxon) world there is something of a class gradation of churches, normally passing down from Episcopalian via Presbyterian and Methodist to Baptist and Pentecostal. It was natural that there should be an affinity of sympathy between small low-class American and European churches near the bottom of their social scale and disenchanted Christians within the colonial world, and something which was a pretty peripheral religious phenomenon in the United States could become in the colonial context a very much more central one. A little appreciated religious enthusiast in Philadelphia might help generate, hardly aware of his good fortune, a major movement in another continent.

It is too early to assert with confidence that an epoch of creative independency in Africa is now effectively over. The whole structure of African society and religion is far too unstable for such a judgement and the emergence of new movements in several parts of the continent in clearly post-independence conditions is undeniable. Yet it is hard not to see a fairly strong link between the movement at its most powerful and two admittedly extended historical moments: the first, that immediately subsequent to the full impact of the colonial system; the second the colonial collapse and the movement back to black initiative and self-rule. That a comparable third context may shortly emerge – or indeed in some places has already emerged – it is at present impossible to assert or to deny with confidence. It seems plausible, however, to suggest that the tendency of the 1970s appears to be against the foundation of clear-cut churches and towards the wider phenomenon of what one may call the religious movement. This would not only be related to the diminished rigidity of the historic churches but also to the advancing influence of Catholicism in most parts of Africa. Catholicism seems fairly strongly inimical to the founding of new churches but it is, on the other hand, very open to the emergence of new movements. This is not only a matter of what goes on within its own boundaries. In a society where the Catholic Church is fairly strong, Protestant churches appear considerably less likely to break apart. The phenomenon of the multiplication of churches is a very Protestant one and Protestants seem to indulge in it most freely in situations where the Protestant ethos is dominant. When Africans in west and south began to multiply churches so uninhibitedly they were acting in a very characteristic Protestant manner and in societies only very slightly touched, if at all, by the Catholic experience. The rapid growth of a Catholic ethos in modern Africa may well be subtly undermining the option of ecclesiastical independency even within fully Protestant ranks. The new religious movement will tend instead to take less the model of a Protestant 'church' and rather more one of a Catholic 'order', 'devotion' or monastic community – rather as Revival in East Africa has long done. Nevertheless the Protestant principle is so strong in Africa and the Protestant community (all churches added together) so much larger in many countries than the Catholic that one must not expect the one pattern of revitalisation wholly to oust the other. One may all the same anticipate that the passing of the tensions of the era of political independence and the advance of popular Catholicism may well between them have brought near to a close the age of independency as a major ecclesiastical phenomenon in African Christianity.

5

Between politics and prayer

Twenty-six years form a fairly short space of time in institutional history and when that span is as close to us as is that which we have been considering, it is bound to be somewhat tricky to discern and assess the more truly significant shifts in the character of communities. Some of the communities we have been studying did not even exist at the beginning of the period and many others have unquestionably altered profoundly. There were indeed areas of some ecclesiastical stability existent in 1950 – the main Protestant churches close to the English-speaking west coast from Sierra Leone to Calabar, Anglicans and Methodists in the Cape, Catholics in Masaka or Ufipa – in such places change could be relatively slight in the following quarter century, but the overall picture is very different. Quantitatively the African Christian community advanced from something in the range of 25 million to one towards 100 million; geographically its spread grew, particularly into the sudanic belt, and its balance altered away from the far south; the number of separate denominations and churches greatly increased, so did the structures within existing churches and the relations between them. Beneath all this there were shifts in concern, in religious language, in almost everything.

The 1950s, the Indian summer of colonialism, were also the last decade in which the missionary movement publicly called the tune within Africa's ecclesiastical scene. Its numbers had greatly grown in the years since the Second World War, its leadership was sagacious and innovative, generally cooperative with government but able to update its own older institutions effectively and add to them imaginative new ones – a Radio ELWA, a Lovanium university, a Mindolo Ecumenical Foundation, a Nyegezi Social Training Centre. However, beneath the intellectual and institutional surface, the 1950s were a time of mounting tension between mission church leadership and the underlying forces within society. It was a tension which was not overcome either at the level of popular consciousness or at that of institutional responsibilities by a new liberalism in some mission spokesmen and the considerable loyalty of many mission-educated leaders. Major explosions were multiplying. In the 1950s, it might be said, the independent churches never had it so good. The tide was flowing their way through most of the decade and it is the age in which they came closest to the centre of

258

society, able on occasion to compete with the mission churches for the majority allegiance of an area, to be worthwhile allies of a political movement or – alternatively – to challenge the claims of the politicians to speak for the multitude. It could be that the mission churches were rescued in the nick of time from a state of affairs in which their white leadership was losing touch more and more with their black mass membership by the coming of political independence. Without this the rise of religious independency in the following years might have been far more startling. Political independence produced an Africanisation of mission-church leadership and a less generally sympathetic attitude on the part of politicians towards independent churches. The subsequent shift did not take place overnight, but by the second half of the 1960s the independent churches had retreated a fair distance from the centre of the scene, even if they were markedly growing in some areas, among them Ghana, where hitherto their presence had been rather insignificant.

In the 1960s one could argue, to strike a simple if paradoxical contrast, that the mission churches in their turn had never had it so good. Their former pupils were now in the seats of power, their institutions were mostly still in their own hands – enriched indeed both from government and from overseas agencies by larger subsidies than ever before – they basked in the beams of black bishops while the missionary personnel was unreduced and their mission freedom even enlarged. Mission–state confrontation in the 1960s was very much the exception, and at no time had the churches grown faster. The threat of religious independency was markedly less felt in most areas after the middle of the decade; there were no more major schisms and a growing sense that there was room enough for all. Even in Kenya, where the independent bodies were far stronger than in most countries, there could be no doubt that the more influential Christian leaders in national life did not come from their ranks but from those of the historic churches – a John Gatu, a Raphael Ndingi, a Henry Okullu.

Nevertheless, it would be a little too paradoxical to claim the 1960s as, without severe qualification, a golden age for the mission churches. There were important exceptions. The greatest of all mission churches was the Catholic Church in Zaire and for it the 1960s was not a good time. The 1950s had been; its massive institutional strength had been tempered by new liberal insights and a more intellectual approach. Its credibility had probably gained from there being in Brussels after 1954 a rather less compliant government. African ordinations were multiplying fast. But it remained a profoundly paternalist and colonialist (though by no means settler) church and it had the greatest difficulty in readjusting to political independence. It weathered storm after storm in the 1960s but with declining morale and efficiency. While the Kimbanguist Église was not comparable in size, its spirit was probably a great deal better.

For the West African coast too one has to express reservations. Here religious independency had been at its most apolitical. With very strong pre-1950 roots, it may to some extent have suffered from the straight pre-independence political activities of the 1950s; its dynamism rather resurrects itself in the decisively post-independence world – the Ghana of the mid-1960s, the eastern Nigeria of civil war and its aftermath.

For southern Africa a caveat must again be registered, if for quite other reasons. Here the black political revolution never arrived and the mounting wave of religious independency would seem to support a claim that the mission churches elsewhere were rescued, rather than threatened, by the triumph of black nationalism. David Mudiwa, a successful Methodist evangelist and preacher in Rhodesia, began to suffer from chronic stomach aches and to get into frenzies in 1963, a period of acute political tension.[1] A spirit medium diagnosed the trouble as the work of a spirit who wished to make him its medium. By 1965, the year of UDI, he held no more church services and his chapel had become a guest-house for the clients who came to consult his spirit *Kafudzi*. His story has its symbolic value. South of the Zambezi the 1960s were certainly not a golden age for the mission churches and they had their losses, yet the more resilient among them probably managed to adjust to the harsher climate – at odds with white government, under suspicion from black nationalism – without severe shipwreck among their following and even with·ultimate gain. At the same time the movement of religious independency seemed with the years to run somewhat out of steam.

By and large the 1970s were a far more obviously abrasive decade for almost all the churches. Islam in its turn seemed now never to have had it so good, benefiting from a very different balance in international politics. It is certainly not hard to compile a fairly lengthy list of ecclesiastical woes. How far did they really affect the life of the churches? Probably rather less than the historian of events might suppose. By the 1960s the churches were still a force for innovation but they were also, and more massively, a force for conservation. Their younger missionary wing and their more prestigious institutions might still be identified with the winds of change, but behind them the ever-growing mass Christianity of countryside and even high-density urban area was a force of its own, conservative but far from static, less and less amenable to control either from government or from the ecclesiastical superstructure. It was that superstructure which chiefly felt the wind in the 1970s. Even the small professional elite which had proved so invaluable at the time of independence remained almost as Christian and as indispensible. Idi Amin's coup was in January 1971. By 1975 the control of Uganda's army and of the cabinet was fairly clearly in Muslim hands, but the senior civil servants, the academics, the doctors and school teachers remained overwhelmingly Catholic or Anglican and they could not be easily replaced. A certain sense of solidarity between the professional class and the senior clergy was of importance here. And if the church growth rate was rather lower than in the previous decade the number of ordained clergy was mounting a good deal faster. The effect of this was still, however, more a matter of undergirding the superstructure than one of shepherding the base far removed from any professional elite. The quality of pastoral work doubtless varied a very great deal but by and large the seemingly endless network of small local congregations, Catholic, Protestant or independent, continued their work and worship – it is safe to say – infrequently taught by their priests and little deterred by any intrusion of the great world of power and policy less than such a disaster as struck the villagers of Wiriyamu at one moment, Hutu settlements up and down Burundi at another.

The independent churches are as permanent a feature of the picture in half the countries of Africa as are the mission churches. Many split too often; some disappear as the generation which created them dies off; others flourish and extend their boundaries. But with the exception of a very few of the most considerable and institutionalised, they are returning towards the periphery of society – albeit a fairly considerable periphery. It could be argued that, effectively, this is where many a mission church is too, and not a bad place to be in countries where the establishment/elite (however it be defined) is small in the extreme, the 'underprivileged' the great majority. All in all the ex-mission church is still, however, likely to be distinguished by the wider range of its membership, its more frequent ability to cross the borders of class, tribe and state. It is also true, nonetheless, that it is not only the independent church which can often fairly be described as 'tribal' for a number of Protestant mission churches may equally qualify for that description.[2]

From this point of view Roman Catholicism provides the greatest contrast, and its massive evolution across these twenty-five years in numbers, institutions and attitudes must constitute one of the central themes of African Christian history, in somewhat sharp contrast with the spread and maturing of the movement of independency. The one has a maximum of professionalism, financial support, foreign personnel and central control, the other the exact opposite of each. In the overall picture the main-line Protestant churches have nothing quite so striking to offer – they fall, perhaps sensibly, between the two but they are also somewhat pressed upon from either side. The Catholics, in their post-conciliar renewal, have stolen much of the Protestant thunder upon the one hand – vernacular liturgy, scripture translation, social concern – the independents upon the other – self-support, self-ministry, self-government. But any hard line between 'Protestant' and 'independent' is increasingly breaking down and some of the most imaginative efforts of Protestant missionaries in the 1970s have been precisely to help the independents. As regards Catholicism, while it has gone

261

from strength to strength on account of its institutional coordination, its missionary numbers, and the movement of revitalisation derived from the Vatican Council, its prospects remain the most enigmatic. What the sequel to a major decline in the missionary force, now shortly inevitable, is likely to be remains unpredictable, though the impact of the earlier stages of that decline is already clear enough.

It seems a good deal easier to generalise about the 1950s than about the 1970s. Politically and ecclesiastically Africa becomes steadily more diverse across these twenty years. A certain uniformity in colonial and mission policies appears in the post Second World War period. There was a new-found orthodoxy and it was certainly something of a shock to find South Africa unwilling to conform to it. Since then the collapse of the immediate post-independence régimes has left a continent in which, at least for the time being, divergent courses are steadily less veiled. There is simply no unity of predicament, of opportunity or of responsibility. Perhaps the sheer complexity and degree of hard diversification now apparent in African Christianity is the best proof of its having taken root. The only safe generalisation about its condition in the 1970s seems to be that one cannot generalise, that there is very little one can say which is not banal and yet sufficiently widely true to make sense at continental level. The total impression of these years is one not just of expansion but of expansion into a new scale of complexity.

Yet the life of all the churches has to relate to certain realities and there are two contrasting poles of experience which can never be very far away from the efforts and aspirations, whether articulated or merely groping, of an African Christian community. One is prayer and the other is politics. In one way or another the churches have to live with both and between them. *Prima facie*, and bearing in mind the depth of mutual involvement of the missionary movement and colonialism, they made the leap across the divide of political independence with such signal skill and success as would gain the appreciation of the Vicar of Bray. They were helped in this by some inherent existing diversity of Christian political attitudes, as well as by the continued need of the state for ecclesiastical and missionary cooperation. More recently Christians have had to live with many other major political changes, often unpredictable and un-nerving. In the 1950s they had to reconcile their Christianity with their nationalism; in the 1970s they have been faced with what can be still harder alternatives in the midst of a Hutu–Tutsi war, the mounting conflict between white and black power all across southern Africa, Marxist revolution, or a national confrontation between a military dictator and the bishops. For the most part government was a good deal more ruthless towards the end of the period than in its earlier years, though for a Kikuyu that might hardly seem to be the case. The wise bishop grows wary. If there is undoubtedly at times a tendency for the churches to withdraw into otherworldliness from any sort of political involvement, there is also, both in the colonial and post-colonial periods, a good deal of ecclesiastical conformism with local political orthodoxy whatever it may be, so long as it is not too blatantly awful (or even when it is). Both are inevitable. More interesting are the attempts to provide some sort of genuinely independent voice of guidance in secular affairs. This has been done by a number of outstanding individuals, by Christian newspapers such as *Target*, organisations such as the Christian Institute, missionary groups such as the Maryknoll Sisters or the Burgos Fathers. It has been done with more institutional weight by Christian Councils and Catholic Bishops' Conferences. On the surface and in terms of the moment, the political power of the churches seems considerably weaker in the 1970s than in the 1950s or early 1960s, if only because they are frequently faced with more dictatorial governments which have long disposed of most other independent organisations. A surface judgement may still be deceptive. The church's political power in the 1950s was that, principally, of a subcontractor for schools and medicine, a junior partner with the colonial establishment which the dominant partner could not afford to offend too frequently or profoundly. At the time of independence its weakness *vis à vis* the state was usually clear enough: its leadership was too foreign, its local clergy too few, its powers of popular mobilisation too limited, its financial dependence upon government for its institutions too considerable, for it to have very much freedom to manoeuvre.

In some ways after fifteen years of independence and a certain amount of bashing, the situation is less clear. Having lost many of their institutions, the churches remain a good deal less vulnerable. What power they have is now more locally based and they have in many cases grown in popular credibility as much as governments have declined in that commodity. Politics have become a bad joke in many an up-country area where administration has manifestly declined in capacity and is riddled with the corruption of the capital. If military régimes may make for rather more efficiency, people do not exactly identify with them. The main churches in the meantime have continued to provide the one recognisable alternative structure; they may offer a more objective network of information and assessment, a still useful range of services – particularly rural hospitals – and some possibility of advancement and of contact with the world beyond. They also provide, at some personal danger, the only alternative personality with continuing national significance to that of the current president – Malula, Zoa, Luwum. If the churches are bashed from time to time by African governments in the 1970s, it is really because they are politically strong – not in immediate action, but in resilience, in the confidence of many people, in their potentiality to carry through significant social programmes of medium size. Many a government continues to find that there is no reasonable alternative to accepting this fact of life and keeping what ecclesiastical friends it may.

The very small church cannot, of course, claim such a status. The range of political options open to the independent churches has nevertheless been considerable, especially in the period of their greatest political influence 1956–66. Only a few, however, have ever consciously chosen another course than that of a fairly careful political neutrality beyond a rough willingness to be loosely associated with the cause of black power in the years around 1960. More consequential could be the innate tendency in some to provide for their members a total society in which no room remained for significant outside links or secular political commitment. The mystical liturgy of a Khambule, the internal politics of many a Zion city, the meticulous organisation of Aiyetoro in the days of its greatness, all effectively prohibit participation in the non-religious politics of a wider society. Such was most obviously the experience of Lumpa in its years of crisis. It began as a revival within the Presbyterian Church centred upon one charismatic figure. By the late 1950s it had developed into a 'church of the people', a large-scale peasant religion with no clear politics but no total withdrawal either, an apparent ally for what was at the time a somewhat dislocated black nationalism. By the early 1960s Lumpa had become instead a sharply withdrawn minority group, concentrating upon the world to come, suspicious of and suspected by the majority of its neighbours. The hasty political mobilisation of UNIP led straight to civil war. Lumpa illustrates both the tendency of the 1950s of independent church and nationalism to pull somewhat together, and that of the 1960s to pull fairly clearly apart while the latter found in the mission churches a more accommodating partnership. The independent church without foreign capital, secular expertise or significant plant and a more or less tribal base had no political goods worth offering government. It might well have little choice in practice between being anti-political and suppression or apolitical and in the terms of national life insignificant.

It is difficult to assess how deeply disillusionment with politics after independence brought individuals and whole segments of society back to the search for religious values, but it is hard to doubt that such has often been the case, just as in South Africa through the whole of the period disillusionment with white rule and every black attempt to shift it goes far to explain the passionate quest of so many for Zion. Take the Kasai, that large central province of Zaire, always falling somewhat between the claims of the capital and the Bakongo to its west, Katanga and its mines to the south, Kisangani and its more radical politics to the east. Kasai gained nothing from independence, not even notoriety, and it endured some wretched massacres from Lumumba's henchmen for supporting the wrong political party. Thereafter it had no reason to love either the central government or its Lumumbist opponents. It does not seem surprising to find that in the early 1960s it became something of a religious goldmine of a populist kind. It was not that it now felt at one with the institutional Catholic Church and its very authoritarian representatives, the Scheut Fathers, Belgium's national missionary society, though they had built up what was numerically a particularly massive church in the province. While Kasai had never been a major Kimbanguist area, Kimbanguism was growing there steadily enough, but it was joined, first by Maranke's Vapostori, who found here one of their most fertile fields, then and on a far larger scale by Jamaa which literally swept the province after 1962, to the bewilderment of the Catholic clergy unable to decide whether this was an ally or an enemy. Disillusioned, it would seem, alike with the political and the ecclesiastical kingdom, Kasai Baba and Mama sought refuge instead in the delights of Franciscan *communitas*. The interinvolvement of politics, institutional and non-institutional religion, is here evident enough, but across the continent as a whole with the rise and fall of a multitude of religious and political movements there are far too many variables at work to propose any single consistent pattern of interpretation.

No church can wholly escape a political dimension to its behaviour but for few churches are politics a primary concern. It is far more in terms of prayer that they understand themselves, hold the loyalty of their members and discover a future laced with hope. This is essentially true even of those missions whose initial attraction has seemed most clearly educational or medical. Within a few years the core of their most effective membership becomes not schooling children but church-going matrons. It is impossible to understand very much about churches without taking very seriously indeed a sociology of prayer, and it could be argued that it was precisely because the mission-church leadership tended to get away from this central axis of ecclesial meaning, preoccupied with school management, scientific medicine, radio stations and printing presses that the independent churches were able time and again to steal their clothes and grow very effectively as just this and little else: churches of prayer.

The prayer of the independent churches is without doubt most frequently prayer for healing or for deliverance from witchcraft or sorcery, but it also includes prayer for a variety of other purposes, spiritual and material. Much the same can be true of Christian prayer in other continents and churches. While the preoccupation with healing is particularly weighty here, it would be a mistake to characterise the prayer of the independents almost exclusively under this heading. Praise, thanksgiving and the confession of sin are also important elements within it. In the first place, while incorporating all the main traditional elements of public Christian prayer, it seems to obtain its special character from its ability to create a public liturgy which makes full cultural sense to its participants in terms of the symbol, gesture and language it incorporates. There is a reaction here to the liturgical poverty of many western missions as well as a reappropriation of traditional symbols. The splendid and moving liturgies which have been evolved in many churches do suggest affinities with the orthodox worship of eastern Europe, the Middle

265

East and Ethiopia, in contrast to the rather rationalised and privatised patterns of prayer more characteristic of modern Protestantism. The core of all this is essentially liturgy, that is to say *public* prayer. It is a liturgy which seems to be triggered off very especially by the holiest of Christianity's traditional language: Alleluia, Hosanna, Amen. Its most expressive form is to be found in the solemn communal liturgy of a holy place, a centre of group pilgrimage. The role of the mountain of prayer, the new Jerusalem, the place where the people of God can be completely themselves, separate from their unbelieving neighbours, dressed in their characteristic uniforms, able to celebrate the great festivals of their church, provides one of the major poles of prayer: communal liturgy.

A very different pole is that of absolutely personal prayer. Isaiah Shembe, when he first came to the holy mountain of Nhlangakazi, his son declared, 'spent ten days in prayer, day and night. He lived here without food, taking only occasionally some water and some unleavened bread, and he prayed for forgiveness, for our fathers also'.[3] It was a not uncommon experience. Personal prayer had been a significant and moving part of much African traditional religion. At times indeed it seemed to flow out from a soul *naturaliter christiana*. There is a true spiritual continuity between this and the prayer of African Christians as we see it expressed, for instance in the work of the Cameroonian Jesuit poet, Englebert Mveng.[4] In meditation and the wrestling of the soul with its God all the churches and all the religions meet, finding a secret strength which the historian cannot assess nor Caesar crush. Unpolitical as intense prayer may be in intention, the power it provides ensures that it will often not be so in consequence. The power of prayer certainly held Michael Tanzi to his monastic cell in Leicestershire remote from all the political contests of his time, but it kept Simon Kimbangu cheerful through thirty years of a Belgian prison and it gave Janani Luwum the divine calm to face Idi Amin, the Thomas of Canterbury of the twentieth century. So devoutly a Christian prayer as the *Tukutendereza Yezu* of the Revival could become in the circumstances of Amin's Uganda, by the empty grave of the archbishop outside Namirembe Cathedral, a timeless statement with unambiguously timely implications.

Far from such prayer is the preoccupation with immediate temporal benefit of a sort one finds rather too frequently in the independent churches of West Africa and elsewhere. There is a tendency here to privatise prayer in a rather unhealthy way. A little book *The Uses of Psalms*, published by the Christian Bookshop, Lagos, illustrates what is a common approach: 'Psalm 10. To Drive Away Evil Spirits: This psalm is specially made to drive away all illness, especially smallpox. The psalm should be read by 12 midnight three times in a new pot full of water and the sufferer to bathe with it. The holy name is ELI, JEHOVAH-NISSI.' Similar things were advised by Oshitelu of the Church of the Lord (Aladura).[5] Furthermore there seems a strong tendency in west coast independency for prayer, public and private, to become quite excessively client-centred; indeed it looks as if many of the new churches of the 1970s in Ghana and Nigeria could as well be regarded as clinics providing a spiritual therapy to individuals as churches centred upon a public liturgy in which the individual is caught up and forgotten in the worship of God.

The solemn celebration of the Good Friday and September festivals in Lekganyane's Zion Christian Church, the January and July festivals of the Amanazaretha, 6 April for the Kimbanguists, and many other such feasts inevitably recall the round of traditional Catholic or orthodox liturgy. Their consideration needs complementing by one of the growth in prayer forms, pilgrimages and monastic communities within the Catholic Church in Africa. New liturgies such as that of Ndzon-Melen in Cameroon, new pilgrimage centres, new monasteries and convents have been springing up across the continent, drawing on the experience of the independents and African traditional religion as well as that of Catholic liturgical and contemplative sources. Benedictine and Cistercian monasteries such as those of Dzogbegan in Togo, Bouaké in Ivory Coast, Koubri in Upper Volta and Lumbwa in Kenya, together with the far more numerous female communities, some more contemplative, some more active, have done a good deal to draw the Catholic Church back to being manifestly a 'church of prayer'.[6] One of the most interesting new ventures here is the Cistercian monastery at Awhum near Enugu begun by Fr Abraham Ojefua, important particularly in that while its basic character is pure Cistercian, the initiative has not been one of a foreign foundation but of a purely local growth. While monasteries and pilgrimage centres provide an important stiffening for the structure of prayer and a locale for its more formal and solemn manifestations, still more important is the prayer life of the village church, for it is this which provides the continuity of local community and the basic sense of Christian identity for the great majority of ordinary people.

In the past some missionary societies made sure that every village centre in which they had a following was provided with a little church, regardless of the presence of a school; other missionary societies seldom built churches but only schools which could then be used for worship. Representatives of the latter may possibly be regretting it now. The symbolic significance of the buildings was not inconsiderable and a study of how the two patterns worked out might well prove informative. Certainly, if in many countries in the past the mission churches must have struck observers as networks of schools, today they can hardly continue at all as other than a network of prayer houses. What has to be considered is how effectively the ex-mission church has adapted to this basic requirement of viability.

Each in its own way, the churches in these years have had to struggle with the contrasting claims of structure and of *communitas*: a structure largely derived from above, a communion from below. It is a problem faced both by mission and independency. The history of a 'successful' independent church is, to a considerable extent, one of how a small *communauté de base* with some intense shared religious insights and fellowship becomes a 'church' – an ongoing network of congregations held together by an 'objective' order of name, ministry, stabilised particular tradition. The history of a 'successful' mission church is, to a considerable extent, one of how a network of ministers with a name and hard historic order effectively found room for a multitude of self-generating *communautés de base* – small worshipping, face-to-face congregations. One has community and is searching for institution; one has institution and is searching for community.

The historian is almost compelled to focus his attention upon institutions, their rise, adaptation and fall, though he will endeavour to widen the range of what can pass as institution, but community as such is hardly matter for history. Yet the religious interest of institutions mostly depends upon the extent to which they express or generate community, and no community can long exist without institutionalisation. It is here worth suggesting a rough distinction between aspects of ecclesiastical institution which may exist almost regardless of community and those which appear as closely correlative to the latter. Institutional positions firmly held by an outsider, regarded as the preserve of the professionally trained, and maintained by full salaries at a level which places their occupants in the elite rather than the mass are characteristic of the first type. They are seldom open to women. Positions which have always been held by a local, maybe part-time, have been more or less generated by immediate needs, are ill paid or unpaid and probably filled by the enthusiastic amateur rather than the graduate, are characteristic of the latter. They are often filled by women. There has been immense institutional growth in both types in our period, but our history has tended towards preoccupation with the former, including especially the degree of 'Africanisation' achieved of hitherto missionary-type functions. We have, however, in regard to the independent churches, catechists, Manyano, Jamaa, and other topics had a fair amount to say about the latter type too; it is about this that we should add something here, for it provides a certain structural index for *communitas*.

A first question to be registered is how different in reality is the role of a catechist in a mission church from that of a minor prophet or apostle in an independent church, and how different the communities they serve might be. It seems probable that the contrast could be more easily overstated than understated, and might well be diminishing in the course of the period. One major contrast was that between the control of the catechist by a firm missionary organisation and a certain unpredictably charismatic impulse in the prophet-apostle. The overall trend of these years would, however, seem to be towards a diminution both in that control and in that impulse. The ratio between missionary (or even well-educated ordained minister) and number of church members was getting steadily bigger in most places, the likelihood of significant supervision of a local rural congregation by an outsider steadily less. On the other side there is a very clear shift in second generation independency from prophet to pastor, coupled with a slight rise in levels of education. Certainly a range of organisational patterns survives and is particularly noticeable in the large town, contrasting the Roman Catholic community with a few massive and expensive buildings and very large congregations and, at the other extreme, a community such as that of Cherubim and Seraphim with a mass of tiny buildings and small congregations. One still stresses the rare but highly qualified priest (probably a foreigner), the other a rich chaos of unpaid ministers. In the one the lay–clergy divide is maximal, in the other minimal. But in the former this is so much the case that in practice, when one moves away from the town church or the large old-fashioned rural mission station, still lumbering on, it almost diappears in the simple factual absence of clergy. If church life is to exist at all, a pattern not unlike that of the more stabilised independent body emerges instead. This becomes particularly clear in areas which political conditions have swept pretty well clean of regular clergy for some years, but in which the 'mission church' keeps going regardless, even flourishing: the southern Sudan, northern Mozambique, northern Angola, much of eastern Zaire, have all been cases in point during prolonged periods of war and governmental breakdown.

The 'mission church' and the 'independent church' continue, however, to have their own characteristic problems within this common condition – problems relating to the different ends from which they have entered. The problem for the independent is continuity of ministry. Its existence has probably derived from two things: the spiritual power of the founder upon the one hand, an absolutely basic need of local *communitas* upon the other. As the church grows larger, the latter is bound to diminish. When the founder dies, there may not be enough to hold the whole together and there is a schism. Such schisms really follow the natural pattern of division between kinship lineages. When the original 'ancestor' dies, two or more spiritual lineages naturally go their own way – one following a son of the founder, others his leading assistants. The church and its structures have not as yet acquired sufficient independent status as against the claim of personality and immediate spiritual experience. If the church survives at all this will, however, be acquired sooner or later – the Christ Apostolic Church or the Kimbanguist Église are examples here. Unity is then no longer ensured principally by a living leader but rather by the dead founder, his legacy, his tomb, the sense of a historic tradition one has the duty to adhere to.

The problem for the mission church is how to get its structures low enough and how to accommodate to them its sacramental and disciplinary rules. An old and not abnormal Catholic mission-parish in eastern Buganda in the 1960s had fifteen catechists; without them its work would have been quite impossible but not one of them was a communicant member of the church. They were all cut off from full membership by marital or other irregularities of one sort or another. While Protestant churches have theoretically a good deal more room for ministerial flexibility and some have it in practice too, the basic rural problems of numbers, poverty, many small local communities, rapid growth and rules unrelated to African marriage customs remain much the same. The Tiv Church in 1967 had 37 pastors to cope with 1,367 places of worship, 11,829 communicants and an average Sunday attendance of 162,884.

Catholic and Protestant tend all the same to have to face rather different problems. The Protestant one all along has been that of the low level of literacy and the near impossibility of establishing a pattern of religion so deeply dependent upon reading a book among a non-reading rural populace: the bourgeois character of Protestantism stood it in bad stead when it got away from Fourah Bay, Lovedale and Alliance High School unless it could find creative ways of retaking ritual into its system. The Catholic problem has been all along that of coping with very rigid structure, a system of church life in which the clergy dominate. Celibacy and the long seminary training just did not take well in most areas. The answer was the catechist, the Trojan of the modern African Catholic Church, but his very centrality has involved a profound shift away from post-tridentine clerical structures and sacramentalism. The shift has been masked by the size and vitality of the expatriate missionary body. While the eucharist may, in a positive sense, have made less mark on African Catholicism than Catholic tradition would have one anticipate, the function of sacramental confession has not been insignificant on moral life even at village level, and it happily carries far less legalistic a note than many a Protestant system of 'discipline'.

The churches may have been right to settle for a double level of sacramental identification: a large, relatively open baptismal one, and a small, tight eucharistic one. They did not, of course, always do so, being initially extremely scrupulous about the admission to baptism. Rivalry, schooling, and the observable fact that such scrupulosity did not eliminate subsequent 'backsliding' drove most churches, however, towards a policy of fairly easy baptismal membership. As marriage laws and (for some Protestant churches) many other regulations remained firm and unyielding, a large gap developed between the communicants and the congregation. This clearly presented additional problems when the church's local ministers could not themselves be included in the former. However the problem here was to a considerable extent resolved pragmatically by the withdrawal of the priest. No priest, no communion. In the absence of an ordained minister, the unity of the village congregation reasserted itself in forms of non-eucharistic worship. In practice independent churches mostly follow a similar pattern: communion is either no part of their worship or a rare, very special, occasion.

The traditional ecclesiastical pattern stressed a moderately strong sense of exclusivity – neither the Catholic nor the Protestant missionary used to favour any mixing of their following in religious matters. And there are independent churches which have cultivated an even greater degree of religious and social separatism than was seriously advocated by the 'historic' churches. Officially the frontiers between the churches were, then, sharply enough defined, as were those between Christianity and 'paganism'. In practice things were usually different. At the start of our period Protestant and Catholic missionaries in the same region might not even be on speaking terms, but they had seldom succeeded in preventing a considerable degree of mixed marriage: the fact that such marriages usually brought with them practical excommunication was seldom a deterrent. In many areas the to-ing and fro-ing between different bodies has been pretty steady[7] so that while exclusivity is characteristic of the institution, inclusivity seems a good deal more characteristic of the community. Here groups like Masowe's Apostles, the Aiyetoro Apostles or Lumpa are rather untypical. It could be argued that the immediate political and social impact of religion depends largely upon brands of exclusivity – in doctrine, organisation, manners. Only a religious body with some sort of a hard edge can have a message with an impact or political 'clout', though the import of its exclusivity will vary. When Johane Maranke destroyed the bull dedicated to his own family spirits he was underlining a hard frontier between his church and traditional religion, and by so doing he was making his church at least potentially significant even in political terms. Members of the Revival fellowship did much the same when they refused bridewealth, Lenshina's followers when they refused to send their children to school, Catholic bishops when they controlled half the schools of a country and the main university of Zaire. In one way or another religious boundaries stimulate social change, create political problems and generate political power. Inclusivity, on the other hand, is essentially apolitical and it is in this direction that African Christianity, not wholly unlinked with African traditional religion, seems predominantly to tend beneath the plethora of denominational difference. The very multiplicity of churches generates its own tolerance.

The tolerance may become specifically ecclesiastical too. It may be a mistake to regard many of the new independent religious bodies in West Africa as 'churches' at all. They are rather what they call themselves – an 'order', a 'Brotherhood', a 'Praying Circle', a 'Prayer House', a 'Spiritual Clinic'. The significance of such terms is not to be undervalued, particularly within an increasingly Catholic ecclesiastical context. Some may develop with time into a clear church with a permanent membership in principle

271

divided from that of other churches; but for many people a probably temporary attachment to such a body is by no means incompatible with continued membership of a more 'historic' church. There is a great fluidity within the African religious and ecclesiastical scene though there are also important cleavages and majority traditions which are not easily displaced.

The most enduring impression given by a wide ranging survey of the African churches in these years would seem to be the steady expansion of what might be called 'village Christianity' in contrast to 'mission Christianity', inclusivist rather than exclusivist, mass rather than elite, community generating structure, rather than structure creating community; yet never without structure, never without its lines of demarcation, even on occasion as exclusivist as can be. There is no doubt that in 1950 there were already extant large and significant areas of 'village Christianity', even within the mission churches and we illustrated it initially with a picture of Anglican Kyagwe. Nevertheless there was still something relatively exceptional about this, at least in the distance which the process of evolution had advanced. The decisive factors would seem to be length of time since the Christian conversion of a fair nucleus of people, the total numerical size of the community, the presence or absence of regular foreign supervision. While the first generation of Christians remains ascendant, while numbers are fairly low and European clergy vigilant, what may a little harshly be described as the missionary straitjacket remains the dominant form which the new community appears to exhibit. The only way out may be independency. In 1950, outside the west coastal strip, parts of South Africa and a few inland areas such as Buganda, that was still the preponderant impression, particularly for those many parts of Africa where evangelisation only got seriously under way after the First World War, if not still later. Turn from 1950 to the 1970s and a map of 'third generation Christianity' would have to cover a vastly enlarged amount of the continent; numbers have escalated and, outside towns, the missionary force is increasingly thin on the ground. As 'missionary Christianity' recedes as a viable social option 'village Christianity' simply takes over. In the 1920s and 1930s that take-over would probably have meant schism and an independent church; by the 1960s such a formality was ceasing to be necessary. There was simply a profound spiritual and social readjustment which the African clergy, growing in numbers admittedly but still far too few, could do precious little about. Theoretically they might have wished to continue the straitjacket, and indeed one of the most fascinating themes for African Christian history could be the tension between elitist and clerical patterns adopted by a minority and the ongoing surge of populist religious consciousness. This is particularly important for the west coast and it could be claimed that while the 'Sierre Leonean' model appeared and still appears as from one point of view a remarkable achievement, from another it was rather the dam to hold back the flood. The

Fourah Bay ideal of the black-coated Protestant gentleman was too absurdly Anglo-Saxon to be creative and in few places has Christianity advanced less in the interior than Sierra Leone and Liberia. The death of President Tubman in 1971 and the immediate abandonment by his successor of frock coat and tie mark the belated end of an era which impeded rather than facilitated the growth of African Christianity and contributed not a little to the noticeable gap in Protestant West Africa between the old establishment of the coast and the new churches of the interior. There was, after all, more than one variety of straitjacket.

The Msinga district of Natal beside the Tugela river is renowned for the conservatism of its inhabitants, untouched by the old Lutheran mission a few miles away. Then in January 1962 a local prophet by the name of Hezekiya Ndlovu set up on Mount Hlonga 'The New Church Step to Jesus Christ Zion in South Africa', and within a few years the homesteads around were sporting red flags bearing a blue cross to indicate their new religious commitment.[8] The march of village Christianity had eaten up another little piece of rural Africa without the slightest publicity. In this case it was done in the immediate interests of a small new independent church; elsewhere it might be done by a Protestant evangelist or Catholic catechist. The result might not be so different in the three cases – a religion combining a strong sense of the one God of judgement and mercy, some personal attachment to Christ, a deep belief in the value of baptism, the use of the Bible as a source of guidance, a sharing in the Christian tradition of prayer and ritual, all combined with a continuing acceptance of much traditional social and religious practice. Village Christianity may tolerantly co-exist with traditional beliefs in spirits and witchcraft or it may desperately challenge the behaviour which follows from them but it lives either way within the world of such things, as mission Christianity does not; yet it tempers them too with another vision which has somehow to attain the mastery from within. This is a world in which the frontier between Christian and non-Christian is a moving one, and moves not only between people but within them and in both directions.

> Umfundisi uzale inyanga,
> inyanga izale umfundisi.

> The pastor begat a herbalist
> The herbalist begat a pastor.

So they say in Natal.[9] Nannungi in Buganda was a Christian chief, his daughter a spirit-diviner. Kiganira Ssewennyana, a prophet-diviner, has been hailed more recently as a remarkable example of contemporary Ganda religion, but he is the son of a devout Christian catechist and was so brought up.[10] Village Christianity is not a static conception and it may move several ways. In some places it will have a strongly Catholic character, in another Methodist, in a third Zionist, elsewhere – where ecclesiastical mobility has

273

been considerable – it will be denominationally syncretistic as well as religiously syncretistic. It is not discussed here as an ideal condition but simply as a fact, the reality for a large part alluded to by the rough statement that a hundred million Africans are now Christian.[11] It was a good deal less in evidence when in 1950 that figure was only twenty-five million. For the intervening years, at least as regards Catholics and Anglicans, its advance could probably be charted in a rough but not unreliable way by the decline in ecclesiastical marriage rates. Its vast, amorphous mass of devotion, cult, belief, superstition, new bonds of fellowship so often structured in ways that hardly accord with the rules of Rome, Geneva or Canterbury, may prove the most enduring ecclesiastical legacy of this quarter century. As the effective control of the western churches declines, one has the strong impression that the model of historic Ethiopia increasingly prevails: village Christianity with very little superstructure had been present there all along together with much symbolic ritual now making its way right across the continent.

The archbishops and theological colleges, the schools, the projects for development and ecumenism, the academic theology and international connections, the conferences and the policy statements, the conflicts with government and the cooperation: all these have their considerable importance and the ecclesiastical historian, like the journalist, will only too willingly provide an account of them. The underlying social history of the church is less easy to write, yet it will still provide the heart of the matter and in its shifts and stresses, its sick areas and new sources of life, it is likely to control the superstructure rather more decisively than the latter can control it. The interlocking of the two, community and structure, for the shaping of significant prayer in a world of politics, is what ecclesiastical history must be all about.

Notes

Chapter 1   1950

1 *The Times*, 5 April 1950.
2 'A note on various international African meetings', *African Affairs*, vol. 53 (April) 1954 pp. 113–18.
3 J. H. Huizinga, 'Africa, the continent of to-morrow', *African Affairs*, vol. 49 (April) 1950 pp. 120–8.
4 *The Times*, editorial, 14 April 1950.
5 Albert Luthuli, *Let my people go*, London: Collins 1962, p. 101.
6 *The Times*, 18 December 1949.
7 Alan Paton, *Apartheid and the Archbishop*, London: Jonathan Cape 1973 p. 191.
8 *The Times*, leader, 30 September 1950.
9 Jacques Louis Hymans, *Léopold Sédar Senghor. An intellectual biography*, Edinburgh: Edinburgh University Press 1971, pp. 86–7.
10 *African Affairs* (Quarterly notes) vol. 49 (Jan.) 1950 pp. 22–3.
11 See *A.B.A.K.O. 1950–1960, Documents*, Les Dossiers du CRISP.
12 Huizinga, 'Africa, the continent of to-morrow', *African Affairs*, vol. 49 (April 1950 p. 124.
13 *The Times*, letter, 4 August 1950.
14 *The Times*, 4 December 1949.
15 *The Times*, 5 April 1950.
16 *The Times*, 22 April 1950.
17 Fergus MacPherson, *Kenneth Kaunda of Zambia*, London: Oxford University Press 1974, pp. 70 and 81.
18 Missionary Statute, Decree-Law no. 31,207, 5 April 1941, article 19. See Appendix I to my *Wiriyamu* (1974), pp. 135–53.
19 See, for instance, the remarks of John Paul in *Mozambique, memoirs of a revolution*, Harmondsworth: Penguin 1975, pp. 28–9 and elsewhere.
20 See the study of Marvin Markovitz, *Cross and sword. The political role of Christian missions in the Belgian Congo 1908–1960*, Stanford: Hoover Institution Press 1973.
21 *African Affairs* (Quarterly notes) vol. 49 (July) 1950 p. 182.
22 Max Warren, *Social history and Christian mission*, London: SCM Press 1967, pp. 33–4.
23 'A survey of the year 1950', *International Review of Missions*, vol. 157 no. 40 (Jan.) 1951 p. 52.
24 Paton, *Apartheid and the Archbishop*, p. 117.
25 *The Times*, 19 July 1950.

26 *Die Kerkbode*, 6 July 1948 and 23 February 1949, quoted in Paton, *Apartheid and the Archbishop*, pp. 170 and 189.
27 *The Times*, 8 April 1950
28 Quoted in M. Wilson and L. Thompson (eds.) *Oxford History of South Africa*, vol. 2 1971 p. 395.
29 Michael Scott, *A time to speak*, London: Faber 1958 p. 121.
30 *African Affairs*, vol. 49 (Oct.) 1950 p. 261 (Review of Freda Troup, *In face of fear. Michael Scott's challenge to South Africa*).
31 *African Affairs* (Quarterly Notes) vol. 49 (April) 1950 p. 89.
32 Alan Paton, *Hofmeyr*. London: Oxford University Press 1964 p. 435.
33 Monica Wilson, 'Z. K. Matthews: a man for reconciliation'. *South African Outlook*, July 1968; repr. in F. Wilson and D. Perrot (eds.), *Outlook on a century*, pp. 557–9.
34 Quoted by Peter Walshe, *The rise of African nationalism in South Africa*, London: C. Hurst 1970 p. 344; the whole of ch. 13, 'Ideological influences, the ferment of 1939–1952', is important for our theme.
35 Luthuli, *Let my people go*, pp. 235–8.
36 Roger Anstey, *King Leopold's legacy*, London: Oxford University Press 1966 p. 221.
37 John Marcum, *The Angolan revolution* vol. 1, Cambridge, Mass.: Harvard University Press 1969 pp. 105–8.
38 Richard Gray, *The two nations* . . , London: Oxford University Press 1960 p. 329; Lawrence Vambe, *From Rhodesia to Zimbabwe*, London: Heinemann 1976.
39 Adrian Hastings, 'John Lester Membe', in T. O. Ranger and John Weller (eds.), *Themes in the Christian history of Central Africa*, London: Heinemann 1975 p. 191; see also David J. Cook, 'Church and state in Zambia: the case of the African Methodist Episcopalian Church', in E. Fasholé-Luke *et al.*, *Christianity in independent Africa*, London: Rex Collings 1978 pp. 285–303.
40 A Catholic missionary could claim in 1961 that of the 'environs de Stanleyville' 'on peut dire que de vastes territoires ont été là-bas *totalement* convertis au Kitawala.' Sectes dans l'est du Congo ex-Belge, in Muséum Lessianum, *Devant les sectes non-chrétiennes*, 1961 p. 96. For Kitawala in Zaire see especially Hans-Jürgen Greschat, *Kitawala: Ursprung, Ausbreitung und Religion der Watch-Tower-Bewegung in Zentral Afrika*, Marburg: N. G. Elwert 1967, Part II; Jacques E. Gérard, *Les fondements syncrétiques du Kitawala*, Brussels: CRISP 1969.
41 Martial Sinda, *Le messianisme congolais*, Paris: Payot 1972 pp. 116–22; and Efraim Andersson, *Messianic popular movements in the Lower Congo*, Uppsala: Alqvist and Wiksell 1958.
42 Munayi Muntu-Monji, 'Nzambi wa Malemba, un mouvement d'inspiration kimbanguiste au Kasai', *Cahiers des religions africaines* vol 8 (July) 1974 p. 234. It is very curious that, at least within two years, Joseph Diangienda, son of Kimbangu and himself at the time a secret Kimbanguist, was actually a member of the secretariat (*cabinet*) of the governor of Kasai, M. Peigneux. See Henri Desroche and Paul Raymaekers, 'Départ d'un prophète, arrivée d'une église', *Archives de Sciences sociales des religions*, vol. 42, 1976 p. 139.
43 Marcum, *The Angolan revolution*, 1, 76–83; Alfredo Margarido, 'The Tokoist Church and Portuguese colonialism in Angola', in R. H. Chilcote (ed.), *Protest and resistance in Angola and Brazil*, Berkeley and Los Angeles: University of California Press 1972, pp. 29–52; Maria Helena Gil, *Les messianismes*

d'Angola, Paris, École pratique des Hautes Études, diplôme, VIe section 1972, 124–61.

44 Gideon S. Were, 'Politics, religion and nationalism in Western Kenya 1942–1962: Dini ya Msambwa revisited', in B. A. Ogot (ed.), *Politics and nationalism in colonial Kenya*, Nairobi: East African Publishing House 1972 pp. 85–104. For a similar incident in 1947, involving the death of three policemen, see Jocelyn Murray, 'The Kikuyu spirit churches', *Journal of Religion in Africa* vol. 5 no. 2, 1973 p. 215. For a major study of Dini ya Msambwa see Audrey Wipper, *Rural Rebels*, Nairobi 1977.

45 There is an unpublished life by J. R. Kigongo Dam-Tibajjina (copy held in Department of Religious Studies, University of Aberdeen); see also F. B. Welbourn, *East African rebels*, London: SCM Press 1961 pp. 77–110.

46 John Waliggo gives some account of the movement in 'Ganda traditional religion and Catholicism in Buganda, 1948–1975', in Fasholé-Luke *et al.* (eds.), *Christianity in Independent Africa*, pp. 413–16.

47 Edward Ullendorff, *The Ethiopians*, London: Oxford University Press 1960 pp. 97–115; John Pawlikowski, The Judaic spirit of the Ethiopian Orthodox Church, *Journal of Religion in Africa* vol. 4 no. 3, 1972 pp. 178–99.

48 Edward Ullendorff, *Ethiopia and the Bible*, London: Oxford University Press 1968 pp. 74–9, 82–7, 131–45.

49 Taddasse Tamrat, *Church and state in Ethiopia 1270–1527*, Oxford: Clarendon Press 1972 pp. 249–50.

50 John Markakis, *Ethiopia: anatomy of a traditional polity*, Oxford: Clarendon Press 1974 pp. 111–37.

51 Negaso Gidada with Donald Crummey, 'The introduction and expansion of Orthodox Christianity in Qélém Awraja, Western Wälläga, from about 1886 to 1941', *Journal of Ethiopian Studies* vol. 10 no. 1, 1972 pp. 103–12.

52 Tsehai Brhaneselassie, 'The life and career of Dajazmač Balča Aba Näfso', *Journal of Ethiopian Studies* vol. 9 no. 2, 1971 pp. 173–89.

53 Mikre-Sellassie Gabre Ammanuel, *Church and missions in Ethiopia in relation to the Italian war and occupation and the second world war*, University of Aberdeen, Ph.D. thesis 1976 pp. 279–325.

54 S. K. B. Asante, 'West Africa and the Italian invasion of Ethiopia', *African Affairs*, vol. 73 (April) 1974 pp. 204–16.

55 For the general history of Christian missions in Africa prior to 1950 see, *inter alia*, C. P. Groves, *The planting of Christianity in Africa*, London: Lutterworth, vols. 2, 3 and 4, 1948–58; Stephen Neill, *Christian missions* (Pelican History of the Church, 6) Penguin 1964; Geoffrey Moorhouse, *The missionaries*, London: Eyre Methuen 1973; Roland Oliver, *The missionary factor in East Africa*, London: Longman 1952; J. F. A. Ajayi, *Christian missions in Nigeria 1841–1891* London: Longman 1965; E. A. Ayandele, *The missionary impact on modern Nigeria 1842–1914* London: Longman 1966; Ruth Slade, *English-speaking missions in the Congo Independent State (1878–1908)*, Brussels: Académie royale des Sciences coloniales 1959; Marcia Wright, *German missions in Tanganyika 1891–1941*, Oxford: Clarendon Press 1971; C. F. Hallencreutz (ed.), *Missions from the north*, Oslo, etc: Universitetsforlaget 1974; G. B. A. Gerdener, *Recent development in the South African mission field*, Pretoria: N. G. Kerk-Uitgewers 1958.

56 See above pp. 22–4; A. Paton, *Apartheid and the Archbishop*.

57 On Oldham see J. W. C. Dougall, 'J. H. Oldham', *International Review of Mission* vol. 233 no. 59 (Jan.) 1970 pp. 8–22; R. Oliver, *The missionary factor in*

East Africa, pp. 250–72; W. A. Visser't Hooft, *Memoirs*, London: SCM Press 1973 pp. 39–42, 77–9; for Max Warren see his autobiography, *Crowded canvas*. London: Hodder and Stoughton 1974.

58 These are very rough estimates; it is really impossible to obtain reliable church statistics for membership on an interdenominational and continental basis. Figures given can be for different things. For example, they may include or may exclude catechumens, 'backsliders' and so forth. Certainly many more people usually claim church allegiance than the church in question is prepared to recognise. In general the figures provided by the Protestant churches tend to be more restrictive than do the Catholic ones. Figures obtained from a government census are again always higher than the churches publish. For some estimates for 1950 or thereabouts see C. P. Groves, *The planting of Christianity in Africa*, vol. 4 pp. 323–4; David B. Barrett, 'AD 2000 – 350 million Christians in Africa', *International review of Mission*, vol. 233 no. 59 (Jan.) 1970 pp. 39–54; E. J. Bingle (ed.), *World Christian Handbook*, London: World Dominion Press 1952.

59 For accounts of the main Protestant churches in Africa one may refer (over and above the works listed in note 55 above) to the following: Efraim Andersson, *Churches at the grass-roots: a study in Congo Brazzaville*, London: Lutterworth 1968; David B. Barrett *et al.* (eds.) *Kenya Churches Handbook*, Kisumu: Evangel Publishing House 1973; F. L. Bartels, *The roots of Ghana Methodism*, London: Cambridge University Press 1965; E. M. Braekman, *Histoire du Protestantisme au Congo*, Brussels: Éd. de la Librairie des Éclaireurs Unionists 1961; E. P. T. Crampton, *Christianity in Northern Nigeria*, Zaria, privately printed, 1975; Anthony J. Dachs (ed.), *Christianity south of the Zambezi, 1.* Gwelo: Mambo Press 1973; Hans W. Debrunner, *A church between colonial powers: a study of the church in Togo*, London: Lutterworth 1965; Carl-Johann Hellberg, *Missions on a colonial frontier west of Lake Victoria*, Lund: Gleerups 1965; Peter Hinchliffe, *The Anglican church in South Africa*, London: Darton, Longman and Todd 1963; Peter Hinchliffe, *The church in South Africa*, London: SPCK 1968; R. Macpherson, *The Presbyterian Church in Kenya*, Nairobi: PCEA 1970; John McCracken, *Politics and Christianity in Malawi 1875–1940*, London: Cambridge University Press 1977; Margaret Nissen, *An African church is born. The story of the Adamawa and Central Sardauna Provinces in Nigeria* [Denmark, 1968]; T. O. Ranger and John Weller (eds.) *Themes in the Christian history of Central Africa*, London: Heinemann 1975; Noel Smith, *The Presbyterian Church of Ghana 1835–1960*, Accra: Ghana Universities Press 1966; John V. Taylor, *The growth of the church in Buganda*, London: SCM Press 1958; John V. Taylor and Dorothea A. Lehmann, *Christians of the Copperbelt*, London: SCM Press 1961; Jaap van Slageren, *Les origines de l'Eglise évangélique du Cameroun*, Yaoundé: CLE 1972; M. Louise Pirouet, *Black Evangelists, the Spread of Christianity in Uganda 1891–1914*, Rex Collings, London 1978.

60 South African census, 1946.

61 Norman Goodall, *A history of the London Missionary Society 1895–1945*, London: Oxford University Press 1954 pp. 245–62, 281–91; Isaac Schapera, Christianity and the Tswana. *Journal of the Royal Anthropological Institute*, 1958 pp. 1–9.

62 E. G. K. Hewat, *Vision and achievement 1796–1956. A history of the foreign missions of the churches united in the Church of Scotland*, London: Nelson 1960.

63 Gordon Hewitt, *The problems of success: a history of the Church Missionary Society 1910–1942*, vol. 1, London: SCM Press 1971.

64 Isaac Schapera (ed.), *Livingstone's missionary correspondence 1841–56*, London: Chatto and Windus 1961 pp. 106–8, 240–1.
65 Bengt Sundkler, *Zulu Zion and some Swazi Zionists*. Uppsala: Gleerups, and London: Oxford University Press 1976, p. 252; again, two separate Methodist churches were established in Southern Rhodesia, one by British missionaries and one by American.
66 George Wayland Carpenter, *Highways for God in Congo*. Leopoldville: La Librairie Evangelique au Congo 1952 pp. 85–8.
67 *Africa is here. Report of the North American Assembly on African Affairs, Springfield Ohio, 1952*, pp. 12–13.
68 *Max Warren, Social history and Christian mission*. London: SCM Press 1967 pp. 146–53, 179–80.
69 Stephen Neill, *Christian missions*, 460; John V. Taylor, *Christianity and politics in Africa*, London: Penguin 1957 p. 11; J. V. Taylor, *The growth of the church in Buganda*, 71, 92–3.
70 John McCracken, *Politics and Christianity in Malawi*, 273–85.
71 *Ibid*. 278.
72 Matei Markwei, 'Harry Sawyerr's patron (Bishop T. S. Johnson)', in M. E. Grasswell and E. Fasholé-Luke (eds.) *New Testament Christianity for Africa and the world*, London: SPCK 1974 pp. 179–97; T. B. Adebiyi, *The beloved bishop. The life of Bishop A. B. Akinyele*, Ibadan: Daystar Press 1969.
73 From an editorial in the *South African Outlook* of 1894. See Francis Wilson and Dominique Perrot, *Outlook in a century: South Africa 1870–1970*, Lovedale: Lovedale Press 1973 p. 1.
74 Alexander Kerr, *Fort Hare 1915–1948*. London: C. Hurst 1968; For Neil Macvicar see R. H. W. Shepherd, 'Neil Macvicar', *South African Outlook*, Jan. 1950, repr. in Wilson and Perrot (eds.), *Outlook on a century*, pp. 545–7; for Professor Matthews see above, pp. 27–8, and Monica Wilson, *South African Outlook*, July 1968, repr. in Wilson and Perrot (eds.), pp. 557–9; for Jabavu see A. Kerr, *South African Outlook*, December 1959, repr. in Wilson and Perrot (eds.), pp. 550–3; and the first chapters of Noni Jabavu, *The ochre people*, London: John Murray 1963.
75 Besides John V. Taylor, *The growth of the church in Buganda*, pp. 125–41, see L. W. Brown, *Relevant liturgy*, London: SPCK 1965 p. 54; Adrian Hastings, *Christian marriage in Africa*, London: SPCK 1973 pp. 103–4, 155–8.
76 Taylor, *The growth of the church in Buganda*, p. 140, and photographs opposite p. 144.
77 Margaret Nissen, *An African church is born*, p. 245.
78 *International Review of Missions* vol 157 no. 40 (Jan.) 1951 p. 48 (A survey of the year 1950).
79 Darrell Reeck, *Deep Mende*, Leiden: E. J. Brill 1976 pp. 72–6.
80 Adrian Hastings, 'John Lester Membe'; Roderick J. Macdonald, 'Reverend Hanock Msokera Phiri', *African Historical studies* vol. 3 no. 1, 1970 pp. 75–87; J. L. C. Membe, *A short history of the AME Church in Central Africa 1900–1962*. [Kitwa, Zambia], 1969; Walton R. Johnson, *Worship and Freedom*, London: International African Institute 1977.
81 Catherine Ellen Robins, *Tukutendereza: a study of social change and sectarian withdrawal in the Balokole revival of Uganda*, Columbia University, Ph.D dissertation 1975; Max Warren, *Revival: an enquiry*, London: SCM Press 1954; Max Warren, *Crowded Canvas*, pp. 199–201; R. Macpherson, *The Presbyterian Church in Kenya*, pp. 125–8.

82 Carl-Johann Hellberg, 'Andereya Kajerero: the man and his church', *Occasional Research Papers* (Makerere University, Department of Religious Studies and Philosophy) 8, (*c.* 1973), paper 71, p. 22; for a more friendly picture of Revival in Buhaya, with a larger time-scale see Bengt Sundkler, *Bara Bukoba. Kynka och miljö*, Uppsala, 1974 pp. 175–209.

83 For the missionary growth of the Catholic church in Africa see, among many others, Simon Delacroix, *Histoire universelle des Missions Catholiques*, Paris: Grund 1956–9, vols. 3 and 4; Henry Koren, *The Spiritans*, Pittsburgh: Duquesne University Press 1958; Adrian Hastings, *Church and mission in modern Africa*, London: Burns & Oates 1967; Antonio Brásio, *Historia e Missiologia inéditos*, Luanda: Instituto de Investigacao Cientifica de Angola 1973; John Todd, *African mission: a historical study of the Society of African Mission*, London: Burns & Oates 1962; Francois Renault, *Lavigerie, l'esclavage Africain et l'Europe 1868–1892*, Paris: E. de Boccard 1971, 2 vols.; W. E. Brown, *The Catholic Church in South Africa*, London: Burns & Oates 1960; Michael Gelfand (ed.), *Gubulawayo and beyond*, London: Geoffrey Chapman 1968; Hubert P. Gale, *Uganda and the Mill Hill Fathers*, London: Macmillan 1959; F. de Meeûs and R. Steenbergher, *Les missions religieuses au Congo Belge*, Anvers: Éd. Zaire 1947; Pierre Legrand and Benoît Thoreau, *Les Bénédictins au Katanga*, Lophen-les Bruges: Abbaye de Saint-André 1935; Michael Kratz, *La mission des Rédemptoristes belges au Bas-Congo*, Brussels: Académie royale de sciences d'Outre-mer, 1968; Karl Müller, *Histoire de l'église Catholique au Togo 1892–1967*, Lomé: Éd. Librairie Bon Pasteur 1968; Ian Linden, *Catholics, peasants and Chewa resistance in Nyasaland 1889–1939*, London: Heinemann 1974. The *Annuaire de l'Église Catholique en Afrique*, published annually in Paris by the Office National de Publications Catholiques is a mine of information; see also the *Revue du Clergé Africain*, published bi-monthly by the Jesuits from Mayidi, Zaire. The influential theologian Fr Denis was editor and principal contributor from its foundation in 1946 until 1966. The Belgian missionary journal *Grands Lacs* (Namur) is also full of valuable information for the 1940s and 1950s – see in particular its 100-page issue on the Catholic Church in the Congo, April 1950.

84 There have, of course, been other American Catholic missionaries working in Africa in several of the international societies, notably Holy Ghost Fathers in Arusha, Tanzania, but they have never been very numerous.

85 Adrian Hastings, 'From mission to church in Buganda', in his *Mission and ministry*, London: Sheed and Ward 1971, pp. 144–76; A. Hastings, 'Ganda Catholic spirituality', *Journal of Religion in Africa* vol. 8 no. 2 1976, pp. 81–91; John Waliggo, *The Catholic Church in the Buddu Province of Buganda, 1879–1925*. University of Cambridge, Ph.D dissertation 1976.

86 For Igboland see John Jordan, *Bishop Shanahan of Southern Nigeria*, Dublin: Clonmore & Reynolds 1949; F. K. Ekechi, *Missionary enterprise and rivalry in Igboland 1857–1914*, London: Frank Cass 1972; there is as yet no considerable published study on Catholicism in Ufipa.

87 Legrand and Thoreau, *Les Bénédictins au Katanga*, pp. 215–16; *The Tablet*, 3 June 1950 p. 440.

88 Johannes Fabian, *Jamaa, a charismatic movement in Katanga*, Evanston: Northwestern University Press 1971 pp. 21–7. The leading Belgian missiologist Pierre Charles at once warmly welcomed the work of Tempels; see his *Études missiologiques* Brussels: Desclée de Brouwer 1956 pp. 266–72.

89 Ruth Slade Reardon, 'Catholics and Protestants in the Congo', in C. G. Baëta

(ed.), *Christianity in tropical Africa*, London: Oxford University Press 1968 p. 90. For de Hemptinne's influence see also Bruce Fetter, *The creation of Elisabethville 1910–1940*, Stanford, California: Hoover Institution Press 1976, especially pp. 103–9.

90 Markowitz, *Cross and sword*, pp. 44–5.

91 Georges Hardy, *Un apôtre d'aujourd'hui. Le Révérend Père Aupiais . . .* , Paris: Larose 1949.

92 *African Affairs*, vol. 54 (April) 1955 p. 143; Renault, *Lavigerie*, I pp. 226–33; Roger Fouquer, *Le docteur Adrien Atiman, médicin-catéchiste au Tanganyika*, Paris: Spes 1964.

93 Elizabeth Isichei, *One man in his time: Michael Tanzi*, Jos Conference on Christianity in independent Africa, unpublished paper, September 1975. Mimeo.

94 Léopold Sédar Senghor, *Prose and poetry*, London: Oxford University Press 1965, pp. 42–3.

95 For a comprehensive bibliography of African independent church movements see Harold Turner, *Bibliography of new religious movements in primal societies*, vol. 1: *Black Africa*, Boston, Mass.: G. K. Hall 1977; for a general discussion of their character see Bengt Sundkler, *Bantu prophets in South Africa* 2nd ed., London: Oxford University Press 1961; H. W. Turner, 'A typology for modern African religious movements', *Journal of Religion in Africa* vol. 1 no. 1, 1967 pp. 1–34; David Barrett, *Schism and renewal in Africa*, Nairobi: Oxford University Press 1968; Hans-Jürgen Greschat, *Westafrikanische Propheten*, Berlin: Dietrich Reimer 1974; Marie-France Perrin Jassy, *Basic community in the African church*, Maryknoll N.Y.: Orbis Books 1973; R. C. Mitchell, 'Towards the sociology of religious independence', *Journal of Religion in Africa* vol. 3 no. 1, 1970 pp. 2–21. The study of religious independency in Africa has been somewhat misled by the over-hasty generalisations of D. Barrett, too easily accepted as an authoritative guide to the subject. For a masterly rebuttal of some of his theses see V. Neckebrouck, *'Le Onzième Commandement'*, *Etiologie d'une église indépendante au pied du mont Kenya*, Immensee, Switzerland, 1978.

96 George Shepperson and Thomas Price, *Independent African: John Chilembwe . . .* , Edinburgh: Edinburgh University Press 1958, *passim*, for Joseph Booth; Sundkler, *Zulu Zion*, pp. 16–67, for Le Roux; also J. D. Y. Peel, *Aladura: a religious movement among the Yoruba*, London: Oxford University Press 1968, pp. 63–9, 105–12; Robert W. Wyllie, 'Pioneers of Ghanaian pentecostalism: Peter Anim and James McKeown', *Journal of Religion in Africa*, vol. 6 no. 2, 1974 pp. 109–22.

97 Adrian Hastings, *Mission and ministry*, chapter 12; R. L. Wishlade, *Sectarianism in Southern Nyasaland*, London: Oxford University Press 1965, pp. 99, 143; Harold Turner, 'African religious movements and Roman Catholicism', in H.-J. Greschat and H. Jungraithmayr (eds.), *Wort und Religion*, Stuttgart: Evangelischer Missionsverlag 1969, pp. 255–64; B. A. Pauw, *Religion in a Tswana chiefdom*, London: Oxford University Press 1960, pp. 222–4. The most complete and extended comparison between a Catholic and a Protestant missionary approach in a particular area, with the growth of independency in mind, is that of M. L. Daneel, *Old and new in Southern Shona independent churches*, The Hague: Mouton 1971 (vol. 1), 185–277.

98 For traditional African religious ritual, see for example Victor Turner, *The ritual process*, London: Routledge & Kegan Paul 1969; Godfrey Lienhardt, *Divinity*

and experience. The religion of the Dinka, Oxford: Clarendon Press 1961; Axel-Ivar Berglund, *Zulu thought-patterns and symbolism*, London: C. Hurst 1976; for a basic discussion of ritual in African independent churches, see Sundkler, *Bantu prophets*, chapter 6; for a Catholic pattern see Adrian Hastings, 'Ganda Catholic spirituality'.

99 Sundkler, *Bantu prophets*, p. 294.
100 E. E. Evans-Pritchard, *Nuer religion*, Oxford: Clarendon Press 1956, chapter 12; J. M. Middleton, *Lugbara religion*, London: Oxford University Press 1960 pp. 258–64.
101 G. C. Oosthuizen has argued insistently for the non-Christian or significantly less than Christian character of the movements; see his *Post-Christianity in Africa*, London: C. Hurst 1968, and *The theology of a South African messiah*, Leiden: E. J. Brill 1967; on this see B. Sundkler's reply (in regard to Shembe), Zulu Zion, pp. 190–205.
102 George Shepperson, Ethiopianism past and present, in C. G. Baëta (ed.), *Christianity in tropical Africa*, pp. 249–68.
103 For a fine study of the style of J. G. Shembe see James W. Fernandez, The precincts of the prophet. A day with Johannes Galilee Shembe. *Journal of Religion in Africa* vol. 5 no. 1, 1973 pp. 32–53.
104 M. L. Daneel, *Old and new in Southern Shona independent churches*, vol. 1, pp. 288–93.
105 Daneel, *Ibid*. p. 376; for a further study of Bishop Mutendi see M. L. Daneel, *Zionism and faith-healing in Rhodesia*, the Hague: Mouton 1970.
106 Daneel, *Old and new*, vol. 1, pp. 304–9.
107 *Ibid*. p. 319; for further accounts of the Maranke Apostles see Bennetta Jules-Rosette, *African apostles*, Ithaca: Cornell University Press 1975; Mary Aquina (A. K. H. Weinrich), 'The people of the Spirit: an independent church in Rhodesia', *Africa* (London) vol 37 no. 2, 1967 pp. 203–19; Marshall W. Murphree, 'Religious interdependence among the Budjga Vapostori', in D. Barrett (ed.), *African initiatives in religion*, Nairobi: East African Publishing House 1971 pp. 171–80.
108 Clive Dillon-Malone, *The Korsten basketmakers: a study of the Masowe Apostles ...*, Fordham University, Ph.D dissertation 1975; see also Cyril Dunn, 'Black Christians build an ark', *The Observer* (London) 26 June 1955 p. 13.
109 See R. W. Wishlade, *Sectarianism in Southern Nyasaland*; Shepperson and Price, *Independent African*; Roderick MacDonald, 'Religious independency as a means of social advance in Northern Nyasaland in the 1930s', *Journal of Religion in Africa*, vol. 3 no. 2, 1970 pp. 106–29; John McCracken, *Politics and Christianity in Malawi 1875–1940*, pp. 184–220 and 273–85.
110 Monica Wilson, *Communal rituals of the Nyakyusa*, London: Oxford University Press 1959 pp. 190–7; T. O. Ranger, *The African churches of Tanzania*, Nairobi: East African Publishing House (1969); T. O. Ranger, 'Christian independency in Tanzania', in D. Barrett (ed.), *African initiatives in religion*, pp. 122–45.
111 F. B. Welbourn, *East African rebels*, pp. 31–58.
112 For the origins of independency in Kenya see Jocelyn Murray, *The Kikuyu female circumcision controversy*, University of California, Los Angeles, Ph.D. dissertation 1974; F. B. Welbourn, *East African rebels*, Part III; Jocelyn Murray, 'The Kikuyu Spirit churches', *Journal of Religion in Africa* vol. 5 no. 2, 1973 pp. 198–234; F. B. Welbourn and B. A. Ogot, *A place to feel at home*, London: Oxford University Press 1966, Part III: 'The African Israel Church, Nineveh';

Walter H. Sangree, *Age, prayer and politics in Tiriki, Kenya,* London: Oxford University Press 1966, pp. 170–223; D. B. Barrett *et al.* (eds.), *Kenya Churches Handbook*, Kisumu, Kenya: Evangel Publishing House 1973. V. Neckebrouck. '*Le Onzième Commandement*', Immensee, 1978. The last, a study of the AIPC, is the most important work hitherto published on religious independency in Kenya.

113 Jocelyn Murray, 'The Kikuyu Spirit churches', p. 234.

114 J. B. Webster, *The African churches among the Yoruba, 1888–1922*, Oxford: Clarendon Press 1964

115 B. M. Haliburton, *The prophet Harris*, Harlow: Longman 1971; and an important critical review of this work by Sheila S. Walker in *The International Journal of African Studies* 8, 1975, Supplement A pp. 73–9.

116 B. Holas, *Le séparatisme religieux en Afrique noire (L'example de la Côte d'Ivoire)*, Paris: Presses Universitaires de France 1965; René Bureau, 'Le prophète Harris et la religion harriste (Côte d'Ivoire)', *Annales de l'Université d'Abidjan* (Serie F) 3, 1971 pp. 31–196. For a definitive study of the Prophet Harris we await the work of David Shank.

117 C. G. Baëta, *Prophetism in Ghana*, SCM Press 1962; James W. Fernandez, 'Rededication and prophetism in Ghana', *Cahiers d'Études Africaines* vol. 10 no. 2, 1970 pp. 228–305 – a study of Wovenu; K. A. Opoku, 'Changes within Christianity, with special reference to the Musama Disco Cristo Church', in Fasholé-Luke *et al.* (eds.), *Christianity in independent Africa*, pp. 111–21.

118 J. D. Y. Peel, *Aladura: a religious movement among the Yoruba*; H. W. Turner, *African independent church*, 2 vols., Oxford: Clarendon Press 1967; R. C. Mitchell, 'Religious protest and social change: the origins of the aladura movement in Western Nigeria', in R. I. Rotberg and A. A. Mazrui (eds.) *Protest and power in Black Africa*, New York: Oxford University Press 1970 pp. 458–96.

119 Martial Sinda, *Le messianisme Congolaise et ses incidences politiques*, Paris: Payot 1972, part 2; Georges Balandier, *The sociology of Black Africa . . .*, trans. D. Garman, London: Andre Deutsch 1970, 389–409.

120 Munayi Muntu-Monji, 'Nzambi wa Malemba', p. 254.

121 Within the vast literature now devoted to Kimbangu and Kimbanguism, the following is offered as a highly selective bibliography for the prophet himself and the early stages of his movement: (1) Werner Ustorf, *Afrikanisch Initiative. Das aktive Leiden des Propheten Simon Kimbangu*. Bern: Herbert Lang 1975 – by far the most comprehensively documented major study; (2) Marie-Louise Martin, *Kimbangu. An African prophet and his church*, Oxford: Blackwell 1975 – close to the official viewpoint of the *Église* led by his son today; (3) Efraim Andersson, *Messianic popular movements in the Lower Congo*, Uppsala 1958 – a very valuable and scholarly work, particularly important in that it dates from before both the institutional development of the Église and the spate of writing on the subject from the period of independence; (4) Paul Raymaekers, 'Histoire de Simon Kimbangu, prophète, d'apres les ecrivains Nfinangani et Nzungu (1921)', *Archives de Sociologie des Religions* vol. 16 no. 1, 1971 pp. 15–42 – a vitally important early Kimbanguist text; (5) Damaso Feci, *Vie cachée et vie publique de Simon Kimbangu selon la littérature coloniale et missionaire belge*, Brussels: Les Cahiers du CEDAF, no. 9–10, 1972; (6) E. Libert, Les missionaires chrétiens face au mouvement kimbanguiste, documents contemporains (1921). *Études d'Histoire Africaine* (Louvain) 2, 1971, pp. 121–54; (7) Cecilia Irvine, 'The birth of the Kimbanguist movement in the Bas-Zaire 1921', *Journal of Religion in Africa* vol. 6 no. 1, 1974 pp. 23–76; (8) A. Geuns,

'Chronologie des mouvements religieux indépendants au Bas-Zaire, particulièrement du mouvement fondé par le prophète Simon Kimbangu', *Journal of Religion in Africa* vol. 6 no. 3, 1974 pp. 187–222; (9) P. H. J. Lerrigo, 'The "prophet movement" in the Congo', *International Review of Missions* vol. 11 (April), 1922 pp. 270–7 – valuable as a very early account by a not unsympathetic outsider, which includes eye-witness material.

122 Jules Chomé, *La passion de Simon Kimbangu*, Brussels: Présence Africaine 1959, p. 91.

123 Kimbangu was admitted to hospital on the afternoon of 9 October and was guarded throughout his last three days by two detectives. It is certain that he was baptized just before his death by Soeur Eudoxie, a Catholic Sister of Charity. It is also certain that he refused all medicine. For a scrupulously careful and sensitive assessment of the evidence for his final days and state of mind see H. Desroche and P. Raymaekers, 'Départ d'un prophète, arrivée d'une église. Textes et recherches sur la mort de Simon Kimbangu et sur sa survivance', *Archives de Sciences Sociales des Religions* 42, pp. 117–62.

Chapter 2 1951–1958

1 Among recent studies on Mau Mau see Robert Buijtenhuijs, *Le mouvement 'Mau-Mau': une révolte paysanne et anti-coloniale en Afrique noire*, the Hague & Paris: Mouton 1971, and two chapters in the symposium *Politics and nationalism in colonial Kenya*, ed. Bethwell Ogot (Nairobi: East African Publishing House 1971) by O. W. Furley, 'The historiography of Mau Mau', pp. 105–33, and B. A. Ogot, 'Revolt of the elders: an anatomy of the loyalist crowd in the Mau Mau uprising 1952–56', pp. 134–48.

2 The continuity between the events of 1954–5 and the founding of the Democratic Party has not been properly recognised. For all this see Colonial Office White Paper, *Uganda Protectorate. Buganda* (Cmd 9320) London: HMSO November 1954; D. A. Low, *Political parties in Uganda 1949–62*, London: Athlone Press 1962; D. A. Low, *The mind of Buganda*, London: Heinemann 1971, pp. 175–6; John Waliggo, 'Ganda traditional religion and Catholicism in Buganda 1948–1975', in E. Fasholé-Luke *et al.* (eds.), *Christianity in independent Africa*, London: Rex Collings 1978, pp. 413–25.

3 *African Affairs*, vol. 52 (April) 1953 p. 111.

4 See the account of this episode in Michael Scott, *A time to speak*, London: Faber 1958, pp. 281–4; for Nkumbula's burning of the White Paper see *African Affairs*, vol. 52 (July) 1953 pp. 232–3.

5 *African Affairs*, vol. 52 (October) 1953 pp. 266–72.

6 M. Nicholson, 'Return to the new Nigeria', *African Affairs*, vol. 54 (October) 1955 p. 298.

7 'Un plan de trente ans' is an extract from the *Dossiers de l'Action Sociale Catholique* for February 1956; for a complete collection of Van Bilsen's papers from 1954 to 1958 see Antoine A. J. Van Bilsen, *Vers l'indépendance du Congo et du Ruanda-Urundi*, Kraainem 1958. Van Bilsen's thirty-year plan may be compared with the twenty to twenty-five year target for Tanganyika's self-government suggested by a UN Visiting Mission in 1954, accepted by Nyerere, but rejected by the British government as too short.

8 Jacques Hymans, *Léopold Sédar Senghor*, Edinburgh: Edinburgh University Press 1971 p. 156.

9 W. Kistner, 'The 16th of December in the context of nationalist thinking', in Theo Sundermeier, *Church and nationalism in South Africa*, Johannesburg: Ravan Press 1975 pp. 85–6.

10 Tom Mboya, *Freedom and after*, London: André Deutsch 1963 p. 14.

11 One may refer to such discussions as those of Mboya in *Freedom and after*, pp. 19–24; Lawrence Vambe in the first four chapters of *From Rhodesia to Zimbabwe*, London: Heinemann 1976.

12 See for example the case of Molin Tengani, a strongly Christian chief, and the M'Bona cult in southern Nyasaland as described by M. Schoffeleers, 'The history and political role of the M'Bona cult among the Mang'anja', p. 88 in T. O. Ranger and I. Kimambo (eds.), *The historical study of African religion*, London: Heinemann 1972.

13 Cf. Kenneth Kaunda, *Zambia shall be free*, London: Heinemann 1962 pp. 147–9; David Cook, 'Church and State in Zambia: the case of the African Methodist Episcopal Church', in Fasholé-Luke *et al.* (eds.), *Christianity in independent Africa*, pp. 285–303.

14 *African Affairs*, vol. 52 (April) 1953 p. 97.

15 Bengt Sundkler, *Zulu Zion and some Swazi Zionists*, Uppsala and London: Oxford University Press 1976, chapter 6.

16 Kwame Nkrumah, *I speak of freedom*, London: Heinemann 1961 p. 118.

17 *Africa is here*. Report of the North American Assembly on African affairs, Wittenberg College, Springfield, Ohio, June 1952 p. 16.

18 *Présence Africaine*, 1956 pp. 157–8; see also the Congolese statement of June 1956 from the *Conscience Africaine* group in P. Boigny, *Les Chrétiens devant le Congo*, Brussels: La Pensée Catholique 1956 pp. 38–51.

19 Albert Luthuli, *Let my people go*, London: Collins 1962 pp. 131–2.

20 Walter Carey, *Crisis in Kenya*, London: Mowbray 1953, p. 20 and p. 30.

21 See Patricia Chater, *Grass roots: the story of St. Faith's Farm*, London: Hodder & Stoughton; Guy Clutton-Brock and Molly Clutton-Brock, *Cold Comfort confronted*, London: Mowbray 1972, chapters 3 and 4.

22 See K. Nyamayaro Mufuka, *Mission and politics in Malawi*, Kingston Ontario: Limestone Press 1977 pp. 147–76.

23 Gonville ffrench-Beytagh, *Encountering darkness*, London: Collins 1973 p. 71.

24 Roland Oliver, *How Christian is Africa?* London: Highway Press 1956 p. 24; besides John V. Taylor's *Christianity and politics in Africa*, Penguin 1957, the following illustrate this strand of thinking: Adrian Hastings, *White domination or racial peace*, London: Africa Bureau 1954; J. H. Oldham, *New hope in Africa*, London: Longmans 1955; Max Warren, *Caesar the beloved enemy*, London: SCM Press 1956; Alfred de Soras, *L'Église et l'anticolonialisme*, Paris: Action populaire 1957.

25 L. Aujoulat, *Aujourd'hui l'Afrique*, Paris: Casterman 1958. For the reference to his 'black heart', from an election handout, see Edward Mortimer, *France and the Africans 1944–1960: a political history*, London: Faber 1969 p. 215.

26 J. Mfoulou, 'The Catholic church and Camerounian nationalism', in Fasholé-Luke *et al.* (eds.), *Christianity in independent Africa*, pp. 216–27. See also Englebert Mveng, *Histoire du Cameroun*, Paris: Présence Africaine, 1963 pp. 433–43; Richard A. Joseph, *Radical Nationalism in Cameroun, Social origins of the U.P.C. Rebellion*, London: Oxford University Press 1977 pp. 258–61.

27 M. Twaddle, 'The Democratic Party of Uganda as a political institution', in Fasholé-Luke *et al.* (eds.) *Christianity in independent Africa*, pp. 255–66.

28 *Problèmes sociaux et missions*, Louvain 1953 p. 82.

29 *The Church to Africa, Sword of the Spirit*, London, 1959, contains a useful collection of African pastorals of the 1950s. For a hostile reaction to a 1953 Madagascar Pastoral on the right to independence see Francois Mejan, *Le Vatican contre la France d'Outre Mer? Paris*: Librairie Fischbacher 1957. See also Colin Morris' comments on a forthright Pastoral issued by the Bishops of Northern Rhodesia in January 1958, *The hour after midnight*, London: Longmans 1961 pp. 154–5.

30 Bildad Kaggia, *Roots of freedom 1921–1963*, Nairobi: East African Publishing House 1975, 70; see also the unpublished study by Jocelyn Murray, *The origins and spread of the 'Dini ya Kaggia' (Kenya)* (University of Aberdeen, African Studies Group seminar, 1976).

31 Harry Thuku, *Harry Thuku: an autobiography*, Nairobi: Oxford University Press 1970 pp. 69–70.

32 There is a little book entitled *Kikuyu martyrs*, by E. M. Wiseman (London: Highway Press 1958). For an admirable discussion of the Christian Kikuyu during Mau Mau one may refer to E. N. Wanyoike's life of his grandfather, the Rev Wanyoike Kamawe, entitled *An African pastor* (Nairobi: East African Publishing House 1974), chapter 7, 'Conflict of loyalties'.

33 *African Affairs* vol. 52 (April), 1953 p. 95. For the restrained approach of the CMS, already at this early stage, see its pamphlet *Mau Mau*, published April 1953.

34 *African Affairs*, vol 56 (October), 1957 p. 258.

35 The quoted phrases come from Bishop Carey's *Crisis in Kenya*, p. 37, written in 1952; this sort of talk went on for many years up to, and beyond, the foolish speech of the Governor, Sir Patrick Renison, in May 1960 describing Kenyatta as 'the leader to darkness and death'. For Kariuki's visit to Lokitaung see Jeremy Murray-Brown, *Kenyatta*, London: Allen and Unwin 1972 pp. 291–2.

36 For the churches and Bantu education see Alexander Kerr, 'The Bantu Education Act', *South African Outlook*, June 1954, repr. in F. Wilson and D. Perrot (eds.), *Outlook on a century*, pp. 513–16, and J. M. MacQuarrie, 'Has missionary education failed?', *South African Outlook*, October 1954, repr. in Wilson and Perrot, *Outlook on a century*, pp. 516–20; Alan Paton, *Apartheid and the Archbishop . . .* , London: Jonathan Cape 1973, chapter 27; W. E. Brown, *The Catholic Church in South Africa*, London: Burns and Oates 1960, pp. 340–1, 346–8.

37 G. C. Grant, 'The liquidation of Adams College', in David M. Paton (ed.), *Church and race in South Africa*, London: SCM Press 1958 pp. 51–93.

38 See Alexander Kerr, 'Never accept defeat', *South African Outlook*, December 1959, repr. in Wilson and Perrot, (eds.), *Outlook of a century*, pp. 521–5; and Monica Wilson, 'Z. K. Matthews: a man for reconciliation, *South African Outlook*, July 1968, repr. in Wilson and Perrot, (eds.) pp. 557–9.

39 *Naught for your comfort*, London: Collins 1956; for another book coming out of the Sophiatown of the 1950s see Bloke Modisane, *Blame me on history*, London: Thames and Hudson 1963.

40 *Naught for your comfort*, p. 234.

41 Colin Morris, *The hour after midnight*, London: Longmans 1961.

42 Quoted in Paton, *Apartheid and the Archbishop*, p. 283.

43 *African Affairs* vol. 56 (October), 1957 p. 258.

44 Paton, *Apartheid and the Archbishop*, pp. 279–80; for Clayton see also Roger Lloyd, *The Church of England 1900–1965*, London: SCM Press 1966 pp. 496–513.

45 *Pastoral Letters*, Southern African Catholic Bishops' Conference, pp. 14 and 16.

286

46 Thus there were 5,502 Catholic missionary priests in Black Africa in 1949, and 8,703 in 1959 (*CIPA*, Rome, no. 187, 5 March 1964, p. 72); it is difficult to obtain comparable figures on the Protestant side, but here too the growth in numbers was certainly very considerable. See E. J. Bingle, *World Christian Handbook*, 1957 edn, London: World Dominion Press 1957, especially pp. xviii–xix; see also Bengt Sundkler, *The Christian Ministry in Africa*, London: SCM Press 1960 pp. 331–2.

47 E. P. T. Crampton, *Christianity in Northern Nigeria*, Zaria, 1975.

48 J. P. Jordan, 'Catholic education and Catholicism in Nigeria', *African Ecclesiastical Review*, vol. 1 no. 2, 1960 p. 61.

49 Henry Weman, *African music and the church in Africa* Uppsala: Lundeqvistska Bokhandeln, 1960.

50 C. P. Groves, *The planting of Christianity in Africa*, London: Lutterworth, vol. 4 1958 pp. 290–4.

51 Norman A. Horner, *Cross and crucifix in mission*, New York: Abingdon 1965, pp. 105, 114–15, for the contrast between Catholic and Protestant; see also F. G. Welch, *Training for the ministry in East Africa*, Limuru, Kenya: St Paul's United Theological College 1963, pp. 86–7.

52 F. L. Bartels, *The roots of Ghana Methodism*, London: Cambridge University Press 1965, pp. 223–6.

53 For the Protestant figures see Bengt Sundkler, *The Christian ministry in Africa*, pp. 324–9; the Catholic figures are from *Status Seminaristarum Indigenarum 1959–1960*, Rome: Propaganda Fide 1960; they are those of the 1958–9 column. They do not include those studying in religious orders, but these were extremely few. There were, however, a number of Oblates of Mary Immaculate in South Africa and Jesuits in the Congo.

54 Roland Oliver, *How Christian is Africa?* p. 10.

55 A. G. Blood, *The history of the Universities' Mission to Central Africa*, vol. 3, *1933–1957*, London: UMCA 1962 pp. 383–97.

56 Adrian Hastings, *Church and mission in modern Africa*, London: Burns & Oates 1967 pp. 221–3; John V. Taylor, *The growth of the church in Buganda*, London: SCM Press 1958, pp. 124–41; Bengt Sundkler, *The Christian ministry in Africa*, London: SCM Press 1960 pp. 64–8; Francis Nolan, 'History of the catechist in Eastern Africa', in A. Shorter and E. Kataza (eds.), *Missionaries to yourselves, African catechists today*, London: Geoffrey Chapman 1972 pp. 25–9.

57 Mia Brandel-Syrier, *Black woman in search of God*, London: Lutterworth Press 1962; Farai David Muzorewa, 'Through prayer to action; the Rukwadzano women of Rhodesia', in T. O. Ranger and John Weller (eds.), *Themes in the Christian history of Central Africa*, pp. 256–68; B. Sundkler, *The Christian ministry in Africa*, pp. 336–7.

58 Note the First Leaders' Meeting for the Apostolate of the Laity in Africa held at Kisubi, Uganda, in December 1953. It was organised for the whole of Africa.

59 Brian Garvey, *The development of the White Fathers's mission among the Bemba-speaking peoples, 1891–1964*, London University, Ph.D. dissertation 1974, pp. 311–12; Colman Cooke, *The Roman Catholic Mission in Calabar 1903–1960*, London University, Ph.D. dissertation, 1977, p. 248.

60 Brandel-Syrier, *Black woman in search of God*, p. 28.

61 *Ibid.*, pp. 30–2, 92–6, 160, 205–12. For Mrs Paul see B. A. Pauw, *Christianity and Xhosa tradition*, Cape Town: Oxford University Press 1975 pp. 264–91.

62 Jaap Van Slageren. *Les origines de l'Église Évangélique du Cameroun*, Yaoundé, 1972, pp. 223–30.

63 Johannes Fabian, *Jamaa. A charismatic movement in Katanga*, Evanston: Northwestern University Press 1971; Vincent Mulago and T. Theuws, *Autour du mouvement de la 'Jamaa'*, Limete (Zaire) (1960); Willy De Craemer, *The Jamaa and the Church. A Bantu Catholic movement in Zaïre*, Oxford: Clarendon Press 1977.

64 *Des prêtres noirs s'interrogent* (Rencontres, 47), Paris: Les Éditions du CERF 1956; Alexis Kagame, *La philosophie bantu-rwandaise de l'être*, Brussels: Académie Royale des Sciences Coloniales 1956.

65 *Christianity and African culture*, Accra 1955.

66 *The Church in changing Africa*. Report of the All Africa Church Conference, Ibadan. New York: International Missionary Conference 1958.

67 Walter Freytag, 'Changes in the patterns of western missions', in R. Orchard (ed.) *The Ghana Assembly of the International Missionary Council, 1958*, p. 140.

68 M. L. Daneel, *Old and new in Southern Shona independent churches*, the Hague: Mouton, vol. 2, 1974 p. 67.

69 H. W. Turner, *African independent church*, Oxford: Clarendon Press 1967, vol. 1, pp. 110–98.

70 Haldor E. Heimer, 'The church suited to home needs . . . A look at the people of two churches in Luluabourg', Congo, in R. T. Parsons (ed.), *Windows on Africa*, Leiden: E. J. Brill 1971 p. 25.

71 J. D. Y. Peel, *Aladura: a religious movement among the Yoruba*, London: Oxford University Press 1968 p. 219.

72 See, for instance, the discussion in Daneel, *Old and new*, vol. 2, pp. 56–67.

73 Already in 1950 a British administrative officer could only describe the Aiyetoro achievement as 'astonishing' and 'astounding'; see C. E. E. B. Simpson, 'An African village undertakes community development on its own', *Mass Education Bulletin* (London) vol. 2 no. 1, 1950 pp. 7–9; for the development of Aiyetoro see S.O.A. Authority, *The happy city of the Holy Apostles' Community, 'Aiyetoro'*, Lagos (1966); Elizabeth M. McClelland, 'The experiment in communal living at Aiyetoro', *Comparative Studies in Society and History* vol. 9 no. 1, 1966 pp. 14–28; Stanley R. Barrett, 'Crisis and change in a West African Utopia', in E. B. Harvey (ed.), *Perspectives on modernization*, Toronto: University of Toronto Press 1972 pp. 160–81; Stanley R. Barrett, *The rise and fall of an African Utopia: A wealthy theocracy in comparative perspective*, Waterloo, Ontario: Wilfrid Laurier University Press 1977.

74 See chapter 1, pp. 77–8.

75 Authority, *The happy city*, p. 37.

76 Sundkler, *Zulu Zion*, p. 282.

77 *Ibid*, pp. 86 and 89.

78 Bohumil Holas, *Le séparatisme religieux en Afrique noir. (L'example de la Côte d'Ivoire)*, Paris: Presses Universitaires de France 1965 pp. 241–2, 245, 270–2.

79 The best existing study of Lenshina is that of Andrew Roberts, 'The Lumpa Church of Alice Lenshina', in R. I. Rotberg and A. A. Mazrui (eds.), *Protest and power in Black Africa*, New York: Oxford University Press 1970 pp. 513–68; see also John V. Taylor, 'Saints or heretics', in *Basileia, Walter Freytag zum 60 geburtstag*, Stuttgart 1961; Dorothea Lehmann, 'Alice Lenshina Mulenga and the Lumpa Church', in J. V. Taylor and D. Lehmann, *Christians of the Copperbelt*, London: SCM Press 1961 pp. 248–68; Garvey, *The development of the White Fathers' mission*, pp. 350–71.

80 For Mai Chaza see Marie-Louise Martin, 'The Mai Chaza Church in Rhodesia',

in D. B. Barrett (ed.), *African Initiatives in religion*, pp. 109–21; comparison can also usefully be made with the career of the Nyasaland diviner Chikanga. See Alison Redmayne, 'Chikanga: an African diviner with an international reputation', in Mary Douglas (ed.), *Witchcraft confessions and accusations*, London: Tavistock Publications 1970 pp. 103–28.

81 See Louis Oger, *Lumpa Church: the Lenshina movement in Northern Rhodesia*, Serenje, Zambia (1960), mimeo, p. 1; see also Garvey, *The development of the White Fathers' mission*.

82 George Shepperson and Thomas Price, *Independent African* . . . , Edinburgh: Edinburgh University Press 1958 pp. 147–59; Jane Linden and Ian Linden, 'John Chilembwe and the new Jerusalem', *Journal of African History* 12 (4), 1971, 629–51; T. O. Ranger, 'The Mwana Lesa movement of 1925', in T. O. Ranger and John Weller (eds.), *Themes in the Christian history of Central Africa*, pp. 45–75.

83 Garvey, *The development of the White Fathers' mission*, pp. 331–49; Taylor and Lehmann, *Christians of the Copperbelt*, pp. 106–8, 191.

84 B. A. Ogot, in F. B. Welbourn and B. A. Ogot, *A place to feel at home*, London: Oxford University Press 1966, pp. 21–71; D. B. Barrett *et al.* (eds.) *Kenya Churches Handbook*, Kisumu: Evangel Publishing House 1973.

85 Max Warren, *Revival: an enquiry*, London: SCM Press 1954, p. 106.

86 René Bureau. 'Le prophète Harris et la religion harriste (Côte d'Ivoire)', *Annales de l'Université d'Abidjan* (Serie F) 3, 1971, pp. 62, 69, 78.

87 John M. Janzen and Wyatt MacGaffey, *An anthology of Kongo religion* . . . , Lawrence, Kansas: University of Kansas 1974, pp. 63–5.

88 Francois M'Vuendy, *Le Kimbanguisme de la clandestinité à la tolérance, (1921–1959)*, École Pratique des Haute Études, Paris, memoire, 1969.

89 The text of the letter is to be found in Henri Desroche and Paul Raymaekers, 'Départ d'un prophète, arrivée d'une église', *Archives de Sciences Sociales des Religions* vol. 42, 1976 pp. 148–59.

90 Janzen and MacGaffey, *An anthology of Kongo religion*, pp. 123–7.

Chapter 3   1959–1966

1 Paul Raymaekers, 'L'Église de Jésus-Christ sur la terre par le prophète Simon Kimbangu: contribution à l'étude des mouvements messianiques dans le Bas-Kongo', *Zaire* (Brussels) vol. 13 no. 7, 1959 p. 682.

2 Quoted in R. I. Rotberg, *The rise of nationalism in Central Africa*, Cambridge, Mass.: Harvard University Press 1967 p. 293

3 Willard Jackson, 'The "Union des Populations du Cameroun" in rebellion: the integrative backlash of insurgency', in R. I. Rotberg and A. A. Mazrui (eds.), *Protest and power in Black Africa*, New York: Oxford University Press 1970 pp. 671–92; E. Mveng, *Histoire du Cameroun*, Paris, 1963 p. 440.

4 William B. Anderson, 'The role of religion in the Sudan's search for unity', in D. B. Barrett (ed.), *African initiatives in religion*, Nairobi: East African Publishing House 1971 pp. 73–92; Oliver Allison, *Through fire and water*, London: CMS 1976; Mohamed Omer Beshir, *The Southern Sudan. Background to conflict*, London: C. Hurst 1968.

5 *Nouvel Observateur*, March 1967.

6 M. Crawford Young, 'Rebellion and the Congo', in Rotberg and Mazrui (eds.), *Protest and Power in Black Africa*, pp. 969–1011; Benoît Verhaegen, *Rébellions*

au Congo. Brussels and Kinshasa: CRISP and IRES, 2 vols. 1966 and 1969.

7 See the letter of the Abbé Placide Tara, of April 1964, in Verhaegen, vol. 1, pp. 162–5.

8 See the document in Verhaegen, vol. 1, pp. 159–62, relating to the mission of Kilembe. For the wider issue of resentment against the long established and frequently abused political privilege of the Catholic Church see Marvin D. Markovitz, *Cross and sword. The political rise of Christian missions in the Belgian Congo 1908–1960*. Stanford: Hoover Institution Press 1973; Michel Merlier, *Le Congo de la colonisation Belge à l'indépendance*. Paris: F. Maspero 1962, 215–229; Paul Ulwor, Une acculturation religieuse en echec dans l'ancienne colonie belge du Congo. *Revue de Psychologie des peuples* (Le Havre) vol. 23, 1968 pp. 390–421.

9 Herbert Weiss, *Political protest in the Congo*, Princeton, N.J.: Princeton University Press 1967 p. 225.

10 Renée C. Fox, Willy De Craemer and Jean-marie Ribeaucourt, 'The Second Independence': a case study of the Kwilu Rebellion in the Congo. *Comparative Studies in Society and History* vol. 8 no. 1, 1965 p. 105. For an early general account of the effect of the 1964 risings on the Church see *Herder Correspondence*, Missionary losses in Congo disorders during 1964. March 1965 pp. 89–93.

11 Muriel Horrell, *Action, reaction and counter-action*. Johannesburg: South African Institute of Race Relations 1974 p. 52.

12 Monica Wilson and Leonard Thompson (eds.), *The Oxford History of South Africa*, vol. 2, 1971 p. 523.

13 Thomas Okuma, *Angola in ferment*. Boston: Beacon Press 1962, 1; Basil Davidson, *In the eye of the storm*, rev. ed., Harmondsworth: Penguin Books 1975, 178–9; René Pelissier, *Résistance et révoltes en Angola (1845–1961)*, privately printed, (?1975), vol. 3, pp. 1146–51.

14 Antonio de Figueiredo, *Portugal: fifty years of dictatorship*, Harmondsworth: Penguin Books 1975 p. 210.

15 A. J. Wills, *An introduction to the history of Central Africa*, London: Oxford University Press 1973 ed. p. 370.

16 Victor Le Vine, 'The coups in Upper Volta, Dahomey and the Central African Republic', in R. I. Rotberg and A. A. Mazrui (eds.), *Protest and power in Black Africa*, 1035–71.

17 K. Nyamayaro Mufuka, *Mission and politics in Malawi*, Kingston, Ontario: Limestone Press 1977 pp. 185–95; Brian Garvey, *The development of the White Fathers' mission among the Bemba-speaking peoples, 1891–1964*, University of London, Ph.D dissertation 1974 p. 377.

18 Kenneth Kaunda, *Zambia shall be free*, London: Heinemann 1962 pp. 145–7; Colin Morris, *The hour after midnight*, London: Longmans 1961 pp. 54–7, 134–42, 158–61; Lawrence Vambe, *From Rhodesia to Zimbabwe*, London: Heinemann 1976 pp. 102–4, 232; Brian Garvey, *The development of the White Fathers' mission*, p. 378; Peter Fry, *Spirits of protest*, Cambridge: Cambridge University Press 1976 p. 114.

19 Patricia Chater, *Grass Roots. The story of St. Faith's Farm in Southern Rhodesia*, London: Hodder & Stoughton 1962 p. 173.

20 *A plea for peace: pastoral instruction on the problem of Rhodesia*. The Catholic Bishops of Rhodesia. London: Geoffrey Chapman 1966 p. 3.

21 John Marcum, *The Angolan revolution*, vol. 1, *The anatomy of an explosion*

(1950–1962), Cambridge, Mass: Harvard University Press 1969, notes by Bishop Dodge, pp. 330–2.

22 The lengthy documentation of his trial many years later can be found in Mario Brochado Coelho, *Em defesa de Joaquim Pinto de Andrade*, Porto: Afrontamento 1971.

23 John S. Peart-Binns, *Ambrose Reeves*, London: Victor Gollancz 1973; a valuable selection from Bishop Reeves' 'Charges' to his diocesan synod, 1952–7, is to be found in David Paton (ed.), *Church and race in South Africa*, London: SCM Press 1958 pp. 9–50.

24 Peart-Binns, *Ambrose Reeves*, p. 235.

25 Dutch Reformed Church, *Christian principles in multi-racial South Africa. A report of the Dutch Reformed Conference of church leaders*. Pretoria: DRC 1953 pp. 15–17.

26 International Commission of Jurists, Geneva. *The trial of Beyers Naudé. Christian witness and the rule of law*. London: Search Press 1975 p. 65.

27 *Ibid*, p. 73.

28 *Herder Correspondence*, 'A crisis of conscience in South Africa', May 1964 pp. 153–6.

29 Leslie Cawood, *The Churches and race relations in South Africa*, Johannesburg: South African Institute of Race Relations 1964 pp. 12–13.

30 *Unity and freedom in the new Tanganyika*, Tabora: Tabora Mission Press December 1960; *Actes de la VIe Assemblée plénière de l'Episcopat du Congo*, Leopoldville 1961.

31 R. C. Fox, W. De Craemer and J. -M. Ribeaucourt, 'The second independence', p. 91.

32 M. Crawford Young, 'Rebellion and the Congo', p. 997; *Congo 1964: political documents of a developing nation*, introd. Herbert Weiss. Princeton, N.J.: Princeton University Press.

33 See note 40 to chapter 1.

34 Marie-Louise Martin, *Kimbangu. An African prophet and his church*, Oxford: Basil Blackwell 1975, pp. 101–2, 126–7.

35 Mary Benson, *Tshekedi Khama*, London: Faber & Faber 1960, pp. 300–4.

36 L. B. Greaves, *Carey Francis of Kenya*, London: Rex Collings 1969, p. 189.

37 For an interesting local study of the schools issue in these years see Colin Leys, *Politicians and policies: an essay on politics in Acholi Uganda, 1962–65*, Nairobi: East African Publishing House 1967, pp. 83–91.

38 J. S. Pobee, 'Church and state in Ghana 1946–1966', in J. S. Pobee (ed.), *Religion in a pluralistic society*, Leiden: E. J. Brill 1976, pp. 121–44.

39 F. B. Welbourn, *Religion and politics in Uganda 1952–1962*, Nairobi: East African Publishing House 1965, chapters 5–8; Michael Twaddle, 'The Democratic Party of Uganda as a political institution', in E. Fasholé-Luke *et al.* (eds.), *Christianity in independent Africa*, London: Rex Collings 1978 pp. 255–66; D. A. Low, *Political parties in Uganda 1949–62*, London: Athlone Press 1962; L. A. Fallers (ed.), *The King's men. Leadership and status in Buganda on the eve of independence*, London: Oxford University Press 1964; Dan Mudoola, 'Religion and Politics in Uganda: the case of Busoga, 1900–1962, *African Affairs*, vol. 77 (January) 1978, pp. 22–35.

40 The letter, entitled *Church and state: guiding principles*, was published both in English and in Luganda by the Marianum Press, Kisubi.

41 Frederick Mutesa (Kabaka of Buganda), *Desecration of my kingdom*, London: Constable 1967, p. 16.

42 For the Rwandan revolution see Ian Linden, *Church and revolution in Rwanda*, Manchester: Manchester University Press 1977, pp. 249–82; also René Lemarchand, *Rwanda and Burundi*, London: Pall Mall Press 1970, though the author's overall estimate of the contrast between the two countries must be greatly modified in the light of post-1970 developments in Burundi; see also *Herder Correspondence*, 'Church and revolution in Rwanda', September-October 1964, pp. 292–3.

43 James Fernandes, 'Rededication and prophetism in Ghana', *Cahiers d'Études Africaines* (Paris) vol. 10 no. 2, 1970 pp. 229–31; for a comparable example of state recognition of an independent church, one can recall the funeral of the Apostle Oduwole of the Church of the Lord (Aladura) in Liberia in April 1965. President Tubman attended the funeral and flags were flown at half mast. See H. W. Turner, *African independent church*, Oxford: Clarendon Press 1967, vol. 1 p. 157.

44 Ndabaningi Sithole, *Obed Mutezo*, Nairobi: Oxford University Press 1970.

45 Andrew Roberts, 'The Lumpa Church of Alice Lenshina', in R. I. Rotberg and A. A. Mazrui (eds.), *Protest and Power in Black Africa*, New York: Oxford University Press 1970 pp. 513–68; Wim. M. J. van Binsbergen, 'Religious innovation and political conflict in Zambia: a contribution to the interpretation of the Lumpa rising', *African Perspectives* 1976 no. 2, pp. 101–35; Fergus MacPherson, *Kenneth Kaunda of Zambia: the times and the man*, London: Oxford University Press 1974 pp. 410–11, 442–3.

46 Martial Sinda, *Le messianisme congolais et ses incidences politiques – Kimbanguisme – Matsouanisme – autres mouvements*, Paris: Payot 1972 pp. 282 283.

47 Efraim Andersson, *Churches at the grass-roots: a study in Congo-Brazzaville*, London: Lutterworth Press 1968 pp. 58–62.

48 F. L. Bartels, *The roots of Ghana Methodism*, Cambridge: Cambridge University Press 1965 pp. 293–314.

49 Eliewaha Mshana, 'The changing shape and pastoral ministry of the Evangelical Lutheran Church in Tanzania, 1955–1975', unpublished paper of the Jos Conference on Christianity in Independent Africa, 1975.

50 Elfriede Strassberger, *Ecumenism in South Africa 1936–1960*, Johannesberg: South African Council of Churches 1974; Peter Bolink, *Towards church union in Zambia*, Franeker: T. Wever 1967.

51 Bolink, *Towards church union*.

52 R. Macpherson, *The Presbyterian Church in Kenya*, Nairobi: Presbyterian Church of East Africa 1970 pp. 142–4.

53 Ogbu Kalu, 'Church unity and religious change in Africa', in E. Fasholé-Luke et al. (eds.), *Christianity in independent Africa*, pp. 164–75.

54 *Ibid*, p. 167.

55 For Ghana's Council of Churches see F. L. Bartels, *The roots of Ghana Methodism*, pp. 287–9; for Kenya see John Lonsdale, Stanley Booth-Clibborn and Andrew Hake, 'The emerging pattern of church and state cooperation in Kenya', in Fasholé-Luke et al. (eds.), *Christianity in independent Africa*, pp. 267–84.

56 John Gratian, *The relationship of the Africa Inland Mission and its national church in Kenya between 1895 and 1971*, New York University Ph.D. dissertation 1974 pp. 298–302.

57 For the increasing polarisation between Protestant missionaries over ecumenical issues in the 1960s see Adrian Hastings, 'Mission and unity, from Edinburgh

via Uppsala to Nairobi', in *The faces of God. Reflections on church and society*, London: Geoffrey Chapman 1975 pp. 68–94.

58. For important seminars at Mindolo in 1962 and 1963 on African independent churches, and on marriage and family life, see Victor E. W. Hayward (ed.) *African independent church movements*, London: Edinburgh House Press 1963; *Report of the All-Africa Seminar on the Christian home and family*, Geneva: World Council of Churches 1963.

59 John V. Taylor and Dorothea Lehmann, *Christians of the Copperbelt*, London: SCM Press 1961 pp. 38–50.

60 John Mbiti, 'Some African concepts of christology' in G. F. Vicedom (ed.), *Christ and the younger churches*, London: SPCK 1972 pp. 51–62, first published in German in 1968 in P. Beyerhaus *et al. Theologische Stimmen aus Asien, Afrika und Lateinamerika* III, Munich.

61 See, for instance, Sir Kenneth Grubb's comments in the preface to *World Christian Handbook*, London: World Dominion Press, 1962 edition.

62 David M. Beckmann, *Eden Revival Spiritual Churches in Ghana*, St Louis Missouri: Concordia Publishing House 1975 p. 38.

63 Gailyn Van Rheenen, *Church planting in Uganda: a comparative study*, South Pasadena, California: William Carey Library 1976.

64 For one example see M. L. Daneel, *Old and new in Southern Shona independent churches*, the Hague: Mouton, vol. 2, 1974 pp. 13–46.

65 E. P. T. Crampton, *Christianity in Northern Nigeria*, Zaria, privately published 1975.

66 D. C. Dorward, 'Religious aspects of socio-economic stratification in modern Tiv society'. Unpublished paper, London University, School of African and Oriental Studies, 1974.

67 The *African Ecclesiastical Review* (*AFER*) published quarterly from Katigondo Seminary, Uganda, from January 1959, and from January 1972 from Gaba Pastoral Institute, located in Kampala until its removal to Eldoret, Kenya (P.O. Box 908) at the beginning of 1976. Its pages are a gold-mine for the evolving shape of the African Catholic Church in these years. The most influential representative of progressive Catholicism in the late 1950s was probably Guy Mosmans, PB. His *L'Église à l'heure de l'Afrique*, Tournai: Casterman 1961, was a reprint of articles written 1956–60 whilst Mosmans was Provincial of the Belgian White Fathers.

68 *Proceedings, East African Lay Apostolate Meeting, Nyegezi (Tanganyika), 21–27 August 1961*, Rome 1962.

69 Its full report was published in the *African Ecclesiastical Review*, vol. 6 no. 4 1964 pp. 33–420.

70 Among them Stephen Mbunga in Tanganyika and Patrick Kalilombe from Nyasaland, both men who would be very influential as rectors of major seminaries in a few years time; see also G. Ngango, 'Langue liturgique et catholicité, in *Personalité africaine et catholicisme*, Paris: 1963 pp. 131–52.

71 Vincent Donovan CSSp was a missionary in Tanganyika; his article is in *AFER* vol. 1 no. 3, 1959 pp. 169–77; he was answered very angrily by Thomas Slevin CSSp., a missionary in Nigeria, in *AFER* vol. 2 no. 2, 1960 pp. 126–31; Donovan replied in July 1960 *AFER* vol. 2 no. 3, 1960 pp. 242–7.

72 Tharcisse Tshibangu, *Théologie positive et théologie spéculative*, Louvain: Publications Universitaires de Louvain 1965.

73 Adrian Hastings, 'The ministry of the Catholic Church in Africa, 1960–1975', in Fasholé-Luke *et al.* (eds.) *Christianity in independent Africa*, pp. 26–43.

74 Robert Roelandt, 'The situation of the church in the Congo', *AFER*, vol. 3 no. 3, 1961 pp. 212–20.
75 *Actes de la VIe Assemblée Plénière de l'Épiscopat du Congo*, Léopoldville 1961.
76 The ten largest societies of missionary priests in Africa in 1964 were as follows: White Fathers, 2,183; Holy Ghost Fathers, 1,929; S.M.A, 780; Jesuits, 756; O.M.I. Oblates, 616; Scheut, 611; Franciscans, 499; Capuchins, 471; Mill Hill, 452; Verona, 328 (*CIPA – Informations* (White Fathers, Rome) no. 219, 8 May 1964, 193).
77 For the full figures see Adrian Hastings, note 73 above, p. 31.
78 For a minor literary masterpiece see the account of one such school, Kit Elliott, *An African school, a record of experience*, London: Cambridge University Press 1970. For the overall Catholic position on education at the end of this period see *Catholic education in the service of Africa*, Report of the Pan-African Catholic Education Conference Leopoldville, 16–23 August 1965 Tournai: Casterman 1966.
79 Aylward Shorter and Eugene Kataza (eds.) *Missionaries to yourselves. African catechists today*, London: Geoffrey Chapman 1972.
80 See Resolution VI of the Pan-African Catechetical Study Week, *AFER*, vol. 6 no. 4, 1964 p. 419.
81 In Eastern Africa a major programme of 'putting across' Vatican II, sponsored by AMECEA, the joint board of bishops of five countries, began in May 1966 with a fortnightly bulletin *Post-Vatican II*, published from Kipalapala, Tanzania; it lasted for two years and systematically worked through the conciliar documents; some 5,000 copies were sent out to all the dioceses of Eastern Africa.
82 Georges Conus, *L'Église d'Afrique au Concile Vatican II*, Immensee, Switzerland: Nouvelle Revue de Sciences Missionaire 1975.
83 Martin West, *Bishops and prophets in a Black city*, Cape Town: David Philip 1975 pp. 37–41.
84 Peter Dirven, *The Maria Legio. The dynamics of a breakaway church among the Luo of East Africa*, Pontifica Universitas Gregoriana (Rome), doctoral dissertation in missiology 1970; Peter Dirven, 'A protest and a challenge: the Maria Legio breakaway church in West Kenya', *AFER* vol. 12 no. 2, 1970 pp. 127–36; Marie-France Perrin Jassy, *Basic community in the African churches*, Maryknoll, NY: Orbis Books 1973.
85 L. J. Suenens, *A heroine of the Apostolate*, Dublin: C. J. Fallen 1956.
86 Eden Revival Church of Ghana, *Handbook: Christianity original re-enacted*, Accra: the Church. (?1971); Beckmann, *Eden Revival*; Ferdinand Akuffo, *Ghanaian pentecostalism*, University of Oxford, D. Phil. thesis 1976.
87 See the following studies by Guy Bernard: (1) with P. Caprasse, 'Religious movements in the Congo: a research hypothesis', *Cahiers Économiques et Sociaux (Kinshasa)* vol. 3 no. 1, 1965 pp. 49–60; (2) '*Les églises congolaises et la construction nationale*', *Revue de l'Institut de Sociologie* (Brussels) vol. 23 nos. 2–3, 1967 pp. 241–7; (3) 'Diversité des nouvelles églises congolaises', *Cahiers d'Études Africaines* (Paris) vol. 10 no. 2, 1970 pp. 203–27; (4) 'La contestation et les églises nationales au Congo', *Canadian Journal of African Studies* vol. 5 no. 2, 1971, 145–56.
88 The report of the twelve wise men, in Janzen and MacGaffey, *An Anthology of Kongo religion*, pp. 136–9.
89 Wyatt MacGaffey, *The beloved city*, a commentary on a Kimbanguist text, *Journal of Religion in Africa* vol. 2 no. 2, 1969 p. 141.

90 See above, p. 77; M. L. Daneel, *Old and new in Southern Shona independent churches*, the Hague: Mouton, vol. 1, 1971 pp. 332–339.
91 Bennetta Jules-Rosette, *African apostles. Ritual and conversion in the Church of John Maranke*, Ithaca, NY: Cornell University Press 1975, pp. 217–24.
92 Haldor E. Heimer, 'The church suited to home needs. A look at the people of two churches in Luluabourg, Congo,' in R. T. Parsons (ed.), *Windows on Africa: a symposium*, Leiden: E. J. Brill 1971 pp. 21–37.
93 A. Lanzas and G. Bernard, 'Les fidèles d'une "nouvelle église" au Congo', *Genèvé-Afrique* vol. 5 no. 2, 1966 pp. 189–216.
94 *Ibid*, p. 207.
95 See above, p. 76; H. Haselbarth, 'The Zion Christian Church of Edward Lekganyane', in *Our approach to the Independent Church movement in South Africa*, Mapumulo, Natal: Missiological Institute, Lutheran Theological College 1966. Mimeo.

Chapter 4 1967–1975

1 *The Church and developing society of Tanzania, Message of the Bishops for the centenary of the Church 1868–*, Ndanda Mission Press 1968, p. 3; see also Bishop Trevor Huddleston's *The state of Anglo-Tanzanian relations*, London: Africa Bureau 1968; Sylvain Urfer, *Socialisme et église en Tanzanie*, IDOC-France 1976.
2 Henry Makulu was chairman of the All Africa Conference on Churches and vice-principal of Mindolo Ecumenical Foundation; he was later chairman of Zambia's Public Service Commission. *Education, development and nation-building in independent Africa* was published by SCM Press in 1971.
3 B. M. Khaketla, *Lesotho 1970*, London: C. Hurst 1971 pp. 283–98, 336–7.
4 John Lonsdale, Stanley Booth-Clibborn and Andrew Hake, 'The emerging pattern of church and state cooperation in Kenya', in E. Fasholé-Luke *et al.* (eds.), *Christianity in Independent Africa*, London: Rex Collings 1978, pp. 267–84.
5 Ian Linden, *Church and revolution in Rwanda*, Manchester: Manchester University Press 1977, pp. 284–6.
6 The *Osservatore Romano* of 13 May 1971 put the number of foreign church workers in Zaire at the time as approximately 2,500 priests, 560 brothers, and 3,100 sisters – 6,160 in all. There were also, undoubtedly, many foreign lay people in the service of the church.
7 Pro Mundi Vita, *Church and 'authenticity' in Zaïre* Special Note 39, March 1975; 'Duel in Zaïre', in *The Month*, May 1972 pp. 131–2; Ngindu Mushete, 'Authenticity and Christianity in Zaire', in Fasholé-Luke *et al.* (eds.) *Christianity in Independent Africa*, pp. 228–41; Kenneth Adelman, 'The church–state conflict in Zaïre, 1969–1974', *African Studies Review* vol. 18 no. 1, 1975 pp. 102–16.
8 Speech of 19 August 1973. *Church and 'authenticity' in Zaïre*, p. 2.
9 Speech of 6 April 1973. *Ibid*, p. 3.
10 *Les relations entre l'Église et l'État au Zaire*, Brussels, Études Africaines du CRISP 1972.
11 Good examples of authoritarian missionary practice can be found in Mary Douglas, *The Lele of the Kasai*, London: Oxford University Press 1963 pp. 264–6.

12 Telegram of State Commissioner of Political Affairs, dated 6 November 1974. *Church and 'authenticity' in Zaire*, p. 10.
13 Address by the State Commissioner of Political Affairs, 4 December 1974. *Ibid*, p. 11.
14 James Burns, 'Freedom for tyranny', *The Tablet*, 8 January 1977; Suzanne Cronje, *Equatorial Guinea – the forgotten dictatorship*, London: Anti-Slavery Society, 1976.
15 Akiiki B. Mujaju, 'The political crisis of church institutions in Uganda', *African Affairs*, vol. 75 (Jan.) 1976 pp. 67–85.
16 For the position of Jehovah's Witnesses see Sholto Cross, 'Jehovah's Witnesses in East and Central Africa', in Fasholé-Luke *et al.* (eds.) *Christianity in Independent Africa* pp. 304–15; Bryan R. Wilson, 'Jehovah's Witnesses in Kenya', *Journal of Religion in Africa* vol. 5 no. 2, 1973 pp. 128–49; J. R. Hooker, 'Witnesses and Watchtower in the Rhodesias and Nyasaland', *Journal of African History*, vol. 6 no. 1, 1965 pp. 91–106; Norman Long, 'Religion and economic action among the Serenje-Lala of Zambia', in C. G. Baëta (ed.), *Christianity in tropical Africa*, pp. 396–413; Tony Hodges, *Jehovah's Witnesses in Central Africa*, London: Minority Rights Group 1976.
17 See articles in *The Observer* (London), 7 December 1975, and *The Times*, 24 December 1975.
18 Godfrey Morrison, *Eritrea and the Southern Sudan*, London: Minority Rights Group, 3rd edition 1976; Louise Pirouet, 'The achievement of peace in Sudan', *Journal of Eastern African Research and Development* vol. 6 no. 1, 1976, pp. 115–45.
19 *Africa Contemporary Record 1968–1969*, ed. C. Legum and J. Drysdale, p. 553; see the analysis of Biafran newspaper propaganda by Andrew Walls, 'Religion and the press in "the Enclave" in the Nigerian Civil war', in Fasholé-Luke *et al.* (eds.), *Christianity in Independent Africa*, pp. 207–16. For a balanced contemporary church assessment of the war see *Herder Correspondence*, The Nigerian Tragedy, November 1968 pp. 327–32.
20 Broadcast by Ojukwu, 10 August 1967, A. H. M. Kirk-Greene (compiler), *Crisis and Conflict in Nigeria*, London: Oxford University Press, 2 vols. 1971, vol. 2, p. 154.
21 Ojukwu's Ahiara Declaration of 1 June 1969 stressed this theme. See Kirk-Greene, *Crisis and conflict*, vol. 2, p. 383.
22 *Ibid*, p. 379.
23 E. A. Ayandele, 'The "Humanitarian" Factor in Nigerian Affairs', *Nigerian Opinion*, Ibadan, July 1969, p. 446.
24 A. E. Afigbo, 'The missions, the state and education in South-eastern Nigeria, 1956–1971', in Fasholé-Luke *et al.* (eds.), *Christianity in Independent Africa*, pp. 176–92; Colman M. Cooke, 'Church, state and education: the Eastern Nigeria experience 1950–1967', in *ibid* pp. 193–206.
25 For developments prior to 1970 see René Lemarchand, *Rwanda and Burundi*, London: Pall Mall Press 1970; for subsequent events, *Conflict in Burundi*, Pro Mundi Vita Special Note 25 April 1973; Jeremy Greenland, 'Black racism in Burundi', *New Blackfriars* vol. 54 no. 641 (Oct.), 1973, pp. 443–51; René Lemarchand and David Martin, *Selective genocide in Burundi*, London: Minority Rights Group 1974.
26 For the course of the Mozambique war see Adrian Hastings, 'Some reflections upon the war in Mozambique', *African Affairs* vol. 73 (July) 1974 pp. 263–76.
27 The 'Message to the people of South Africa' has been published in many places,

e.g., F. Wilson and D. Perrot, *Outlook on a century*, Lovedale 1973, pp. 683–8.

28 For the grants controversy see (1) the correspondence between B. J. Vorster and the churches in *Pro Veritate*, July 1971 pp. 14–25; (2) Adrian Hastings, 'Christianity and revolution', *African Affairs*, vol. 74 (July) 1975 pp. 347–61; (3) Kenneth Sansbury, *Combatting racism*, British Council of Churches 1975; (4) Elizabeth Adler, *A small beginning. An assessment of the first five years of the Programme to Combat Racism*, Geneva: World Council of Churches 1974; (5) Wolfram Weisse, *Sudafrika ünd das Antirassismusprogramm*, Bern: Herbert Lang 1975; (6) Darill Hudson, *The World Council of Churches in International Affairs*, Leighton Buzzard: Faith Press, 1977 pp. 59–128.

29 The Presbyterian Church of South Africa withdrew from the World Council of Churches. For the Anglican position see the memorandum presented to the Anglican Consultative Council meeting in Dublin. *Partners in Mission*, London: SPCK 1973 pp. 26–9.

30 Bishop Alphaeus Zulu of Zululand, a member of the praesidium of the World Council of Churches, is an African Christian who has opposed the making of grants throughout.

31 For the trial of Dean Gonville ffrench-Beytagh see his own book, *Encountering darkness*, London: Collins 1973.

32 Beyers Naudé made this point clear in his trial. See International Commission of Jurists, Geneva, *The trial of Beyers Naudé*, London: Search Press 1975.

33 A full account of the trial has been published: see preceding note.

34 *Christian Action Journal* (London), 'The happenings at Hammanskraal', Spring 1975 pp. 16–21.

35 *The Tablet*, 7 February 1970.

36 Oswin Magrath, *Unity of the clergy*, 1971, privately published. This was recognised by the Catholic hierarchy in a very remarkable statement early in 1977.

37 See the lengthy documentation in *Namibia now*, IDOC–International 1973, vi, 'The Churches'; for the background see Lothar Engel, *Kolonialismus und Nationalismus im Deutschen Protestantismus in Namibia 1907 bis 1945*, Bern: Herbert Lang and Frankfurt: Peter Lang 1976.

38 Colin Winter, *Namibia: the story of a bishop in exile*, Guildford: Lutterworth Press 1977.

39 *Diario de Noticias* (Lisbon), 6 December 1959.

40 Cesare Bertulli, *Croce e spada in Mozambico*, Rome: Coines Edizioni 1974 pp. 127–9; White Fathers, *Mozambique, une église, signe de salut . . . Pour qui?* (a very valuable 400-page mimeographed collection of documents produced by the White Fathers Generalate, Rome, in early 1973) pp. 199–202.

41 See many incidents described in John Paul, *Mozambique, memoirs of a revolution*, Harmondsworth: Penguin Books 1975, e.g. pp. 122–3; W. Burridge, WF, in *The Guardian*, 3 August 1973.

42 *Africa Contemporary Record 1968–9*, pp. 399–400; Bertulli, *Croce e spada*, pp. 130–1.

43 *Mozambique, une église, signe de salut . . . ?* p. 2.

44 The complete documentation of the trial of Fathers Sampaio and Mendes is to be found in *O Julgamento dos Padres do Macuti*, Porto, 1973; for Mucumbura see International Defence and Aid Fund, *Terror in Tete*, 1973, ch. 3 and Appendix 3.

45 Adrian Hastings, *Wiriyamu*, London: Search Press 1974; *Terror in Tete*; Franz Ansprenger *et al.*, *Wiriyamu, Eine Dokumentation zum Krieg in Mozambique*, Munich: Kaiser-Gruneweld 1974; *The Guardian*, 23 April 1974.

46 *The Guardian*, 16 April 1974; *The Times*, 17 April 1974; Adrian Hastings, 'Portugal's other rebellion', *The Observer* (London) 21 April 1974.

47 *Mozambique Revolution* (London), Independence issue, no. 61.

48. A statement of the Bishop of Nampula (Manuel Pinto) issued just after independence, July 1975, entitled 'Reflexion sobre la Iglesia de Mozambique', is to be found in *Misiones Extranjeras* (Madrid), Nov.–Dec. 1975 pp. 482–95. Further valuable post-independence documentation of church–state relations in Mozambique is to be found in the same periodical, issues of Jan.–Feb. 1976 pp. 33–5; March–April 1976 pp. 155–61; May–June 1976 pp. 263–77. See also *Mozambique. A church in a socialist state in time of radical change* (African Dossier 3), Brussels: Pro Mundi Vita, Jan.–Feb. 1977.

49 The bishops' statement is given in part in *The Tablet*, 27 July 1974; for a first national meeting of black priests, brothers and nuns in Angola, held at Huambo 17–22 March 1975 see *Misiones Extranjeras* (Madrid), Nov.-Dec. 1975 pp. 524–9; for background see J. Sanches, 'Les missions catholiques et la politique de l'état portugais', *Spiritus* (Paris) 1972 pp. 370–82; see also the Angolan documents in *Mozambique, une église, signe de salut*, pp. 110–20.

50 *A call to Christians*, 7 June 1969.

51 *A message and appeal from church leaders to the Christian people of Rhodesia*, 1969 p. 4.

52 Dieter B. Scholz, 'The Catholic Church and the race conflict in Rhodesia', in Anthony J. Dachs (ed.), *Christianity south of the Zambezi*, Gwelo: Mambo Press 1973 p. 201; for the Catholic position see also *Herder Correspondence*, 'The Church and the Rhodesian conference', June 1970 pp. 166–71; R. H. Randolph, *Church and state in Rhodesia, 1969–1971*, Gwelo: Mambo Press 1971: Donal Lamont, *Speech from the dock*, Leigh-on-Sea, Essex: Kevin Mayhew Ltd. 1977.

53 Norman Thomas, 'Inter-church co-operation in Rhodesia's towns, 1962–72', in T. O. Ranger and John Weller (eds.), *Themes in the Christian history of Central Africa*, London: Heinemann 1975 pp. 238–55.

54 *Africa Contemporary Record 1970–71*, ed. Colin Legum, p. B552.

55 Guy Clutton-Brock and Molly Clutton-Brock, *Cold Comfort confronted*, London: Mowbrays 1972; Didymus Mutasa, *Rhodesian Black behind bars*, London: Mowbrays 1974.

56 *The Guardian*, 11 April 1975, and elsewhere.

57 *The Tablet*, 22 June 1974; *Africa Contemporary Record 1970–71*, p. B 533.

58 *The Times*, 1 April 1974; *The Observer*, 28 April 1974; *The Times*, 28 June 1974.

59 See three reports published by the Catholic Institute of International Relations (CIIR) in London: *The man in the middle: torture, resettlement and eviction* 1975 and *Civil war in Rhodesia*, 1976, both compiled by the Catholic Commission for Justice and Peace in Rhodesia; *Racial discrimination and repression in Southern Rhodesia* (compiled by the International Commission of Jurists) 1976.

60 For a criticism of the Catholic bishops as inadequately radical see Roger Riddell in *The Month*, May 1977 pp. 155–60.

61 A. R. I. Doi, 'Islam in Nigeria: changes since independence', in Fasholé-Luke *et al.* (eds.), *Christianity in independent Africa* pp. 334–53.

62 Ali A. Mazrui, 'Religious strangers in Uganda: from Emin Pasha to Amin Dada', *African Affairs* vol. 76 (Jan.) 1977 pp. 21–38.

63 Akiiki B. Mujaju, 'The political crisis of church institutions in Uganda', *African Affairs*, vol. 75 (Jan.) 1976 pp. 67–85.

64 As for instance on the Catholic side in Eugene Hillman and Adrian Hastings, 'A missionary correspondence', *New Blackfriars*, August 1967, p. 602.

65 *Ecumenical Press Service*, 20 June 1974, p. 11. For the moratorium issue see R. Elliott Kendall, 'On the sending of missionaries: a call for restraint', *International Review of Mission* vol 64 no. 253 (Jan.) 1975 pp. 62–6, and several articles in International Review of Mission vol. 64 no. 254 (April) 1975.

66 P. W. Brierley, *UK Protestant Missions Handbook*, London: Evangelical Missionary Alliance 1973 (this does not include the USPG figures which were obtained separately); *North American Protestant Ministries Overseas 1968*, Waco, Texas, 8th edition, and Edward R. Dayton (ed.), *Mission Handbook: North American Protestant Ministries Overseas 1976*, Monrovia, California: MARC, 11th edition; see also R. Elliott Kendall, 'The missionary factor in Africa', in Fasholé-Luke *et al.* (eds.), *Christianity in independent Africa* pp. 16–25.

67 The total number of Protestant expatriate church workers in South Africa in 1973 was 1,400. David Bosch, 'The feasibility of a moratorium on missions in the South African context'. Unpublished paper (?1975).

68 John Gration, *The relationship of the Africa Inland Mission and its national church in Kenya between 1895 and 1971*, New York University, Ph.D dissertation 1974 pp. 282–342.

69 In 1974 the Diocese of Kimberley and Kuruman, with rather few clergy, decided to abolish the colour bar between white and black clerical stipends (*USPG Network*, June 1974); in this it was exceptional, 'In the Diocese of Natal, for example, black priests earn only between one third and a half of the stipend of the white priests.'

70 A. G. Blood, *The history of the Universities' Mission to Central Africa*, vol. 3, *1933–1957*, London: UMCA 1962 pp. 51–2.

71 Tom Tuma, 'Major changes and developments in Christian leadership in Busoga, Uganda, 1960–1974', in Fasholé-Luke *et al.* (eds.), *Christianity in Independent Africa*, pp. 74–7; Catherine Ellen Robins, *Tukutendereza: a study of social change and sectarian withdrawal in the Balokole revival of Uganda*, Columbia University, Ph.D dissertation 1975.

72 The main publications of African theology on the Protestant side in this period are the following: Bolaji Idowu, *Olódùmarè. God in Yoruba belief*, London: Longmans 1962, *Towards an indigenous church*, London: Oxford University Press 1965, *African traditional religion. A definition*, London: SCM Press 1973; G. G. Baëta, *Prophetism in Ghana*, London: SCM Press 1962; Harry Sawyerr, *Creative evangelism*, London: Lutterworth Press 1968, *God: ancestor or creator?* London: Longman 1970; Mark Glasswell and E. Fasholé-Luke (eds.), *New Testament Christianity for Africa and the world. Essays in honour of Harry Sawyerr*, London: SPCK 1974; Kwesi Dickson and Paul Ellingworth (eds.), *Biblical revelation and African beliefs*, Maryknoll NY: Orbis Books 1969; John S. Mbiti, *African religions and philosophy*, London: Heinemann 1969; *Concepts of God in Africa*, London: SPCK 1970, *New Testament eschatology in an African background*, London: Oxford University Press 1971. For an African conservative evangelical critique of 'African theology' see Byang H. Kato, *Theological pitfalls in Africa*, Kisumu, Kenya: Evangel Publishing House 1975. Dr Kato was General Secretary of the Association of Evangelicals of Africa and Madagascar. One should also consult such periodicals as the *Sierra Leone Bulletin of Religion, Orita* (Ibadan) and *Africa Theological Journal* (Makumira). For a fine example of a widening concern among the younger generation of

African theologians see the Ghanaian John Pobee's 'The cry of the centurion – a cry of defeat', in Ernst Bammel (ed.), *The trial of Jesus. Cambridge studies in honour of C. F. D. Moule*, London: SCM Press 1970 pp. 91–102.

73 Basil Moore (ed.), *Black theology. The South African voice*, London: C. Hurst 1973; David Bosch, 'Currents and cross currents in South African black theology', *Journal of Religion in Africa* vol. 6 no. 1 1974 pp. 1–22; Manas Buthelezi, 'African theology and black theology', in *Relevant theology for Africa. Report on a consultation at Mapumulo, Natal, September 1972*, pp. 18–24; Simon Gqubule, 'What is black theology?', *Journal of Theology for Southern Africa* 1974 pp. 16–23. For an interesting series of contributions to the theological debate, see the chapters by Desmond Tutu, Samuel Kibicho, Christian Gaba, Gabriel Setiloane, Laurenti Magesa and Sidbe Sempore in part II of E. Fasholé-Luke *et al.* (eds.) *Christianity in independent Africa*; see also the wide-ranging review of Edward Fasholé-Luke, 'The quest for an African Christian theology', *The Ecumenical Review*, vol. 27 no. 3, 1975 pp. 259–69.

74 Brian Garvey, *The development of the White Fathers' mission among the Bemba-speaking peoples 1891–1964*, University of London, Ph.D dissertation 1974 pp. 350–71.

75 Boniface Luykx, *Culte chrétien en Afrique après Vatican II*, Fribourg: Immensee 1974; Paul van Thiel, in *African Ecclesiastical Review*, vol. 3 no. 2, 1961 pp. 144–7, vol. 6 no. 3, 1964 pp. 250–7, vol. 8 no. 1, 1966 pp. 53–62; G Riordan and O. Hirmer, 'African liturgical music', *African Ecclesiastical Review* vol. 8 no. 2, 1966 pp. 130–3; Stephen Mbunga, 'Church music in Tanzania', *Concilium*, February 1966, pp. 57–60; Jakob Baumgartner, 'Liturgie in Shona', *Neue Zeitschrift für Missionswissenschaft* vol. 32 no. 1, 1976 pp. 62–7; A. M. Jones, *African hymnody in Christian worship*, Gwelo, Rhodesia: Mambo Press 1976.

76 Adrian Hastings, 'The ministry of the Catholic Church in Africa, 1960–1975', in Fasholé-Luke *et al.* (eds.) *Christianity in independent Africa*, pp. 26–43, and P. A. Kalilombe, 'The African local churches and the world-wide Roman Catholic Communion', in *ibid*, 79–95; Aylward Shorter and Eugene Kataza, *Missionaries to yourselves. African catechists today*, London: Geoffrey Chapman 1972; Adrian Hastings, *Church and ministry*, Gaba, Uganda: Pastoral Institute 1972. This is no. 25 of Gaba's 'Pastoral Papers' of which the whole series throws much light on the pastoral needs and preoccupations of these years. *Congo–Kinshasa 1969*, Brussels: Pro Mundi Vita 1970, surveys the Catholic Church in Zaire immediately preceding the *kulturkampf* with Mobutu. For two other recent major surveys of parts of the Catholic Church see F. J. Verstraelen, *An African church in transition: from missionary dependence to mutuality in mission*, 2 vols., Leiden: 1975, a case study of the Roman Catholic Church in Zambia; and *'Let my people go'* – *a survey of the Catholic Church in Western Nigeria*, Brussels: Pro Mundi Vita 1974.

77 The public debate over a married clergy in Africa began about 1964. See Adrian Hastings, 'The church in Afro-Asia today and tomorrow', *African Ecclesiastical Review* vol. 6 no. 4, 1964 pp. 293–4, and Theo Slaats, 'The ministry of the priesthood', *African Ecclesiastical Review*, vol. 7 no. 4, 1965 pp. 337–45. The public Catholic debate on polygamy really began with a paper of Eugene Hillman submitted by Bishop Durning of Arusha to a meeting of the AMECEA bishops in 1967. See *Pastoral perspectives in Eastern Africa after Vatican II*, Nairobi: AMECEA 1967, appendix, 'Polygamy considered', pp. 127–38.

78 The regional episcopal conference of Central Africa and Cameroon 1969 – see

Adrian Hastings, 'Celibacy in Africa', *Concilium*, October 1972 pp. 151–6.

79 *Status Seminaristarum Indigenarum 1974–1975*, Rome: Propaganda Fide 1975.

80 David Bosch, 'The feasibility of a moratorium on missions in the South African context'.

81 *Osservatore Romano*, 13 May 1971.

82 The figures derive from the *Annuario Statistico della Chiesa 1969–74*; see René Laurentin, 'Données statistiques sur les Chrétiens en Afrique', *Concilium* no. 126, June 1977 pp. 119–31.

83 For a picture of one not untypical post-Vatican II missionary priest, Wim Smulders SJ, who died in 1975 aged 44, see Anthony Bex, *St. Peter's Harare*, Gwelo, Rhodesia: Mambo Press 1976; for another see Bernard Joinet, *Le Soleil de Dieu*.

84 G. A. C. van Winsen, 'Ethiopian Christianity', *Zeitschrift für Missionswissenschaft*, vol. 11, 1974 pp. 124–33.

85 Paul Jenkins, 'Christianity and the churches in Ghanaian history, a historiographical essay', in J. O. Hunwick (ed.), *Proceedings of the Seminar on Ghanaian historiography and historical research*, Legon 1977 pp. 124–33.

86 Adrian Hastings, *Christian Marriage in Africa*, London: SPCK 1973; Benezeri Kisembo, Laurenti Magesa, and Aylward Shorter, *African Christian marriage*, London: Geoffrey Chapman 1977; *Family life and marriage among Christians in sub-Saharan Africa*, Brussels: Pro Mundi Vita 1976.

87 Hastings, *Christian marriage*, p. 143.

88 Hastings, *Christian marriage*, p. 139; for the other side of what these Morogoro statistics imply in the growth of 'village Christianity' see James L. Brain, 'Ancestors as Elders in Africa – Further Thoughts', *Africa* 1973, pp. 122–32, especially pp. 129–31.

89 Brian Gogan, 'Ibo Catholicism: a tentative survey', *African Ecclesiastical Review*, vol. 8 no. 4, 1966 pp. 346–58.

90 Bernard Mels, 'An example of fruitful adaptation in Africa: the "Jamaa" at Luluabourg', *Christ to the World* (Rome) vol. 9 no. 6, 1964 pp. 500–4.

91 The full text of the condemnation is to be found in Tharcisse Tshibangu, *Le propos d'une théologie africaine*, Kinshasa: Presses Universitaires de Zaire 1974 pp. 41–7; for a very hostile account see also Placide Mukendi, 'La Jamaa et son avenir', *Revue du Clergé Africain* (Mayidi, Zaire) vol. 26 no. 2, 1971, pp. 142–68; for a more sympathetic account see Willy De Craemer, 'A sociologist's encounter with the Jamaa', *Journal of Religion in Africa* vol. 8 no. 3, 1976 pp. 153–74.

92 One well-known Zairean priest remarked to me in 1977, 'Of course I am sympathetic – my father and mother are both members of *Jamaa*'.

93 *The Tablet*, 29 March 1975.

94 For a perceptive review of the condition of African Catholicism at the end of our period see the series of articles, mostly by African priests and bishops, in *Concilium*, June 1977, entitled: 'Les Églises d'Afrique, quel avenir?'

95 See above, pp. 77–8; Clive Dillon-Malone, *The Korsten basketmakers: a study of the Masowe Apostles*, Fordham University, Ph.D. dissertation 1975; Bennetta Jules-Rosette, Marropodi: an independent religious community in transition', *African Studies Review* vol. 18 no. 2, 1975 pp. 1–16.

96 Dillon-Malone, *The Korsten basketmakers*, p. 346, see also p. 324.

97 Stanley Barrett, *The rise and fall of an African Utopia: A wealthy theocracy in comparative perspective*, 1977.

98 Martin West, *Bishops and prophets in a Black city*, Cape Town: David Philip 1975 p. 2.
99 Bengt Sundkler, *Zulu Zion and some Swazi Zionists*, Uppsala: Gleerups 1976 pp. 288–303.
100 Martin West, *Bishops and prophets*, chapter 8, 'The rise and fall of A I C A', pp. 142–70; Danie Van Zyl, *God's earthenware pots*, Johannesburg: Christian Institute of Southern Africa 1968; Danie Van Zyl, 'Bantu prophets or Christ's evangels', *Pro Veritate* vol. 5 no. 5, 1966 pp. 6–9; *ibid*, vol. 5 no.6, 1966 pp. 10–13.

Chapter 5   Between politics and prayer

1 Peter Fry, *Spirits of protest*, Cambridge: Cambridge University Press 1976 pp. 38–42.
2 Laurence Henderson, 'Protestantism, a tribal religion', in R. T. Parsons (ed.), *Windows on Africa: a symposium*, Leiden: E. J. Brill 1970 pp. 61–80.
3 H.-J. Becken, 'On the holy mountain', *Journal of Religion in Africa*, vol. 1 no. 2, 1967, p. 144.
4 E. Mveng, *L'Art d'Afrique noire, liturgie cosmique et langage religieux*, Yaounde: Editions Cle 1974; E. Mveng, *Balafon, poemes*; Yaounde: Editions Cle 1972.
5 M. O. Moses, *The uses of psalms*, Lagos: Christian Bookshop, n.d.; H. W. Turner, *African independent church*, Oxford: Clarendon Press 1967, vol. 2, pp. 72–6.
6 'Monasticism in the Africa of Tomorrow', *Herder Correspondence* September–October 1964, pp. 260–3; Mary Aquina Weinrich, 'An aspect of the development of the religious life in Rhodesia', in T. O. Ranger and John Weller (eds.), *Themes in the Christian history of Central Africa*, London: Heinemann 1975 pp. 218–37; M. A. Weinrich, 'Western monasticism in independent Africa', in E. Fasholé-Luke *et al.* (eds.), *Christianity in independent Africa*, London; Rex Collings 1977 pp. 000–76.
7 Marshall Murphree, 'Religious interdependence among the Budjga Vapostori', in D. B. Barrett (ed.), *African initiatives in religion*, Nairobi: East African Publishing House 1971 pp. 171–80.
8 H. -J. Becken, 'A healing church in Zululand: "The New Church Step to Jesus Christ Zion in South Africa"', *Journal of Religion in Africa*, vol. 4 no. 3, 1972 pp. 213–22.
9 Bengt Sundkler, *Zulu Zion*, Uppsala: Gleerups 1976 p. 261.
10 John V. Taylor, *The growth of the church in Buganda*, London: S C M Press 1958 p. 111; Peter Rigby, 'Prophets, diviners and prophetism: the recent history of Kiganda religion', *Journal of Anthropological Research*, vol. 31 no. 2, 1975 pp. 116–43; John Waliggo, 'Ganda traditional religion and Catholicism in Buganda', in Fasholé-Luke *et al.* (eds.), *Christianity in independent Africa*, pp. 413–25.
11 For the general discussion of 'village Christianity' see particularly Darrel Reeck, *Deep Mende*, Leiden: E. J. Brill 1976; M. W. Murphree, *Christianity and the Shona*, London: Athlone Press 1969; B. A. Pauw, *Christianity and Xhosa tradition*, Cape Town: Oxford University Press 1975; T. O. Ranger, 'The churches, the nationalist state and African religion', in Fasholé-Luke *et al.* (eds.), *Christianity in independent Africa*, pp. 479–502; Adrian Hastings, *African Christianity*, London: Geoffrey Chapman 1976.

Bibliography

Adebiyi, T. Bayo. *The beloved bishop. The life of Bishop A. B. Akinyele 1875–1968*. Ibadan: Daystar Press Nigeria 1969.

Adelman, Kenneth. 'The church–state conflict in Zaire: 1969–1974', *African Studies Review*, vol. 18 no. 1, 1975 pp. 102–16.

Adler, Elizabeth. *A small beginning. An assessment of the first five years of the programme to combat racism*. Geneva: World Council of Churches 1974.

Afigbo, A. E. 'The missions, the state and education in South-eastern Nigeria 1956–1971', in E. Fasholé-Luke *et al.* (eds.) *Christianity in Independent Africa*, pp. 176–92.

Africa is here. Report of the North American Assembly on African Affairs. Springfield, Ohio 1952.

Akuffo, Ferdinand W. B. *The indigenization of Christianity: a study in Ghanaian pentecostalism*. University of Oxford, D.Phil. thesis 1976.

Ajayi, J. F. A. *Christian missions in Nigeria 1841–1891. The making of a new elite*. London: Longmans 1965.

Allison, Oliver. *Through fire and water*. London: Church Missionary Society 1976.

Anderson, John E. *The struggle for the school. The interaction of missionary, colonial government and nationalist enterprise in the development of formal education in Kenya*. London: Longman 1970.

Anderson, William B. 'The role of religion in the Sudan's search for unity', in David B. Barrett (ed.), *African initiatives in religion*, pp. 73–92.

Andersson, Efraim. *Messianic popular movements in the Lower Congo* (Studia Ethnographica Upsaliensia xiv). Uppsala: Almqvist & Wiksell, and London: Kegan Paul, 1958.

Churches at the grass roots. A study in Congo-Brazzaville. London: Lutterworth Press 1968.

Annuaire de l'Église Catholique en Afrique Francophone. Published annually: Paris: L'Office National de Publications Catholiques.

Ansprenger, Franz, *et al. Wiriyamu, Eine Dokumentation zum Krieg in Mozambique*. Munich: Kaiser-Gruneweld 1974.

Anstey, Roger. *King Leopold's legacy: the Congo under Belgian rule 1908–1960*. London: Oxford University Press 1966.

Asante, S. K. B. 'West Africa and the Italian invasion of Ethiopia'. *African Affairs*, vol. 73 (April) 1974 pp. 204–16.

Aujoulat, L. *Aujourd'hui l'Afrique*. Paris: Casterman 1958.

Authority, S. O. A. *The happy city of the Holy Apostles' Community 'Aiyetoro'*. Lagos: Eruobodo Memorial Press (?1966).

Ayandele, E. A. *The missionary impact on modern Nigeria 1842–1914. A political and social analysis*. London: Longmans 1966.

Baëta, C. G. *Prophetism in Ghana: a study of some 'spiritual' churches*. London: SCM Press 1962.

(ed.) *Christianity in tropical Africa*. London: Oxford University Press for the International African Institute 1968.

Balandier, Georges, *The sociology of Black Africa: social dynamics in Central Africa*, trans. D. Garman. New York: Praeger, and London: Andre Deutsch 1970.

Barrett, David B. *Schism and renewal in Africa: an analysis of six thousand contemporary religious movements*. Nairobi and London: Oxford University Press 1968.

'AD 2000 – 350 million Christians in Africa', *International Review of Mission*, vol. 59 no. 233 (Jan.) 1970 pp. 39–54.

(ed.) *African initiatives in religion. 21 studies from East and Central Africa*. Nairobi: East African Publishing House 1971.

Barrett, David B., Mambo, George K., McLaughlin, Janice, and McVeigh, Malcolm J. (eds.). *Kenya Churches Handbook: the development of Kenyan Christianity 1948–1973*. Kisumu: Evangel Publishing House 1973.

Barrett, Stanley R. 'Crisis and change in a West African Utopia', in E. B. Harvey (ed.), *Perspectives on modernization*. Toronto: University of Toronto Press 1972, pp. 160–81.

The rise and fall of an African Utopia: A wealthy theocracy in comparative perspective. Waterloo, Ontario: Wilfrid Laurier University Press 1977.

Bartels, F. L. *The roots of Ghana Methodism*. London: Cambridge University Press 1965.

Baumgartner, Jakobo. 'Liturgie in Shona'. *Neue Zeitschrift für Missionswissenschaft*, vol. 32 no. 1, 1976 pp. 62–7.

Becken, Hans-Jürgen. 'On the holy mountain: a visit to the New Year's Festival of the Nazaretha Church on Mount Nhlangakazi, January 1967', *Journal of Religion in Africa*, Vol. 1 no. 2, 1967 pp. 138–49.

'A healing church in Zululand: "The New Church Step to Jesus Christ Zion in South Africa"'. *Journal of Religion in Africa*, vol. 4 no. 3, 1972 p. 213–22.

Beckmann, David M. *Eden Revival Spiritual Churches in Ghana*. St Louis, Missouri: Concordia Publishing House 1975.

Benson, Mary. *Tshekedi Khama*. London: Faber & Faber 1960.

Berglund, Axel-Ivar. *Zulu thought-patterns and symbolism* (Studia Missionalia Upsaliensia XXII). London: C. Hurst & Co. 1976.

Bernard, Guy. 'Les églises congolaises et la construction nationale', *Revue de l'Institut de Sociologie* (Brussels) vol. 23 nos. 2–3, 1967 241–7.

'Diversité des nouvelles églises congolaises', *Cahiers d'Études Africaines* (Paris) vol. 10 no. 2, 1970 pp. 203–27.

'La contestation et les églises nationales au Congo', *Canadian Journal of African Studies*, vol. 5 no. 2, 1971 pp. 145–56.

Bernard, Guy and Caprasse, P. 'Religious movements in the Congo: a research hypothesis', *Cahiers Économiques et Sociaux* (Kinshasa) vol. 3 no. 1, 1965 pp. 49–60.

Bertulli, Cesare. *Croce e spada in Mozambico*. Rome: Coines Edizioni 1974.

Bex, Anthony. *St. Peter's Harare*. Gwelo, Rhodesia: Mambo Press 1976.

Binsbergen, Wim M. J. van. 'Religious innovation and political conflict in Zambia: a contribution to the interpretation of the Lumpa rising', *African Perspectives*, 1976 no. 2, pp 101–35.

Blood, A. G. *The history of the Universities' Mission to Central Africa*. Vol. 3. *1933–1957*. London: UMCA 1962.

Boigny, P. *Les Chrétiens devant le Congo*. Brussels: a Pensée Catholique 1956.

Bolink, Peter. *Towards church union in Zambia*. Franeker: T. Wever 1967.

Bosch, David. 'Currents and cross currents in South African black theology', *Journal of Religion in Africa* vol. 6 no. 1, 1974, pp. 1–22.
'The feasibility of a moratorium on missions in the South African context'. MS. of address (?1975).

Braekman, E. M. *Histoire du Protestantisme au Congo*. Brussels: Éditions de la Librairie des Éclaireurs Unionistes 1961.

Brandel-Syrier, Mia. *Black woman in search of God* London: Lutterworth Press 1962.

Brásio, Antonio. *Historia e missiologia inéditos e esparos*. Luanda: Instituto de Investigação Cientifica de Angola 1973.

Brierley, P. W. *U.K. Protestant Missions handbook*. London: Evangelical Missionary Alliance 1973.

Brown, Leslie W. *Relevant liturgy. Zabriskie Lectures 1964*. London: SPCK 1965.

Brown, William Eric. *The Catholic Church in South Africa from its origin to the present day*. London: Burns & Oates 1960.

Buijtenhuijs, Robert. *Le mouvement 'Mau-Mau'; une révolte paysanne et anti-coloniale en Afrique noire*. The Hague and Paris: Mouton 1971.

Bureau, René. 'Le prophète Harris et la religion harriste', *Annales de l'Université d'Abidjan* (Serie F) 3, 1971, pp. 31–196.

Buthelezi, Manas. 'African theology and black theology', *Relevant theology for Africa. Report on a consultation at Mapumulo, Natal, September 1972*, pp. 18–24.

Carey, Walter. *Crisis in Kenya. Christian common sense on Mau Mau and the colour-bar*. London: A. R. Mowbray 1953.

Carpenter, George Wayland. *Highways for God in the Congo. Commemorating seventy-five years of Protestant missions 1876–1953*. Leopoldville: La Librairie Evangelique au Congo 1952.

Catholic Institute of International Relations. *The man in the middle: torture, resettlement and eviction* (compiled by Catholic Commission for Justice and Peace in Rhodesia). London 1975.
Civil war in Rhodesia (compiled by Catholic Commission for Justice and Peace in Rhodesia). London 1976.
Racial discrimination in Southern Rhodesia (compiled by the International Commission of Jurists). London 1976.

Cawood, Leslie. *The churches and race relations in South Africa*. Johannesburg: South African Institute of Race Relations 1964.

Charles, Pierre. *Études missiologiques* (Muséum Lessianum, Section Missiologique no. 33). Brussels: Desclée de Brouwer 1956.

Chater, Patricia. *Grass roots. The story of St. Faith's Farm in Southern Rhodesia*. London: Hodder & Stoughton 1962.

Chomé, Jules. *La passion de Simon Kimbangu 1921–1951*. Brussels: Présence Africaine 1959

Church Missionary Society. *Mau Mau*. London 1953.

Clutton-Brock, Guy and Clutton-Brock, Molly. *Cold Comfort confronted*. London: Mowbrays 1972.

Coelho, Mario Brochado. *Em defesa de Joaquim Pinto de Andrade*. Porto: Afronamento 1971

Colonial Office. *Uganda Protectorate, Buganda*. Cmd. 9320. London: HMSO 1954.

Bibliography

Congo 1964: Political Documents of a Developing Nation. Compiled by CRISP, introduction by Herbert Weiss. Princeton, N.J.: Princeton University Press 1966.

Conus, Georges. L'Église d'Afrique au Concile Vatican II. Immensee [Switzerland]: Nouvelle Revue de Science Missionaire 1975.

Cook, David J. 'Church and state in Zambia: the case of the African Methodist Episcopal Church', in E. Fasholé-Luke et al. (eds.), Christianity in Independent Africa, pp. 285–303.

Cooke, Colman M. The Roman Catholic Mission in Calabar 1903–1960. University of London, Ph.D. dissertation 1977.
'Church, state and education: the Eastern Nigeria experience 1950–1967', in E. Fasholé-Luke et al. (eds.), Christianity in independent Africa, pp. 193–206.

Crampton, E. P. T. Christianity in Northern Nigeria. Zaria, privately printed 1975.

Cross, Sholto. 'Independent churches and independent states: Jehovah's Witnesses in East and Central Africa', in E. Fasholé-Luke et al. (eds.), Christianity in independent Africa, pp. 304–15.

Dachs, Anthony J. (ed.) Christianity south of the Zambezi. I. Gwelo, Rhodesia: Mambo Press 1973.

Dam-Tibajjina, J. R. Kigongo. 'The life of Archpriest Reverend Father Spartas R. S. Ssebanja Mukasa'. [1969?]. Mimeo.

Daneel, M. L. Zionism and faith-healing in Rhodesia (Afrika-Studiecentrum Leiden, Communication 2). The Hague: Mouton 1970.
Old and new in Southern Shona independent churches. I Background and rise of the major movements. The Hague: Mouton 1971. II. Church growth – causative factors and recruitment techniques. Mouton 1974.

Davidson, Basil. In the eye of the storm. Angola's people. Harmondsworth: Penguin Books 1975 (1st ed. 1972).

Dayton, Edward R. (ed.). Mission Handbook. North American Protestant Ministries overseas 1976. Monrovia, California: MARC, 11th edition 1976.

Debrunner, Hans W. A church between colonial powers: a study of the church in Togo. London: Lutterworth Press 1965.

De Craemer, Willy. 'A sociologist's encounter with the Jamaa', Journal of Religion in Africa, vol. 8 no. 3, 1976, pp. 153–74.
The Jamaa and the Church. A Bantu Catholic movement in Zaire (Oxford Studies in African Affairs). Oxford: Clarendon Press 1977.

Delacroix, Simon. Histoire universelle des Missions Catholiques. Paris: Grund, vols. 3 and 4, 1956–9.

Desroche, Henri and Raymaekers, Paul. 'Départ d'un prophète, arrivée d'un église. Textes et recherches sur la mort de Simon Kimbangu et sur sa survivance', Archives de Sciences Sociales des Religions, vol. 42, 1976, pp. 117–62.

De Wolf, Jan, J. Differentiation and Integration in western Kenya. A study of religious innovation and social change among the Bukusu. Mouton: The Hague 1977.

Dickson, Kwesi and Ellingworth, Paul (eds.). Biblical revelation and African beliefs. Maryknoll, NY: Orbis Books 1969.

Dillon-Malone, Clive. The Korsten basketmakers: a study of the Masowe apostles, an indigenous African religious movement. Manchester University Press 1978.

Dirven, Peter J. 'A protest and a challenge: the Maria Legio breakaway church in West Kenya', African Ecclesiastical Review, vol. 12 no. 2, 1970 pp. 127–33.
The Maria Legio: the dynamics of a breakaway church among the Luo of East Africa. Pontifica Universitas Gregoriana (Rome), doctorate in missiology 1970.

Doi, A. R. I. 'Islam in Nigeria: changes since independence', in E. Fashole-Luke *et al.* (eds.), *Christianity in independent Africa*, pp. 334–53.

Dorward, D. C. 'Religious aspects of socio-economic stratification in modern Tiv society'. Seminar paper, University of London, School of Oriental and African Studies 1974.

Dougall, J. W. C. 'J. H. Oldham', *International Review of Mission*, vol. 59 no. 233 (Jan.), 1970 pp. 8–22.

Douglas, Mary. *The Lele of the Kasai*. London: Oxford University Press 1963.

Dunn, Cyril. 'Black Christians build an ark'. *The Observer* (London) 26 June 1955 p. 13.

Dutch Reformed Church. *Christian principles in multi-racial South Africa. A report of the Dutch Reformed Conference of Church Leaders*. Pretoria: DRC 1953.

Eden Revival Church. *Handbook: Christianity original re-enacted*. Accra: the Church (?1971).

Ekechi, Felix K. *Missionary enterprise and rivalry in Igboland 1857–1914*. London: Frank Cass 1972.

Elliott, Kitt. *An African school. A record of experience*. Cambridge: Cambridge University Press 1970.

Engel, Lothar. *Kolonialismus und Nationalismus im Deutschen Protestantismus in Namibia 1907 bis 1945*. Bern: Herbert Lang, and Frankfurt: Peter Lang 1976.

Evans-Pritchard, E. E. *Nuer religion*. Oxford: Clarendon Press 1956.

Fabian, Johannes, *Jamaa. A charismatic movement in Katanga*. Evanston: Northwestern University Press 1971.

Fallers, L. A. (ed.). *The king's men. Leadership and status in Buganda on the eve of independence*. London: Oxford University Press 1964.

Fasholé-Luke, Edward; Gray, Richard; Hastings, Adrian and Tasie, Godwin (eds.). *Christianity in independent Africa*. London: Rex Collings 1978.

Feci, Damaso. *Vie cachée et vie publique de Simon Kimbangu selon la littérature coloniale et missionaire Belge*. Brussels: Les Cahiers du Centre d'Étude et de Documentation Africaines, no. 9–10, 1972.

Fernandez, James W. 'Rededication and prophetism in Ghana', *Cahiers d'Études Africaines* (Paris) vol. 10 no. 2, 1970 pp. 228–305.
'The precincts of the prophet. A day with Johannes Galilee Shembe', *Journal of Religion in Africa*, vol. 5 no. 1, 1973 pp. 32–53.

Fetter, Bruce. *The creation of Elisabethville 1910–1940*. Stanford, California: Hoover Institution Press 1976.

ffrench-Beytagh, Gonville. *Encountering darkness*. London: Collins 1973.

Figueiredo, Antonio de. *Portugal: fifty years of dictatorship*. Harmondsworth: Penguin Books 1975.

Fouquer, Roger. *Le docteur Adrien Atiman, Médecin-catéchiste au Tanganyika. Sur les traces de Vincent de Paul*. Paris: Spes 1964.

Fox, Renée C., De Craemer, Willy and Ribeaucourt, Jean-Marie. 'The second independence: a case study of the Kwilu rebellion in the Congo', *Comparative Studies in Society and History*, vol. 8 no. 1, 1965 pp. 78–110.

Freytag, Walter. 'Changes in the patterns of Western missions', in R. K. Orchard (ed.), *The Ghana Assembly of the International Missionary Council. 1958*. Selected Papers. London: Edinburgh House Press 1958.

Fry, Peter. *Spirits of protest: spirit mediums and the articulation of consensus among the Zezuru of Southern Rhodesia*. Cambridge: Cambridge University Press 1976.

Furley, O. W. 'The historiography of Mau Mau', in B. A. Ogot (ed.), *Politics and nationalism in colonial Kenya*. Nairobi: East African Publishing House 1972 pp. 105–33.

Gale, Hubert P. *Uganda and the Mill Hill Fathers*. London: Macmillan 1959.

Garvey, Brian. *The development of the White Fathers' mission among the Bemba-speaking peoples, 1891–1964*. London University, Ph.D dissertation 1974.

Gelfand, Michael (ed.). *Gubulawayo and beyond: Letters and journals of the early Jesuit missionaries to Zambesia (1879–1887)*. London: Geoffrey Chapman 1968.

Gérard, Jacques E. *Les fondements syncrétiques du Kitawala* (Collections Études Africaines, 1). Brussels: Centre de Recherche et d'Information Socio-Politiques 1969.

Gerdener, G. B. A. *Recent development in the South African mission field*. Pretoria: N. G. Kerk;Uitgewers 1958.

Geuns, André. 'Chronologie des mouvements religieux indépendants au Bas-Zaïre, particulièrement du mouvement fondé par le prophète Simon Kimbangu', *Journal of Religion in Africa*, vol. 6 no. 3, 1974 pp. 187–22.

Gil, Maria Helena. *Les messianismes d'Angola, Contributions à l'inventaire des messianismes et millénarismes d'Afrique noire*. École Pratique des Hautes Études, diplôme, VIe Section 1972.

Glasswell, Mark E. and Fasholé-Luke, Edward W. (eds.). *New Testament Christianity for Africa and the world. Essays in honour of Harry Sawyerr*. London: SPCK 1974.

Gogan, Brian. 'Ibo Catholicism: a tentative survey', *African Ecclesiastical Review*, vol. 8 no. 4, 1966 pp. 346–58.

Goodall, Norman. *A history of the London Missionary Society 1895–1945*. London: Oxford University Press 1954.

Gqbule, Simon. 'What is black theology?', *Journal of Theology for Southern Africa*, 1974 pp. 16–23.

Grant, G. C. 'The liquidation of Adams College', in David M. Paton (ed.) *Church and race in South Africa*. London: SCM Press 1958 pp. 51–93.

Gration, John. *The relationship of the Africa Inland Mission and its national church in Kenya between 1895 and 1971*. New York University, Ph.D. dissertation 1974.

Gray, Richard. *The two nations. Aspects of the development of race relations in the Rhodesias and Nyasaland*. London: Oxford University Press for the Institute of Race Relations 1960.

Greaves, L. B. *Carey Francis of Kenya*. London: Rex Collings 1969.

Greenland, Jeremy J. 'Black racism in Burundi', *New Blackfriars*, vol. 54 no. 641 (Oct.) 1973 pp. 443–51.

Greschat, Hans-Jürgen. *Kitawala. Ursprung, Ausbreitung und Religion der Watch-Tower-Bewegund in Zentral Afrika* (Marburger theologische Studien 4). Marburg: N. G. Elwert 1967.

Westafrikanische Propheten. Morphologie einer religiösen Spezialisierung (Marburger Studien zur Afrika-und Asienkunde, Serie A: Afrika – Band 4). Berlin: Dietrich Reimer 1974.

Groves, Charles Pelham. *The planting of Christianity in Africa*. London: Lutterworth Press, 4 vols. 1948–58.

Haliburton, Gordon MacKay. *The prophet Harris, a study of an African prophet and his mass-movement in the Ivory Coast and the Gold Coast 1913–1915*. Harlow: Longman 1971.

Hallencreutz, Carl F. (ed.). *Missions from the North. Nordic Missionary Council 50 years*. Oslo etc.: Universitetsforlaget 1974.

Hardy, Georges. *Un apôtre d'aujourd'hui. Le Révérend Père Aupiais, provincial des Missions africaines de Lyon*. Paris: Larose 1949.

Haselbarth, H. 'The Zion Christian Church of Edward Lekganyane', *Our approach to the Independent Church Movement in South Africa*. Mapumulo, Natal: Missiological Institute, Lutheran Theological College 1966. Mimeo.

Hastings, Adrian. *White domination or racial peace*. London: Africa Bureau 1954.
'The church in Afro-Asia today and tomorrow', *African Ecclesiastical Review*, vol. 6 no. 4, 1964 pp. 287–98.
Church and mission in modern Africa. London: Burns & Oates 1967.
Mission and ministry. London: Sheed & Ward 1971.
'Celibacy in Africa', *Concilium* October 1972 pp. 151–6.
Church and ministry (Pastoral Papers 25). Gaba, Uganda: Pastoral Institute 1972.
Christian marriage in Africa. London: SPCK 1973.
'Some reflections upon the war in Mozambique', *African Affairs*, vol. 73 (July) 1974 pp. 263–76.
Wiriyamu. London: Search Press 1974.
'John Lester Membe', T. O. Ranger and John Weller (eds.) *Themes in the Christian history of Central Africa*, pp. 175–94.
The faces of God. Reflections on church and society. London: Geoffrey Chapman 1975.
'Christianity and revolution', *African affairs*, vol. 74 (July) 1975 pp. 347–61.
African Christianity. London: Geoffrey Chapman 1976.
'Ganda Catholic spirituality', *Journal of Religion in Africa*, vol. 8 no. 2, 1976 pp. 81–91.
'The ministry of the Catholic Church in Africa, 1960–1975', in E. Fasholé-Luke *et al.* (eds.), *Christianity in independent Africa*, pp. 26–43.

Hayward, Victor E. W. (ed.). *African independent church movements*. London: Edinburgh House Press 1963.

Heimer, Haldor E. 'The church suited to home needs. A look at the people of two churches in Luluabourg, Congo', in R. T. Parsons (ed.), *Windows on Africa. A symposium*. Leiden: E. J. Brill 1971, pp. 21–37.

Hellberg, Carl Johan. *Missions on a colonial frontier west of Luke Victoria* (Studia Missionalia Uppsalensia VI). Lund: C. W. K. Gleerup 1963.
'Andereya Kajerero: the man and his church', *Occasional Research Papers* (Makerere University, Department of Religious Studies and Philosophy) vol. 8, paper 71 (?1973).

Henderson, Laurence. 'Protestantism: a tribal religion', in R. T. Parsons (ed.), *Windows on Africa: a symposium*. Leiden: E. J. Brill 1971, pp. 61–80.

Hewat, Elizabeth G. K. *Vision and achievement 1796–1956. A history of the foreign missions of the churches united in the Church of Scotland*. London: Nelson 1960.

Hewitt, Gordon. *The problems of success: a history of the Church Missionary Society 1910–1942. I. In tropical Africa, the Middle East, at home*. London: SCM Press for the Church Missionary Society 1971.

Hillman, Eugene. 'Polygamy reconsidered', Appendix to *Pastoral perspectives in Eastern Africa after Vatican II*. Nairobi: AMECEA 1967 pp. 127–38.

Hinchliff, Peter. *The Anglican Church in South Africa*. London: Darton, Longman & Todd 1963.
The church in South Africa (Church History Outlines). London: SPCK 1968.

Hodges, Tony. *Jehovah's Witnesses in Central Africa* (Minority Rights Group Report 29). London: Minority Rights Group 1976.

Bibliography

Holas, Bohumil. *Le séparatisme religieux en Afrique noire. (L'example de la Côte d'Ivoire)*. Paris: Presses Universitaires de France 1965.

Hooker, J. R. 'Witnesses and Watchtower in the Rhodesias and Nyasaland', *Journal of African History*, vol. 6 no. 1, 1965 pp. 91–106.

Horner, Norman A. *Cross and crucifix in mission*. New York: Abingdon 1965.

Horrell, Muriel. *Action, reaction and counter-action*. Johannesburg: South African Institute of Race Relations 1971.

Huddleston, Trevor. *Naught for your comfort*. London: Collins 1966.
The state of Anglo-Tanzanian relations. London: Africa Bureau 1968.

Hudson, Darrill. *The World Council of Churches in international Affairs*, Leighton Buzzard: Free Press, 1977.

Hymans, Jacques Louis. *Léopold Sédar Senghor. An intellectual biography*. Edinburgh: Edinburgh University Press 1971.

Idowu, E. Bolaji. *Olódòmarè. God in Yoruba belief*. London: Longmans 1962.
Towards an indigenous church. London and Ibadan: Oxford University Press 1965.
African traditional religion. A definition. London: SCM Press 1973.

International Commission of Jurists, Geneva. *The trial of Beyers Naudé. Christian witness and the rule of law*. London: Search Press 1975.

International Missionary Council. *The Church in changing Africa. Report of the All-Africa Church Conference, Ibadan*. New York: IMC 1958.

International Review of Missions. A survey of the year 1950. *International Review of Missions*, vol 40 no. 157 (Jan.) 1951.

Irvine, Cecilia. 'The birth of the Kimbanguist movement in the Bas-Zaire 1921', *Journal of Religion in Africa*, vol. 6 no. 1, 1974 pp. 23–76.

Isichei, Elizabeth. 'One man in his time: Michael Tanzi', Jos Conference on Christianity in independent Africa, unpublished paper, September 1975. Mimeo.

Jabavu, Noni. *The ochre people. Scenes from a South African life*. London: John Murray 1963.

Jackson, Willard. 'The "Union des Populations du Cameroun" in rebellion: the integrative backlash of insurgency', in R. I. Rotberg and A. A. Mazrui (eds.), *Protest and Power in Black Africa*, pp. 671–92.

Janzen, John M. and MacGaffey, Wyatt. *An anthology of Kongo religion: primary texts from lower Zaïre* (Publications in Anthropology, 5). Lawrence, Kansas: University of Kansas 1974.

Jenkins, Paul. 'Christianity and the churches in Ghanaian history, a historiographical essay', in J. O. Hunwick (ed.), *Proceedings of the Seminar on Ghanaian historiography and historical research*. Legon, 1977, 124–133.

Johnson, Walter R. *Worship and freedom: a Black American church in Zambia*. London: International African Institute 1977.

Joinet, Bernard, *Le Soleil de Dieu en Tanzanie, Prêtre en pays Socialiste*, Propos recueillis par Jean-Claude Petit, Cerf, Paris 1977.

Jones, A. M. *African hymnody in Christian worship*. Gwelo, Rhodesia: Mambo Press 1976.

Jordan, John P. *Bishop Shanahan of Southern Nigeria*. Dublin: Clonmore & Reynolds 1949.
'Catholic education and Catholicism in Nigeria', *African Ecclesiastical Review* vol. 2 no. 1, 1960, pp. 60–2.

Joseph, Richard K. *Radical Nationalism in Cameroun. Social Origins of the U.P.C. Rebellion*. London: Oxford University Press 1977.

310

Jules-Rosette, Bennetta. *African apostles. Ritual and conversion in the Church of John Maranke*. Ithaca: Cornell University Press 1975.
'Marropodi: an independent religious community in transition', *African Studies Review* (Boston) vol. 18 no. 2, 1975 pp. 1–16.

Kagame, Alexis. *La philosophie bantu-rwandaise de l'Être*. Brussels: Académie Royale des Sciences Coloniales 1956.

Kaggia, Bildad. *Roots of freedom 1921–1963. The autobiography of Bildad Kaggia*. Nairobi: East African Publishing House 1975.

Kalilombe, P. A. 'The African local churches and the world-wide Roman Catholic communion', in E. Fasholé-Luke *et al.* (eds.), *Christianity in independent Africa*, pp. 79–95.

Kalu, Ogbu. 'Church unity and religious change in Africa', in E. Fasholé-Luke *et al.* (eds.), *Christianity in independent Africa*, pp. 164–75.

Kato, Byang H. *Theological pitfalls in Africa*. Kisumu, Kenya: Evangel Publishing House 1975.

Kaunda, Kenneth. *Zambia shall be free*. London: Heinemann 1962.

Kendall, R. Elliott. 'On sending of missionaries: a call for restraint', *International Review of Mission*, vol. 64 no. 253 (Jan.) 1975 pp. 62–6.
The end of an era, Africa and the Missionary London: SPCK 1978.

Kerr, Alexander. 'The Bantu Education Act', *South African Outlook*, June 1954, repr. in F. Wilson and D. Perrot (eds.), *Outlook on a Century*, pp. 513–16.
Never accept defeat. *South African Outlook*, December 1959, repr. in F. Wilson and D. Perrot (eds.), *Outlook on a Century*, pp. 521–5.
Davidson Don Tengo Jabavu. *South African Outlook*, August 1963; repr. in F. Wilson and D. Perrot (eds.), *Outlook on a Century*, pp. 550–2.
Fort Hare 1915–48. London: C. Hurst 1968.

Khaketla, B. M. *Lesotho 1970*. London: C. Hurst 1971.

King, Kenneth J. *Pan-Africanism and education, a study of race, philanthropy and education in the southern states of America and East Africa*. Oxford: Clarendon Press 1971.

Kirk-Greene, A. H. M. (comp.). *Crisis and conflict in Nigeria: a documentary sourcebook*. 2 vols. London: Oxford University Press 1971.

Kisembo, Benezeri, Magesa, Laurenti, and Shorter, Aylward. *African Christian marriage*. London: Geoffrey Chapman 1977.

Kistner, W. 'The 16th of December in the context of nationalist thinking', in Theo Sundermeier (ed.), *Church and nationalism in South Africa*. Johannesburg: Ravan Press 1975.

Koren, Henry J. *The Spiritans*. Pittsburgh: Duquesne University Press 1958.

Kratz, Michaël. *La mission des Rédemptoristes belges au Bas-Congo. La période des semailles*. Brussels: Académie royale de sciences d'Outre-mer 1968.

Kupalo, Ancilla. 'African Sisters' congregations', in E. Fasholé-Luke *et al.* (eds.), *Christianity in independent Africa*, pp. 122–35.

Lamont, Donal. *Speech from the dock*. Leigh-on-Sea, Essex: Kevin Mayhew Ltd. in association with the Catholic Institute for International Relations, London, 1977.

Lanzas, A. and Bernard, Guy. 'Les fidèles d'une "nouvelle église" au Congo', *Genève-Afrique*, vol. 5 no. 2, 1966 pp. 189–216.

Laurentin, René. 'Données statistiques sur les Chrétiens en Afrique', *Concilium* June 1977 pp. 119–31.

Lee, Annabelle. 'African nuns – an anthropologist's impressions', *New Blackfriars*, vol. 49 no. 573 (May) 1968 pp. 401–9.

Bibliography

Legrand, Pierre and Thoreau, Benoît. *Les Bénédictins au Katanga: vingt-cinq ans d'apostolat, 1910–1935*. Lophem-les Bruges: Abbaye de Saint-André 1935.

Lehmann, Dorothea. 'Alice Lenshina Mulenga and the Lumpa Church', in J. V. Taylor and Dorothea Lehmann, *Christians of the Copperbelt*, pp. 248–68.

Lemarchand, René. *Rwanda and Burundi*. London: Pall Mall Press 1970.

Lemarchand, René and Martin, David. *Selective genocide in Burundi*. London: Minority Rights Group 1974.

Lerrigo, P. H. J. 'The "prophet movement" in the Congo', *International Review of Missions*, vol. 11 (April) 1922 pp. 270–7.

Le Vine, Victor. 'The coups in Upper Volta. Dahomey and the Central African Republic', in R. I. Rotberg and A. A. Mazrui (eds.), *Protest and Power in Black Africa*, pp. 1035–71.

Leys, Colin. *Politicians and policies: an essay on politics in Acholi, Uganda 1962–65*. Nairobi: East African Publishing House 1967.

Libert, E. 'Les missionaires chrétiens face au mouvement kimbanguiste, Documents contemporains 1921', *Études d'Histoire Africaine* (Louvain) 2, 1971, pp. 121–154.

Lienhardt, Godfrey. *Divinity and experience. The religion of the Dinka*. Oxford: Clarendon Press 1961.

Linden, Ian. *Catholics, peasants and Chewa resistance in Nyasaland 1889–1939*. London: Heinemann 1974.

Church and revolution in Rwanda. Manchester: Manchester University Press 1977.

Linden, Jane and Linden, Ian. 'John Chilembwe and the new Jerusalem', *Journal of African History*, vol. 12 no. 4, 1971, pp. 629–51.

Long, Norman, 'Religion and socio-economic action among the Serenje-Lala Zambia', in C. G. Baëta (ed.), *Christianity in Tropical Africa*, pp. 396–413.

Lonsdale, John, Booth-Clibborn, Stanley and Hake, Andrew. 'The emerging pattern of church and state cooperation in Kenya', in E. Fasholé-Luke *et al.* (eds.), *Christianity in independent Africa*, pp. 267–84.

Low, D. A. *Political parties in Uganda 1949–62*. London: Athlone Press 1962.

The mind of Buganda: documents on the modern history of an African kingdom. London: Heinemann 1971.

Luykx, Boniface. *Culte chrétien en Afrique après Vatican II*. Fribourg: Immensee 1974.

Luthuli, Albert. *Let my people go: an autobiography*. London: Collins 1962.

McClelland, Elizabeth M. 'The experiment in communal living at Aiyetoro', *Comparative Studies in Society and History*, vol. 9 no. 1, 1966 pp. 14–28.

McCracken, John. *Politics and Christianity in Malawi 1875–1940*. London: Cambridge University Press 1977.

MacDonald, Roderick J. 'Reverend Hanock Msokera Phiri', *African Historical Studies* (Boston) vol. 3 no. 1, 1970 pp. 75–87.

'Religious independency as a means of social advance in Northern Nyasaland in the 1930s', *Journal of Religion in Africa*, vol. 3 no. 2, 1970 pp. 106–29.

MacGaffey, Wyatt. *The beloved city: a commentary on a Kimbanguist text. Journal of Religion in Africa*, vol. 2 no. 2, 1969 pp. 129–47.

MacPherson, Fergus. *Kenneth Kaunda of Zambia: the times and the man*. London: Oxford University Press 1974.

MacPherson, Robert. *The Presbyterian Church in Kenya*. Nairobi: Presbyterian Church of East Africa 1970.

MacQuarrie, J. M. 'Has missionary education failed?' *South African Outlook* October 1954, repr. in F. Wilson and D. Perrot (eds.), *Outlook on a Century*, pp. 516–20.

Makulu, Henry. *Education, development and nation-building in independent Africa*. London: SCM Press 1971.

Marcum, John. *The Angolan revolution*. Vol. 1. *The anatomy of an explosion (1950–1962)*. Cambridge, Mass.: Harvard University Press 1969.

Margarido, Alfredo. 'The Tokoist Church and Portuguese colonialism in Angola', in R. H. Chilcote (ed.), *Protest and resistance in Angola and Brazil: comparative studies*. Berkeley and Los Angeles: University of California Press 1972, 29–52.

Markakis, John. *Ethiopia: anatomy of a traditional polity*. Oxford: Clarendon Press 1974.

Markovitz, Marvin D. *Cross and sword. The political rise of Christian Missions in the Belgian Congo 1908–1960*. Stanford, California: Hoover Institution Press 1973.

Markwei, Matei. 'Harry Sawyerr's patron (Bishop T. S. Johnson)', in N. E. Glasswell and E. W. Fasholé-Luke (eds.), *New Testament Christianity for Africa and the world*, pp. 179–97.

Martin, Marie-Louise, 'The Mai Chaza Church in Rhodesia', in D. B. Barrett (ed.), *African initiatives in religion*, pp. 109–21.
Kimbangu. An African prophet and his church, trans. D. M. Moore. Oxford: Basil Blackwell 1975.

Mary Aquina [A. K. H. Weinrich]. 'The people of the Spirit: an independent church in Rhodesia', *Africa* (London) vol. 37 no. 2, 1967, pp. 203–19.

Mazrui, Ali A. 'Religious strangers in Uganda: from Emin Pasha to Amin Dada', *African Affairs*, vol. 76 (Jan.) 1977 pp. 21–38.

Mbiti, John S. 'Some African concepts of Christology', in G. F. Vicedome (ed.), *Christ and the younger churches*. London: SPCK 1972, pp. 51–62, first published in German in 1968 in P. Beyenhovs *et al. Theologische Stimmen aus Asien, Afrika und Lateinamerika* III, Munich.
African religions and philosophy. London: Heinemann 1969.
Concepts of God in Africa. London: SPCK 1970.
New Testament eschatology in an African background: a study of the encounter between New Testament theology and African traditional concepts. London: Oxford University Press 1971.

Mboya, Tom. *Freedom and after*. London: A. Deutsch 1963.

Mbunga, Stephen. 'Church music in Tanzania', *Concilium*, February 1966 pp. 57–60.

Meeûs, F. de, and Steenbergher, R. *Les missions religieuses au Congo belge*. Anvers: Éditions Zaïre 1947.

Méjan, Francois. *Le Vatican contre la France d'Outre Mer?* Paris: Librairie Fischbacher 1957.

Mels, Bernard. 'An example of fruitful adaptation in Africa: the "Jamaa" at Luluabourg'. *Christ to the World* (Rome) vol. 9 no. 6, 1964 pp. 500–4.

Membe, J. L. C. *A short history of the AME Church in Central Africa 1900–1962*. (Kitwe): Zambia: AME Church 1969.

Merlier, Michel. *Le Congo de la colonisation belge a l'indépendance*. Paris: F. Maspero 1962.

Bibliography

Mfoulou, J. 'The Catholic church and Camerounian nationalism', in E. Fasholé-Luke *et al.* (eds.), *Christianity in independent Africa*, pp. 216–27.

Middleton, John M. *Lugbara religion. Ritual and authority among an East African people*. London: Oxford University Press for the International African Institute 1960.

Mikre-Sellassie Gabre Ammanuel. *Church and missions in Ethiopia in relation to the Italian war and occupation and the second world war*. University of Aberdeen, Ph.D dissertation 1976.

Mitchell, Robert Cameron. 'Towards the sociology of religious independency', *Journal of Religion in Africa* vol. 3 no. 1 1970 pp. 2–21.
'Religious protest and social change: the origins of the aladura movement in West Nigeria', in R. I. Rotberg and A. A. Mazrui, (eds.), *Protest and Power in Black Africa*, pp. 458–496.

Modisane, Bloke. *Blame me on history*. London: Thames and Hudson 1963.

Mohamed Omer Beshir. *The Southern Sudan. Background to conflict*. London: C. Hurst 1968.

Moore, Basil (ed.) *Black theology. The South African voice*. London: C. Hurst 1973.

Moorhouse, Geoffrey. *The missionaries*. London: Eyre Methuen 1973.

Morris, Colin. *The hour after midnight*. London: Longmans 1961.

Morrison, Godfrey. *Eritrea and the Southern Sudan. Aspects of wider African problems*. London: Minority Rights Group, 3rd ed., 1976.

Mortimer, Edward. *France and the Africans 1944–1960: a political history*. London: Faber 1969.

Moses, M. O. *The uses of psalms*. Lagos: Christian Bookshop n.d.

Mosmans, Guy. PB, *L'Église à l'heure de l'Afrique*. Tournai: Casterman 1961.

Mufuka, K. Nyamayaro. *Mission and politics in Malawi*. Kingston, Ontario: Limestone Press 1977.

Mujaju, Akiiki B. 'The political crisis of church institutions in Uganda', *African Affairs*, vol. 75 (Jan.) 1976 pp. 67–85.

Mukendi, Placide. 'La Jamaa et son avenir', *Revue du Clergé Africain* (Mayidi, Zaïre) vol. 26 no. 2, 1971 pp. 142–68.

Mulago, Vincent and Theuws, T. *Autour du mouvement de la 'Jamaa'* (Orientations Pastorales, 1). Limete [Zaïre]: Centre d'Études Pastorales [1960?].

Müller, Karl. *Histoire de l'église catholique au Togo 1892–1967*. Lomé: Éditions Librairie Bon Pastuer 1968.

Munayi Muntu-Monji. 'Nzambi wa Malemba, un mouvement d'inspiration Kimbanguiste au Kasai', *Cahiers des Religions Africaines* 8 (July) 1974 pp. 231–55.

Murphree, Marshall W. *Christianity and the Shona*. London: Athlone Press 1969.
'Religious interdependence among the Budjga Vapostori', in D. B. Barrett (ed.), *African initiatives in religion*, pp. 171–80.

Murray, Jocelyn. 'The Kikuyu Spirit churches', *Journal of Religion in Africa*, vol. 5 no. 2, 1973 pp. 198–234.
The Kikuyu female circumcision controversy, with special reference to the Church Missionary Society's 'sphere of influence'. University of California, Los Angeles, Ph.D. dissertation 1974.
'The origins and spread of the "Dini ya Kaggia" (Kenya)', University of Aberdeen African Studies Group, Seminar paper 1976. Mimeo.

Murray-Brown, Jeremy. *Kenyatta*. London: Allen & Unwin 1972.

Museum Lessianum. 'Sectes dans l'est du Congo ex-belge', in *Devant les sectes non-chrétiennes. Rapports et compte rendu de la XXXe Semaine de Missiologie, Louvain 1961*. Paris: Desclée de Brouwer [1962?], pp. 91–101.

314

Mutasa, Didymus. *Rhodesian Black behind bars*. London: Mowbrays 1974.
Mutesa, Frederick. *Desecration of my kingdom*. London: Constable 1967.
Muzorewa, Farai David. 'Through prayer to action. The Rukwadzano women of Rhodesia', in T. O. Ranger and John Weller (eds.), *Themes in the Christian history of Central Africa*, pp. 256–68.
Mveng, Englebert. *Histoire du Cameroun*. Paris: Présence Africaine 1963.
M'Vuendy, François. *La Kimbanguisme de la clandestinité à la tolérance (1921–1959)*. Ecole Pratique des Hautes Études, Paris, Diplôme 1969.
Negaso Gidada with Crummey, Donald. 'The introduction and expansion of Orthodox Christianity in Qélém Awraja, Western Wälläga, from about 1886 to 1941', *Journal of Ethiopian Studies* vol. 10 no. 1, 1972 pp. 103–12.
Neckebrouck, V. *Le onzième Commandement. Etiologie d'une église indépendante au pied du mont Kenya*. Immensee: Switzerland 1978.
Neill, Stephen. *Christian missions* (Pelican History of the Church, 6). Harmondsworth: Penguin Books 1964.
Ngango, Georges. 'Langue liturgique et catholicité', in *Personalité africaine et Catholicisme*. Paris: Presence Africaine 1963 pp. 131–51.
Ngindu Mushete. 'Authenticity and Christianity in Zaïre', in E. Fasholé-Luke et al. (eds.), *Christianity in independent Africa*, pp. 228–41.
Nissen, Margaret. *An African church is born. The story of the Adamawa and Central Sardauna Provinces in Nigeria*. [Denmark, printed by Purups Grafiske Hus, Viby] 1968.
Nkrumah, Kwame. *I speak of freedom*. London: Heinemann 1961.
Nolan, Francis. 'History of the catechist in Eastern Africa', in A. Shorter and E. Kataza (eds.), *Missionaries to yourselves*, pp. 1–28.
Oger, Louis. *Lumpa Church: the Lenshina movement in Northern Rhodesia*. Serenje, Zambia: [White Fathers' Mission] (?1960).
Ogot, B. A. 'Revolt of the elders: an anatomy of the Loyalist crowd in the Mau Mau uprising 1952–56', in B. A. Ogot (ed.), *Politics and nationalism in colonial Kenya*. Nairobi: East African Publishing House 1972, pp. 134–48.
Okuma, Thomas *Angola in ferment*. Boston: Beacon Press 1962
Oldham, J. H. *New hope in Africa*. London: Longmans 1955.
Oliver, Roland. *How Christian is Africa?* London: Highway Press 1956.
The missionary factor in East Africa. London: Longman 1952; 2nd ed., London: Longman 1965.
Oosthuizen, G. C. *The theology of a South African messiah. An analysis of the hymnal of 'The Church of the Nazarites'*. Leiden: E. J. Brill 1967.
Post-Christianity in Africa. London: C. Hurst 1968.
Opuku, K. A. 'Changes within Christianity, with special reference to the Musama Disco Cristo Church', in E. Fasholé-Luké et al. (eds.), *Christianity in independent Africa*, pp. 111–21.
Paton, Alan. *Hofmeyr*. London: Oxford University Press 1964.
Apartheid and the Archbishop. The life and times of Geoffrey Clayton, Archbishop of Cape Town. London: Jonathan Cape 1973.
Paul, John. *Mozambique. Memoirs of a revolution*. Harmondsworth: Penguin Books 1975.
Pauw, B. A. *Religion in a Tswana chiefdom*. London: Oxford University Press for the International African Institute 1960.
Christianity and Xhosa tradition. Belief and ritual among Xhosa-speaking Christians. Cape Town: Oxford University Press 1975.
Pawlikowski, John. 'The Judaic spirit of the Ethiopian Orthodox Church: a case

study in religious acculturation', *Journal of Religion in Africa*, vol. 4 no. 3, 1972 pp. 178–99.

Peart-Binns, John S. *Ambrose Reeves*. London: Victor Gollancz 1973.

Peel J. D. Y. *Aladura: a religious movement among the Yoruba*. London: Oxford University Press 1968.

Pélissier, René. *Résistance et révoltes en Angola (1845–1961)*, 3 vols. Privately published (?1975).

Perrin Jassy, Marie-France. *Le communauté de base dans les églises africaines*. Bandundu, Zaire, 1970; Eng. trans., *Basic community in the African churches*. Maryknoll, N.Y.: Orbis Books 1973.

Pinto, Manuel. 'Reflexion sobre la Iglesia de Mozambique', *Misiones Extranjeras* (Madrid), Nov.–Dec. 1975 pp. 482–95.

Pirouet, Louise M. 'The achievement of peace in Sudan', *Journal of Eastern African Research and Development* (Nairobi) vol. 6 no. 1, 1976 pp. 115–45.
Black Evangelists, the Spread of Christianity in Uganda 1891–1914, London: Rex Collings 1978.

Prêtres noirs s'interrogent (Rencontres, 47). Paris: Les Éditions du CERF 1956.

Pro Mundi Vita. *'Let my people go' – a Survey of the Catholic Church in Western Nigeria*, Brussels: Pro Mundi Vita 1974.
Mozambique. A church in a socialist state in time of radical change (African Dossier 3). Brussels: Pro Mundi Vita 1977.

Randolph, R. H. *Church and state in Rhodesia, 1969–1971*. Gwelo: Mambo Press 1971.

Ranger, T. O. *The African churches of Tanzania* (Historical Association of Tanzania, Paper no. 5). Nairobi: East African Publishing House (?1970).
'Christian independency in Tanzania', in D. B. Barrett (ed.), *African initiatives in religion*, pp. 122–45.
'The Mwana Lesa movement of 1925', in T. O. Ranger and John Weller (eds.), *Themes in the Christian history of Central Africa*, pp. 45–75.

Ranger, T. O. and Weller, John (eds.). *Themes in the Christian history of Central Africa*. London: Heinemann 1975.

Raymaekers, Paul. 'L'Église de Jésus-Christ sur le terre par le prophète Simon Kimbangu: contribution à l'étude des mouvements messianiques dans le Bas-Kongo', *Zaïre* (Brussels) vol. 13 no. 7, 1959 pp. 675–756.
'Histoire de Simon Kimbangu, prophète, d'apres les écrivains Nfinangani et Nzungu (1921)', *Archives de Sociologie des Religions*, vol. 16 no. 1, 1971 pp. 15–42.

Reardon, Ruth Slade. 'Catholics and Protestants in the Congo', in C. G. Baëta (ed.), *Christianity in tropical Africa* pp. 83–100.

Redmayne, Alison. 'Chikanga. An African diviner with an international reputation', in M. Douglas (ed.), *Witchcraft confessions and accusations*. London: Tavistock Publications 1970 pp. 103–28.

Reeck, Darrel. *Deep Mende*. Leiden: E. J. Brill 1976.

Reeves, Ambrose. 'Selections from the charges to his Diocesan synod, 1952 to 1957', in D. M. Paton (ed.), *Church and race in South Africa*. London: SCM Press 1958 pp. 9–50.

Renault, François. *Lavigerie, l'esclavage Africain et l'Europe 1868–1892*. Paris: E. de Boccard 1971, 2 vols.

Riordan, G. and Hirmer, O. 'African liturgical music', *African Ecclesiastical Review* vol. 8 no. 2, 1966 pp. 130–3.

Roberts, Andrew. 'The Lumpa Church of Alice Lenshina', in R. I. Rotberg and A. A. Mazrui (eds.), *Protest and Power in Black Africa*, pp. 513–68.

Robins, Catherine Ellen. *Tukutendereza: a study of social change and sectarian withdrawal in the Balokole revival of Uganda*. Columbia University, Ph.D. dissertation 1975.

Roelandt, Robert. 'The situation of the Church in the Congo', *African Ecclesiastical Review*, vol. 3 no. 3, 1961 pp. 212–20.

Rotberg, Robert I. *The rise of nationalism in Central Africa. The making of Malawi and Zambia 1873–1964*. Cambridge, Mass.: Harvard University Press 1967.

Rotberg, Robert I and Mazrui, Ali A. (eds.), *Protest and power in Black Africa*. New York: Oxford University Press 1970.

Sanches, J. 'Les missions catholiques et la politique de l'État portugais', *Spiritus* (Paris) 1972 pp. 370–82.

Sangree, Walter H. *Age, prayer and politics in Tiriki, Kenya*. London: Oxford University Press for the East African Institute of Social Research 1966.

Sansbury, Kenneth. *Combating racism*. London: British Council of Churches 1975.

Sawyerr, Harry. *Creative evangelism. Towards a new Christian encounter with Africa*. London: Lutterworth Press 1968.

God: ancestor or creator? Aspects of traditional belief in Ghana, Nigeria and Sierra Leone. London: Longman 1970.

Schapera, Isaac 'Christianity and the Tswana', *Journal of the Royal Anthropological Institute*, July–December 1958 pp. 1–9.

(ed.). *Livingstone's missionary correspondence 1841–1856*. London: Chatto & Windus 1961.

Schoffeleers, Matthew. 'The history and political role of the M'Bona cult among the Mang'anja', in T. O. Ranger and I. Kimambo (eds.), *The Historical study of African religion*. London: Heinemann 1972 pp. 73–94.

Scholz, Dieter B. 'The Catholic Church and the race conflict in Rhodesia', in A. J. Dachs (ed.), *Christianity South of the Zambezi*, pp. 199–211.

Scott, Michael. *A time to speak*. London: Faber & Faber 1958.

Senghor, Léopold Sédar. *Prose and poetry*. London: Oxford University Press 1965.

Shepperson, George. 'Ethiopianism past and present', in C. G. Baëta (ed.), *Christianity in tropical Africa*, pp. 249–68.

Shepperson, George and Price, Thomas. *Independent African: John Chilembwe and the origins, setting and significance of the Nyasaland Native rising of 1915*. Edinburgh: Edinburgh University Press 1958.

Shorter, Aylward and Kataza, Eugene (eds.). *Missionaries to yourselves. African catechists today*. London: Geoffrey Chapman 1972.

Simpson, C. E. E. B. 'An African village undertakes community development on its own', *Mass Education Bulletin* (London) vol. 2 no. 1, 1950 pp. 7–9.

Sinda, Martial. *Le messianisme congolais et ses incidences politiques – Kimbanguisme – Matsouanisme – autres mouvements*. Paris: Payot 1972.

Sithole, Ndabaningi. *Obed Mutezo, the Mudzimu Christian nationalist*. Nairobi: Oxford University Press 1970.

Slaats, Theo. 'The ministry of the priesthood', *African Ecclesiastical Review*, vol. 7 no. 4, 1965 pp. 337–45.

Slade, Ruth [Reardon]. *English-speaking missions in the Congo Independent State (1878—1908)*. Brussels: Académie royale des sciences coloniales 1959.

Smith, Noel. *The Presbyterian Church of Ghana 1835–1960. A younger church in a changing society*. Accra Universities Press 1966.

Soras, Alfred de. *L'Église et l'anticolonialisme*. Paris: Action populaire 1957.

Bibliography

South African Catholic Bishops' Conference. *Pastoral Letters*. Pretoria: SACBC (?1967).

Status Seminaristarum Indigenarum 1959–1960. Rome: Propaganda Fide 1960.

Stenning, Derrick J. 'Salvation in Ankole', in M. Fortes and G. Dieterlen (eds.), *African systems of thought*. London: Oxford University Press for the International African Institute 1965 pp. 258–75.

Strassberger, Elfriede. *Ecumenism in South Africa 1936–1960, with special reference to the mission of the church*. Johannesburg: South African Council of Churches 1974.

Suenens, Leon J. *A heroine of the Apostolate (1907–1944). Edel Quinn, envoy of the Legion of Mary to Africa*. Dublin: C. J. Fallon 1956.

Sundkler, Bengt G. M. *The Christian ministry in Africa*. London: SCM Press 1960.
Bantu prophets in South Africa. 2nd. ed., London: Oxford University Press for the International African Institute 1961.
'Chief and prophet in Zululand and Swaziland', in M. Fortes and G. Dieterlen (eds.) *African systems of thought*, pp. 276–90.
Zulu Zion and some Swazi Zionists. Uppsala: Gleerups, and London: Oxford University Press 1976.

Taddasse Tamrat. *Church and state in Ethiopia 1270–1527*. Oxford: Clarendon Press 1972.

Taylor, John V. *Christianity and politics in Africa*. London: Penguin Books 1957.
The growth of the church in Buganda. London: SCM Press 1958.

Taylor, John V. and Lehmann, Dorothea A. *Christians of the Copperbelt: the growth of the church in Northern Rhodesia*. London: SCM Press 1961.

Thomas, Norman E. 'Inter-church co-operation in Rhodesia's towns 1962–72', in T. O. Ranger and John Weller (eds.), *Themes in the Christian history of Central Africa*, pp. 238–55.

Thuku, Harry. *Harry Thuku: an autobiography*, with assistance from Kenneth King. Nairobi: Oxford University Press 1970.

Todd, John Murray. *African mission: a historical study of the Society of African Missions*. London: Burns & Oates 1962.

Tsehai Brhaneselassie. 'The life and career of Dajazmač Balča Aba Näfso', *Journal of Ethiopian Studies*, vol. 9 no. 2, 1971 pp. 173–89.

Tshibangu, Tharcisse. *Théologie positive et théologie spéculative: position traditionnelle et nouvelle problématique*. Louvain: Publications universitaires de Louvain 1965.
Le propos d'une théologie africaine. Kinshasa: Presses Universitaires du Zaïre 1974.

Tuma, Tom. 'Major changes and developments in Christian leadership in Busoga, Uganda, 1960–1974', in E. Fasholé-Luke *et al.* (eds.), *Christianity in independent Africa*, pp. 60–78.

Turner, H. W. *African independent church*. Vol. 1. *History of an African independent church: the Church of the Lord (Aladura)*. Vol. 2. *African independent church: the life and faith of the Church of the Lord (Aladura)*. Oxford: Clarendon Press 1967.
'African religious movements and Roman Catholicism', in H. -J. Greschat and H. Jungraithmayr (eds.) *Wort und Religion – Kalima na Dini*. Stuttgart: Evangelischer Missionsverlag 1969 pp. 255–64.
'A typology for modern African religious movements', *Journal of Religion in Africa*, vol. 1 no. 1, 1967 pp. 1–34.

318

Bibliography of new religious movements in primal societies. 1 *Black Africa.* Boston: G. K. Hall 1977.

Turner, Victor W. *The ritual process: structure and anti-structure.* London: Routledge and Kegan Paul 1969.

Twaddle, Michael. 'The Democratic Party of Uganda as a political institution', in E. Fasholé-Luke *et al.* (eds.), *Christianity in independent Africa,* pp. 255–66.

Ullendorff, Edward. *The Ethiopians.* London: Oxford University Press 1960; 3rd. ed. 1973.
Ethiopia and the Bible. London: Oxford University Press for the British Academy 1968.

Ulwor, Paul. 'Une acculturation religieuse en échec dans l'ancienne colonie belge du Congo', *Revue de Psychologie des Peuples* (Le Havre) vol. 23, 1968 pp. 390–421.

Urfer, Sylvain. *Socialisme et église en Tanzanie.* IDOC – France 1976.

Ustorf, Werner. *Afrikanisch Initiative. Das aktive Leiden des Propheten Simon Kimbangu.* Bern: Herbert Land, and Frankfurt: Peter Land 1975.

Vambe, Lawrence. *From Rhodesia to Zimbabwe.* London: Heinemann 1976.

Van Bilsen, Antoine A. J. *Vers l'indépendance du Congo, et du Ruanda-Urundi. Réflexions sur les devoirs et l'avenir de la Belgique en Afrique Centrale.* Kraainem: 1958.

Van Rheenen, Gailyn. *Church planting in Uganda, a comparative study.* South Pasadena, California: William Carey Library 1976.

Van Slageren, Jaap. *Les origines de L'Église Évangélique du Cameroun.* Yaounde: CLE 1972.

Van Winsen, G. A. C. Ethiopian Christianity. *Zeitschrift für Missionswissenschaft* vol. 11, 1974, pp. 124–33.

Van Zyl, Danie. 'Bantu prophets or Christ's evangels', *Pro Veritate* (Johannesburg) vol. 5 no. 5, 1966 pp. 6–9; *ibid,* vol. 5 no. 6, pp. 10–13.
God's earthenware pots. Johannesburg: Christian Institute of Southern Africa 1968.

Verhaegen, Benoit. *Rébellions au Congo.* Brussels: CRISP and Kinshasa: IRES, 2 vols. 1966 and 1969.

Verstraelen, F. J. *An African church in transition: from missionary dependence to mutuality in mission.* Leiden, 2 vols. 1975.

Waliggo, John. *The Catholic Church in the Buddu Province of Buganda 1879–1925.* University of Cambridge, Ph.D. thesis 1976.
'Ganda traditional religion and Catholicism in Buganda 1948–1975', in E. Fasholé-Luke *et al.* (eds.), *Christianity in independent Africa,* pp. 413–25.

Walker, Sheila. [Review of] *The prophet Harris* by Gordon MacKay Haliburton *The International Journal of African Historical Studies* vol. 8, 1975 pp. 73–9.

Walls, Andrew F. 'Religion and the press in "the Enclave" in the Nigerian civil war', in E. Fasholé-Luke *et al.* (eds.), *Christianity in independent Africa,* pp. 207–16.

Walshe, Peter. *The rise of African nationalism in South Africa: the African National Congress 1912–1952.* London: C. Hurst 1970.

Wanyoike, E. N. *An African pastor: the life and work of the Rev. Wanyoike Kamawe 1888–1970.* Nairobi: East African Publishing House 1974.

Warren, Max. *Revival: an enquiry.* London: SCM Press 1954.
Caesar, the beloved enemy. London: SCM Press 1956.
Social history and Christian mission. London: SCM Press 1967.
Crowded canvas: some experiences of a life-time. London: Hodder & Stoughton 1974.

Bibliography

Webster, James Bertin. *The African churches among the Yoruba 1888–1922*. Oxford: Clarendon Press 1964.

Weinrich, Mary Aquina [A K H] 'An aspect of the development of the religious life in Rhodesia', in T. O. Ranger and John Weller (eds.), *Themes in the Christian history of Central Africa*, pp. 218–37.
'Western Monasticism in independent Africa', in E. Fasholé-Luke *et al.* (eds.), *Christianity in independent Africa*, pp. 554–76.

Weiss, Herbert. *Political protest in the Congo*. Princeton, N.J.: Princeton University Press 1967.

Weisse, Wolfram. *Südafrika und das Antirassismusprogramm*. Bern: Herbert Land 1975.

Welbourn, F. B. *East African rebels*. London: S C M Press 1961.
Religion and politics in Uganda 1952–1962. Nairobi: East African Publishing House 1965.

Welbourn, F. B. and Ogot, B. A. *A place to feel at home: a study of two independent churches in Western Kenya*. London: Oxford University Press 1966.

Welch, F. G. *Training for the ministry in East Africa*. Limuru (Kenya): St Paul's United Theological College 1963.

Weman, Henry. *African music and the church in Africa*. Uppsala: A B Lundeqvistska Bokhandeln for Svenska Institutet for Missionsforskning 1960.
'The new praise in ancient tunes', in P. Beyerhaus and C. F. Hallencreutz (eds.), *The church crossing frontiers. Essays in honour of Bengt Sundkler* (Studia Missionalia Upsaliensia XI). Lund: Gleerup 1969 pp. 177–88.

Were, Gideon S. 'Politics, religion and nationalism in Western Kenya, 1942–1962: Dini ya Msambwa revisited', in B. A. Ogot (ed.), *Politics and nationalism in colonial Kenya*. Nairobi: East African Publishing House 1972 pp. 85–104.

West, Martin. *Bishops and prophets in a Black city. African independent churches in Soweto and Johannesburg*. Cape Town: David Philip, and London: Rex Collings 1975.

White Fathers. *Mozambique, une église, signe de salut . . . Pour qui?* Rome: White Fathers Generalate 1973. Mimeo.

Wills, A. J. *An introduction to the history of Central Africa*. London: Oxford University Press, 3rd. ed. 1973.

Wilson, Bryan R. 'Jehovah's Witnesses in Kenya', *Journal of Religion in Africa*, vol. 5 no. 2, 1973 pp. 128–49.

Wilson, Francis, and Perrot, Dominique (eds.), *Outlook on a century: South Africa 1870–1970*. Lovedale: Lovedale Press with Spro-Cass 1973.

Wilson, Monica. *Communal rituals of the Nyakyusa*. London: Oxford University Press for the International African Institute 1959.
'Z. K. Matthews: a man for reconciliation', *South African Outlook*, July 1968; repr. in Wilson and Perrot, *Outlook on a century*, pp. 557–9.

Wilson, Monica and Thompson, Leonard (eds.), *The Oxford History of South Africa*, vol. 2. Oxford and New York: Clarendon Press 1971.

Winter, Colin. *Namibia: the story of a bishop in exile*. Guildford; Lutterworth Press 1977.

Wipper, Audrey, *Rural Rebels, a study of two protest movements in Kenya*, Nairobi: Oxford University Press 1977.

Wiseman, Edith M. *Kikuyu martyrs*. London: Highway Press 1958.

Wishlade, R. L. *Sectarianism in Southern Nyasaland*. London: Oxford University Press for the International African Institute 1965.

World Council of Churches. *Report of the All Africa Seminar on the Christian home and family life*. Geneva: World Council of Churches 1963.

Wright, Marcia. *German missions in Tanganyika 1891–1941*. Oxford: Clarendon Press 1971.

Wyllie, Robert W. 'Pioneers of Ghanaian pentecostalism. Peter Anim and James McKeown', *Journal of Religion in Africa*, vol. 6 no. 2, 1974 pp. 109–22.

Young, M. Crawford. 'Rebellion and the Congo', in R. I. Rotberg and A. A. Mazrui (eds.), *Protest and power in Black Africa*, pp. 969–1011.

Index

Index

Index